MW00777288

GHOSTS of GREYSTONE

BEVERLY HILLS

Once you open this book
you'll find THE TRUTH
Outweighs your BELIEF!

GHOSTS of GREYSTONE

GREYSTONE

BEVERLY HILLS

CLETE KEITH

edited by Stephen Vittoria

An imprint of Those Keith Brothers, Inc.

An imprint of Those Keith Brothers, Inc.
1112 Montana Ave Suite 823
Santa Monica CA 90403

Library of Congress Control Number:2019907342

Publisher's Cataloging-In-Publication Data
(Prepared by The Donohue Group, Inc.)

Names: Keith, Clete, author.
Title: Ghosts of Greystone : Beverly Hills : dramatic eyewitness accounts
/ Clete Keith.
Description: First edition. | Santa Monica, CA : Linseed Press,
[an imprint of Those Keith Brothers, Inc.], 2020.
Identifiers: ISBN 9781733155908 (hardcover) |
ISBN 9781733155915 (paperback) | ISBN 9781733155922 (ePub) |
ISBN 9781733155939 (Kindle) | ISBN 9781733155946 (PDF)

Subjects: LCSH: Haunted houses--California--Beverly Hills. | Ghosts--California--
Beverly Hills. | Supernatural--Anecdotes. | LCGFT: Anecdotes. | BISAC: BODY, MIND
& SPIRIT / Supernatural (incl. Ghosts)
Classification: LCC BF1472.U6 K45 2020 (print) | LCC BF1472.U6 (ebook) | DDC
133.12979493--dc23

Cover design by Angie Alaya
Cover Copyright © 2020 Those Keith Brothers, Inc.
Cover image courtesy of University of Southern California,
on behalf of the USC Libraries Special Collections.
Edited by Stephen Vittoria
Interior book design by Rob Guillory
Proofreading by Jennifer Grubba and Martha Mayakis

The author is available for speaking engagements.
"Ghosts of Greystone – Beverly Hills" books may be purchased
in bulk for educational, business, fund-raising, or sales promotional use.
For more information: contact@ghostsofgreystone.com
or
Ghosts of Greystone
1112 Montana Ave Suite 823
Santa Monica CA 90403

FIRST EDITION, October 2020

Printed and bound in the United States of America

This book is dedicated to all the brave individuals who came forward and shared their incredible stories, knowing full well they might face ridicule, disbelief, or even a snicker or two behind their backs. This book is also dedicated to the spirits who reside at Greystone… this extraordinary estate—whether inside the mansion or on its spacious grounds; whether earthbound by choice or trapped in a realm by circumstance. It is with honor that we shine a bright light into your world, illuminating the evidence that life after life does indeed exist.

If you are reading this, then you are blissfully unaware what is creeping up behind you.

– Unknown

CONTENTS

CONTENTS

FOREWORD

As a Senior Forensic Specialist with the Beverly Hills Police Department, now recently retired after 37 years, one of my duties was to respond to crime scene investigations throughout the 5.6-square-mile City. These crime scenes varied from murder, suicide, robbery, to a variety of other types of crimes that needed forensic examination. In addition to my regular forensic duties, I was the Police Department historian, dealing with an opulent history, starting in 1906 when the Rodeo Land and Water Company was renamed the City of Beverly Hills.

I have spent decades traversing and conversing with residents; some of whom happen to be celebrated, in this so-called small-town community. I have become familiarized with many stories from individuals involving strange and unique paranormal experiences in various older, historical homes in Beverly Hills. Many are eager to share experiences and emotions they felt, others are very guarded in revealing those events, worried about how they may be perceived.

As a field scientist, I'm inclined to seek reasoning as to these paranormal experiences. The common denominator tends to be that each situation involves an aspect of the macabre or depicts death in some bizarre manner. In researching my book entitled *Beverly Hills Confidential: A Century of Stars, Scandals and Murders,* my co-author and I reexamined many sensational stories of the past century, which involved some very notorious murders occurring in this world famous, tightknit community. The Doheny Murder is one we shared with our readers, which had a cast of individuals and of course two dead bodies. This murder occurred in 1929, within the thick walls of the renowned Doheny Estate known simply as Greystone Mansion, because of the somber grey stone appearance. This Tudor revival mansion, built in 1928, is situated on the hillside with its bold stateliness overlooking the City of Beverly Hills. It also reminds me of the type of mansion that you see in an old movie during a moonless night with heavy rains pounding and of course, a murder takes place. The residence, which drew much attention, was built by Edward L. Doheny as a wedding gift for his son, Ned Jr., and wife, Lucy. The mansion's grandeur reminds one of the wealthy ambiances of celebrity homes of the past.

I have known Clete Keith for many years, and we have worked together on various projects for the City of Beverly Hills. His knowledge of Greystone Estate is impressive, trustworthy, and enlightening. More importantly, it would be hard to find anyone more qualified to write this book. He has extensively researched, documented, and interviewed a vast number of individuals who have experienced mysterious activity inside the mansion and on the grounds of the estate. These ghostly encounters have embraced the emotions and experiences described by the various individuals revealed during actual interviews. They shake you into a believer of the supernatural and beyond. As a scientist, it's critical to rely on evidence, whether it be recordings, photo images, video, etc. However, the accounts of so many people taking place in one residence are quite fascinating and revealing, which should bring this paranormal activity into mainstream science.

So sit back, hold on, and get ready for the unexplained activity on a palatial residence with a rich history, in a rich town…oh yeah, and I can't forget the main characters…the Ghosts of Greystone!

—Clark W. Fogg

Beverly Hills Police Department, Sr. Forensic Specialist 1982-2019
Author, *Beverly Hills Confidential: A Century of Stars, Scandals and Murder*

PREFACE

In the 1960s, my great uncle, Wes, was living with his wife, Margie, in a small cottage by the sea in Cambria, California. Riddled with cancer, Wes slipped out of their bed late one night while Margie slept. He grabbed his .22 caliber rifle, sat down on the front porch facing the ocean and shot himself in the head. How's that for an opening story? If it piqued your interest, you're in for one heck of a ride.

Years later in the 1970s, Margie had a stroke and was placed in a nursing home. My mother and father drove up from Los Angeles to pack Aunt Margie's belongings, clean her cottage, and sell it to pay for her care. During the garage cleanup, they heard three loud knocks at the front door. My dad went to see who was there. The front stoop was empty. He figured it was probably kids playing a prank. They continued cleaning and again heard three loud knocks. This time, Dad hurried to check. Again, nothing. Back in the garage he asked my mother, "You heard that, right?" Emphatically, my mother said, "Of course I did." Clearly, he was ready to leave, "Let's get the hell out of here." And they left. My dad didn't want to know who or what it was. I think he had an idea—and that idea was unsettling. Mom was convinced it was Wes. That didn't seem to frighten her and, in fact, years later, there were times she felt she could see and feel spirits on the other side. Their story of that mysterious knocking was the first time I'd heard anything about ghosts, spirits, hauntings, or someone trying to connect from the other side.

The second incident informing me about the possibilities of ghosts happened in the late 1970s. I was traveling with other actors while performing a play and became friendly with an actress named Pam. One day she invited me over to her apartment in Beverly Hills to have a glass of wine and chat. I grabbed my guitar and headed over. Her apartment was beautifully furnished with a piano and a large sofa with an accompanying coffee table. There were candles lit and placed throughout the living room. One large candle on the coffee table had a fancy clear glass housing. It was all very refined. It was like an apartment set in a movie. We enjoyed the wine and talked about our play and various acting techniques. At one point in the conversation she suddenly informed me that her apartment was haunted.

Now, at this point in my life, I knew of only one ghost experience: the story above passed down from my Mom and Dad. Pam started detailing her experiences one after another. "I woke up one night to find a woman standing at the foot of my bed. She was solid and smiling down at me." Of course, I'm wondering if her story is legitimate or not. "What did she look like?" I asked. Pam told me she was wearing a long white dress. Also at this point in my life, I didn't know much about ghosts if anything, but that description sure sounded like the typical ghost answer. In fact, I was waiting for her to say, "Then her eyes turned red, she floated above me and howled like a demon!" I asked Pam, "Did you freak out?" She shook her head calmly. "No, the woman was comforting in a way. I wasn't scared. It was a friendly vibration. I went back to sleep." *Went back to sleep?* I tell you what, if I woke up and saw a ghost woman hanging out at the end of my bed in the dead of night, I think I'd vibrate something out into the back end of my pajamas!

But Pam wasn't done with her stories. "I had a friend over one night and we both heard the piano play by itself," she said. Oh boy, here we go. This is yet another typical ghost story—I woke up and there's a candelabra on the piano and Liberace is playing while sipping a spritzer. I asked her, "What song was being played?" Pam said that it wasn't a song, just some notes. At this point, I'm just going along with it. Who knows what's real and what isn't? I was trying hard not to be judgmental. Pam is a very intelligent person. We start smoking some weed and she breaks out a book entitled *Seth Speaks*. She starts elaborating on how Seth channels spirits. I'm high, also buzzed from the wine, and suddenly realize I'm in over my head. I'm staring at the cover of *Seth Speaks* with this freaky lady supposedly "channeling." Her mouth is slightly open, and her eyes are staring off into the great beyond. I'm uncomfortable, I'm high, and in typical twenty-three-year-old know it all fashion, I start making fun of the woman who showed up in her bedroom. "Doesn't she have anything better to do than to watch you sleep?" Pam is smiling, but not responding. I'm not done. "And as far as the piano goes, did you open the top to see if there were any mice inside with top hats doing some high kicks on the strings?" I finish with a wise guy smirk. Again, no response. I take one last look at the book cover. "And what the hell happened to her? She looks like she ate some bad shrimp." Pam waits a long moment to answer. "You shouldn't make fun of the ghosts." I try and reassure her that I'm not making fun of them as I hold up the book. "But seriously, look at her face." Suddenly the glass housing around the large candle explodes! I mean, it completely shatters the glass. Pam is frozen, staring at the candle as it keeps burning. She looks over to me. She's horrified. I'm high as a kite and my heart is racing. Pam manages to utter, "That's never happened before," as she's fixated on the shards of broken glass. Now, did I mention that I'm high? I'm all tingly and I feel my ass pucker up in fear. Not a good combination now that the weed has really kicked in. I manage to stand up, grab my guitar, offer Pam some gibberish-like reassurance, and bolt out the door. As I drive away into a spinning L.A. night, I'm imagining Pam fending off her lady in white, the dancing mice, and the constipated-looking spirit channeler spitting up shrimp.

My third and final paranormal incident happened when my mother was almost eighty years old and dying from Parkinson's disease. Mom was an actress and we moved her into the Motion Picture & Television Fund home for full-time care. She initially shared a room with a woman named Peggy—the mother of a well-known actor. Mom and Peggy became friends. Unfortunately, Peggy was declining fast. Eventually, Mom was moved into her own room. I arrived to visit Mom and all the nurses were busy, running around more than usual. I asked at the nurses' station what was going on. "Peggy just died." I asked her if she contacted her son. She nodded and said he was on his way—but the nurse seemed confused. She looked at me and I could see she wanted to tell me something. I asked the nurse if everything was okay. She shook her head, "No. Something is weird. The nurses' station keeps getting a call from the phone next to Peggy's bed. It rings and when I pick it up, there's no one there. I had our telephone technician come out and check and everything is fine. I don't understand what's happening."

I had a feeling I knew exactly what was going on. And strangely, I also felt the nurse knew but didn't want to say it out loud because that might make it real. I pushed the envelope a bit: "Well, you know what this is, don't you?" She just stared at me, and then finally, "It's Peggy." I said, "She's still in the room and doesn't know she's passed. She's confused, so she's calling the front desk for help." The nurse kept shaking her head. "No. No. Don't say that. I don't want to hear that. No."

I walked into Peggy's room. Her body had been removed by this time. I moved close to her bed. "Hi, Peggy. You've passed, honey. You're out of the body. You need to go to the light. Look up in the corner of the room and you will see a white light. Go to that light. You'll be okay. You're loved. Just go to the light." I stood there and said a silent prayer. When Peggy's son and wife arrived, they spent some time with the nurses getting the details and they eventually left. I went to see the nurse again and asked, "Still getting calls from her bed?" She shook her head. "No. It stopped ringing." I smiled and went to visit Mom.

Flash forward to the late 1990s. The City of Beverly Hills hired me to work in the Recreation and Parks division, now known as Community Services. My assignments included helping with special events such as the Beverly Hills Art Show and Winter Wonderland—a snow event where we would blow one hundred tons of shaved ice on ramps in a lush city park (after all, this is palm tree populated Beverly Hills!). In 2003, my role expanded to include helping with the Park Ranger program. Part of my duties was to assist with various events as well as help oversee motion picture filming and still photography shoots in and around the famous Greystone Mansion—a Tudor revival estate surrounded by distinctive Italian Renaissance-inspired gardens.

I shared an office in the gatehouse, a small building at the south end of the Greystone Park property. At that time, I knew nothing of Greystone's history or of the paranormal activity connected with the estate. My parents' story of that mysterious knocking, my evening with the exploding candle, and the story of Peggy's departure was light years ago and I'd never given it another thought. But as the years passed, Greystone staff, City employees, as well as patrons of the park would occasionally tell me their stories of spirits and odd occurrences in and around the mansion.

Our office constantly fielded calls from numerous Hollywood movie and television production companies interested in filming paranormal reality shows at Greystone. The stories of "strange" activity in the mansion had become legendary, thanks in part to the internet that is now chock-full of ghostly stories about the Greystone estate and Doheny Mansion. As a result, there was no shortage of production companies and visitors wanting to spend the night performing investigations. All those calls were referred to me. My direction then, and still to this day, is to say, "No... no filming overnight at this location." Trucks rolling in and filming all night with noisy equipment and crews chattering simply doesn't sit well with the gazillionaire neighbors who pay a huge amount in taxes and expect privacy and quiet nights. Also, the City of Beverly Hills doesn't want to draw attention to the notorious murder/suicide that took place inside the mansion. Murder? Suicide? Yep.

In fact, that particular bloody incident has always been the fuel of paranormal fire at Greystone. When people visit the park and mansion and ask about the "incident," our instructions are, "DON'T discuss it!" Obviously, I can't feign ignorance and say, "What murders?" Instead I say, "Ned and his secretary, Hugh, did die in the mansion, but the specific details as to why are still not clear and probably never will be." Then I quickly redirect them to the incredible and sprawling views of Los Angeles.

In all my time at the mansion, I've never had someone come up to me and say, "I see this 46,000 square foot mansion was built in the English Tudor style. Can you elaborate a bit about the neoclassic and Gothic architecture?" Never. Not once. Nada. But guess what is the number one question I've been asked over the years: "Is this place haunted?" Followed closely by the usual litany of queries, *"Are there ghosts in the mansion?—Have you seen or heard things?—Is it scary inside?—Do you have any proof that spirits actually exist in there?"* And of course, "Where are the restrooms?"

Having spent more than twenty years at Greystone, I've been paranormally educated about the property by events that have happened to myself, co-workers, former City staff, and visitors from various walks of life. Many people have stories, some incredible, and those stories bring forth even more valid questions.

One early morning in November of 2017, with my retirement looming, I prayed for guidance to transition to the next chapter of my life. I awoke suddenly at 3:00 a.m. (also known as "dead time" in many paranormal circles) and the idea came to me that I should journal all the mysterious experiences and stories I've been told since working at Greystone. I gazed into the darkness, recalling my tours of the mansion, the strange incidents, and the countless unearthly stories—and then it hit me: *write a book!* That way, those of us who have worked at Greystone will have our solid documentation recorded, and the visitors who've experienced these peculiar happenings will know that their stories are forever detailed in these pages. Also, for those captivated by this amazing and historic location, but can't visit in person, this book will shed some intriguing light on what's really taking place within the confines of this bygone and erstwhile estate.

The truth lies in the following pages, as told by the people who lived it, in their own words. These folks are eyewitnesses to Greystone's lively paranormal activity. No hearsay, but rather all real events. What you're about to experience are the actual accounts from more than eighty-five people totaling nearly three hundred stories.

Finally, it's time for you to be the judge. So wait for the dead of night, pour yourself a warm cup of tea, find a quiet dark room and a comfortable chair, turn on a single reading light, and slowly turn to chapter one... I dare you!

—Clete Keith
Santa Monica, Fall 2020

INTRODUCTION

Having committed to writing about the strange phenomena at Greystone, I wanted *Ghosts of Greystone—Beverly Hills* to reveal this amazing location like no other. My intention is to share the ghost stories I gleaned from hours upon hours of extensive interviews, while also providing the reader with a brief background of the infamous family that occupied these extraordinary and historic grounds. It is my intention that the historical information will shed important contextual light on how influential and affluent the Doheny family was, especially in the 1920s and 1930s.

Let us delve into the history of the Doheny family and examine what might be the possible causes for what has been regarded as "paranormal activity" at the Greystone Estate.

A (VERY) BRIEF HISTORY

In 1892, Edward Laurence Doheny, and his friend, Charles Canfield, were the first to discover oil in the City of Angels. They seized an opportunity to venture down to Tampico, Mexico, and on February 9, 1916, struck oil at one site that eclipsed the production of all the other wells in the nearby fields combined, making Doheny's company the largest producer of oil worldwide—and making Edward Doheny one of the wealthiest men in the world. Among the many real estate acquisitions that he and his wife, Carrie Estelle Betzold, purchased were the 429 acres that became the Doheny Ranch, which is now part of Beverly Hills proper.

Edward gave a 12.58-acre parcel to his son, Ned, and wife, Lucy, as a wedding gift. On February 15, 1927, construction began on the 46,054 square foot, 55-room Greystone Mansion, at a cost of $1,238,378.00, bringing the total cost of the land and estate to $3,166,578.00 (equal to approximately $46 million in 2020). In its time, Greystone was known as the Hearst Castle of Southern California. Ned, Lucy, and their five children, Lucy, Edward ("Larry"), William, Patrick, and Timothy, moved into the mansion in September of 1928. Less than five months later, Ned would be lying dead on the floor of his new home.

■ *What We Know… or Think We Know*

On the night of February 16, 1929, Ned and his secretary and friend, Hugh Plunkett, were involved in a spirited discussion that turned deadly. The facts remain sketchy to this day, but in all likelihood, the events that took place on this evening were the result of mounting pressure from the Teapot Dome scandal.

In the 1920s, Albert Fall—the Secretary of the Interior under President Warren G. Harding—secretly leased the federal oil reserves of the infamous Teapot Dome oilfields (35 miles north of Casper, Wyoming) to oil tycoon Harry F. Sinclair of the Mammoth Oil Company. Fall also secretly leased the Elk Hills and Buena Vista Hills oil reserves in the San Joaquin Valley of California to Edward L. Doheny (Pan American Petroleum Company). Doheny sent his son, Ned, and his trusted friend and employee, Hugh Plunkett, to New York to deliver $100,000 to Fall as a loan (read: "gift"), which also gave Doheny access to the Department of the Interior's naval oil reserves worth $100 million. The subsequent US Senate inquiry into the leases concluded that Sinclair and Doheny's so-called loans were indeed bribes and further government probes were launched to expose the unfolding scandal. Both Ned and Hugh were due to testify. Hugh was extremely distressed about the situation and believed he was a prime candidate to take the fall for Doheny. On the evening of February 16, 1929, Hugh arrived at Greystone, secured a weapon from the Gun Room, and confronted Ned.

Clark Fogg, former Senior Forensic Specialist at the Beverly Hills Police Department Crime Lab, describes in *Beverly Hills Confidential: A Century of Stars, Scandals and Murder,* what he believed took place on that fateful night: "It's quite possible Hugh Plunkett didn't intend to kill his boss. The tragedy may have been an accidental murder/suicide. An examination of the crime scene images taken that night of the incident suggests that an emotionally charged conversation ensued between Plunkett and Doheny. A possible scenario: since the firearm was a Colt Bisley single-action revolver (single-action revolvers require less trigger-pull than double-action firearms), as Plunkett pointed the firearm at Doheny, it could have accidentally discharged. With Doheny falling out of the chair and blood gushing from his head wound, Plunkett decided to end all outside pressures by ending his life as Mrs. Doheny and the doctor approached him in the hallway outside the guest bedroom."

The case, which was open and shut in forty-eight hours, was found to be a murder-suicide in which Hugh Plunkett went berserk and killed his benefactor. End of story. But certainly not the end of the story as far Greystone Mansion was concerned.

Photo: Marc Wanamaker / Bison Archives

(L-R) Edward L. Doheny, Jr., Mrs. Carrie Doheny, and Edward L. Doheny, Sr., leaving Los Angeles Federal Court during the Teapot Dome trial. November 1, 1924

"Teapot Dome Scandal"—Postscript: The Supreme Court declared the leases fraudulent and illegally acquired. The Court invalidated the leases and they were returned to the US Navy. Albert Fall was convicted of conspiracy and accepting bribes and sentenced to one year in prison— the first presidential cabinet member to go to prison. Doheny and Sinclair were not convicted of paying the bribes, although Sinclair was convicted of jury tampering. Prior to the Watergate scandal, the Teapot Dome Scandal was regarded as the most sensational political disgrace in American history.

■ *More Tragedies*

Unfortunately, there were more unnatural deaths in and around Greystone. A woman servant killed herself inside the mansion's meat locker on the second floor of the servants' wing, near the kitchen. She slit her wrists in the meat locker so her blood would go directly down the built-in drain, making sure that fellow workers and friends wouldn't have to clean up after her. This story was considered a rumor when I started working at Greystone, and I had no way of verifying it. That is, until Steven Clark, a retired Park Ranger Supervisor, revealed to me that back in 2001, a woman visited the grounds and told him that her grandmother had worked at the mansion as a maid. Without any further prompting, she proceeded to tell Clark that her grandmother was a close friend of the maid who had committed suicide inside the meat locker.

A second servant was said to have been impregnated out of wedlock by someone on the property during a time when it was very shameful to do so. Being shunned by society, not to mention that this was a very Catholic household, she hanged herself in a room in the servants' wing.

Another verified death was a triangle love affair between Doheny mansion employees: a family driver, another male staff person, and a female staff person, which resulted in the woman's murder by strangulation. The police report states that she was wrapped in a carpet and removed from the mansion through the servants' wing door.

A young girl who was a friend of the Doheny daughter, Lucy, fell to her death from Lucy's second floor room window onto the terrace. (Other "sightings" in this book might shed light on a different story of her demise.)

A distraught man committed suicide on the property in 2003 by shooting himself in the head. I witnessed his body still seated in place on a bench near the willow pond, just minutes after he ended his life.

We don't know very much about the construction of the mansion outside of the practical: the architect was Gordon Kaufmann and the builder was P.J. Walker and Company of San Francisco. But there are rumors and unanswered questions that continue to swirl. Did anyone die during the time it was being built? What about the land on which Greystone sits, and all the countless lives possibly lost on this property dating back hundreds of years? (Indigenous burial grounds are recorded in the nearby Hollywood Hills and surrounding areas.) On these counts, the jury is still out.

■ *Is Greystone Mansion Haunted?*

The question remains: did these tragedies set in motion any kind of paranormal activity? There are many books and articles that discuss this historic location, but not one focuses on the ghostly and spectral events. Why? Perhaps the topic is taboo. Or much is based on hearsay. Or there's a lack of evidence. People are quick to say "there are no such things as ghosts." Possibly they're not prepared to believe if they haven't seen it with their own eyes. Religion also plays a part. I understand all these opposing points of view. Boy, do I understand. I hear them all the time.

But, if Greystone is haunted, WHERE'S THE PROOF? And maybe, just as important, WHY IS IT HAUNTED? Was it spawned by the bloodshed that took place on that fatal night of February 16, 1929? Like a lightning rod, it signaled, dare I say, beckoned, the spirits to engulf the mansion? Or were they already there, waiting to wield their influence? Did the spirits manipulate people to behave in certain ways, shaping the circumstances that led to all the brutal deaths at this location?

■ *Theories*
One belief is that places like Greystone are haunted because spirits are drawn to locations where they experienced an intense emotional event during their physical life. The emotional trauma or joy solidifies their connection to that exact time and place, whether it's good experiences drawing them back to a happy time, or a horrific incident that forces them to relive a tragedy or disturbing ordeal repeatedly.

■ *A Portal. Huh?*
Could Greystone be the site of a portal—a spiritual highway used by spirits to enter a specific location? A ghost door, so to speak. It is said that battlefields, hospitals, and locations where violent acts (such as murder and plunder) have occurred can form a portal. Two well-known psychics, Peter James and Chris Fleming, entered the mansion a decade apart, pointed to the exact same location and said, "Do you know you have a portal here?" All I will say is that over the years I have taken some amazingly bizarre and strange photographs in that specific area—and I've experienced some "interesting" interactions to say the least.

How to Navigate This Book
After much consideration, I finally decided the best way to disclose the paranormal events that have taken place in and around this large eighteen-acre property was to break down the locations into chapters. Each section of the mansion and grounds will have interviews related

to that specific location and will include descriptions that will help you recreate the ambience of that particular setting. In the appendix there are floor plans for each of the mansion's four floors, plus a map with an overview of the estate grounds to provide you with the big picture.

Offering great historical context, the Greystone Historical Report was written at the request of the Beverly Hills City Council, and delivered to the council on August 30, 1984. It is a fifteen-part history of the Greystone Estate and the Doheny Ranch. This report comprises information about the Doheny family, the purchase of the 429-acre property, the construction of the mansion and its grounds in the late 1920s, a description of the mansion and its grounds upon their completion in 1928, and intriguing glimpses of the Doheny family's lifestyle at Greystone. Also included are comments by Ned Doheny's youngest son, Timothy, as well as Sam Schultz, who was Mrs. Battson's (née Lucy Doheny) chauffeur for more than 50 years (Ned's wife, Lucy Doheny, changed her last name when she married her second husband, Leigh Battson, in 1932). Very few people are aware of this edifying document, let alone have read the full report. I've selected pertinent aspects of this report allowing you to peek behind the curtain to get a feel for the family and the property.

I've spent many hours interviewing the people whose stories appear in this book, doing my best to organize their conversations and take into account their attempt to explain the unexplainable. In the case of interviewees who were Hispanic and did not speak English, I used interpreters to help me through my questioning process, and I adjusted the wording, when required, for a better translation.

For authenticity, I brought as many witnesses who were willing, back to the exact location where they had their experience. Whether inside the mansion or on the grounds, this helped most interviewees to recall their incident, especially if it happened years ago. It also seemed to heighten their senses and emotions, being back at the scene of the so-called crime.

You'll find many of the stories are from past and present Park Rangers—individuals who over the years have had the most access to the mansion. At some point during their shifts, rangers will enter the mansion for any number of reasons, from security sweeps to checking on events, and trust me, there are some who go inside and get out as fast as possible. All the stories in this book—with the exception of the one that happened to me—are based on interactions I've had with fellow city workers, film crews, guests, and patrons.

FINAL THOUGHTS

From the book's inception, I knew there would be individuals who would be reticent about coming forward to tell their stories and would not be comfortable divulging their names. In those cases, I've respected their wishes and not disclosed their identities. There were some individuals who refused to speak to me at all, and I took their reluctance as an indication that their stories were most likely true, or why else would they stay silent? When that was the case, those stories have been told from a third person perspective, as are also stories told to me by an interviewee about a person I couldn't track down or is no longer alive. I contacted several police officers and a district attorney for their personal stories. All refused to talk to me except for one Beverly Hills police officer who agreed to meet me at Greystone mansion to relive his encounter, but only if I did not reveal his name.

I'm thrilled to share with you these personal accounts about this iconic location. I have held on to many of these stories for years, waiting for the right situation to divulge these exhilarating experiences. This book is that situation. Over the years, when I talk to people I meet at Greystone about some of the paranormal narratives, I receive the furrowing of a brow, or worse, a slight smile of condolence in fear that my screws have indeed come loose. I can't tell you how many people say to me, "I'd love to spend the night inside the mansion!" To those people, I say, this book will be your best opportunity.

INTRODUCTION

So let's enter the gate at 501 Doheny Road…we'll take it nice and slow…
and if you think you see dark shadows lurking, or hear the hooves of a
horse pulling a stagecoach approaching, or hear someone or something
whisper, "Get out!"—try not to panic… it's just the Ghosts of Greystone.

Grand Entry

I'm like freaking out and I'm still tingling and I'm just like, "Okay, you're crazy, it's in your head." Then I look at my arm and it's got a red scratch on it!
— Ranger M.M.
    Greystone Park Ranger

Photo: Chris Keith

Many motion pictures and television shows have been filmed in this iconic entryway, including *Spider-Man* and *Spider-Man 3*, *The Social Network*, *The Disorderly Orderly*, *National Treasure: Book of Secrets*, *Charlie's Angels: Full Throttle*, *Rock Star*, *All of Me* starring Steve Martin and directed by Carl Reiner, *The Golden Child* starring Eddie Murphy, *The Loved One*, *The Gilmore Girls*, *Garfield: A Tail of Two Kitties*, and last but not least, the most fitting of them all: *Ghostbusters 2*.

Walking into the Grand Entry, you're immediately awestruck by the elegance of the architecture. You pause to take in the beauty—the elaborate detail of the woodwork on the bannisters and archways, all hand carved by European artisans. The work is magnificent.

Greystone Historical Report

The mansion's interior displays this same pleasing mix of good proportion, exquisite craftsmanship, grandeur, yet intimacy. Located beneath a porte-cochere, the double front doors were plate glass covered with a hand wrought iron grillwork, which displayed the initials ELD. These doors opened into the stair landing. To the right, a set of stairs led to the second floor. Most visitors, however, descended the broad grand stairway to the first floor hallway, which ran the full length of the mansion, roughly east to west.

While grand and imposing, children will be children. Especially young boys. They looked at the marble stairs as the perfect angle for their new ride. They would grab whatever they felt would race down the stairs the fastest and jump onboard. Screams of joy and laughter must have filled these halls as they slid down their homemade rollercoaster—until mom caught wind of what was going on.

Greystone Historical Report

"We used to slide down the grand staircase, the big stairway near the front door, on suitcases and cardboard boxes, whatever would slide."

—Timothy Doheny

The Grand Entry, with its beautiful and striking features, turned out to be a very peculiar location when it came to interviewing the eyewitnesses. It proved to be one of the most active areas in the mansion in terms of paranormal activity. I kept wondering why. Is it because the interviewees are coming into "their" home? It was as if the visitors were being "checked out" by the spirits. It was common during the interview process that witnesses would take a deep breath as they crossed the threshold into the Grand Entry as if their original experience from a day ago, a week ago, or even decades ago, still brought a chill to their spine.

"Unseen Legs"

Gabriel Jara's story is enough to give anyone chills. Ranger Gabe is quite reserved. In fact, when considering which rangers to approach regarding the mansion's paranormal activity, Gabe was not high on the list—he's that reserved. He never mentioned anything about spirits or the paranormal, and his daily patrols of Greystone Park didn't allow him much time inside the mansion. I was reminded that when he was selected for the Ranger Program, he spent many hours training at Greystone. One day I took a chance and asked him if he ever witnessed any paranormal activity. A slight smile broke across his face, "Several, actually." He agreed to be interviewed. We stood face-to-face in the Grand Entry as he told me his story with sincerity and urgency. By the time Gabe finished, we both had major chills.

GABRIEL JARA
(Lead Park Ranger)

> Gabriel: *This was after an event, around one in the morning. As we shut everything down,* [co-worker and fellow Ranger] *Steve Clark realizes he forgot his lunchbox in the house. He goes back inside with his flashlight and I wait for him at the front entrance. It's pretty dark and it seems*

like he's taking a lot of time. Gazing around, I look up to the second-floor landing and I suddenly see this white, I don't know, ghost figure. He's not wearing clothes. It is just a completely solid white figure. It looks like a man wearing a hat, a big hat—also white. I recall that very well. And all I can see is from the waist up. I can't see his legs. Maybe he has them, maybe he doesn't, I'm not sure. And he is looking directly at me. So right away I look down because I'm like, "What did I just see? Did I really see a ghost or an evil spirit?" I look up again because this can't be real. And it was still there— looking right at me, straight at me!

Gabe takes a long pause and he had that million-mile stare that went right through me.

Gabriel: *And that just scared the living hell out of me. And that's when Steve shows up from inside the house. He was tired and couldn't wait to leave. He alarms the house and we get out. I wanted to say something, but I didn't. I thought, "Maybe I'm just seeing things," you know? I'm dead tired, it's my imagination. Maybe I should have looked back but I was way too scared. I've never told that story to anybody.*

"Whisper"

I discovered through the writing of this book that Ranger Juan Andrade has a strong sensitivity when it comes to the paranormal. His experiences are not confined to just the mansion. As a young boy, he remembers having visions—one particular vision was a grown-up Juan working at a very large property. "I remember a beautiful garden full of hedge groves, kind of like a maze with red bricks," he tells me warmly. "It was high up on a hill with no other homes visible. It was beautiful. I also remember a stream and flowing water." Juan spent many of his childhood days at the Doheny residence located at 8 Chester Place, in the historic West Adams District of Los Angeles, where his mother worked. This 10,500 square-foot mansion was purchased by Edward L. Doheny, Sr. in 1901, for $120,000—the equivalent in 2020 of nearly $4 million. Years later, when Juan visited Greystone for a tour of the mansion, the grounds looked incredibly familiar to him, like he was returning home. But he had never stepped foot in Greystone. When Juan applied for the ranger job, he realized his boyhood visions of a large property was indeed Greystone. Possibly Juan was coming home.

Photo: Chris Keith

JUAN ANDRADE

(Park Ranger Supervisor)

Juan: *It was early in the morning, maybe a quarter to seven. I open the Richie Rich gates[1] and the front door. As I walk inside, I hear what sounds like a group of people whispering. I can't figure out what is going on. Then I hear one of the voices clearly say, "He's in the house." I stop and listen*

1 The "Richie Rich" gates, with the initial "R" on each ornamental metal gate, were installed in 1994 for the film of the same name starring Macaulay Culkin. They separate the West Courtyard from the Inner Courtyard.

5

and I'm thinking, "Who is in the mansion?" But I don't hear the voices anymore. I flip on the lights and disarm the security system. I walk back to the main door and wait, but I hear nothing. Like I said, when I first walked in, it sounded like a group of people were whispering very, very low. I never heard footsteps moving away. Nothing. And I'm just standing there waiting for something to happen. It's completely quiet. I want to see if I hear anything else. There was nothing. But boy, it gave me chills.

Greystone Historical Report

"Right by the front door, there was a night watchman. And of course, there was a gatekeeper. There were people on duty all the time. That was during the Lindbergh thing [the kidnapping and subsequent death of Charles Lindbergh's infant son in 1932]. There were threatening notes and letters and things. Phone calls. But nothing really happened."
—Timothy Doheny

"TOUCHED BY A SPIRIT"

From the look on Chanh Hang's face as he told me the following story, it's clear that the incident still haunts him to this day. Chanh is a man of great integrity and I have no reason to doubt him, especially when you read my story after this one. The incident in question took place on a Friday night after a performance of "The Manor"—a staged play that's performed in the mansion—loosely based on the trials and tribulations of the Doheny family. When the show was over, Ranger Chanh checked to make sure everyone was out of the building and he continued with his regular routine. But on this night, it was anything but routine.

CHANH HANG

(Lead Park Ranger)

Chanh: *Normally, working the play is always the same for me. When it's over, I make one last round to make sure no one is in the mansion. I arm the alarm panel, turn the sconces off, and I'm gone. Simple. But this night was different. When I go to leave, I twist the doorknob to the left, which is normal—but the door won't open. Then with more force, I turn it and push again. I can't get the door to budge.*

Chanh shakes his head, still not believing what took place.

Chanh: *At that moment, to my left side, like from the top of my head, I feel someone run their fingers lightly down to my ear and then off my shoulder. I still can't get the door open! I just freaked out! Suddenly the door opens up like I was now being allowed to exit! I quickly step out and close the door behind me. I grab my flashlight and shine it through that wrought iron and glass door. I see nothing. I try to calm myself down. I open the door, stick my flashlight inside and shine it toward the stairwell to make sure no physical being is there. Then I realize, "The alarm! I have to disarm it before it goes off!" Deep breath and I go inside towards the alarm panel. I'm still facing the stairwell. I shine my flashlight everywhere just to make sure. Nothing. I disarm the panel. It's totally quiet. I scan the second-floor stairs down to the bottom with the light. Nothing. I'm still freaked out trying to figure out what touched me. The alarm pad says it's ready to arm again. I arm the mansion, still facing the stairs. It's totally silent as I move away slowly over to the front door. Now my back is to the door. I reach behind me, turn the doorknob, and slowly walk out backwards, closing the door. I never heard a voice. I never saw anything. Just felt fingers down my head and off my shoulders. The mansion is now armed and I slowly backed away.*

"STILL SHOOK UP"

CLETE KEITH

Ranger Chanh's story corroborates my experience with a visiting Australian family. I was leaving for the day when I passed a family—father, mother, a daughter maybe fourteen, and a son around twelve. I overheard the dad say, "*There Will Be Blood* was filmed here." I stopped and asked if they had any questions and we chatted for a few minutes. They were so interested in Greystone, I decided to walk them into the bowling alley to show them where scenes of Paul Thomas Anderson's movie had been shot. They were overjoyed and so appreciative that I decided to treat them to a tour of the rest of the mansion. I told them about the history of the Doheny family along with some of the paranormal stories.

Here are my recollections after the tour:

We are back at the front door of the Grand Entry. I begin to act out Ranger Chanh's story and describe the creepy way he was touched. When I was done, we say goodbye and the daughter hurries out first, followed by the rest of the family. After closing up and heading back to my car, I overhear the mother talking to a ranger. She says that her daughter has experienced something weird and is quite shaken up. Concerned, I immediately offer to talk to her daughter and make sure she is all right. When I find her, she is still shook up. I ask her if she is okay, she says, "I never believed in ghosts. My mom is the one that does, but I don't." She tells me that when I was acting out Ranger Chanh's story of how he was touched on the back of his ear, she felt her hair move to the side and that "something or someone" touched her neck. It completely freaked her out, but she didn't say anything to me or her family at the time.

This is a common theme. On many tours, people who have a paranormal experience, keep it to themselves for a few reasons: they're scared out of their wits; they're afraid of ridicule; or they're so shocked that they question themselves as to whether this happened or not. It explains why she was the first to hurry out of the mansion when I opened the front door. This wonderful family was stopping in Los Angeles to visit Beverly Hills before flying off to vacation in London. After seeing the bowling alley where *There Will Be Blood* was filmed, the father said, "This will be a trip we'll never forget." I think their daughter would agree, but for a totally different reason.

"Strange Energy"

Speaking of corroboration, compare the following story with the previous two stories. I was involved, yet again, and this one was also astonishing. It was one of the hottest days of the summer in 2017. Easily above one-hundred degrees. I was working in the Greystone Gatehouse where my office was at the time. It's a small house at the southern part of the property where - from 1928 to 1955 - the lead security guard would sign in the guests upon entering the estate.

On this blistering day, I heard a knock at the door and opened to find two women in their early twenties, Krizza and Tonje, standing before me, beet red. They had just walked several miles from the Beverly Center, a shopping mall in Los Angeles—in heels! No easy hike in any footwear. They were vacationing from Norway and Greystone was on their list of sites to visit.

I invited them into the air-conditioned office, gave them some cold water, and encouraged them to rest. Being from Norway, they were shocked at the temperature. Once they cooled off, I felt it only fair to take them inside the mansion for a quick look. They were immediately excited, although Krizza seemed a bit apprehensive. Little did I know that soon her apprehension would turn into outright panic.

KRIZZA ELISABETH
(Visitor)

> Krizza: *I felt so much energy when we went into that house. It was like an energy wave hitting me when you opened that door. And I thought everyone felt it. So I was like, "Wow!" It literally felt like wind in my hair. That's the only way to explain it. That's the first feeling I got when you opened the door and we stood inside. And then you were talking, I don't remember what you were talking about, but I remember something pushing on me. It was like so much energy pushing me, so weird, and I felt so heavy and so tired on my feet. And when you told us about that family from Australia, I was feeling someone brush away some of my hair and I put it back behind my ear. Do you remember? I kind of jumped a little bit? And you asked me, "Everything okay?" And I was like, "I don't know, it's nothing. I'm good."*

I remember she said she was "good," but she looked concerned. Really concerned.

> Krizza: *At first I thought I was paranoid. Actually I still feel paranoid today. Months after having felt that energy. But when I felt my hair being touched and no one was behind me, I was terrified because I've always been sensitive to the paranormal. Every time something happened to me in the mansion, Tonje was like, "I want to feel it as well." And I'd say, "Yeah? Be my guest, because I don't want to feel it!"*

"MYSTERIOUS TAPPING"

His colleagues consider Park Ranger Chanh Hang someone who is very much "by the book." He's quiet, very professional, and quite observant. Being in the mansion is not one of his favorite duties. In fact, a relative of Chanh's, who's very sensitive to the spirit world, has advised him that he should get in and get out of the mansion as fast as possible. When Ranger Chanh came to me with the following story, I thought he was joking around, because a few weeks before, another ranger called me in a panic with the exact same story (that ranger's account follows this one). When I interviewed Chanh in the Grand Entry, I realized quickly, by the way he recounted his story, that he was clearly not joking.

CHANH HANG
(Lead Park Ranger)

> Chanh: *I came in to work at six-thirty in the morning. I walk through the courtyard and enter the grand entry to disarm the mansion alarm and turn on the lights. I turn around to leave and as soon as I grab the doorknob, I hear over my left shoulder, the sound of fingers tapping on glass. Not a knock, but fingers tapping—like someone is out there trying to get my attention.*

Chanh took a long moment to gather his next thoughts.

> Chanh: *I'm finally able to isolate the tapping—it is toward the card room, over by the library and those glass door panels… and the tapping sounds like it is on glass, not wood, it is definitely glass. Everything else over there is wood besides those three panels. Remember, at this hour, no one should be in the park. The alarm is on, so if someone managed to hide in the mansion overnight, it will no doubt trigger the alarm. The sound keeps happening and I've worked here long enough that I can recognize wood creaking because the mansion is old. I know the sounds of some rat running across the marble floor, or a window being opened, or a twig that might hit the glass from a tree outside, but this is definitely fingers tapping, clear as day. Listen, it is early morning, crack of dawn, still dark, I'm alone. I just walk out without saying a word. I am not going to play Ghostbusters and investigate who or what is making that tapping noise!*

For Chanh, this was the pièce de résistance.

Chanh: *And then, listen to this—another ranger told me their experience with the exact same sound and said it was isolated in the same area! In the same room. We met that evening and when I demonstrated what I heard on the glass, that ranger said, "Yep, that's exactly what I heard!" Same experience. Two weeks apart.*

"STATIC SHOCK"

(This Ranger prefers not to reveal their identity.)

One night I get a panicked phone call from Ranger M.M., who sounded very nervous and overwhelmed. I quickly turned on my recorder to capture the story. Ranger M.M. was transferred from Greystone to a different Beverly Hills park in part because of the incident that follows.

"RANGER M.M."
(Park Ranger)

Ranger M.M.: *This happened a bit after eight p.m. I turn off the last light inside the mansion and I'm ready to leave when I hear something moving around in the house and I'm like, "What the hell is that?!" I flip on some lights and look around and I don't see anything—but I do hear something making this noise. Something is clearly moving around. It sounds like something scampering, like a rat, a big rat, running up the wall or across the side of the window. And I'm like, "Oh, no. This isn't good. I don't like this." It could either be near the corner of the library or the card room. I'm rattled and I want to get out of the mansion. I turn on the alarm, turn off all the lights, lock up and I'm out. As I get close to the Richie Rich gates, I suddenly feel a static shock! Like static electricity! It's a tingling feeling on my arm and it's not going away. If it's a few seconds, okay, but this shock lasts like two minutes!*

There is a long silence, then a deep nervous breath.

Ranger M.M.: *So now I walk to the ranger truck and my arm is still tingling! I'm driving up to the ranger office, freaking out because it's still tingling! And I'm just like, "Okay, you're crazy. It's in your head." Then I look at my arm and it's got a red scratch on it! I mean bigger than an inch. Now I really started freaking out! I go into the ranger office and the tingling slowly disappears and I'm thinking, "Get over it!" I start typing up my report and I hear that tapping sound again! Against the window! And then the tingling in the arm is back. I call* [Ranger] *John, "Hey, did anything weird ever happen to you up here?" And he says, "Like what?" I told him and he immediately says, "Call Clete." Like, honestly, if I didn't have the scratch, I probably wouldn't have said anything. I would have just thought, "Alright, cuckoo, get over it." But when I saw the scratch...*

In a follow up with Ranger M.M., I asked if after leaving the office and exiting the park, did the tingling stop? Ranger M.M. said, "Yes. Completely." This ranger has since left the Ranger Program and is now working in a different department within the city.

Greystone Historical Report

"Tapestry hung on the wall facing the top landing on the main staircase."
—Sam Schultz, Lucy (Doheny) Battson's
  chauffeur for many years

"ONE BAD DECISION"

There are rules and regulations in place to protect the mansion from damage when it's being used for film shoots or indoor events. The rules cover restrictions such as nailing into wood, painting unauthorized surfaces, moving film equipment inside without floor protection, among many others. Various rangers warn film and event companies that if they don't follow the rules there will be consequences from "Ned."

Lydie Gutfeld was one of those rangers who warned companies about "Ned." A lifeguard at one point prior to her employment with the City of Beverly Hills, Lydie used those skills to remain on alert whenever working at Greystone. When she dealt with film and event companies, they naturally assumed that she and the other rangers were speaking about their immediate boss, named Ned, when in fact, they were speaking of Ned Doheny, the owner of the mansion who was murdered back in 1929. Yeah, that Ned.

In fact, some of the rangers felt like they had a "working relationship" with Ned. They wanted what was best for the property and would give Ned a verbal or mental heads up as to what was going to take place inside the mansion. When I first heard this, it sounded quite bizarre, until I discovered through these interviews that there were several instances where those who disregarded the rules of the mansion did in fact have to deal with the consequences.

LYDIE GUTFELD
(Retired Park Ranger, Camp Counselor)

> Lydie: *Maybe twenty-five years ago, they were filming a movie and the set people painted the wall at the entrance this weird color, and they hung these huge rugs as wall paintings. They didn't tell me that they were going to do that.*

Film companies are notorious like this. But the rules are clear: after completing a final walkthrough with a film company, no changes to the mansion are to be made without the consent of the supervising ranger.

> Lydie: *So I walk in around five a.m., before the crew is allowed inside the house, and I see these rugs and I'm like, "Oh crap, this is not good. Okay, what is going to go wrong today?!" They start rolling cameras and nothing is going right. Settings on the cameras keep getting messed up, take after take and they're like, "What is going on?! And why isn't the*

electrical generator working?!" No genny, no lights. Nothing went right. Not one thing! It was literally a wasted day of filming because nothing would work!

"WHO MOVED MY HAT?"

I did not meet Luz prior to interviewing her. She was a ranger from 1995 to 2001, but our paths had surprisingly never crossed. I was stunned to find out after our walkthrough of the mansion that she has 21 paranormal stories from her time as a ranger. In fact, when transcribing one of our interviews, I discovered a mysterious voice that joined in on the conversation that we never heard at the time of the interview. Apparently, everyone tries to get in on the act.

As it turns out, Luz is very sensitive to energy and I wonder if that's why she was targeted. Some of her stories left me stunned, not only because they're amazing stories, but because Luz stood her ground and didn't run screaming from the building. Luz would be a good person to have with you in a foxhole. I told her to lead the way through the mansion to where she remembered having her experiences.

Photo: Chris Keith

The railing of the Grand Entry's staircase has decorative carved wooden acorn ornaments on four of its posts.

LUZ RODRIGUEZ

(Retired Park Ranger)

> Luz: *My routine was always the same. I come into the mansion, turn off the alarm, and then go walking around the house checking on various things. I always set my hat on one particular acorn—the one on the left. Then one day, I put my hat on the left cone and made my rounds through the rooms to the kitchen. When I came back up my hat is on the cone on the right. Not where I definitely left it. I was like, "I know I set it there, that's what I do."*

She was very sure of herself, until…

> Luz: *And then I start doubting myself. "Maybe I did set it over there. I could be wrong." And then it happened again. I set it on the left acorn and I know I set it there. I make sure I set it there. I turn off the alarm and go down into the mansion and come back and it was over there on the right acorn! And so I spoke out loud directly to them: "Okay you guys, I get it. I get it." Because my mom would tell me, "Luz, don't be afraid. They're not going to hurt you. Be afraid of the living, not the dead." She told me to just talk to the spirits. So when I come into the house and it happens again, my response is, "Listen, I'm here to make sure your house is okay and everything is safe. I will walk through and leave. I promise." After that, it never happened again. My hat stayed put.*

"A WALK WITH CHRIS FLEMING"

CLETE KEITH

Chris Fleming is the son of former National Hockey League star Reggie Fleming. But that's not why Chris Fleming is well-known. Chris' fame is based on his work as a medium and paranormal researcher—work in these fields jettisoned his career as a television star on A&E, Animal

16

Planet, and guest appearances on many paranormal shows such as *Ghost Adventures.*

I'm not sure what it is about the Grand Entry and the area surrounding that makes it particularly active, but I do remember quite vividly the day that forever changed my research about this location. I walked Chris Fleming and three of his associates inside the mansion. He immediately felt strong energy. Chris said, "Can we go upstairs?" Something was leading him that way. As we took a couple steps away from the Grand Entry and started up the staircase, he suddenly bent over, as if he were in pain, and said, "We've got somebody here with us."

Now when I hear a statement like that, I don't automatically assume it's true just because a person claims to have "abilities" or "the gift."[3] Chris looked at the woman with us, who was also supposedly psychic, and said, "Do you feel that?" And she said, "Yes, I do." He pulled out his digital recorder, turned it on, and said into the recorder, "I know that you're here. I can feel you. Can you tell me your name? Who are you?" He shut the recorder off, played it back. To my astonishment, on the recording[4] was a male voice that did not belong to me or anyone else in the room. It sounded garbled. We played it back several times and couldn't make out exactly what the voice was saying, but there was definitely a voice trying to communicate.

We continued our walk through the mansion. The rest of this Chris Fleming visit is documented in several other chapters.

---

3 "The gift" refers to one's ability to see (clairvoyance), hear (clairaudience), feel or sense (clairsentience) spirits on the other side.
4 Audio recording is non-existent.

"Portal Energy?"

Juan texted me on the night of September 24, 2019. We talked on the phone as this incident was unfolding. I could feel the urgency in his voice. It sounded like he was overwhelmed with what was taking place in the mansion. I stayed on the phone and asked him questions about what was going on and it all seemed so strange but…it's Greystone.

This follow-up interview is quite in depth. He was able to express what he was seeing and feeling. This story starts near the Grand Entry and leads him up to the Second-Floor Landing.

JUAN ANDRADE
(Park Ranger Supervisor)

> Juan: *I was on the job and I walk inside the mansion and I end up right by the main stairs outside of the men's bathroom. There is no one in the grand hallway. All the guests are inside, in the rooms on their tours and I'm keeping an eye on the main entrance door. I turn around to my right and look at the men's bathroom door. At first, I think I'm seeing a laser pointer because it was bright, ruby red. It looked like someone was making a "U" pattern with the laser and then it disappeared. I quickly scan the area for anyone with a laser pointer, but there is nothing. At the same time, I can hear Daniel and Sara* [Park Ranger Supervisor and Venue Coordinator, respectively] *on the second floor, but I know Daniel doesn't carry a laser and he wouldn't point a laser down there anyway. Nobody else is in the grand hall, so I'm puzzled. I look back to the area where I clearly saw this red dot type laser light that had like a tail moving with it, but I still can't find the source. But I clearly saw it. It wasn't in my peripheral vision. It wasn't like a fast thing. No, I saw it. It moved in a circular motion and then it disappeared. It just stopped.*

It's interesting during these interviews how the interviewee works hard, searching their memory banks, to re-create and revisit their experiences in logical detail.

Juan: *I walk up two or three steps on the grand entry staircase and I hear Daniel walk away from the second-floor landing and Sara comes down the stairs and says, "Hey, Daniel was looking for you. He wanted to tell you that he was leaving. I'm heading out, too." But I am still puzzled where that red light came from. I walk up to the top of the grand entry stairs, take out my cell phone and take a picture of the men's bathroom door. And what my cell phone camera does is throw a series of flashes before it takes a picture; so as I'm taking the picture, I can see an orb[5] coming towards me, but my cell phone camera, in the process of flashing, is too slow to pick it up. But I clearly see an orb coming right at me on my phone's screen. It's white. A translucent white. But now I feel like someone is on the second floor, moving around, but I don't see anything. Sara has already grabbed her stuff and left along with Daniel, so there was no one up there. But then what I see is moving skin.*

This didn't make sense, but then again, a lot of things at Greystone sometimes make little sense.

Juan: *You know how the banisters have carved designs and there are crevices? Like open areas? I can see what looks like a skin tone, moving through the bannister. Dark skin. Not black, but maybe my tone. But the vibe is there. I mean, I really feel it. Now all my hair is standing straight up. Someone or something has showed themselves to me and they're on the second-floor landing. And suddenly I start to become very emotional. I want to cry. I feel as if I am watching something I shouldn't see. Someone who is dead. It's just pure grief or sadness. That's the only way I can interpret it. I come down the stairs and that emotion goes away, but I know there is something still up on that second-floor landing. And by now, the guests are starting to leave the mansion so I begin closing up the second-floor landing, turning off the two chandeliers. And again, maybe fifteen minutes later, I clearly feel something up there. The vibe came back very, very strong. There*

---

5 An "orb" is a sphere or ball of light that in theory is representative of energy from a spirit being.

is so much energy that it bothers me. It is very uncomfortable. I feel that it is hurting me. It's almost like being in a science museum and you touch that ball that's sparking like lightning and all your hairs stand up? I've never been hit by lightning, but can you imagine just an electrical field so powerful that it makes all your hairs on your body stand up and you can actually feel it on your skin. It's like that. It feels like a very strong electromagnetic field.[6] So I turn off the lights and as I come back down the stairs, that energy is gone.

Juan was visibly dumbfounded. I waited for him to pull his thoughts together.

Juan: *It was almost as if a portal[7] opened and I was going in and out of that electromagnetic field. I could feel it. I could literally feel the portal! I've never felt anything like this. And it was just so much all at once. I mean, first I see the chandelier phase in and out. Then I see the red orb. I also see someone or flesh moving on the second-floor landing, and then all that electrical energy that is up there. My main concern was that I had a spirit attachment[8] and was going to bring something home with me.*

Ghosts or spirits from the other side have been reported to inhabit the body and energy of human beings.

Juan: *And then as soon as I leave the property, there is this burning sensation around my eye. Like I had burned my eye, around here, all around my left eye. As I am driving home, it slowly went away. But it was the weirdest shit!*

---

6 Electromagnetic fields (EMF) consist of a combination of invisible electric and magnetic fields of force. In the paranormal field, you may feel this as a change in temperature, or a sense of static electricity.

7 A "Portal" is a ghost doorway(s) from another dimension. It allows the spirit world to connect with ours. It is believed that spirits use these to go from one place to another.

8 A spirit attachment is the sort of possession in which a disembodied entity attaches itself to a living person. Almost like a spirit parasite. This spirit attachment does not imply, or is not associated with, a demonic possession. Most spirit attachments are benign.

"Pushed"

Steve Clark, who has since retired from the Ranger Program with the City of Beverly Hills, was extremely competent, intelligent, and experienced in his job. He enforced the rules and made sure the Ranger Program ran efficiently. He could always be counted as a straight shooter and someone who would offer great advice and guidance. We began working for the City at the same time and became great friends. Steve was the ranger on duty when psychic medium, Lisa Williams, filmed her Lifetime network program, *Life Among the Dead,* on an overnight walkthrough in the mansion. When she showed up on this cold, Los Angeles winter night, she met Steve. They shook hands, and then she pointed at his hands saying, "Oh my God, you have the gift." Steve looked at his hands and said, "Oh, no, it's so cold out, I was just rubbing my hands together to stay warm." "No," she said, "You've got the gift!" Steve threw up his hands and said, "I don't want the gift!"

Is it because of this "gift" that Steve was targeted by whatever spirits there are in the mansion? I asked Steve to spend some time with me in the mansion for an extended interview. At the end of our long session and walkthrough, he detailed 13 stories, some of which I find absolutely astounding.

We started at the staircase near the Grand Entry.

STEVEN CLARK
(Retired Park Ranger Supervisor)

> Steven: *We were told the story about a ranger who got pushed down the stairs. That was the iconic Greystone story passed down through the ranger program. Well, it wasn't fabricated, because I met the ex-ranger who's now a District Attorney[9] in California and he verified that he was with the*

---

9 I contacted the ex-ranger/District Attorney, but he would not go on record and talk to me about the incident.

female ranger when she was pushed down the stairs. I mean, he was there actually walking down the stairs with her.

Steve is enthused telling the story regarding what actually happened.

Steven: *Up until then it had been ranger legend. But the two rangers were going down the staircase right here, at the top of the stairs, and the female ranger was hit in the back and got shoved down the stairs. I mean violently. She went head over heels down the stairs. She wanted to quit that day and who could blame her? The funny thing was that her boss wouldn't let her because he didn't have anybody else to cover her shift for the next day. So he made her work here another two days until he could get coverage. And then she was out. She left the job. But this guy, the DA from California, he was the one who was walking with her that day. He completely verified that story without any prompting. He came back to Greystone with his two kids and his wife and I brought him into the mansion. As he tells me that story, I was shocked. I said, "Oh my God, we thought that was urban legend! We didn't know this was a true story!" And he says, "It's true, I was there!"*

Chapter 2

Grand Hall

*I was just so shocked. I saw a long white dress that was literally
floating in front of my eyes!*
— BROOKE PICONE
    FORMER GREYSTONE CAMP COUNSELOR

Photo: Chris Keith

The films *Rock Star, National Treasure: Book of Secrets,
The Muppets, Mercury Rising, Hanging Up, The Disorderly
Orderly*, the Coen Brothers' *The Big Lebowski, Dead
Ringer, Death Becomes Her, Spider-Man 3, There Will Be
Blood* directed by Paul Thomas Anderson, *The Astronaut's
Wife* starring Charlize Theron and Johnny Depp, and
Star Trek Into Darkness directed by J.J. Abrams, were all
filmed in the Grand Hall.

The Grand Hall certainly lives up to its name—an extensive hallway
that spans almost the entire length of the mansion's first floor. What
immediately catches the eye is the iconic black-and-white marble floor
that imbues it with a striking beauty. You can almost imagine the sound
of Hugh Plunkett's oxfords striking against the marble as he abruptly
rushed to confront Ned Doheny on that fateful night.

Imagine the east hallway back in 1928, when this section was adorned with Chippendale wallpaper and furnishings that included English-style chairs and tables throughout. The library, east alcove, and dining room occupy this side of the hall. Situated at the west end of the hall is the living room, south guest room (aka the Murder Room), and the north guest room (aka Doll Room). Furnishings were in the Venetian-style and Italian paintings decorated the walls. Along with the unique furnishings in the Grand Hall, this area of the mansion took on a unique and festive splendor during the holiday season. Timothy Doheny recalls Christmas and his mother's penchant for giving out an excessive number of gifts.

Greystone Historical Report

"Usually they put the tree out in the hallway, near the main entrance overlooking the terrace. They put it in the west corner. I remember people passing out presents and dozens of kids running into each other. My mother had a propensity for giving lots of presents, most of them junk. You'd get lots of them, at least ten or twelve of them."

—Timothy Doheny

"DISEMBODIED NED"

After this interview, I showed Luz a photo that shocked her.

LUZ RODRIGUEZ
(Retired Park Ranger)

Luz: *I'm outside cleaning the windows on the terrace and I look up and there is someone standing inside the mansion. At first, I think it's someone at the grand entry door or maybe it's a reflection of someone standing behind me. But when I look back, there is no one there. I saw who I believe to be Ned Doheny standing right here in the middle of the grand hallway. But I couldn't see his shoes. He was cut off somehow, like you couldn't see his whole body, definitely not most of his legs. He was almost floating and kind of see-through, transparent. He was wearing a reddish smoking jacket. He had a mustache. His hair is neatly combed. And he just stood there, looking at me—for a long time. I still get chills! And I was just like, "Okay, Hi Ned. This is weird." And then I thought, "My mind is playing tricks," you know? "It can't be." But it was like he was not fully materialized.*

I show Luz the murder/suicide photo of Ned Doheny. She just stared at it. Shocked. The photo shows Ned, deceased, lying on the floor, bloodied, in what looks like a smoking jacket.

Luz: *Is that smoking jacket red?!*

I tell her all the photos are in black and white, so we don't know. She is absolutely stunned having never before seen the photo. She holds out her arm to me. "Goose bumps!"

"My Name Is Emily"

CLETE KEITH

While we're on the topic of apparitions in the mansion, I have my own story to share. This one not only adds to the evidence I've collected pointing to the presence of a young spirit in the mansion, but it possibly gives us her name. It all begins with me accompanying a television crew on a walkthrough of the mansion so they could plan an upcoming shoot. As I watched the crew, I noticed a woman looking over at me. She appeared unnerved. I knew right away that something had taken place and she was anxious. She broke away from the rest of the crew and approached me.

In a hushed tone, her first question was, "Is this place...you know?" And I said, "No, I don't know." I knew what she was talking about, but I always prefer to let people tell me their story first before I volunteer any information involving spirit activity. She lowered the sound of her voice even more and said, "I mean, are there ghosts in here?" I still wouldn't divulge any information, "Why do you ask?" And she said, "Ever since I was a little girl, I was able to see and hear, even sense ghosts around me. But when I turned fifteen (she was in her thirties at this time), it got too much for me to handle, so I shut it down. I couldn't take it anymore. But when I walked into this house and I was standing here with the crew, this little girl ran up to me and said, "My name is Emily! It's Emily! My name is Emily!"

It became obvious to this woman that the rest of the crew could not see or hear the little girl. She realized it was happening again, just as it had when she was a young girl. She told me she casually broke away from the group, stepped behind a wall where she couldn't be seen, turned to the little girl and said, "Okay, your name is Emily. Okay, I got that, but you've got to stay away from me! Please, don't do this to me. Stay away." She backed away from the little girl, shaken by what had just taken place, and walked back to the crew. Then she asked me point blank, "Is this place haunted?" I said, "Yes." The questions kept coming: "Did a little girl die here?" I said, "Yes." She asked, "Was her name Emily?" I said, "We don't know." She took a long pause, looked me dead in the eyes and said, "It's Emily."

From that day on, I've called the spirit "Emily." Whenever I walk into the mansion, I say, "Hi Emily. It's Clete." If I'm there at night, I say, "Emily, you can come out and talk to me if you want." I've never seen her, but that woman finally gave a name to the spirit—and according to my research—has been seen as many as five times.

"MYSTERY GUNSHOT"

A young man in his twenties, Martin did not work at Greystone very long before this next experience. Normally, Martin was very quiet and kept to himself, but there were days he talked to me about the experiences he was having when he cleaned inside the mansion. He told me stories of being haunted in his youth and how he would flee his house in tears, waiting outside until his older brother came home to comfort and reassure him. Now he felt, for better or for worse, the spirits were trying to connect with him while he worked in the mansion. Does Martin have abilities to draw the spirits to him? I can't say, but he confided in me about what was taking place and how he was struggling to get through each day in the mansion. Martin has always struck me as a deeply sincere man, but unfortunately was clearly living in fear of what he might witness on any given day.

MARTIN J. PEREZ
(Janitorial Services)

> Martin: *This happened in the Grand Hall. I was passing through and suddenly BANG—I honestly thought "someone fired a shot in the house." I stopped dead. It had that echo sound a gunshot would have bouncing off the walls. And it was so loud. Really loud. I couldn't tell if it was coming from upstairs or the bottom floor. Like I said it echoes. But no one was in the house. It's weird because they have the play[1] and they perform it on the staircase, and they have the guy shooting with that snap-bang sound from the gunshot! I honestly felt that I heard the same thing by the staircase. Snap! Bang! It really scared me.*

Martin now has a job with another company and no longer works at Greystone. I'm sure he's very relieved. I've left my recorder running inside the mansion when it's closed at night, and I've captured several remarkable

---

1 When Martin mentions "the play," he's referring to "The Manor"—a play performed in the mansion in which a gun is fired.

recordings[2] of what appears to be exactly what Martin heard—a loud gunshot ringing out.

Greystone Historical Report

"Greystone is a beautifully laid-out machine for living," states Dr. David Gebhard, professor of Architectural history and director of the Art Galleries at the University of California at Santa Barbara. [1984]

Indeed, Greystone offers seven uniquely designed Georgian fireplaces, exquisite paneling and ceilings, plus incredible antique-inspired furniture. For its time, Greystone Mansion was also a thoroughly modern and practical building.

"DON'T BE AFRAID"

I interviewed Dalila right in the middle of the Grand Hall—for her, ground zero of this next experience.

DALILA PEREZ
(Janitorial Services)

> Dalila: *I'm mopping the floors in here and I turn around because I am feeling very cold air on my face and right through my body. Like something blowing cold air right at you. I feel like it passes right through me. So I stood right here with the mop and I say, "Oh my God. I don't know what it is, but I cannot be afraid. I have to finish cleaning." It's the same thing I told Elva* [a co-worker] *when I was training her for three days. "The first thing you're going to feel when you stand right here, right in the middle of the grand hall, you're going to feel that fresh air." She was like, "Don't*

---

2 Audio recording exists in author's collection.

tell me that!" But I tell her, "Don't be afraid! But trust me, when you start mopping this place, and you're by yourself, you will feel it." Then on the first week, she calls me the moment she felt it—"Dalila, I'm afraid!" I say, "Why?" Elva says, "I just feel the same thing you said I was going to feel." I asked her, "What do you feel?" She was nervous, "I feel a lot of cold air, fresh air, but cold, right in the middle where you told me!" So I told her again, "Don't be afraid. That's okay. It's normal. Don't be afraid." She says, "That's not normal! I'm afraid! I'm outta here!" I said, "Just finish what you're doing fast and get out of there. But if you cannot handle it, just go." But Elva was very afraid. She finished and left in a hurry.

"MAN IN WHITE"

MARTIN J. PEREZ

(Janitorial Services)

Martin: *I was outside the card room looking in from the terrace to the grand hall. With the reflection of the light outside, it's kind of hard to see in, so you have to cup your hands to get a better look. It was early in the morning. The piano tuner was scheduled and I see him at the front door with Steve Clark* [Park Ranger Supervisor]. *Then I see this tall man, all dressed in white, with his head down and his hands in his pockets, walking through the grand hall. He was a tall white male. As Steve and the piano tuner walked down the main entrance staircase, this man in white walked right past Steve and up the staircase toward the entrance. Obviously, Steve and the piano tuner didn't see him. So I went around to the front door and the man in white was no longer there. I waved at Steve and rushed over to catch him before he left the mansion. And I said, "Hey, Steve, who's the other guy?" And he's like, "What other guy? The piano tuner?" I said, "No, this guy was all dressed in white and he was very tall. You didn't see him?" And Steve said, "No… I felt something, but I didn't see anything." But I did—he just walked right past Steve. I couldn't tell if he went upstairs or just faded away.*

I questioned Steve about this incident, and he said he did feel something out of the ordinary, but he didn't want to look. Remember, Steve doesn't want anything to do with the paranormal. He simply continued on with the piano tuner and the task at hand.

> Martin: *But I clearly saw him. He was a solid figure. Caucasian, really pale. It kind of tripped me out. I was like, "Whoa!" No way it was a reflection from the outside, because I was looking with my hands cupped against the window and my head was literally right up against the glass, so there's no possible way. It just makes you think like maybe this is the thing that's following me around because it's always here on the first floor So who knows? Another mystery in the mansion.*

"FLOATING WHITE DRESS"

When Brooke Picone was a child, she attended the Beverly Hills theatre camp at Greystone named "Catskills" after the famous summer resort area in New York State. Eventually she became one of their main camp counselors. I brought her back to the mansion to relive several moments that took place many years ago. I was captivated, not only by Brooke telling this particular story, but at just how astonished she is, to this day, at what took place that night on March 3, 1991. We walked into the Grand Hall so she could show me exactly where her incident took place.

BROOKE PICONE
(Beverly Hills "Catskills" Camp Counselor)

> Brooke: *This was one night during the week and it was probably around nine or ten p.m. I was with my boyfriend, Brehnen Knight, who was a ranger. We were in the mansion making sure all the windows were shut. Obviously, the park is closed. So there's nobody's in the park and there's nobody in the house. We come inside here and Brehnen goes to the restroom. I'm waiting for him right here in the middle of the grand hall. I look over*

and down the hallway to that glass door—and remember, it's pretty dark inside the house. The only lights that were coming into the mansion would be the city lights.

Brooke took this unique pause as she stared down the hallway to the glass door. I could see the memory of that night was flooding back. Then she turned back to me.

Brooke: *All of a sudden, from this direction, right here, on the left, I see this little girl—she was small, maybe eight years old just floating outside, past that window. And when I say she wasn't walking—she wasn't, she was floating, like literally ten inches or a foot off the ground. And she's wearing a long white dress and you can't see any feet coming through. She's just floating! I honestly don't even remember if I saw any type of face. I was just so shocked I saw a long white dress that was literally floating in front of my eyes! And then she was gone! I told Brehnen and he said that he had seen her before, too. And I'm like "What?!" I just thought it was so weird and strange, yet kind of expected from this place. And even when I told other people years later, they always said, "Yeah, that's the little girl in the white dress!"*

Chapter 3

Card Room and Terrace

I think to myself, what did I just see? Did I see a girl? A real person? I have to step outside for a little fresh air. Get myself together.

— CHANH HANG
   GREYSTONE LEAD PARK RANGER

Photo: Chae Yi

The Prestige starring Christian Bale and Hugh Jackman, *Guilty by Suspicion* with Robert DeNiro and Annette Bening, *The Witches of Eastwick* starring Jack Nicholson, Cher, and Susan Sarandon, *Air Force One* starring Harrison Ford as President James Marshall, and finally, *Hard to Kill* with Steven Seagal, were films shot in the Card Room.

On my first visit inside the mansion, I remember walking into the Grand Entry, and I was immediately taken aback by the historic architecture and stunning woodwork. But then I was drawn to the three doors with lead-paned windows in the adjacent Card Room. It was nearly dusk and the beauty of the room, highlighted with the Terrace view, was picture-perfect. Most visitors to Greystone, who enter the mansion the way I did, have a similar visceral reaction—one that can only be described as spectacular. But while the beauty is awesome, and in its day was a place for fun and games, the Card Room is not immune from the many strange and unexplainable occurrences so prevalent at Greystone Mansion.

Greystone Historical Report

Straight ahead, three archways of intricately carved and highly polished oak led into the marble floored card room, complete with a now-vanished fountain. From the card room, three round-arched French doors opened onto a stone terrace overlooking the estate's sweeping front lawn and all of Beverly Hills.

Card Room

Natural light pours into the picturesque Card Room from the leaded glass doors facing the Terrace, making it the perfect space for family and friends to gather to play games and cards. The east and west walls of this room, now painted white, were once adorned with Italian landscapes. At one time, the center of the room was host to a small, stone fountain, which was eventually removed and replaced with chairs and gaming tables.

"In Shock"

Dan Hernandez and I have been friends for nearly twenty years. He's a hard-working, stand-up guy, who climbed his way up the ladder to Park Ranger Supervisor. When he began telling me his story that took place in the Card Room, he was calm and calculated, but by the time we stepped outside to the Terrace to finish the story, he was completely animated. Of course, my questions didn't help calm him down. I kept saying, "Wait, so you come out here and what happened?! How is that possible?!" Dan was able to place himself right back in the drama of his experience, and at the same time, he was still trying to figure out how this event could have actually taken place.

DANIEL HERNANDEZ

(Park Ranger Supervisor)

> Daniel: *My week started on a Sunday. This happened about eight in the morning. Nobody was in the park, which opens at ten a.m. I open up the inner courtyard and walk in through the front door and disarm the alarm of the mansion. We hosted a wedding the night before, so I walk down into the card room and I look at the marble floor to see what damages there are from the wedding. The room is dirty, and it could use some clean up. I follow up outside to check on the condition of the terrace. I exit the front door of the mansion and walk around to the terrace. It was clear that I need to wash down the slate because the spillage was bad. When I look over to the card room, all the doors are open—open to the terrace! I was just in the card room a minute ago and they were all closed. I was in shock.*

I could see it now, during the interview, the shock on his face and in his voice. It's like he time-traveled back and was feeling the exact same overwhelming emotions of that original moment.

> Daniel: *I immediately get on the phone and call Steve Clark, the ranger who worked the night before. And it's not like I was calling him to say, "Hey, you didn't lock up those card room doors!" I was calling him because I was in shock! I really couldn't talk! I finally say, "All these card room doors are open!" He's like, "I could have sworn I latched them and double checked!" And I said, "I'm not calling for that! I'm calling because I'm freaking out over here! This is unreal, they're all open! And I was just in the card room and they were all closed. I'm standing on the terrace and there's no one around. The mansion is empty." Steve interrupts me, "Plus, the alarm could not have been set with these doors open, or ajar, even just an inch."*

I asked Dan, "Could someone, I'm not sure who that would be, but could they somehow have opened the doors in the time you left the Card Room and walked to the Terrace?"

Daniel: *No way. All three doors have canes* [about ten-inch solid metal bars that go into the threshold and another cane that goes into the mount on top] *and each handle has its own lock that you turn. So we're talking about unlatching the canes—twelve of them—and then unlocking all three doors, and getting them open, which isn't easy because they get stuck all the time. So that's like fifteen things to do before you can even open them!*

Like he said, "no way."

Daniel: *"Like I was in shock. It made absolutely no sense. It was just another thing that convinced me that this place is crazy active, and they wanted my attention. Well, they got it!"*

Parting thoughts: Over time, Dan went from being dumbfounded to trying to somehow justify this bizarre and baffling occurrence. The most puzzling aspect of this experience, and there are numerous, is what Ranger Clark stated, that the alarm could not have been set with the doors open or even ajar. In addition, all the doors have complex locking mechanisms. I can personally attest that opening all six doors is a hassle and they're very difficult to open which only added to Dan's confusion and the reason why he was so shocked.

"Shattered Mirrors"

For ten years, the City of Beverly Hills produced sponsored design shows at Greystone. Interior designers would select a room, design it, and present it on display for public visitors. The event was very popular, which meant that a large number of designers and their assistants would navigate in and out of the mansion—redecorating various rooms, hallways, and landings. Quite frankly, it was a logistical nightmare. No doubt the public loved it—but there are others in the mansion, namely the spirits who call this place home, that apparently didn't like the design shows one bit. Items were mysteriously broken and moved out of place from where the very picky designers had placed them. And it happened during every show. The rangers and I knew it wasn't a matter of "if," but "when."

This following story is indicative of the ongoing spirit hijinks. (The mirrors to which Steve is referring, were in one such design show.)

STEVEN CLARK
(Retired Park Ranger Supervisor)

> Steven: *I remember in this one show we lost two mirrors put up on the walls by designers. One mirror over here, on the west wall of the card room, didn't break, the heavy-duty wire just snapped. I mean, those things just don't snap on their own. Two other mirrors broke that year. One of them in here was a big mirror shaped like a star that dropped and crashed to the floor.*

Remember, these items are worth a lot of money. The designers and their assistants are professionals. They not only do this for a living, but they are very diligent and protective of these valuable items.

> Steven: *We looked at the mirror and it was like the wire was cut! It wasn't like the nail pulled out of the wall, which is what you think might happen. But we lost two huge mirrors. That was a particularly weird year, especially for that show. But this type of stuff was always going on!*

"GHOSTLY GIRL"

This is one of the stories I tell everyone because it corroborates several other sightings. For a very quiet guy, Chanh became both excited and anxious as he reenacted what had happened during our interview.

CHANH HANG
(Lead Park Ranger)

Chanh: *It was a Friday. My normal day here at Greystone. I start at ten in the morning and check in with my supervisor. There are no events scheduled, but I still go around the mansion and do my routine tasks— water and check the grounds, feed the fish, check the doors, the windows. Just a visual check of everything. At about 11:20 a.m., I walk over to the front door. First thing I do, out of curiosity, is peek through the left side of the front door, which has glass with iron metal work. I cup my hands and look right through towards the card room. There I see, between those two pillars, the shape of a girl. I'm thinking maybe between age nine to twelve. She has long, straight hair, maybe blonde, and is wearing a polka dot dress. She quickly skips across and hides herself behind the wall next to the library. Now, in my mind, I'm thinking someone's in the mansion! So I unlock the front door, walk down the steps, get to the main hallway and I just stand there for a second trying to hear something, anything. I wait there—no noise. Can't hear any footsteps.*

At times during many interviews, the interviewee will just stop, and I always get the feeling they're trying to talk themselves out of whatever happened, as if they don't believe their own reality, with their own eyes. With Chanh, at this moment, it was one of those times. But he continues. And quite frankly, I'd think we'd all feel the same!

Chanh: *Okay, now I slowly move forward, look over to the left side, toward the library doors. They are closed shut. And I know, working here so many years, there's no way you can open those double doors without making a sound. So I backtrack over to the other side of the library and those two doors that open from the grand hall are also closed. So I attempt to open that door to see if it's a possibility that she might have snuck in without the wood creaking loud. As I inch closer and closer, I step into the card room where I thought the girl would be hiding behind that wall. What do I see?*

An empty room. I step back and think to myself, "What did I just see? Did I see a girl? A real person?" I had to step outside for a little fresh air. Get myself together. I've never seen her again. Many times I've asked myself, "Did I see a girl or did I just see a shadow from the front terrace." I mean she was fully formed and solid. I could see her hair. She had a headband on going across the top of her head. I know she was in a polka dot dress.

I asked Chanh, "How did the little girl move?"

Chanh: *She did like a regular skip and run. It's kind of like a quick run to get away because I think she knew I saw her. It wasn't a slow walk, it's a little girl type of skip and run right across and hid herself behind the wall, at that corner. And that's why I walked in without any fear the first time because I thought she was real.*

Chanh continues to ponder the situation.

Chanh: *But I never figured it out. And until you see it yourself, to try and tell the story to someone who is not a believer, they're going to go, "Yeah, okay..."*

Chanh smiles and rolls his eyes like people will think he's completely crazy.

"MOVING STATUE"

One morning, I received a call from a rattled Park Ranger Supervisor Steve Clark, who explained to me what happened to him earlier that day. Frankly, what he told me didn't sound possible. We were in the midst of the 2013 Design House International Show. The theme for the annual showcase was "Titans of Business and the Best of Design." A brilliant designer, Lisa Turner, titled her room, "The Music Room," because she selected the great Stevie Wonder as her Titan. When I spoke with Steve, he seemed to be both anxious and thunderstruck. I knew he's experienced plenty of strange encounters during his career at Greystone and this one, in the Card Room, was certainly no exception, but he seemed more shocked than normal. As unlikely as his story sounded, I knew him to be a person of great integrity, so I felt compelled to figure out both how it happened and why. We met up in the Card Room—recorder running.

Photo: Mary E. Nichols

STEVEN CLARK
(Retired Park Ranger Supervisor)

Steven: *I opened up the mansion. The sun isn't quite up. It's still dark out. The first thing I do when I come in is to start turning lights on just so I can get through the house. I came this way, east to west in the grand hall, and I just naturally look at the view* [through the Card Room out to the Terrace] *and as I look, I swear, one of the statues moves. It turns as I'm walking. And I stop, and I actually went up to the statue to look at it and I'm like, "Okay, my imagination." I say something to it like, "You just moved! But you're not going to scare me." I mean, I was just being silly. And then I continue turning the lights on. And when Lisa Turner* [the designer] *came in about noon that day, she was all worked up because she said, "Somebody moved my statue away from the wall." I didn't even notice that it moved away from the wall at the time. I just saw it turn to me. And these statues were big, tall, African statues with old ceremonial masks. They don't move easy. They're like hundreds of pounds each! So I told Lisa what happened.*

The story continues with this follow-up interview…

"MOVED BY ITSELF"

I was told that Lisa Turner was angry about someone moving her statues in the abovementioned design show. Like most designers, Lisa is a perfectionist (that's their job) and she noticed it immediately. She heard the story from Steve Clark—that must have been an interesting conversation! Imagine Steve telling her that the statue moved by itself? I decided to get involved. My interview with Lisa about this incident was actually filled with laughter because the entire scenario is just so implausible. The statues are ridiculously heavy and very difficult for someone to move on their own. But it happened and I was determined to get to the bottom of it.

LISA TURNER

(Creative Director of "Interior Obsession")

> Lisa: *I installed these really tall and heavy sculptures by the artist Woodrow Nash. And these sculptures you cannot move on your own. Sometimes two people can't even move them. I had to have my crew install them between the French doors perfectly in line. That morning I came in and they were moved. One was up forward away from the doors and one was back closer to the doors. And what was so strange is that the actual sculptures are called "spirits." I don't know if Woodrow Nash thinks of them as certain warriors*

or whatever, but they were African spirits. We were laughing because how the heck could they have moved? And I could not move them back or put them into position. And at this time, I had no idea that the mansion was supposed to be haunted until, I guess, you and I spoke about it.

I asked Lisa about her thoughts when Steve Clark told her they moved by themselves. At first it was simply laughter.

Lisa: *Poor Steve. I don't remember the exact words, but when he told me that the statues moved by themselves, I looked at Steve with a look like "you got to be kidding me?" Then I pointed to the statues and said, "Why would someone even want to do that?" Even if it was four guys? Why? Are city workers that bored that they hang around until the mansion's closed to move hundreds of pounds of dead weight? It makes no sense. I don't know. It was just very, very, very strange. But the mansion has that feel. I don't care how many rooms you decorate or how much you fill the rooms, it really has this haunted, or actually, cold feeling, to it. Not a warm feel to call home. It's a very different feeling. Again, I don't care what you do to it. You've got all these talented designers, whatever they do, it just never feels like a home, you know? It's like the Twilight Zone.*

After the incident, I told Lisa I would set up a four-camera, infrared system in the room to see if any activity was taking place at night. She had concerns that any activity might be from her African artifacts on display. After viewing the footage, we did not see any movement. I told her what I thought may have caused the statue to slide forward—it was Ranger Steve Clark. And by that I meant some of the documented incidents in the mansion have directly involved Steve. He's sensitive to the energy within the building. Perhaps while he worked at this location, the "spirits" were constantly trying to contact him, trying to get him to interact? In this case, they certainly got him to react to the movement of one massive, three-hundred-pound statue.

"CHILLS"

Frank Turner was at the design show to support his wife. He tells a story of his own that is quite bizarre. I've never heard anything like this happen at Greystone before or since. He didn't even tell Lisa about it until after they returned home.

FRANK A. TURNER, III
(Lisa Turner's Husband)

> Frank: *I'm in the card room that Lisa is designing, and I just returned from touring the home. I'm standing off to the side watching Lisa interacting with some guests and I feel this cool breeze go past me and I get so cold and I say to myself, "What is that? What's going on?" And then I got colder and colder to the point where I start shaking, freezing—and I was going to go tell Lisa, but I'm shaking so much that I didn't want to approach her. I mean my teeth are chattering, I'm so cold.*

I could hear in his voice this incident scared the daylights out of him. And with good reason.

> Frank: *I mean this feels like a serious medical thing. I have to leave. All I could think about was getting in my car and turning on the heat. And that's what I did... I got in my car and I turn the heat up as high as I can. And I remember driving down Highland near Sunset, and I'm still shaking, and I still can't get warm. So now I go to Kaiser Hospital and I tell them, "I'm just shaking. I'm so cold, I don't know what's going on." So I'm in the ER and they start checking my vitals and the doctor says, "Your oxygen is fine. You don't have a fever. But yeah, your hands and extremities are really cold. You could be coming down with something. Take a couple aspirin, go home and get warm."*

I asked Frank what happened when he got home.

Frank: *I got in a hot tub of water. And that's the only thing that worked. After about an hour, I kind of came back to normal. Overall, it lasted about five hours. I've never been that cold in my life. I wasn't sick. I didn't have the flu. But the doctors couldn't explain it. And then a few days later, I went back to the mansion. We were taking things down in the room and Steve Clark was there sharing a little bit about the history of the mansion and the suicides that had occurred, and I said, "Something strange happened to me a few days ago." And that's when it all came out. It was all very bizarre.*

Terrace

Photo: ©SWA/Denise Retallack

Star Trek Into Darkness, directed by J.J. Abrams, used the Terrace during filming as did *Disorderly Orderly* starring Jerry Lewis and *The Fabulous Baker Boys* starring Jeff and Beau Bridges.

The property's most beautiful view is from this location, situated just outside the Card Room. The Terrace overlooks the grounds south of the mansion and beyond—you can see from downtown Los Angeles to the Pacific Ocean. The view is stunning. One can only imagine how breathtaking this vantage point must have been when the Doheny family first moved in and there were no buildings or structures blocking this magnificent vista.

"STARING MAN"

Charlie Ackerman worked for the City of Beverly Hills for almost twenty-eight years. He was working in Project Administration at the time of this incident. Part of his job was to oversee any renovations or structural changes at Greystone. We shared quite a few laughs as he recounted several stories about the paranormal activity at Greystone. This one story was particularly funny because those who knew the gardener, Bob C., had the impression he didn't scare easily.

CHARLIE ACKERMAN
(Retired Building Maintenance Supervisor)

> Charlie: *I remember Bob C., when he was a gardener, which goes way back. I believe the mid–1980s. He was out on the back patio, the terrace, with a blower and he told me that the hair on the back of his neck suddenly just stood up on end! He turned around and instinctually looked up at the windows above the card room* [Lucy Doheny's room] *and there was a guy standing inside, in a white shirt and slacks, staring down at him. Needless to say, it scared the hell out of him! He said he turned the machine off, dropped it, and just ran off. It cracked me up because Bob didn't seem like the kind of guy who would get that spooked that fast!*

Back in those days, nobody went inside the mansion unless there was filming or an official event. So to see someone inside the house, staring down at you, especially someone you didn't recognize, had to be extremely unnerving, as evidenced by Bob C's immediate exit stage left.

One morning we received an email on our *Ghosts of Greystone* website from Vinicio Castro. He wrote to us about several paranormal events he experienced at Greystone and ended his note with, "I appreciate you bringing these things to light." We contacted Vinicio and arranged to meet at Greystone. I was immediately intrigued when I read his email. Vinicio's stories were frightening, baffling, and bizarre. As we stood together on the mansion's Terrace, he told me his stories. Vinicio was convincing. I had no doubt he was telling the truth.

"DARK AND MISTY"
VINICIO CASTRO
(Visitor)

Vinicio: *It was at night on July 4, 2018. Andrea [Flores] and I were standing right here on the terrace. We were looking out at the city. My sister and her boyfriend were also here and he was using night vision binoculars. He aimed it at the center glass door [of the Card Room] and said he saw a small hand on the lower glass pane. He passed me the binoculars and I thought he was saying it was a handprint. But as time went on, we kept looking at that spot and the handprint disappeared. It just wasn't there anymore. So it couldn't have been a handprint because it would still be there. And that really threw us off. It wasn't super scary. It was just odd. So we stayed out here for another ten or fifteen minutes and suddenly I saw what appeared to be a mist or a shadow coming up the steps toward the terrace. These are the steps from down below leading up to the terrace. I took off my glasses and kind of shut and rubbed my eyes because I thought it was a blur either on my glasses or in my eyes. And as I was putting them back on, my sister had a reaction of distress saying, "Oh my*

46

God! Look!" I put on my glasses and we all saw a really dark, misty figure come up the steps, make the turn around the railing, and move towards us. I could see through it with my own eyes. It wasn't a solid, black shadow, it was transparent, like a mist. And this mist wasn't human looking because you couldn't see arms but you could slightly tell where the head was. You couldn't see it walking because it was floating at least five inches off the ground. It kept the same pace moving toward us. As it got closer, we ran. When we turned back around, we didn't see it anymore, but we could still feel its presence. Then, suddenly, it came through us like a breeze, and it wasn't windy at all that night. But at that exact moment it felt like it went right through us. We all felt it and I definitely felt an electrical charge go through my body. It gave me chills.

I asked Vinicio why his group didn't just run away off the Terrace and get the hell out of there.

Vinicio: *At first, when we ran like seven or eight feet away, we weren't looking at it. Then we stopped running to see if it was still there, but we didn't see it anymore—and then suddenly we felt it. We just bunched up and froze. That's when we felt the charge. My hair stood up, I got really bad chills, I felt a vibration throughout my body and my heart was racing. I couldn't believe what we just saw. Everyone else also had chills and we were freaked out. I could tell my sister felt it just by looking at her. She looked frightened. We were all really scared.*

Chapter 4

Living Room and Minstrels' Gallery

I'm telling you, I lost a couple of nights of sleep. I thought it was the
weirdest thing I've ever seen!

— JULIE KAY STALLCUP
GREYSTONE PARK VISITOR

Photo: Chris Keith

Remarkable films were photographed in this elegant living room including *Air Force One*, *The Big Lebowski* starring Jeff Bridges and John Goodman, *Indecent Proposal*, *Town & Country* starring Warren Beatty and Diane Keaton, *The Bodyguard* with Kevin Costner and Whitney Houston, *Charlie's Angels (2000)*, *Flowers in the Attic*, *Garfield: A Tail of Two Kitties*, *The Witches of Eastwick*, *Star Trek Into Darkness*, Oliver Stone's *Nixon* with Anthony Hopkins, *There Will Be Blood* starring Daniel Day-Lewis, and in 1964, *Dead Ringer* starring the legendary Bette Davis.

The Living Room is the largest room in this 46,054-square-foot mansion and it's typically where the family entertained guests. What you first notice upon entering the Living Room are the hand-carved arches and columns inviting you inside. In 1928, the original fireplace on the east wall was an impressive eleven feet tall. Disassembled in the remodel of 1945, a smaller marble fireplace was installed. Two beautiful chandeliers from 1928 remain hanging in the room to this day. The Living Room also holds a secret: set in the carved oak walls are two banks of hidden cabinets used to store liquor during Prohibition. We can just imagine Ned Doheny opening these secret cabinets and pulling out the bottles of scotch for his evening guests as the live music played from the Minstrels' Gallery above.

Greystone Historical Report

"The living room was for parties. Sometimes they put the Christmas tree over there."
—Timothy Doheny

Living Room

"WHITE CLOUD"

Lydie told me the following story as if it were just a matter of fact. Clearly, for a ranger working at Greystone in the late eighties, the bizarre had become quite commonplace! Lydie, as well as a few of the other rangers, had especially strange guidelines for film production companies that were going to shoot inside the mansion; rules that were simple, but must have sounded quite bizarre to the filmmakers.

LYDIE GUTFELD
(Retired Park Ranger / Camp Counselor)

> Lydie: *Literally hundreds of times when I'd go through the mansion on a location scout,*[1] *I'd always make my speech and say, "Listen, you're going to think I'm crazy, but I need to know anything that's going to be changed in*

---

1 A walkthrough with the heads of the film departments, discussing what changes were permitted in each location.

this house because I have to tell Ned what's going on." And they're thinking the whole time that Ned was like a supervisor and I'd say, "No, it's the ghost of Ned Doheny who died here." And they'd be like, "What?" And I'd explain this as a matter of fact, "This house is haunted. And if you want your shoot to go well, you just need to follow my instructions because I'm telling you, if you don't, it'll go bad." And I think it was when they were filming Oliver Stone's film Nixon. *They switched the handles on the French glass doors so they'd be very antique looking—and they didn't tell me. And when I walk in the next day, there's just this white cloud that is literally covering the entire bar. It was just this white, like fog cloud, and the location manager comes in with me and I said, "See, I told you! And that won't go away, so you won't get a good shot!" And they're like, "No, it'll go away."*

What I find interesting here is that they're discussing whether this "white, like fog cloud" will stay or go away, as opposed to, "Holy shit! Do you see what I see?! Run!!"

Lydie: *And then they would take a picture with a Polaroid camera and the fog doesn't show up in the photo, and then like ten minutes later they'd look and there was the white cloud in the photo. I would put my hands in the area of the fog and I couldn't feel anything. I don't know how to explain it. And then sure enough, they would take more Polaroid shots for art direction and props and there was still the white cloud in the photo. And it happened all the time! It was a trip. Ned was definitely there for me. I had my own personal relationship with that guy. I remember just starting to work at Greystone for a month and being told, "Oh, just wait, it'll happen, it'll happen. He will make himself known to you." And I was like, "Ah, whatever. I don't believe in ghosts." And after incidences like that with the fog, I would tell people, whether they believed me or not, "I talk to ghosts for a living. This is what I do!"*

"Voices of Ned and Hugh"

The more paranormal stories I heard at Greystone, the more curious I became. I began watching all the ghost shows on television and checking out what equipment they were using during their investigations. On a whim, I bought an EMF meter (Electromagnetic Field meter), because it's believed the presence of a spirit might be associated with a temperature fluctuation and electromagnetic energy. I also purchased a Spirit Box—a device that produces radio frequency sweeps that generate white noise through which spirits can supposedly speak. I know, it sounds crazy. I thought it was nuts as well, but I figured why not, I'll give it a try.

One night, I talked Ranger Dan Hernandez into going inside the mansion after a night event to try out these new devices. Around 11:00 p.m., as we stood outside the Living Room, I turned on the EMF meter and gave it to Dan. The colored lights on the meter lit up, which let us know an energy field was within range of the device. I said jokingly to him, "Dude, we've got someone here with us!" He put the meter next to a nearby electrical outlet to see if that was the reason for the meter lighting up. There was no reaction on the meter. He pulled it away and stood by the entrance to the room and it started lighting up again. I took the Spirit Box, handed Dan my digital sound recorder, and said, "Let's go inside the Living Room." Dan turned on the recorder and I turned on the Spirit Box and we walked inside. Here's Dan's account of what happened.

DANIEL HERNANDEZ
(Park Ranger Supervisor)

> Daniel: *We turned on the Spirit Box and we were messing around with the output trying to set the AM or FM frequency, and you said, "If there's anybody here with us, would you come toward me and speak into this red light on this device? Is there anyone here with us?" Suddenly through all the white noise the name "Ned" came through plain as day. "Ned." We were stunned that, first of all, the device worked! And secondly, we heard the*

name Ned! Clete, you were so amazed you said, "Did he just say Ned!?" I was just as blown away. I said, "I think he did!" Then you were like, "Ned, thank you! If that was you, please say it again." And in a totally different voice, we heard "Hugh" come through! And as we know, Ned and Hugh were the two men who were in a murder/suicide at Greystone, February 16, 1929. We were both stunned—shocked and amazed when we heard their names.[2]

I recall Dan and me just staring at each other as it became apparent that both Ned and Hugh were actually with us, albeit as ghosts, in the Living Room.

It's hard to describe the feeling you get when, for years, I've heard all these mysterious stories about the murder/suicide—who killed whom, were they lovers, what really happened that fateful night?—all these unanswered questions, and then here they are, both Ned and Hugh, inside the Living Room with us, somehow speaking their names to let us know they were still here. It blew our minds! I asked more questions but there were no answers. I've kept those recordings and listen to them every once in a while, out of sheer disbelief. I still get chills when I hear their two very clear, distinct voices.

"GHOSTLY ORB"

In 2018, I was a ranger during the filming of the series *I Am the Night*, directed by Patty Jenkins, who also directed *Wonder Woman 1984*, *Wonder Woman*, and *Monster*. I was in the inner courtyard, keeping an eye on the crew, when Patty came out of the mansion and walked over to me. She said she'd been told to talk to me if she had any questions about ghosts at Greystone. I said, "Oh, really?" Then I started joking with her. I said, "What do you want to know?" "Are there ghosts here?" she asked.

2 Audio recording exists in author's collection.

"I'm not going to tell you," I said. "Why not?" she wondered. "Because you couldn't handle it." She looked at me like I was nuts. "What are you talking about?" She grabbed my arm and pulled me toward the mansion, she began telling me what had just happened in the Living Room. "We caught an orb as we were filming. You've got to see this!" She sat me down in front of a monitor. Patty called out for the video assistant to play the footage, which I was allowed to record with my phone.[3] What follows is Patty's commentary as we watch the footage, which showed an actress walking into the Living Room.

PATTY JENKINS
(Motion Picture Director)

> Patty: *Here it is. See it flying on the right? See it in that corner?* [calls to the video assistant in another room] *Play it a few more times. Okay. Yeah. Start even a hair earlier. I think it actually comes around the corner there. Back it up a little bit more. There it is! Hold on. That's awesome. Isn't that amazing?* [she points to the entrance ceiling] *Wow! It comes from all the way up there. Look at where it starts!*

Clearly Patty was excited, and I have to admit, so was I. The orb, captured on camera, flies out from the lower ceiling to the left of the entrance, the Minstrels' Gallery is directly above, and drops down, and then flies along the east wall and exits camera right.

> Patty: *Look at where it starts, up there by the ceiling. That's fucking incredible! Look at where it starts from upstairs! I didn't see that before. Look at that. Whoa! That is so cool. It's crazy. Here it comes out of the balcony!*

---

3 Video recording exists in author's collection.

We ran the footage back and forth at least a dozen times, scrutinizing exactly where it appears and exits. Then she was very adamant about coming back to the mansion for a complete tour to get the full experience.

"FLYBY"
CHANH HANG
(Lead Park Ranger)

> Chanh: *It's around six o'clock in the evening and I'm securing the mansion after my patrol. Right with my first step in the door, I feel great energy. My arm has goose bumps and I'm like, "Okay, here we go again." I do my rounds quickly with my flashlight and check the west side door, check the murder room, go into the living room, check the door at the far end, turn around, and suddenly I feel like somebody's watching me. I look around and then up to the minstrel gallery. Nothing. I start walking away, but I feel something prompting me to look up.*

I've heard this from several people I've interviewed where they feel or sense an energy or a spirit that is prompting them to look in a certain direction.

> Chanh: *On my left side I see a round, not solid, almost a clear shiny orb, by the chandelier underneath on the right, fly by me so fast. I recognized that it's an orb. I'm not going to second guess what it was. I've been here too long, right? So I continue walking and I get to almost the center of the main hallway and that's when another orb flies by me again. Fast. I move on… I continue checking the windows, the doors to the card room, the library, all the other rooms and finally get to the main stairs. That's where the alarm panel is located, and another orb is hovering almost at my head level but this one just disappears. It is different from the others. The other two were fast and did like a flyby. So I arm the mansion, hit the last light switch, and walk out. From the moment I stepped in the house, there was*

strong energy. I felt it right away. Even walking around checking the doors and windows I felt it. It wasn't until I left the premises that that feeling went away.

I asked Chanh to detail the orbs a bit more—size, color, anything he remembers.

Chanh: *All three orbs were the same size, maybe like a tennis ball, kind of white with maybe a speck of shiny gold color. And it also had kind of a glow to it. I saw the orb that you showed me in the living room, the one that the director* [Patty Jenkins] *caught on camera. It was just like that.*

Greystone Historical Report

Easily the mansion's most impressive interior space, the living room has a two-story tall ceiling with intricately carved beams, a baronial stone fireplace, and a nearly-story-tall leaded glass bay window.

"GHOST PHOTO BOMB"

Former Ranger John Huybrecht contacted me to say he received an eerie photo from some Greystone visitors who were flipping out. The husband and wife couple believed they captured a ghost image during a recent photo shoot. After reviewing the photo, I contacted Julie and her husband, Darrell, and they agreed to an interview about the photo. They recounted their story at Greystone as we were standing outside the Living Room where their ghostly photo was taken.

JULIE KAY & DARRELL STALLCUP
(Visitors)

Julie: *A friend of mine, Brittney, has a sister who was getting married, so I said, "Let's do a photo shoot with my camera for fun." I'm not a professional photographer. So we go to Greystone, start taking photos, and the ranger* [John Huybrecht] *tells us, "You can't use a professional camera. You have to have a permit." And so the photo in question was the last photo on my camera before he pulled the plug. That's what's kind of weird about it. So then I get home, I upload some pictures* [to a social media site] *and I went out to eat with my girlfriends. All of a sudden, my phone started ringing and my friends are like, "Look over Brittney's left shoulder! There's someone's face in the window!" And I'm like, "Oh my God! This is crazy!" I can barely eat my dinner and my friends are asking, "Where's your original memory card?!" And I was like, "Well, I think it's still in the computer." I call Darrell, "Honey, go look at the last photo on the memory card."*

Darrell: *So I'm home and now Brittney calls and goes, "Oh my God! What's in this picture? Look over my left shoulder!" I go on the Mac and looked at it from the memory card and zoomed in on the face, and I'm like, "Oh my God! The image is on the original." And we were freaking out. We head back to Greystone and meet with Ranger John and we show him the ghost photo. John was silent and just staring at it. Then he says, "This is crazy! Let me see the memory card." He wanted to make sure nobody superimposed the image in Photoshop or whatever. But no, John sees it's on the original memory card.*

With the help of my brother, Chris, we all venture outside to the west door of the Living Room. We try to recreate their photo with people standing in the exact same positions. Could someone standing behind the camera have been the ghostly face/reflection that appears in the photograph? But after thirty minutes of trying to recreate the photo, we realize we can't do it. I show Julie and Darrell a photo on my phone of Ned Doheny that resembles the face in the window. You can see Ned Doheny's photo in the Introduction.

Julie: *I remember when you showed us his photo, I was freaking out: "This picture looks like him! He's got that scowl on his face. It's kind of creepy.*

Darrell, this is scary. Look at that. It's the eyebrows." I'm telling you, I lost a couple nights of sleep. I thought it was the weirdest thing I've ever seen! Somebody spotted it after we posted it, or I would've never known.

Julie starts searching for the photos from that day on her phone.

Julie: *Wait! Wait! Wait! Look at this! Darrell, look at this! See, so here's the others. These are the other shots!*

Julie shows us the other photos that were taken at the same time; all are missing the face in the window.

Julie: *See? Nothing! And it was the last picture of the day because the ranger got mad at us. That is so freaky and weird!*

Photo: Julie Kay Stallcup

Minstrels' Gallery

How could this door close by itself?
— Luz Rodriguez
    Retired Greystone Park Ranger

Photo: Chris Keith

Just off the Second-Floor Landing is the entrance to the Minstrels' Gallery. Directly below, on the first floor, is the entryway to the Living Room with its hand-carved arches and columns that help support this room above. Minstrels' Galleries gained their popularity hundreds of years ago throughout England and Ireland. Primarily found in castles and manor houses, a Minstrels' Gallery, or balcony, housed musicians, originally minstrels, to perform for guests during a gathering. Traditionally, the musicians were discreetly hidden from the guests enjoying themselves below. A memorable, somewhat recent pop culture reference is the quintessential 1975 album, *Minstrel in the Gallery*, by Jethro Tull.

Greystone Historical Report

On this balcony, a band played at parties and the younger children watched the festivities. "I can remember only two incidents with my father," says Timothy Doheny. "One is when he pulled me out of the surf at Hermosa and kept me from drowning. He pulled me out by the hair. The other time was when he carried me out on the second floor gallery above the living room, and we looked down at a party downstairs."

"Startled by the Slam"

On my walk with Luz, we ventured upstairs. As we were walking toward the master suites, I was surprised when she stopped in front of the entrance to the Minstrels' Gallery. She turned and I followed her as she walked down the steps into the balcony. In all the interviews I've conducted, there are only a few rooms where there hasn't been any activity. I thought surely this location was one of them. I was wrong.

LUZ RODRIGUEZ
(Retired Greystone Park Ranger)

Luz: *So I came in here and the door was open like this, maybe two feet. I was just kind of looking down from the balcony into the living room and the door just slammed shut. I mean, like someone threw it shut. And it's a thick, huge door. So I just stood here for a second. Like what just happened!? Because I was so startled by the slam, and then to realize that the door closed on its own. But it's so thick and heavy—how could this door close by itself? So then I thought someone was in here playing a trick on me. I turned the doorknob carefully, 'cause I'm like, "Did it lock? And if it did, I'm going to have to call the fire department to come ladder me down." But it opened. And then I swung it all the way open and there was no one there. And I was like, "Okay, you don't want me up here? I can respect that."*

Knowing that Luz is like a lightning rod for the paranormal, I said, "Let's get out of here before it happens again!" She smiled as we left.

Chapter 5

Murder Room

*Something bad happened and that energy is trapped here. And it
literally echoes through the floor to the room above it.*
— Anonymous Beverly Hills Police Officer

Photo: Chris Keith

On February 1 of 1929, the musical film, *The Broadway Melody,*
opened at Sid Grauman's Chinese Theatre in Hollywood. On
February 14 of 1929, the Saint Valentine's Day Massacre happened in
Chicago—four unknown assailants gunned down five members of the
North Side Gang led by Bugs Moran. On Saturday, February 16 of 1929,
the New York Stock Exchange posted widespread losses—a harbinger of
things to come. Also, on February 16 of 1929, some 3,000 miles away, at
approximately 11:00 p.m., on the first floor of the Doheny Mansion, Ned
Doheny was found shot to death. His secretary, Hugh Plunkett, was lying
face down, also dead, just outside the door to what has become known as
the "Murder Room."

NED DOHENY

Photo: Watson Family Photographic Archive

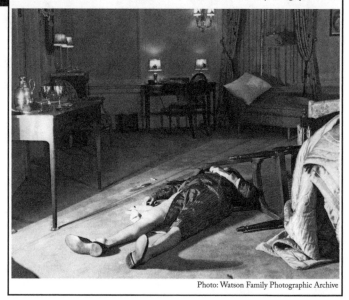

Photo: Watson Family Photographic Archive

Photo: Watson Family Photographic Archive

HUGH PLUNKETT

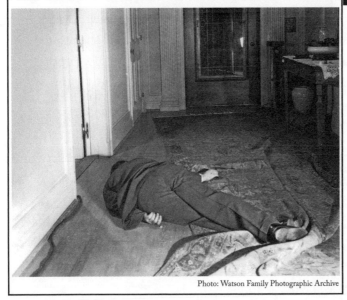

Photo: Watson Family Photographic Archive

Here's an excerpt from the *Los Angeles Times* as they covered the story in retrospect years later:

> Edward Laurence "Ned" Doheny Jr., the 35-year-old heir to an oil family fortune, was found dead, shot through the head, at Greystone Mansion, his 55-room, Tudor-style home in Beverly Hills.
>
> His secretary, Hugh Plunkett, was found nearby, also dead of a bullet wound.
>
> After a brief investigation, authorities ruled that a deranged Plunkett had shot his employer and then turned the gun on himself. But to this day the crime is a source of rumor and speculation. Was it really a murder-suicide or just made to look that way? Was it tied to another scandal?
>
> Doheny was the son of L.A.'s richest man, and that's what led to so many questions that were never answered. Some speculated the killing may have been tied to a huge national corruption scandal, which brought more intrigue.

Here's another account from the Doheny Reference Center at the University of Southern California:

> On the night of February 16, 1929, Hugh Plunkett arrived at the Greystone mansion. He called the house from the gates, and was told by Lucy Doheny that he should not come in. Ignoring her words, he apparently used his pass key to enter the grounds and the house, going to the guest bedroom on the first floor where he often stayed.
>
> Ned Doheny found him there around 10PM. At 10:30, the Doheny family physician, E.C. Fishbaugh, who was in

Hollywood attending a theater performance, received a call from his maid, who told him that he was needed urgently at the Doheny home. Fishbaugh arrived a little before 11 PM, and was greeted by Lucy Doheny, who told him that Plunkett and her husband were in the guest bedroom. As they proceeded down the hallway to the bedroom, they saw the door standing ajar, and Plunkett standing by it. He warned them to come no closer, then shut the door.

Immediately after a shot rang out. When the doctor entered the room, he found Plunkett lying on the floor by the door, shot through the head, the gun lying by his side. Doheny lay on the floor by the beds, next to an overturned chair, barely alive with a gunshot wound to the head.

Various theories, rumors, and stories swirl around this infamous evening. What actually happened that night in this room will probably never be known. Did Hugh shoot Ned out of an act of rage and kill himself? Or did Ned, who had been drinking, shoot his secretary and friend and then turn the gun on himself?

Over the years, this location in the mansion, with windows looking out onto the reflection pond, was used as a guest room, a study, and a game room. It is sometimes referred to as the "South Guest Room."

"EMILY, AGAIN?"

Krizza, the tourist from Norway who we met in Chapter One – "Grand Entry," was on an impromptu tour that I gave to her and her friend, Tonje. I played them an audio clip of voices that were recorded in the Living Room. These voices appear to belong to Hugh and Ned and it's this recording that Krizza refers to below.

KRIZZA ELISABETH
(Visitor)

> Krizza: *Just before when we were outside that room* [Murder Room], *you played us a recording where you captured some voices. When we were listening, it felt like someone was watching us by the door. I thought I heard tip toes, like one step-two steps and then silence. And then again, one step-two steps, and then silence. And she was right behind me. That's what I felt.*

I asked who "she" was and to elaborate on the story: What exactly did she feel?

> Krizza: *It felt like "she" was the spirit. And then she turned around and ran away. That sounds weird, I know, but I could feel the wind from her when she got close to me and turned fast and ran away. Like she had long hair and that's the wind. Do you understand what I mean? Like it was a child. But I remember later you talked about a child* [the story of Emily]. *Okay, and then at some point, someone was pulling on my purse, because I had my purse kind of over one shoulder, across over my body. And I remember that someone pulled me, like she, or he, I don't know, was just playing with me. It's a little bit scary to realize that maybe something else is out there that we don't see. And I can't prove it because you and Tonje didn't feel it. So it's really weird to say, "Okay, I felt something, it was a little girl playing with me, it was playful and scary at the same time, but I don't know if it really was something. I'm positive it was and then again I'm not."*

I love the last phrase she said to me—"I'm positive it was and then again I'm not." It sounds odd; I almost want to say, "Well, did you feel it or not?!" But if I put myself in her place, and something interacted with me that I couldn't see, I think I might feel like my mind is playing tricks on me. Or, finally one of my many screws has come loose. And truth be told,

I had an encounter in the Basement that still has me scratching my head and searching for a screwdriver.

"Who Turned on the Tap?"

LUZ RODRIGUEZ

(Retired Park Ranger)

Luz: *Okay, the murder room. The bathroom faucet turned on by itself. I'm not kidding. When you're on the job in the mansion for a long time, it gets a little boring. It gets a lot boring. So I would wander through the house and I would look carefully through the rooms, the woodwork, the designs, even the bathrooms, I'd look at the detail of the tile work. So in this bathroom* [as we walk inside the Murder Room bathroom], *I'm looking at the bathroom scale. I have my back to the faucet and then I hear the water come on. And I was like, "Why is the water coming on?" The water wasn't just leaking it was really running. So I turn it off and walk out. And I hear it come on again! And so I said, out loud, like I'm talking to myself, "OK guys, you can't play with the water because I'm leaving. We can't leave the water running. So I'm going to turn it off. Leave it off." So I turned it off again, and as I'm leaving, I'm hoping it doesn't happen again. It didn't.* [smiling] *I guess they listen to me.*

"Mysterious Voice"

Ranger John Huybrecht contacted me with a story he said I should investigate and follow up. It was with a visitor who experienced something very strange on his tour of Greystone. Here's the story, directly from Tim, an Englishman who was visiting from London.

TIM BAILEY
(Visitor)

Tim: *I had never heard of Greystone before. I was on vacation with my partner for the Christmas holidays and we met with some friends in Los Angeles. That morning it was suggested we tour Greystone Mansion, saying it's beautiful and has been used in numerous films. So my mind wasn't in a, "Oh, this is going to be spooky," kind of mood. It was more like, "Oh, films have been shot there. This is Hollywood. This is going to be cool."*

I asked him about any past paranormal experiences he may have encountered.

Tim: *I was open-minded about ghosts when I was much younger. But as I've aged, I'm 44 now, I've become more cynical. My view recently has been, "Well, I didn't exist before I was born, so why should I exist after I die?" I have never had a ghost experience before, although I have been in houses before that have felt spooky.*

Tim returned to his recollection. I noted how well he remembered the details.

Tim: *The tour started around 5:30 p.m. Our guide, John, started to explain that the house had quite a history! We were in the murder room on the ground floor, and John was telling us the story of how the owner, Ned, and his "friend" Hugh, had been found shot dead in an apparent murder-suicide. However, lots of mystery and theories have surrounded this. One theory was that Ned and Hugh were lovers. I stood in the middle of the room with my back to the doorway that leads into the main hallway and said out loud, "Well, it was clearly Lucy [Ned's wife] that killed them. I bet she walked in on them!" It's worth noting at this point that I wasn't in a "spooky" frame of mind. I was merely just fascinated by the history of the house. Within seconds I heard a voice that came from the direction of the doorway behind me. Everyone on the tour—there were six of us in total, including John—were all in front of me. I recall it was a light, female voice. It sounded like a young lady. And I'd say it actually sounded English, maybe a little posh. It's annoyed me ever since that I didn't catch what she actually said, but I know it was three short words. And all three words were one syllable. Initially, I was just really surprised and taken aback. I quickly looked in the direction of the voice, but no one was there. And I already knew we were the only people in the house at this time. I quickly nudged my partner who was standing next to me, "Did you hear that?" He hadn't.*

Boy, I was hoping he could remember the three words that were uttered. Or maybe have a sense of what they might have been? All he knew is that they sounded like one syllable each.

Tim: *At this point, John turned and asked me what was wrong, as I think I must have looked rather shocked! It was only after I explained that I heard a voice that he said it was common at Greystone, but that he hadn't heard of that happening in the murder room. The rest of the tour we kept talking about it. But I do think it's telling that this happened before I was aware that place was haunted and before my mindset got spooked. But we all jumped to the conclusion it might have been Lucy. Maybe she was annoyed I had accused her? I don't know, maybe she said, "You are wrong." Or maybe she was saying, "You are right." All I know for certain is I didn't imagine the voice. I think my partner, Tom, was especially spooked by it as he knew that I wouldn't make this up. John, the guide, wasn't surprised at all. He told us of the experiences he has had in the house himself. I'm fascinated to understand what happened, whether I really had a ghostly experience in Beverly Hills, or if there is some other explanation. I'm not a firm believer, but after this, I think I'm more open-minded.*

Regarding the voice Tim heard and his recollection that it may have been with an English accent, Lucy Doheny was born in California and did not speak with an English accent.

"SOMETHING ROTTEN"

Mary, who happens to be one of the nicest, sweetest people you will ever meet, was working as an official photographer at one of the many design showcases hosted at the Greystone Mansion.

She's an exceptionally talented photographer who has worked for the world's finest magazines. Mary has several stories from her time working in the mansion—stories that provided her with an eerie indoctrination.

MARY E. NICHOLS
(Professional Photographer)

> Mary: *The first time I shot in the mansion, I didn't think I'd be willing to come back. I simply wasn't prepared for just how creepy and haunted this place is. I get through the two weeks of the show, but then I think, "I hope they don't ask me again… I don't really want to come back here." And then a year or so passes and you kind of get yourself together, feeling like you can come back and deal with the haunted factor. But I remember telling Steve [Ranger Steven Clark] one night, "We're just tired and it's late and the electricity is kind of going in and out. I think we're just going to make this our last shot." And he goes, "Well, there are ghosts here." And I said, "Steve, the only thing I noticed here is I think there might be a dead animal under the entry to that room where Doheny was killed. There was a strong kind of rotting smell there while I was shooting." And he said, "Well, that's right where one of the bodies was." In a few days, after we all got to know each other, he let me read the first paranormal investigation report and it mentioned that exact smell and location.*

"Boom!"

This story interested me because, from what I've observed, both Martin and Chanh Hang (Park Ranger) have an ability to sense spirits and their energy. So when they're the only ones in the mansion, there's a good chance that something might happen.

MARTIN J. PEREZ
(Janitorial Services)

> Martin: *There was a time with me and Ranger Chanh, in which we are both talking in the center of the grand hall, and I was like, "Hey, Chanh, don't leave me here with these damn ghosts!" You know, we're messing around, joking. He goes, "Yeah, yeah, yeah. I'm gonna leave you here all alone!" Then he told me, "Look, don't worry. We're calm. There's no events, so there's no one in the house." As soon as he said, "There's no one in the house," the murder room door slams shut! Boom!*

At this point in the story, Martin holds out his arm to show me his goose bumps. They're real.

> Martin: *See, it still gives me the chills! As soon as Chanh said that, I swear to God. We both stopped and stared at the murder room door. And Chanh's like, "Forget this, I'm gone!"* [he laughs]. *I was like, "Chanh, no! You can't leave! Don't leave me alone!" But that door really spooked us. I swear, as soon as he said, "There's no one in the house," wham-bam, the murder room door slams shut! It hit so hard it echoed through the whole house.*

I asked Martin what happened next.

> Martin: *Nothing. Chanh takes off. He just leaves me there on my own. And I'm just standing there like, "Ahhh, I guess I have to deal with it... I definitely don't get paid enough!"*

"Golden Egg"

CHANH HANG

(Lead Park Ranger)

Chanh: *I'm in the hallway outside of the murder room. I need to turn the light off. I go in and to my left is that storyboard on the wall, you know what I'm talking about, with the history of the room? Inside the room it's bright, sunlight through the windows. I look at the wall and all I see is like a yellow, maybe more golden light kind of hovering—it's almost like the size and shape of an egg, and it just goes flying* [he gestures a swirling motion over his head] *like this, and then whoosh, over my head. At first, I'm thinking it's the sun reflecting off my badge as I move around.*

Chanh shows me how he walked back and forth looking at the wall to see if the light from the windows was shining off his badge.

Chanh: *I did it like ten times, back and forth, just to see if I turn my body towards the light of the window, if it casts any of that yellow around again, but it didn't. But again, this moving light looked like solid gold. It went from the wall, came right at me, then zipped over my head. Literally, and it was like gone. Like, "What in the world was that?" I even tried my flashlight to shine on my name tag and badge, but I still didn't see anything like that.*

I asked Chanh if he felt anything else, or sensed anything while this was happening, or possibly even before or after the event.

Chanh: *I didn't feel anything—no chills. Nothing. The light, this golden light, was just there, it did its thing, flew over my head, and it was gone as fast as it came. You know, I've told you. I've seen orbs in green and red, but this was a new one! Golden light. Who knows? Strange.*

"JUMPER"

It's Saturday night, February 15, 2020. One month before the Coronavirus (COVID-19) would stop all group activities for the unforeseeable future in the United States. The Mother-Son Dance is being held in the mansion. The boys, all between the ages of six and eleven years old, join their mothers for an evening of dining, DJ dancing, and games. I receive a call from Ranger Juan around 10:30 p.m. He sounds alarmed. I ask him if he is okay and he says, "Actually, not really." We talk about the following story and agree to talk further in the morning. The next day, Juan and I walk over to the Terrace and into the Murder Room bathroom to discuss the events of the prior night.

JUAN ANDRADE
(Park Ranger Supervisor)

Juan: *I was standing outside on the terrace to make a quick phone call during the Mother-Son Dance. Part of our enforcement is not to let any of the kids in the murder room bathroom because we don't want them turning on the faucets or using the toilet. This area is off limits to everybody except for the photographer. He has his camera equipment in there and that's it. And so while I'm out on the terrace, looking at the murder room bathroom window, I see a kid wearing a white, long sleeve shirt, with a collar, literally jumping and nearly hitting the ceiling—and the ceiling is nine feet high. I'm thinking, "What the fuck?" And when I watch him jump, he is perfectly centered in the window and he was going like this.*

Juan shows me what he means: both arms held out away from his body and his head is faced directly down, like what you might see in a sorrowful religious painting.

Juan: *Obviously, I can't see anything below the white curtain that's there, and I can't see his face because he's looking down at the floor—but he is literally jumping above the curtain and I can see his head, his torso, and his arms. I can't see his legs because of the angle. But when he is jumping, it is so high I thought he was going to hit the ceiling. That's how high this kid was going. And his movement is kind of floating up and down. So I'm thinking, "Do they have a trampoline in there?" But that wouldn't work because he would stay up and hang like a couple of seconds and then drop down. I see the kid do this three times in a row. So I'm thinking some kids from the party are getting into the bathroom to pee or something and now they're screwing around.*

I had to stop here because this was intriguing. "Juan," I interrupted, "From what you're saying, this kid jumping was defying gravity. Is that what you're suggesting?"

Juan: *That's exactly it. Jump, hold for a little hang time, and drop.*

We both just stood there for a long silent moment. I motioned for him to continue.

Juan: *So I run in through the west door of the grand hall, opened the bathroom door and I see the photographer packing his stuff up and I said to him, "You know, there shouldn't be any kids in here." And he gave me a weird look and says, "There are no kids in here." I told him, "I just saw from the outside a kid jumping at the window." He tells me, "There haven't been any kids in here this whole night." I look behind the door and I said again, "I just saw this kid from the terrace." And now I can tell I'm pissing him off, "There were no kids in here!" He finished packing up and left. I walked around, trying to figure out how someone could jump like that. Maybe he jumped off the toilet or the sink, which are both nearby the window, but then he'd be jumping at an angle, not straight up.*

Juan was at a loss for words. I then offered, rhetorically, "I guess there's only one explanation." Juan rolled his eyes in agreement. I interpreted his reaction as "Here we go again."

Photo: Clete Keith

Let's break down the possibilities—as you can see in the photo, the top of the curtain is six feet and three inches from the floor. So this child would have to jump high enough for his waist to be level with six feet three inches from the floor. With only twenty inches left to the top of the window, Juan would simply not have been able to see the boy's head, which he did. For Juan to see the boy from his waist up to his head in the window, the boy would have to be standing and jumping from farther back in the room, probably eight to nine feet back from the window. But there wouldn't be anything for the boy to climb on and jump off. And he saw the boy do it three times in a row—jump up, hold in mid-air, and then straight back down. And, most importantly, there was a photographer in the bathroom with his gear spread out on the floor right where the child was jumping. But it was real enough for Juan to run back into the mansion looking for a boy in a white-collared shirt.

Juan: *At the end of the night, when I'm locking up with Patrick* [another Park Ranger], *I didn't say anything at first because I didn't want to scare him. It wasn't until the end—when we got everybody out of the mansion, turned off all the lights, checked all the doors and windows—that I told him what happened. Patrick suggests, "Let's go check it out." So we went into the bathroom and we're trying to rationalize what happened. Just saying how it's not possible. Patrick says he's six foot, two inches tall. He tried duplicating what I said I saw, and he couldn't do it. Not even close. Then it gets freaky when suddenly Patrick says something just touched him, twice, that gave him goose bumps. I felt a cold spot near by him. We just got out of there. But we agreed, it would be impossible for any of these little kids to jump as high as what I saw this one kid do.*

"BLOOD?"

I went to Beverly Hills City Hall and ran into Vilma Lopez, who works for the janitorial service that cleans at Greystone. We started talking about Greystone and I showed her several photos on my phone. One, in particular, is Hugh Plunkett—shot dead in the head and on the floor in a pool of his own blood just outside the ill-famed Murder Room door. Vilma stared at the photo and said, "Andrea has to see this." She told me that she and Andrea had to clean the Murder Room back in November of 2019 and something happened to her just outside the door to the room while she was mopping, but Vilma said Andrea didn't want to talk about it. Vilma told me that Andrea was in their office right next door. That's all I needed to know. So I asked Andrea what happened to her while she was mopping the floor outside the Murder Room. Andrea just looked at Vilma with a look of "thanks for nothing." I pulled up the photo of Hugh on my phone, showed it to Andrea, and told her what we were looking at in the photo. She stared at it, stunned. Then she agreed to tell me what happened and why she was so shocked.

Andrea is a special person. Not only is she kind, very smart, and a professional, she tells me she feels and has seen spirits most of her life and has had her share of experiences at Greystone. But not all of those experiences were warm and fuzzy. In fact, some of her stories are so unnerving that I'm not sure how she keeps coming back to work. It has to be the health insurance!

ANDREA FLORES

(Janitorial Services)

> Andrea: *It was around Thanksgiving last year. There was a lot of light, must have been midday. I was mopping in the hallway at the west end of the grand hall, just outside the murder room door and I saw a stain. A wet stain on the floor. It looked like blood. So I mopped it up—but the water*

was clear when I put the mop in the bucket. It should have dirtied the water, right? And dirtied the mop.

I ask Andrea if she now thinks there was actually blood on the floor or not.

Andrea: *No. There was no blood. But that's what I saw. That's what I mopped up. But like I said, nothing in the water. But now, having seen the murder photo of Hugh for the first time, he's laying in the same spot where I thought I mopped up the blood. I didn't know that he was killed outside the room. I thought that everything happened inside the room. That they were both killed inside. We always had that impression. There was no way for me to know that was the same spot. Your photo amazed me. I feel goose bumps because I didn't expect that. I mean, how could I see something that I didn't know anything about? How could I see it so clear? And I only told Vilma what happened to me, nobody else. But I'm glad I did because maybe the photo confirms what I saw. Maybe they're* [the spirits] *wanting to tell me about what happened that night. Someone wants me to know what happened. That's what I feel those two guys* [Ned and Hugh] *are trying to tell me.*

"CRUSHING PRESSURE"

When discussing the idea of writing this book, Ranger Steve Clark suggested I contact a certain police officer who experienced some paranormal events on a tour conducted by Steve and Ranger Daniel Hernandez. The police officer, whom Steve believes has the "gift," agreed to an interview at the mansion, on the condition that he remain anonymous. When he showed up, I could see that his experience on that mansion tour in question still affects him some years later. As we chatted outside the house, I could sense his great hesitation about going inside.

His whole demeanor changed. He knew it and I knew it. On the original tour, his police partner (we'll call the partner "Bob"), did not mention that Greystone was thought of by many to be haunted. Bob brought him there to see how he would react.

The interview below begins as we're walking toward the Grand Entry. He's discussing his previous visit to the mansion when he came for the tour with Steve and Dan.

ANONYMOUS
(Beverly Hills Police Officer)

> Police Officer: *We arrive at the room, and I can't even breach the door. It's like someone punches me in the face. I finally walk in and I was like, "Whoa!" I have no idea what happened here, but something really bad happened. And that's when Bob and Danny say, "Well, this is the murder room. This is where Mr. Doheny and his assistant were found dead." And I'm like, "Okay, well, that makes sense. Listen, I'm going to stand outside here, and you guys enjoy yourselves 'cause I can't stand it in there." There's just so much pressure and just an overall feeling of dread in that room. I don't like to be in there. I don't want to be in there. It's cool. But I tell them I'll look at it through the window.*

We then walked up to the entrance of the mansion. The officer takes a deep breath as I open the door and we walk inside. We walk down the steps toward the Murder Room. He's feeling the energy beginning to ramp up. I feel nothing.

> Police Officer: *Oh my God!*

We move past the Living Room and he stops outside the Murder Room. I ask him what he's feeling.

Police Officer: *Pressure. Like someone is using their hands and they're just crushing my chest. Pure pressure.*

His breathing is labored and he's very hesitant to enter the room. I ask him if we can go inside the room. (I know, c'mon, give the poor guy a break!) He takes another deep breath and walks inside. He immediately starts coughing and trying to catch his breath.

Police Officer: *There's like a… like an energy that's in here… it's off the charts. Like just off the charts… I've got to stand outside.*

He's visibly uneasy as we walk outside the room. He coughs again and needs to catch his breath. He tries to pull his thoughts together and convey his feelings.

Police Officer: *There's like, I don't know, it felt like sitting on a train, stuff passing by quickly, multi-layered, you can see things behind other things. That's what it feels like passing these rooms. It felt like as we're walking down this way, there was something going along with us, which is why I kept looking in the rooms. But whatever it is, it's back enough out of your peripheral vision so that you're not seeing it. But it's there. That feeling. Something is moving through these rooms.*

"An entity?" I ask.

Police Officer: *Call it whatever you want, but sure, it has to be. Like a shadow—you're not seeing it, but you know something's moving.*

Remember, this is a trained police officer who can look at the hard evidence of a crime scene and break it down with great analytical know-how. But that's because at that moment he's dealing with rock-solid reality: a weapon, blood samples, fingerprints, a body or bodies. But as you can see, at Greystone, where up is down and down is up, he's having a difficult time articulating what he's seeing and feeling. This is common with many of the people I've brought back to the location for an interview or re-creation and then something unexplainable takes place. The interviewees seem mystified and bewildered. This officer is a sharp professional, who is usually very articulate—but standing outside the Murder Room, he's suddenly at a loss for words. Reality has been turned upside down.

> Police Officer: *It's like you're staring at a wall and someone walks by a window and you see the shadow or shadowy effect. You're still seeing something but there's no real definition. It's like a shadowy effect. But conditions can help define the entity, can help track it, usually—if it's dark or darker, or even when the atmosphere's different.*

I nod in agreement because I understand the phenomenon he's trying to explain. In fact, I've read all about it. When nightfall happens and the barometric pressure changes, the pressure within the earth's atmosphere changes. These conditions appear to be conducive to the manifestation of spirits or ghosts.

> Police Officer: *As someone who senses this stuff, you still feel that there's evil in that room. You can't shake it. It could be residual. Obviously two people died. How? Nobody's going to really know that one for sure. But two people died here tragically, and I think that's what's fueling this. And if it was an evil that took over Doheny, or his assistant, or maybe something else was going on here that would have shamed his dad or the Doheny name, well then, the murder/suicide may have trapped that energy in here. And it literally echoes through this entire place, even to the room above where I also felt this energy.*

As we walk up to the Grand Entry door, I have a question that I feel I need to ask. It's not specific to the mansion, but I'm curious to ask a police officer who actually feels and senses spirits. "I'm sure you've visited crime scenes that witnessed violent murders, or even worked locations where someone has passed naturally, or even a car wreck with fatalities… have you ever felt anything, anything spiritual?"

Police Officer: *I don't like dead bodies. That's part of my job and I do what I have to do, but I don't enjoy them. Nobody likes death. Death is an unfortunate, sad part of the job, and we know it's a reality. People pass away, whether by violence, like here, or old age or other circumstances. But in non-violent situations, I've never felt what I feel here. Only complete peace. Like they're finally better off than what they were before. There's sadness, obviously from the people left behind who are distraught, but nothing else. That's its own energy. And then there's the situations you walk into and it's bad. You just know it, like something else was there. Something else helped facilitate this suicide or this death. Those are usually the ones that I really feel something, like dread. Definitely, the suicides. There's also a completely different feeling when you walk in to a murder scene. I've been in houses here in Beverly Hills and I hate searching, 'cause it's like you hit the breach of the doorway and you feel it, the heaviness, an overwhelming bad heaviness. But there's nobody physically there. It's just a room, but I still have that 'ick' feeling. But we've had other officers who are no longer with the department that refused to come in this place… or when we get the alarm calls in the middle of the night from inside the mansion. They refused. Hated coming here.*

Chapter 6

Doll Room

I said, "What is that?" And he said, "That's Mrs. Doheny."
— JOHN HUYBRECHT
   FORMER GREYSTONE PARK RANGER

Photo: Chris Keith

> The motion picture, *The Golden Child*, with Eddie Murphy and directed by Michael Ritchie, was filmed in this room. It was also a location used by the television series *The Gilmore Girls*.

In 1928, this modestly furnished room had a desk, several chairs, and two beds. It earned the name, "Doll Room," in the 1940s because it was where Lucy—Ned Doheny's daughter—displayed her European doll collection. The room is also known as the north guest room.

"Sickly Sweet Perfume"

John Huybrecht was with the Ranger Program for nearly four years. A very kind and well-read man. He loves the rich history of Greystone but didn't quite love the paranormal activity inside the mansion. He told me on more than one occasion that he has a heart condition and if he actually saw an apparition, he might have a heart attack and drop dead on the spot. I laughed the first time I heard this and then quickly realized he wasn't kidding. He said that the spirits must like him because they hadn't yet snuck up and spooked him, which isn't to say he hasn't had his moments. But the most bizarre aspect about John is that he loves horror movies. He's written and directed horror films! He left the Ranger Program and California in early 2019, but I managed to interview him before he moved back home to Wisconsin.

"Perfume is that last and best reserve of the past,
the one which when all our tears have run dry, can make us cry again."
—*Marcel Proust, French Novelist*

JOHN HUYBRECHT
(Former Park Ranger)

John: *About a week or two into my training, I was with Ranger Steve Clark. We were in the doll room moving chairs into the closet. All of a sudden there's this really floral smell, like an old lady's perfume, like something your grandma might wear. And it was really stenchy. At first, I thought it might have been from opening up the closet door, like moth balls, but it wasn't. It smelled very perfumey, like when someone walks past you with cologne and they're wearing way too much? Because when Steve opened the door, the smell, the fragrance just came at you, like a big waft. Heavy... and it wasn't a normal smell, that kind of a thing. And I asked Steve if he could smell that and he said, "Smell it? It's in my lungs." And I said, almost choking, "What the hell is that?" And he said, calmly,*

"Oh, that's Mrs. Doheny. Her dressing room is right above us." Yeah, it smelled sweet and rotten at the same time, like something that went bad.

Investigating smells or odors in a paranormal setting is tricky. Instruments to detect or measure smells don't really exist. Investigators rely on their own sense of smell as well as witness accounts. This also presents a problem because people's sense of smell vary greatly—some are very sensitive to smell and can narrow down and define aromas, while others have difficulty detecting and defining a stench. But in the experience above, both men equally absorbed the stinky perfume!

Ladies Powder Room

I don't know, is there such a thing called a ghost bruising?
— CHANH HANG
    GREYSTONE LEAD PARK RANGER

Photo: Chris Keith

Located to the west of the Grand Entry staircase, this room provided women visitors with a place to freshen their make-up and touch-up their hair upon arrival. The decorations and furnishings in the Ladies Powder Room changed dramatically from Art Deco in 1928 to French Provincial in 1945.

Why were these rooms called *powder rooms*?
In the 1700s, especially in Europe, status was defined by wardrobe and powdered wigs. The wealthy demanded high fashion and wigs became so important to maintaining one's social standing that separate rooms were

devoted to the act of powdering one's wig. Hence, the "powder room," and the name stuck. "Excuse me, but I must powder my wig."

"MYSTERIOUS MARKS"

After the September 11, 2001 attacks, Chae Yi was working at Los Angeles International Airport for a major airline carrier and witnessed layoffs, loss of benefits, and pay cuts. He decided to look for a government job that offered more stability and by 2005, he was working for the City of Beverly Hills as a ranger. By 2007, Chae was a Lead Park Ranger and a great ambassador for the Ranger Program. He works all the major events and often has shifts at the front desk of City Hall. Gregarious and personable, he enjoys chatting to patrons in the parks. We venture over to the mansion to talk about his story. Of all the things he loves about his job, entering the mansion isn't one of them.

Once inside, Chae confided to me that he had a very bizarre story. I also find that his experience has not happened to anyone else and that made it very unique. Chae didn't have photographic proof, but I took him at his word. Little did I know that only four weeks later his story would corroborate another Ranger's story.

CHAE YI
(Lead Park Ranger)

> Chae: *I'm moving tables and chairs, putting them back into the ladies' lounge. A very normal routine. So that night, when I get home, and I am washing up, I was a little surprised to find I have marks on my right wrist. They look like a bruise, but it also looks like it could be burns. I can't figure out what it is. I show it to my wife, and she says, "You have skin cancer." I get really worried. I look up skin cancer online, thinking maybe she's right. I'm also thinking age spots. But when I touch it, it doesn't hurt, it just looks like two bruises, like someone held my wrists really hard and twisted.*

They are circle bruises by the wrist. Really dark red, maybe even more like a plum-ish color. I show it to co-workers the next day and they're making jokes like, "The ghost grabbed you in the mansion!" And I'm like, "No, don't be ridiculous."

I asked Chae how long these bruises lasted.

Chae: *I had it on my wrist and my arm for about a week. So for a couple of days I backtracked, thinking I must have hit something, or I scraped something because it's not going away. I put on ointment, rubbing alcohol, aloe vera, whatever, and it still didn't go away.*

I was surprised this bruise didn't hurt. I asked him if there was any discomfort.

Chae: *There was no pain—no burning, no sensation, just the marks. So I was determined to go to the dermatologist to ask, "Is this a skin cancer?" But all of a sudden, like I said, about a week later, it just disappeared as if nothing had happened. But to this day, I still can't explain how I got this. I really focused on how this could have happened. What did I do that I don't remember doing? All I was moving was chairs and tables. Did I hit myself? Did I bang into something? To have marks like that you would really have to do something obvious, right? On the other hand, if I did, I'd be hurting because there were bruises. It's like something grabbed my wrist when I was working in the mansion. I guess some kind of spirit or something.*

"MORE MYSTERIOUS MARKS"

Now, keep in mind, after all the years of interviews and investigating Greystone, the type of situation that happened to Chae Yi, with the bruising, was never told or reported to me. When I interviewed Chae, the experience was an exception—until four weeks later.

CHANH HANG
(Lead Park Ranger)

Chanh: *This was in the morning during a fall event and Juan* [Park Ranger] *and I are setting up inside the mansion. All the tables and cocktail chairs are in the ladies' lounge* [Powder Room] *closet. After about an hour and a half of setup, I go to the restroom to wash my hands. Some dust and dirt is on my forearm and wrist. But as I wash, there is also a bruising mark, pretty big at the wrist. It doesn't hurt and I didn't notice it was there that morning or before. I just notice it as I wash my hands. And the color worries me because it isn't pink or reddish, it's dark purple. That seems unusual for*

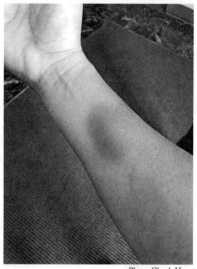

Photo: Chanh Hang

a bruise. A fresh bruise. One of my co-workers, Ranger Chae, had the same type bruising about a month before. And he showed me his bruising on his forearm, by his wrist. When I saw my bruising, I thought back on how his bruising was very similar, even the color. But I don't know, could this be the same entity?

Chanh: *And when I talked to Chae, he doesn't know how it happened, either. All he knows, and me, too, is that we got it at Greystone. He also said it didn't hurt and it wasn't tender. Same with me. It didn't bother me. You know how sometimes you don't recall bumping your hand or how you got it? I have felt bruises before on my knees and arms, but with it being that size, something had to have had a hard impact to give me that type of bruising. And I would have felt that.*

You can see how both rangers struggled to try and figure out exactly what took place, as well as rationalize how it could have happened without any pain—during the injury or after. Very odd.

> Chanh: *I don't know, is there such a thing called a ghost bruising? There's no explanation for it, but it's kind of strange that Chae and I had the same thing a month apart…same arm and bruise and he didn't know how he got it either. At that time, I was making fun of him when he showed me, but then it happened to me!*

I think we can call that ghost karma!

Chapter 8

Formal Dining Room

I can see right through him. And he is wearing black pants and a red smoking jacket. I know it's him. It's Ned.

— Luz Rodriguez
Retired Greystone Park Ranger

Photo: Chris Keith

The Social Network directed by David Fincher, *The Holiday* starring Kate Winslet and Cameron Diaz, *Nothing but Trouble* with Chevy Chase, Dan Aykroyd, and John Candy, *Ghostbusters 2, Nixon,* and *All of Me* were all filmed in this dining room.

Adjacent to the east end of the Grand Hall, surrounded with rustic oak wood paneling, is the Formal Dining Room. When Mr. and Mrs. Doheny entertained dinner guests, this was the room where they formally dined. Back in 1928, the fireplace mantle was black and white

Italian swirled marble. It was replaced with a solid white marble mantel piece during the large-scale redecorating of the mansion between 1944 and 1945. In the center of the room still hangs the original chandelier. The servant's call button, in the middle of the floor, which would have been underneath the dining room table, still remains. When we hear "Formal Dining Room," we might imagine a larger and more grand venue, but Mrs. Doheny wanted intimate rooms making up this 46,000-square-foot mansion.

"See-Through"

On my walk through the mansion with Luz, who is sincere and soft spoken, we visited many rooms, but she was only one of two people I interviewed who led me into this room. For her, this was a very bizarre and impactful incident that took place in 1999.

LUZ RODRIGUEZ
(Retired Park Ranger)

> Luz: [points to the leaded glass door that leads out to the terrace] *See how everything gets hand prints on them? That's why I was wiping down the windows outside of the library and I make my way inside the formal dining room. As I start to walk toward this door that leads out to the terrace, he is standing right here by the door, just looking out.*

The "he" is the figure she saw… and now, standing in the room and reliving the experience after all these years, brings her right back to the feeling and confusion of that exact moment.

> Luz: *I can see right through him. And he is wearing black pants and a red smoking jacket. I know it's him. It's Ned. And I was like, "OK, it's Ned."*

Luz stares at the spot as if she can still see the figure. She tells me that she knows Ned through photographs, and now, here he was in the dining room—albeit "see-through." I'm watching Luz closely as she slowly turns around to me.

Luz: *So I back away from the door, thinking maybe someone got into the house, but I doubt they would be see-through, you know?* [laughs] *It was probably around four in the afternoon when this happened, when I saw Ned. I never had the feeling he saw me; it was a one-way thing. Then I looked down and took a deep breath. When I looked back up, he was gone. This really scared me, but it didn't feel evil or malicious. He disappeared, and I just stood there and finally continued cleaning the windows.*

I'm thinking to myself, "You did what?!" After seeing "Ned," who passed away 70 years prior, and he's now hanging out in the dining room, how many of us would shake like a Chihuahua and run away screaming? But she gathered herself and continued cleaning the windows. Huh?! Talk about cool under pressure! When I asked her if she remembered any other specific details, she described the same apparition she saw in the Grand Hall.

Luz: *From my angle, I could tell he had a dark mustache. Dark hair. And he was wearing a red smoking jacket.*

I bring up the same murder photo of Ned on my phone and we look at it again together.

Luz: *Yeah. That looks like what I saw. Wow. That's amazing.*

"BLACK SHADOW"

In the fall of 2019, the City of Beverly Hills hired several new park rangers. At one point, I sat down with the new crew and discussed the fact that eventually they would have shifts at Greystone. Oftentimes that shift would mean locking up the mansion and the park "by yourself." I could sense that one of the new rangers (we'll call Art) was uncomfortable with what I said. He looked nervous and was looking down as I asked if everybody was okay with that. They all nodded "yes," but Art was quiet and seemed unnerved. I could tell that he was hesitant to talk about anything in front of the other rangers. I told them all that some people have experienced paranormal activity in the mansion. Art looked at me. I could see he was trying to hide his fear. "There's ghosts in there?" I told him the mansion is known to be haunted. Art confided, "I've had my share of activity in my life." It was then that I assumed he most likely had the ability to connect with ghosts. Ranger Juan moved in and said it was time to tour the mansion so the new rangers could see the location for themselves. I went along on the tour. As we walked into the Formal Dining Room, something happened, but it didn't directly involve Art, it involved me.

This was my interview with Juan after the tour was over and just the two of us were in the mansion. We talked in the Formal Dining Room.

JUAN ANDRADE
(Park Ranger Supervisor)

> Juan: *I'm leading a tour for four of the new rangers. We are going room-to-room and you were trailing behind us. When we moved from the dining room into the breakfast room through the connecting door, we all went in first and you were last. As I was standing by the doorway in the breakfast room, I saw a shadow move behind you.*

Juan makes a gesture in the direction in which the shadow traveled. I have him clarify its movements. "So the shadow is moving south away from the threshold behind me?" Juan nods.

Juan: *Yes. As you walked into the breakfast room, I'm watching the shadow in the dining room move behind you.*

I had no clue that Juan, or myself for that matter, were that close to a shadow apparition. I felt nothing.

Juan: *I was maybe five feet from the shadow.*

Now I needed specifics. "How tall was the shadow?" Juan holds up his hand to the height.

Juan: *About three feet tall. It moved right behind you.*

I still need more details. "And tell me, was it transparent and what color was it?" Juan shakes his head "no."

Juan: *It wasn't transparent at all, and it was completely black. So after I noticed the shadow, I walked back into the dining room and I looked around the room, but the shadow was gone. I pretended nothing happened and continued with the tour.*

I'm amazed Juan didn't react. I knew something happened because I know him so well and I could see he looked puzzled. I confirmed again, "My back was to it, but I didn't feel anything." Juan agrees.

Juan: *I didn't feel it either. I didn't get any goose bumps, nothing. I first thought maybe there was a shadow from that door over there in the dining room, but the shadow behind had no relation I could see with the door. I was also wondering why didn't any of the rangers see it.*

I guess the guys who walked into the Breakfast Room weren't looking up. They were looking down at the cork floor, because that's what we were talking about, how it is original to the mansion. I just wonder if they would have seen the black shadow had they been looking my way as I was walking into the Breakfast Room from the Dining Room. Juan just shrugs. I ask Juan his opinion, "Why do you think that shadow was here?"

Juan: *I'm not sure. I feel it was following us and wanted to find out who these four new rangers were. Maybe one of them has an aura about them that attracts the ghosts? And then as we continue on our tour, I notice, out of the corner of my eye, my peripheral vision, orbs moving really slow and then disappearing. And then again, moving really slow and disappearing.*

We start to walk out of the mansion. I ask Juan, "Did any of this scare you at all?"

Juan: *No. I didn't feel scared at all. Maybe I'm just desensitized. Part of the job.*

Chapter 9

Breakfast Room

It was like something out of The Shining.

— CHAD NELSON
   RETIRED GREYSTONE PARK RANGER

Photo: Chris Keith

The Social Network, which won Aaron Sorkin the Oscar® for his screenplay, and the Coen Brothers' *The Big Lebowski,* starring Jeff Bridges and John Goodman, were filmed in this room.

When you enter the Breakfast Room, a cork floor leads to a large bay window facing east, out over what were once gardens and a waterfall that cascaded down to a small lake. In 2015, the once large, nearly one-hundred-year-old leaning eucalyptus trees, abundant in this area, but now likely to fall, were removed to protect the mansion.

Photo: Berkeley Archives

With the sun rising in the east, it was the perfect spot for morning breakfast.

Greystone Historical Report

"This is where we ate most of our meals unless there were a lot of people," remarks Timothy Doheny. "Then it was the dining room."

"PARTY TIME!"

Chad started as a ranger in 1989. On his first day, he was by himself with no assistance. A television movie was filming in the mansion and Chad was responsible to oversee the entire production for Greystone. Chad remembers, "It was pandemonium. Hundreds of extras, people in period costumes, horses crapping all over the place. It was a real nightmare." In the nearly two years he worked as a ranger at Greystone, there were good times and strange times. "It was a lot of fun," he recalled, "a long with a lot of weird stories!"

CHAD NELSON
(Retired Park Ranger)

> Chad: *I was scheduled to open up the mansion. It was early morning and I start to go downstairs and I hear this cocktail party going on. I hear the echo of glasses clinking together and low conversation. And I also hear old-time music playing off towards the kitchen. Like in the breakfast room. In that area. I hear this and I think, "What on earth?" Maybe there's a movie crew in there setting up, and I didn't get the notice, but I didn't see any camera trucks outside, no catering trucks. I didn't see anything outside* [indicating an event or film crew]. *What is going on? I start walking toward the room not knowing what to expect. As I get closer and closer to the sounds, the whole thing didn't sound as you might expect. You would figure it would get louder as you got closer, right? No, it just stayed the same level. It didn't get lower or louder, and it had kind of a sing-songy sound.*

I asked him to elaborate or try and make the sound, just to give me a sense. He made a musical hum sound that might remind you of an old player-piano or an organ-grinder tune.

> Chad: *I kept getting closer and closer to what I presumed was the source but it didn't change. And then when I got to where I thought the sound was coming from and I expected to see what it was, or who was playing what—it just stopped. Gone. But what I heard on my way was like old time music. Like thirties music. Trumpets, you know, stuff you'd hear from the thirties. Maybe even a cocktail party thing. That I remember distinctly. It was like audio from the past somehow…*

Chad took a long pause.

> Chad: *It was like something out of* The Shining.

Jack Nicholson is walking down that empty hallway, and you can hear the music from the ballroom—"Midnight, the Stars and You"—he turns into the full ballroom and the maître d welcomes him, "Good evening, Mr. Torrance." Except when Chad arrived in the Breakfast Room, his movie ended abruptly.

Chapter 10

Kitchen — First Floor

And suddenly, out of nowhere, something brushes me behind my back!
It felt really weird and then I get super, super lightheaded to a point
where I almost faint.
— BRENT JONES
GREYSTONE PARK VISITOR

Photo: Mary E. Nichols

The Witches of Eastwick starring Jack Nicholson, *Death Becomes Her* starring Meryl Streep, *Spider-Man 3*, *The Bodyguard* with Kevin Costner and Whitney Houston, *All of Me*, *Nixon*, and *There Will Be Blood* all filmed scenes in the downstairs kitchen.

At the far eastern end of the Grand Hall, butted up against the Servants' Wing, is the First Floor Kitchen. The chef's pantry is on one side and the flower room is on the other. The Doheny's staffed the kitchen with a first cook, a second cook, a kitchen maid, as well as several women serving. The kitchen was equipped with a large island that filled the middle section, and a massive Magic Chef gas stove with two broilers, a warmer, and eight burners.

Quite a few structural changes have taken place in this section of the mansion. From 2011 through 2012, the servants' dining room, which adjoined the main kitchen, was demolished to make way for a modern catering kitchen, a changing room/bathroom, a dumb waiter elevator, and a storage room.

The kitchen is home to one of the earliest electric refrigerators models made by Westinghouse. Most homes at that time used "ice boxes" to cool their food. The original cabinets and drawers still line the north and eastern walls. Bordering the south wall is a one-piece, twenty-one-and-a-half-foot stainless steel countertop with two inset soap compartments and two sinks. Since stainless steel was in use as early as 1900, and considering Greystone Mansion was built in 1927, it's possible this countertop was one of the largest of its kind in the world. You could dedicate a half-hour to this kitchen on HGTV!

"Source of Energy"

Brehnen Knight is very articulate, with a detailed memory of his time working as a Park Ranger at Greystone. He is always a wealth of information. He told me that back in his day, the interior of the mansion was never rented out for events as it is today. According to Brehnen, "It was absolutely never done. There was a lot more mystique to the place, and it was very, very rare that anyone stepped inside the house." In fact, the only time the mansion was opened back then was for a film shoot. He commented, "As rangers, our job duties were to make sure the production companies and crews didn't mess up the house, and more importantly, that they cleaned and restored the house as they found it." But the hustle and bustle of making a movie wasn't the only problem Brehnen encountered inside the mansion.

BREHNEN KNIGHT
(Retired Park Ranger)

Brehnen: *I remember getting ready to lock up. Everything's closed off and it's a new alarm system. Back then you had green lights to indicate all the zones were closed, and it wouldn't let you set the alarm until you had the green light. One of the places where the alarm would always go off would be the motion sensor in the middle of the hall. Occasionally film crews would put up curtains or fabric that would occasionally set off the alarm. But in this particular case, the alarm was being sensitive and it wasn't allowing me to lock the mansion. The light beam sensor would shine from one end of the hall to the other. This night in question, there was nothing like suits of armor, or curtains, or anything else that could get in the way of the beam, so I'm like, "Okay, whatever." I go back up to the panel and it's still blinking* [not ready to arm]. *At that point I'm talking to myself, "Okay, c'mon, whoever this is, I'm trying to go home. I've got schoolwork to do, knock it off." I go back down the stairs, and by this time I've got all the mansion lights off and I'm holding a flashlight. That's when I definitely saw, what I can only call, a source of energy. Nothing with definitive boundaries. And light is probably the wrong word to describe it, but something that differentiated itself from the background, continually going back and forth from the kitchen to the breakfast room, crossing the light beam sensor, obviously disrupting the alarm panel. It's happening for about five minutes, and I can't set the alarm. And there is clearly a pacing to it, where it goes in one room and then you wait a few seconds and it would reverse motion and go back out to the other one. And I'm just like, "Come on. Really? Really?!" And, of course, I'm not in any hurry to walk down there and tell them* [the spirits] *not to do it. Right?*

Out of curiosity, I asked Brehnen, "So it's darting back and forth. What did you finally do?"

Brehnen: *Well, just before I felt like I'm going to have to yell or scream at it, the light just went away. Gone. But this really stood out to me because this was the only time I actually saw something, with my own eyes—some paranormal evidence or activity that you can't explain. Usually it's doors banging, weird sounds, whatever, but it was never something that I ever physically saw. I mean, I don't know how many false alarms happened, but it was like, "I can't even set this thing," you know? It's a source of energy. In other words, it creates light that is way brighter than the surroundings. And you can imagine looking down that hall with everything shut off at nighttime. It's just so dark. So it didn't take much light to be seen— and what was surprising, it isn't just like a little dot floating around or anything. It's way bigger than that. Let's say, the size of a Frisbee. But it wasn't round... it didn't have round edges, but I'm thinking about size. It didn't have well-defined edges in any way or a sharp shape. It was sort of gaseous, going back and forth. It could have been a servant* [from back in the day] *going from the kitchen to the breakfast room and back, still performing their duties.*

"RESIDUAL MAID"
LUZ RODRIGUEZ
(Retired Park Ranger)

Luz: *There's a lot of energy in the kitchen area. And I think that's why I see servants going back and forth. And it looks like a head maid in a grayish maid's smock. I can literally see her. She's the one I see the most coming in and out of the kitchen area and that flower room area on the other side.*

I walk with Luz into the flower room that's connected to the kitchen. I can see Luz scanning the area as memories of certain "visions" come back to her.

> Luz: *I've seen her in here. I see her doing this over at the sink* [gestures as if she's washing something]. *And then over here, maybe arranging some flowers, and then she moves out into the kitchen. But because it happens so much, I feel like they're not actual entities. Also, because it's like not interacting or scary to me. It's like now I'm the invisible one. It's more residual*[1] *energy.*

What Luz may have seen is a woman performing the same duties as when she was alive and working in the mansion. The paranormal theory is that leftover energy is not in real time. It's like a film loop of energy that plays over and over. Now, that being said, there are others who say it could be an active spirit that, in real time, has come back to perform her former duties in the mansion because she hasn't, as of yet, fully crossed over to the other side. The last possibility is she may not even know she is dead. Believe it or not, that is a scenario I've heard and researched. Sounds unbelievable, right? But it seems likely what Luz is explaining is one of those three scenarios if these spirit energies are actually being witnessed by living-breathing human beings.

An interesting hypothesis was offered by *Live Science's* Benjamin Radford in the November 11, 2011 issue of *Live Science:*

> Many ghost hunters believe that strong support for the existence of ghosts can be found in modern physics. Specifically, that Albert Einstein, one of the greatest scientific minds of all time, offered a scientific basis for the reality of ghosts.

---

1 When someone says "residual," they're referring to remnants of energy within locations left by people who once occupied that space.

A recent Google search turned up nearly 8 million results suggesting a link between ghosts and Einstein's work covering the conservation of energy. This assertion is repeated by many top experts in the field. For example, ghost researcher John Kachuba, in his book "Ghosthunters" (2007, New Page Books), writes, "Einstein proved that all the energy of the universe is constant and that it can neither be created nor destroyed… So what happens to that energy when we die? If it cannot be destroyed, it must then, according to Dr. Einstein, be transformed into another form of energy. What is that new energy? Could we call that new creation a ghost?"

"THE BROOMSTICK"

CHANH HANG

(Lead Park Ranger)

Since 1994, "Music in the Mansion" has presented concerts featuring selected prize-winning international and local artists. From January through June, monthly Sunday concerts are followed by meet-the-artists receptions and a tour of the first floor of the Greystone Mansion. After one of these matinee performances, the guests were gone and Park Rangers Chanh and Gabriel were wrapping up.

Chanh: *Gabriel and I start putting away the tables and chairs and right when we put away the last stack of chairs, we are walking east down the grand hallway, and there's a noise I hear that I will never forget. Moving down the hallway toward the chef's pantry, it sounded like something fell and hit the floor. We both heard it. Loud and clear. First thing I say to him is, "Someone is still in here." I ask Gabriel to check out the library and go towards the dining room and the breakfast room. I'll take the main hall and move towards the pantry. We'll meet in the kitchen.*

I asked Chanh to describe the sound.

> Chanh: *It's like a broomstick falling and hitting against the floor. You know when wood hits the marble floor, it makes that 'Smack!' noise? That's what it sounded like. So when we meet at the kitchen, I asked Gabriel, "Did you notice a broomstick or a mop stick on the floor anywhere?" He didn't. But he goes, "We're going to find the stick. It has to be here somewhere." So we continue looking around—nothing. We walk back into the servants' quarter's hallway and see the janitor's closet is closed. We looked inside. Nothing has fallen on the floor. We walked towards the service corridor, which is now the new remodeled kitchen. Nothing in there either. And even if we found a broomstick in there, it sounded so very close to us, that it still wouldn't make any sense. That sound had to be in the historical kitchen. But after our first sweep when we didn't find anything, Gabriel said, "Okay, let's leave," and I said, "No, way, we can't, because that sound was real. It didn't sound like some ghost slamming a door or something. If someone is still in here, we need to clear this mansion, because I'm leaving in 20 minutes. After I leave, and you think somebody's still in here, you're on your own and you'll have to arm the mansion by yourself. And if they walk out and trip the sensor, you're going to have to get back in here and deal with them. So you either clear it with me or you can do it later." Gabriel goes, "Okay, let's do it now." We continued the search but we didn't find a person, a broomstick, or anything on the floor. Finally, we set the alarm and exited out the service quarters. The alarm never went off. I never did figure it out, but I've never forgotten it either.*

"HELLO?"

CLETE KEITH

Whenever I'm interviewing someone who has experienced possible paranormal activity on the property, it always prompts me to think about other people I've interviewed with regards to that same location. With Ranger Chanh's aforementioned encounter, it made me think of an incident that happened to myself and several co-workers in the kitchen. Not only did it stun me, but after the incident I walked away with incredible evidence that I didn't even know I had at the time of the encounter! Let me explain.

Ranger Steve Clark and I took a fellow city worker, Tim, and his brother, Matt, into the mansion one night. We weren't going to stay the whole night, but we were going to try and be there late. Matt really wanted to visit the mansion. He'd heard a lot about the paranormal activity and was very interested, so I offered, "Okay, Steve and I will take you both in and we'll hang out for a while." So this one evening, near midnight, we brought out a table, and what Steve called trigger objects[2]—a couple glasses of scotch, and cigars, things that both Ned and Hugh enjoyed in their lives in the mansion. We placed them on the table in the Grand Hall and sat down, inviting both Ned and Hugh, or anyone else from the other side, to join us. With my recorder turned on, we sat quietly and waited for a response. Finally, Steve suggested, "Why don't we just walk around and show Tim and Matt the mansion?"

From the Grand Hall, we walk east through the Library, into the Formal Dining Room, the Breakfast Room, and then walk into the historic Kitchen. Tim and I are talking when suddenly Matt turns to me, eyes wide as saucers, and says, "What was that noise just now?" We didn't hear anything. Matt says, "Didn't you just hear somebody say, 'Hello?'" We all said "no"—and it certainly wasn't Matt because he's the one asking the question. I remind them, "I have the recorder going, hopefully we caught something on it." I didn't listen to it there for one simple reason: if I turn off the recorder and something happens, we miss it. I listen after the mansion is in my rearview mirror. We eventually packed everything up

---

2 Trigger objects are objects that are relevant to the specific environment in which you're investigating. They're usually left unattended with the idea that a spirit or ghost might interact with the object, and that interaction may be captured via a video/audio recording and used as evidence.

and went home. Later, at home, when I listened to the recording, there is indeed a voice, clear as the day is long, that utters, "Hello?" And not only does this voice say, "Hello?" but when it says "Hello?" there's an echo to the room, the same echo you hear in the kitchen. I sent the recording to Matt and he said it was exactly what he heard live and in-person. Why the three of us didn't hear it and only Matt did, I don't know. Maybe because we were engaged in conversation and Matt was just looking around and listening.

I was exceedingly happy that I actually captured the recording. It remains one of the best EVP recordings I've ever captured.[3] In the world of parapsychology and ghost hunting, EVPs (Electronic Voice Phenomena) are sounds or voices recorded intentionally or unintentionally on electronic recording devices. It's incredibly clear and sounds like the spirit is right next to us. Who was it? Ned... Hugh... or ???

"THE MISSING PIECE"

Ronda was a guest interior designer at the Fifth Annual Beverly Hills Garden and Design Showcase at Greystone in 2006. The designers are asked to select a room to design. The process takes months to load in their design inspirations for the chosen room's décor. As she was working, I walked into the historic kitchen to see how Ronda was doing. As soon as I spotted her, I could tell she was frazzled. Ronda was quick to say, "Is there something going on here?" Ronda is a no-nonsense individual, so I knew something was up. She is a professional who appears to handle work obstacles with relative ease. So I asked her what she meant, and she began telling me everything that was happening in the kitchen. I have to admit, it sounded farfetched, but not surprising. Her story was bewildering, not only to her, but to her design team as well.

---

3 Audio recording exists in author's collection.

RONDA JACKSON, CID IIDA

(Principal, Décor Interior Design)

Ronda: *Two things stood out that I remember distinctly. One, how cold the kitchen was. I think you and I talked about when energy is in a room and the spirits aren't happy, how it gets very, very cold. You kind of get that chilly effect.*[4] *The second thing was when you saw the crazy expression on my face, it was because as we were trying to finish the room, a piece of tile had disappeared. I had laid out the exact amount of tile for a pattern all across the center kitchen island so my design team would know exactly where to place each piece. They showed up to work, started on the countertop and we were missing one piece. Even after cleaning up, and unloading and offloading, we never found that piece of tile. It wasn't something that could have easily disappeared. We would've heard it hit the floor if it had fallen. So I had to camouflage that area in the photo with a tray and tea towel. But, yeah, the tile walked off! Never did find it. It was literally gone!*

There was more…

Ronda: *We were also putting cups, coffee mugs, and plates in the cabinets—and I was quite meticulous about how I was arranging things. I would leave the room and come back and things would be disheveled or out of order. We ended up making curtains and just kind of closing it all off because we couldn't make it work. I guess "they" didn't like my selection of tea cups and dishes.*

Ronda also mentioned to me some photos she took. I asked her about what they revealed.

Ronda: *There were all sorts of orbs in the photographs. I remember you and I had a lengthy conversation about the orbs. I guess when you're not sure what you're confronted with, you almost have to accept it. It's one thing to*

---

4 It is said that when an entity tries to manifest, it draws all the heat around it to use for energy. Thus, the area becomes very cold.

be able to solve a problem because you know what the problem is, but to have things that you don't understand and can be considered complex or taboo, it makes it really challenging. The showcase was a huge opportunity. I don't even know today if I would've done anything differently. I definitely wasn't expecting the place to be haunted!

After my interview, several months later, I came across some scribbled notes from when I first walked in to talk to Ronda that day in the kitchen. Her conversation with her team regarding finishing up placing the tile: "You've got to finish this up," she said. And they replied, "We will when we get all the pieces." To which Ronda replied, "Well, I just placed out all the pieces for you." She looked and saw a piece was missing and said to them, "Come on guys, where is it?" And they said, "We just got here! We didn't touch it!" Ronda then tells me several days later that she was so frustrated with the tile and the cabinets and the "spirits or whatever" interfering that she said out loud to the unseen perpetrators, "I'm trying to make this kitchen look nice. Would you please allow me to do that?!" After that, she said the room eventually did warm up. "Actually," she said, "it got very toasty in there. So we did something right!"

"GET OUT NOW!"
CHANH HANG
(Lead Park Ranger)

Chanh: *I remember it was a Friday. Ranger Steve was in the firehouse office. It was maybe about three-thirty or four in the afternoon. We didn't have any events, but a few lights were still on in the mansion. So my routine on Friday evening is to close the mansion early and make sure I check the lights, windows, and all the doors before I set the alarm. So I enter the grand entry, and walk down over to the west side of the mansion to start from that end. As I get to the kitchen, Steve calls me on the radio. "375*

[Chanh's radio number at Greystone], *what's your 20?" I tell him, "Hey Steve, I'm inside the mansion closing up." Then I hear him say, "Chanh, can you 10-9?"* [repeat your transmission]. *I say, "I'm in the kitchen." He asks a third time, "Chanh, I can't make out anything." All of a sudden, I hear white noise. That's not expected on this type of radio. This is a two-thousand-dollar radio that we carry. Either the transmission is clear, or it doesn't go through. So then I hear* [Ranger] *Chae chime in, "Chanh, you've got to speak up. I can't hear you." Steve comes back on the radio, "Get out! Get out now!" I'm like, "Copy that." So I quickly walk up the servants' quarters and exit out to the east courtyard. I stand there and Steve, who looked concerned, meets me right there and says, "Chanh, where were you in the mansion?" I tell him I was in the chef's pantry turning the lights off. He says, "Is there something wrong with your radio?" So I clicked the mic and I go, "Radio check." He hears it from his radio loud and clear. He thought maybe my battery was low. I check—it wasn't. But like I said, even if the battery was low, it wouldn't make white noise. Steve wonders, "Did you hear me on the radio?" I say, "I heard you fine, I heard Chae fine, but then nothing but a bunch of static." Steve tells me that he couldn't really hear me. And then I told him after the static "I finally heard you say "Get out! Get out now!" Steve just stares at me and says, "I'm glad you're okay," and he walks away. But it was really weird, and it has never happened again.*

When I realized Chanh didn't press Steve about the "Get out! Get out now!" message, I immediately contacted Steve about this event. He was confident it wasn't him yelling over the radio, "Get out! Get out now!" So I asked if it wasn't him over the radio telling Chanh to "Get out," then who was it? He didn't have an answer.

"Catch My Fall"

Brent is a hair stylist who was on a private tour with eight other friends. He was very interested in the mansion and told me about some paranormal incidents that happened to him in the past. When I asked him to elaborate, he told me and then asked me not to share it with anyone. Obviously, I will honor his wishes. All I will say, though, is that it was quite graphic and very disturbing. At Greystone that night, this following event was one of two that took place with Brent.

BRENT JONES
(Visitor)

> Brent: *As you know, we're on the tour. I walk through the door of the kitchen, turned around and face towards the group who are coming in and crowding around. I think it's like maybe six people in front of me and my back is right up against the wall. And suddenly, out of nowhere, something brushes me behind my back! It felt really weird and then I get super, super lightheaded to a point where I almost faint. I mean, I have to step my foot out to catch myself because I almost fell forward. I was scared I was going to bust my head open if I didn't catch my fall. I think so much was just going on, people talking and all that, I didn't have a chance to let it register what was happening. But I thought, "That was kind of weird." I know we're on a tour of a mansion that's famous for being haunted, so that was kind of strange in itself, but really, that kind of suddenly feeling lightheaded doesn't happen to me every day. You know what I'm saying? So that was just strange.*

"Ooooohhhhh!"

It came to my attention that Glenda and Tony had an experience in the mansion when working a wedding. They were part of the catering staff. They agreed to meet me at Greystone to record an interview. They were very interested in going back inside the mansion, yet, you could tell when I greeted them that they were still unnerved by what took place several years prior on that evening in the kitchen area. We chatted as we made our way through the mansion and into the kitchen. They couldn't believe that three years had passed since that evening in 2016.

GLENDA DOPAZO & TONY KELLAM
(Catering Vendor Employees)

Tony: *Basically, the wedding is over. Glenda and I are told by our boss to come back down here and clean up any leftover cocktail glasses or anything like that down here or in the back of the house out on the terrace. It was probably around seven or eight at night.*

Glenda: *Tony is trying to open other doors to get outside and I was like, "Uh, Tony, I don't think we should be trying to open any doors." So we meander into the dining room. Tony goes over to the glass door that opens out to the terrace and tries to open it.*

Tony: *Yeah, it was weird. I was trying to open that door and it simply wouldn't open. I guess it was locked. And I jokingly said to Glenda, "Oh, maybe the ghost locked it."*

Glenda: *But then I hear a sound that was like a combination of a man lamenting and the wind. But there was no wind. Put those sounds together and it was what you might typically think a ghost would sound like, "Oooooohhhhhh!" Like that. And that long. About four to five seconds. So I immediately start looking at all the windows to make sure there are no cracks. No window was open because, of course, the first thing my mind started to do was try to rationalize what I just heard. I was like, "It has to be the wind." So I asked Tony if he heard the sound. He didn't.*

Tony: *I wasn't listening. I was looking out the door and focusing on how to get outside. And Glenda says, "Did you hear that sound!?"*

Glenda: *And I was like, "I don't think we should be here!" And then suddenly it happens again, "Ooooooooooohhhhhhhhh," but stronger this time. And then Tony stood up and goes, "Shut the fuck up! Oh my God! Did you hear that?!" And I said, "Yes! That's the same sound I told you I heard!"*

Tony: *I was so focused on trying to get outside I didn't hear it the first time. But it was this groaning male, "Ooooooooaaaaahhh!" Kind of windy, almost like the Tarzan yell, but with multiple voices all at once. I remember wanting to check it out.*

Glenda is now getting very excited as she relives that moment from three years ago—the feelings have obviously come back full force.

Glenda: *Not me! I was feeling like we shouldn't linger. Everything's locked, so we know there's nobody in here. It's completely dark, and actually I've heard that there might be ghosts, and I just felt like we shouldn't be in here. And I knew our staff had gone. So basically, it's just us down here.*

Tony: *And that's when we both were kind of onboard like, okay, something's happening. Let's go!*

Glenda: *Yeah, you got a little nervous too at the end. You were like, "I think we should get out of here! I think we should go!!"*

Tony: *And so we discussed like should we stay, or should we go? We were both kind of torn.*

Glenda: *No. I was like, "Let's go!" And you said, "Hold on. Let's look through here." And we peeked in the crack of the door somewhere and I remember seeing a long, dark, black hallway and I said, "No way! Let's go!" So we walked back into the butler's pantry, just outside the kitchen and we started looking for any air blowing or open windows—we wanted to find a rational reason. But there was no airflow anywhere.*

Glenda points to the windows in the Kitchen.

> Glenda: *We looked everywhere for cracks or open windows. And I was thinking maybe it was this exhaust fan above the double sinks. Maybe this fan moved, you know...and made this unworldly sound. But it was obvious, this thing wasn't moving. I kept thinking, "There's got to be something open."*

> Tony: *We're just looking around, but I remember feeling that the sound was now coming from down the hall.*

> Glenda: *All over. It seemed like it was coming from all over.*

Tony agrees and now we're walking toward the Grand Hall. Glenda looks back up toward the windows.

> Glenda: *Of course, in my mind, I'm looking towards the windows, but it's not like it came from the windows. It's just me trying to figure out, or justify, that it must be the wind.*

Tony moves into the Grand Hall and he still seems slightly confused when trying to analyze what took place. He stares down the hallway, almost as if he is expecting it to happen again. I asked him if he remembers any more details about the voice or the sound.

> Tony: *It felt like it was down the hall because it was an echoey, rich, deep sound with a windy reverb type thing.*

> Glenda: *Yes. It was a rich* [she lowers her voice and mimics what she heard]. *A very deep, soooouunnnd, you know? But I think before that, I was feeling that energy. I definitely had the chills when I heard it.*

> Tony: *It's hard to know if it's the fear or the mind or what. I was certainly excited by it. It did feel like there was something here.*

Glenda: *So we left, and we were sort of processing and talking about it. And we literally were texting until four in the morning, talking, telling each other the different research we have found online and sending photos and saying, "Look at this! Check this out!"*

Tony is now quiet and thinking back to that frightening moment.

Tony: *Like there was a story within the voice. It felt like there was something with it. Like there was an intelligence there.*

Glenda: [nods in agreement] *It felt like it was a suffering voice. Like it was suffering with anger, hurt, and pain, all in one. It wasn't like a, "Hey, get out of here!" sort of voice or feeling.*

Tony: *It sounded like it was a sentient being. Like there's a story behind the groaning and moaning.*

Glenda: *I think that was the first time that I ever actually heard something that could have been a spirit. And again, I think what resonated with me the most was that anger and pain. I don't know if it was trying to reach out to us. It felt more like, "Get out of here!" And in my mind, I just thought, "I don't want to hear it anymore! Let's go!"*

Chapter 11

Room 120

*You could hear them coming straight towards the door, but there was
no one there.*

— Luz Rodriguez
  Retired Greystone Park Ranger

Photo: Chris Keith

Greystone Historical Report

The serving girls also ran the two telephone switchboards,
one of which was located between the servants' hall and
breakfast room on the first floor.

We call this "Room 120" because the numbers "120" are at the top of the door. We believe when the American Film Institute was housed in the mansion (from 1969 to 1982 and the City leased it to them for $1 per year), they put the number there to distinguish it from all the other rooms. We're not clear as to why they singled out this particular room. However, we do know that in 1929 it served as a telephone operator's room. "Betsy, ring me Fairfax-2717, please."

"Room 120" was also originally known as a wrapping room for gifts. It's a tiny room in the downstairs Servants' Wing, just off the hallway. The room is lined with drawers and cabinets (currently filled with extension cords, light bulbs, and other assorted electrical equipment). A janitor's closet is also close by in that same hallway.

"SOMETHING IN THERE?"

Elva is a quiet sweet woman. I believe she has the ability to sense paranormal energy and spirits. She is very religious, which can be problematic given that certain religions frown on any kind of communication with those who have passed. Elva doesn't want to communicate with any spirits or any "thing" on the other side. She arrives at work about twenty minutes early, sits in her car, and says her prayers before she enters the mansion. When she first started working at Greystone, she would bring Holy Water with her as protection. So you're wondering: have things happened to her in the mansion? She certainly believes so and finds that the activity in the mansion fluctuates—there are times when she feels the energy and times when she feels nothing. She has good days and bad days that are usually dictated by the energy or spirit activity inside the mansion. While she has a wonderful sense of humor, there have been times when activity in the mansion is far from humorous. She tells this story with a straight-to-the-heart honesty. Her attitude is pleasingly frank: "This is what I heard. I don't know why it happens to me. I don't want to talk to spirits. I just want to do my job and leave."

ELVA
(Janitorial Services)

Elva: *Do you know where my closet is? Where I keep all my stuff? Across from that is the one-twenty on the door? The rangers use that for whatever they have inside. There is a little lock that locks the door. I'm walking by and I hear banging from inside. Really loud banging. Not like a knock. It was loud, like pounding. So I told one of the rangers that I could hear banging inside. "Naw, there's nothing in there," he said. "Well, okay, maybe you think it's nothing, but that's what I heard." And I made sure I went back and looked. The door is locked. There is no way you can go inside there and lock yourself in. But there has to be something in there. How that happened, I don't have any idea. It just happened that once and I never heard anything again. I just kept praying. My prayer is my weapon and I go according to the Bible. "You don't talk to dead people." That goes against God. So that's what I do. Every time I go there, I just want to be on the safe side. So I pray not to bother me. I'm only doing this because I need to work. But to me, I don't want to mess with it because if you look for it, you'll find it.*

"Hallway Footsteps"
LUZ RODRIGUEZ
(Retired Park Ranger)

Luz: *We used to call it the gift-wrapping room. It was also the kind of place to just get away. We had an old-fashioned rotary phone in there that actually worked, so when there was filming, you could go in there and make phone calls. But from inside you could hear footsteps up and down the hallway when no one was around. I swear I could hear footsteps of spirits walking around, for some reason, especially during filming. You could hear them coming straight towards the door, but there was no one there.*

I asked her how she knew these were "spirit footsteps" and not just someone in the flesh walking by.

Luz: *I'd hear footsteps coming down the hallway, coming straight towards the door, and I would quickly step out of the room and there was no one there. I mean, you could hear the steps, but there was no one there just a second later!*

Chapter 12

Servants' Wing — First Floor

As soon as I heard it, chills just shivered up my spine. I ran out the front door of the house! I was really scared.

— MARTIN J. PEREZ
JANITORIAL SERVICES

Photo: Chris Keith

Beginning at the east end of the mansion, both on the first and second floor, is the Servants' Wing. When you enter this subterranean area, you walk in from just outside the chef's pantry. You immediately notice the black and white checkered linoleum floor that spans the length of this hallway. Room 120 is on the left side of the hallway, and the door on the right, when opened, reveals a large combination safe that housed all the silver and gold placement settings for family dining. There's a green panel switch plate on the wall that allowed the staff to turn on the lights to the lake, waterfalls, north terrace, formal garden, cypress lane, and other areas on the property. On that same wall is an "annunciator"—also known as the servant call system display. Every room in the mansion had a designated number, so when a button was pushed by a family member or guest from a specific room, a small arrow would point to that number, alerting the servants that service was requested.

Greystone Historical Report

The service wing jutted off this end of the mansion at a northerly angle, and it included a butler's pantry, kitchen, flower room, servants' dining room, maids' sitting room, and maid's rooms, plus a service stairway to the second floor.

"SCREAM" (PART ONE)

I remember very well when Dan called me about this experience. It was early on a Sunday morning. He was dumbfounded. "Clete, you're not going to believe this." I've heard this initial line from dozens of people ready to tell me what strange thing just rankled their reality at Greystone. And this particular one, coming from Dan, and judging by his bewildered tone, I knew it must have been bizarre. I met him in the mansion and he walked me through his experience. Once he finished telling me his story, I thought it was indeed bizarre, especially as it began with him sitting on the toilet.

DANIEL HERNANDEZ
(Park Ranger Supervisor)

> Daniel: *I came to work, unarmed the mansion, walk through to the new kitchen to use the restroom. Our day porter, Martin, was mopping the floor in the grand hall. So I'm in the restroom when suddenly I hear a little girl scream.*

This threw me totally off guard. I immediately say, "What!?"

Daniel: *Yeah. A scream. So I get outside quickly to see if I could hear or see anyone in the park, around the mansion, or setting up for a party in the neighborhood. Nothing. But it's early Sunday morning, close to 8:30. So I go back inside to Martin and ask him, "Did you hear something?" He says, "The little girl scream?" So he heard it too. It sounded like it came from the servants' hall and it was definitely a little girl.*

I asked Dan about Martin's reaction.

Daniel: *Yeah, Martin's reaction was kind of normal, but his body language said something else. He told me things were happening here to him quite often.*

"SCREAM" (PART TWO)

MARTIN J. PEREZ
(Janitorial Services)

Martin: *Yeah, it was early in the morning. The park wasn't even opened yet. No people around whatsoever. As I was just doing my thing of cleaning, this girl's scream echoes through the whole house. It was like a high pitch, but it echoed. Dan heard it, too. I think he went outside first. I'm not exactly sure where it happened, because it just echoed all over the place. It was just so... As soon as I heard it, chills just shivered up my spine. I ran out the front door of the house! I was really scared. I'm like, "Damn, did I just hear that!?" And I needed to get out and catch a breather and get a drink of water, and Dan is there and he says, "Hey, do you have someone in the house?" I was like, "No, I have no one in here." He goes, "Because I heard someone screaming." And I'm like, "You heard that too!?" This girl's scream was loud and it was in the house, close by, and it echoed in kind of a weird way.*

I asked him if that was unusual to hear something like that.

Martin: *During the time I was here, working all over, especially in the room where the murder scene happened, or in the library, or here in the center of the grand hall and pretty much the whole first floor, I always felt as if someone was following me. Following me everywhere and trying to touch me. Because I could feel the hairs on my arms just move. It kind of felt like a spider web on your arm, but it wasn't. Yeah, but boy, that girl's scream really scared me.*

"OPENED WINDOWS"

BREHNEN KNIGHT
(Retired Park Ranger)

Brehnen: *Most of the stuff that I've experienced, in general, was either by the kitchen, the breakfast room, or the maid's quarters in the servants' wing. Also, where the film companies park their generator truck in the AFI parking lot over by the koi pond. There's a small courtyard down below and that's the laundry room* [it's also known as the laundry pit and is secured and off limits to the public]. *There's a set of windows there where the film grips would pull power cables for filming because it didn't get in the way of people walking on it. A lot of those windows would be open. So at the end of a day's shooting, they would have to unhook the cable, pull it out, and then I would go back and lock the windows. I just knew after years of filming, that's what you look for first. So the park is empty and everyone is gone. I would always go down there to make sure those windows were closed and locked—both on the first and second floor of the servants' wing. And I have to make it back to the other end of the mansion to set the alarm, and invariably, by the time I got back to the alarm panel, the system would relay that one or two of the windows were now unlocked.*

So I turn around and go back to lock those windows, which were in fact unlocked—after, I know, minutes before, I locked them.

"Closer and Closer"

GABRIEL JARA

(Lead Park Ranger)

Gabriel: *About five or six years ago, maybe 2014, I'm working on a Sunday alongside one of the new park rangers. His name is Raul. And this is a daytime wedding. And so, we go inside the mansion through the east door, the servants' wing door, and we are trying to access the door that leads to the servants' dining room in the servant hallway downstairs. As we are trying to unlock that door, we start hearing a loud bang coming through the walls, and it just kept coming closer and closer and we both look at each other like, "What the hell is that?!" And as it comes closer, and closer, we're like, "What do we do!?" We look at each other and we run out the door! Some people working the wedding outside are looking at us like, "What happened?" And we tell them and it scared them as well. I don't know, I mean, it sounded like somebody was hitting that wall and it just kept coming closer and closer to us, and that's when we just split. And here's the crazy thing, probably not even a year later, Raul quit. Not sure if it had anything to do with that day, but I'll tell you, if I have to go into that house for anything, I'm always on the lookout. It haunts me to this day.*

"Voices in the Night"

This story is so compelling. I was riveted as Steve unwrapped the details. It also offers credence to the fact that the paranormal activity in the mansion is so unpredictable. I've gone inside the mansion countless times anticipating that something unnerving will literally be right around the corner—and nothing happens. Activity seems to happen when you least expect it. And remember, when it's at night inside the mansion, there's a fear factor that emanates from deep within all of us and affects our imagination… but also fuels the anticipated connection with the spirits—it's almost an invitation to them: "Okay, I'm here, show yourself." The bottom line: it's one thing to enter in the daytime, quite another at night. In this account, a last-minute decision on Steve's behalf turned out to be a big mistake.

STEVEN CLARK
(Retired Park Ranger Supervisor)

Steven: *So this is the night we had the Prince and Princess of Monaco here doing a fundraiser, I think a Saturday in October 2014. And it is late. Two-thirty or three in the morning and it is just after we closed everything up. I get all my gear and I'm outside the mansion, "Shit, I forgot my lunch box." It's in the refrigerator in the servants' wing. And by then, I'm out of uniform. I grab my keys; I don't even think I have my flashlight. I'm thinking I can run up, get my lunch box and come back down. So I go in through the servant's entrance and it is dark. I don't know why I didn't turn the lights on. I just came in the door and I'm maybe halfway up the staircase when I start hearing two men talking. I can't tell from where. I just hear voices in the house. And I'm like, "Oh my God!" And I stop and I listen. There's someone in the house! And I can't tell if it is upstairs or downstairs because it is just mumbling and talking. Two mumbling voices. So I'm going up the servant's staircase very quietly to see if the voices are upstairs. And as I move up, it seemed like the voices are getting farther away. So I come back down, and I didn't turn on the lights because now I'm just listening. I don't think they are in the kitchen, but now I'm sure and I'm like, "Oh shit, there's two people here!" But I can't hear what they're saying—but it's two distinct male voices. And I'm thinking, "I'm not going to turn the lights on. I'm not going to surprise them. I'll go back to my car, get my phone and call the police." And then, being really quiet, just as I'm ready to go out the door, I hear one of the guys starts to sing. It sounded like he was singing an old twenties, acapella song. So I sneak out, get my phone, call the police and I'm like, "Hurry, hurry, there's somebody here!" They show up and I'm like, "There are two people inside." So we go in and start looking around. We went in the kitchen. We went everywhere, searched the whole house. And they're like, "Were the lights on?" And I'm like, "No." And the cops ask, "Why would two guys be talking in the dark?" I reply, "I don't know." I didn't think about that. I just heard voices, and then the singing. I go through the entire house with them—closets, rooms, hallways, upstairs and down. Nothing. Their final analysis is the house is empty. There is nobody here. As they started to leave, I was like, "Sorry, but I know what I heard."*

"HIDDEN CONVERSATIONS"

ELVA

(Janitorial Services)

Elva: *It was morning, maybe around eight-thirty. The park was closed. I was about to enter the mansion through the servants' door into the kitchen when I heard two people talking inside. There was a man's voice and a lady's voice, and I was like, "Maybe [Ranger] M.M. is here, or someone else is inside." But when I went into the mansion, there was nobody there. And I know they were having a conversation because I heard very clear a woman and a guy talking. What they said, I cannot tell you because I did not understand what they're talking about…but I know there's two people talking. I think it was English. I thought they're having coffee or something. But when I went inside and looked, and nobody was there.*

"MISSING A HEAD"

JUAN ANDRADE

(Park Ranger Supervisor)

Juan: *I'm working a Saturday night event back in May of 2019. I'm there to oversee the breakdown and clean up. I'd say it's around nine o'clock and the event is over. I'm in the catering kitchen checking on things. As I'm walking out, I look to my left, and I see a little... a small person. Maybe four feet tall. And it isn't my peripheral vision. It isn't out of the corner of my eye. I turn around and see it straight on. I can't tell the sex. It's white, almost translucent, and right away it takes off running. I can't see the whole body, I just see parts of it. It is all white, except it's missing a lot of details. It was missing a head and some body parts. I only saw a quick glimpse before it ran off. But as it's running, it just disappears. And again, it wasn't out of the corner of my eye. I made direct visual contact. No goose bumps and my hair wasn't standing on edge. Nothing. I didn't even feel scared. All of a sudden it was there and then it was gone. It was like this little kid was running or maybe looking at me or chasing me or just following me. I don't know. But as soon as it saw me, it ran away. That's my first time I've ever seen a white figure!*

As with most sightings on this property, the witnesses find themselves trying to rationalize why it happened to them. Juan is aware he has a sense or a way of sensing spirits, but it still surprises him when it actually happens.

Juan: *Maybe the spirits are feeding off my energy... I might be very susceptible to kids because I have a young daughter and we're close. Maybe they're picking up on that, I don't know. It was a child. It was small and it was looking right at me. I could see its elbow so clearly as it turned and ran away—isn't that weird? And then boom, it disappeared.*

"WAVING"

This is a very interesting encounter as the entity interacted in normal fashion with one of our visitors.

CHAE YI
(Lead Park Ranger)

> Chae: *It was early February 2020, and we are doing a regularly scheduled ten o'clock tour. About forty-five minutes into the tour we're in the main kitchen and I realize that somebody from the tour walked off and I have to go find him. When I find him in the downstairs hallway, he tells me that he saw a little kid on top of the staircase by the servants' quarters, who was waving at him. And I said, "Can you tell me more about him?" He said the young boy had been standing on the staircase, he had curly hair and he was waving at him. The person telling me this was with his mom on the tour and he had special needs. But he kept on pointing down the hallway to the staircase by the servants' quarters. He said, "Right there, right over there. He was right there, lots of curly hair waving at me. So I was waving back at him." He went on to tell me that "he was about so big, maybe three feet tall."*

As Chae told me the story, I realize that this type of interaction doesn't happen often. I asked him about that.

> Chae: *You're right, I get all different types of people on these tours where they see and feel things. But this is the first time I ever had an encounter where someone on the tour actually saw a spirit or an image. As a matter of fact, I remember that I had goose bumps because he kept saying, "Right there, for sure. I saw him. I'm not lying. A little boy with curly hair waving at me and I was waving back at him."*

"JOHN, PAUL, GEORGE, RINGO, AND GABE"

When Gabriel experienced this event, the park had been closed for more than two hours.

GABRIEL JARA
(Lead Park Ranger)

> Gabriel: *I don't mind saying, this was a really scary, spooky incident. It's late and I was by myself closing up the mansion after an event. After closing everything up, I go out to the courtyard and walk around the mansion to make sure all the lights are off. On this night I notice one of the lights is still on in the servants' wing. This is not that unusual. Rangers are always talking about after they're sure they turned everything off, they go outside and see a light on. So I'm like, "Oh no, here we go." I grab my flashlight. I have to do it. I don't want to, but I have to go in there and turn it off. That's my job.*

I ask Gabriel if it's possible that he left a light or any lights on.

> Gabriel: *Well, it's possible…but, regardless, I have to go back in. So I open the front entrance door to the grand entry. I've got my flashlight and all the lights are off as I walk through the main hallway into the servants' wing. And right when I open the servants' wing door, I hear music playing. And you wouldn't believe what's playing. It's the Beatles! Is that crazy? I swear, a song from the Beatles is playing. I don't remember which song. I like the Beatles, but I don't know the names of their songs. And I don't know where the music is coming from. It's definitely not coming from outside. The light I saw is still on, but you know what, I wasn't going to turn it off!*

I had several immediate thoughts. First of all, I'm wondering, "Why the Beatles?" Why not something from the era of the 1920s or 1930s? Could it be the Beatles are so popular, even those on the other side dig their music?! Secondly, maybe someone left their phone behind or an iPod or something and John, Paul, George, and Ringo are gracing him via iTunes.

But Gabriel says he doesn't think so. He saw nothing out on a table, or the floor, but he doesn't say he searched everywhere by any means.

> Gabriel: *I ran out and immediately called my supervisor and said, "You know what, I'm sorry, but I'm by myself, and there's music playing inside the mansion and I have no idea where it's coming from. Somewhere in the servants' wing, I think, and it's playing the Beatles!" All I hear is, "What!?" And I tell him that the music was definitely not coming from outside the mansion. It was right when you open that door to the servants' wing on the first floor. Right in that room and I want nothing to do with that! I mean, that's crazy. I feel crazy even telling you.*

I remind Gabriel this is Greystone. He smiles and nods in agreement.

> Gabriel: *I've only told that story to maybe a handful of people. You can see why. But it was just super scary. Really super scary.*

"She's Hitting Me!"

When I walk people through the mansion, I always tell this story because it's so crazy and so descriptive. Of course, it happened to Steve Clark who never wants anything to do with the ghosts, spirits, entities, the paranormal, supernatural, or anything other than rock-solid reality— and yet poor Steve experienced his share of encounters at Greystone. To recount this particular experience, Steve and I walk into the Servants' Wing downstairs and he narrates this story. It's now humorous to tell, but I can't imagine having this happen while I'm doing a walkthrough!

STEVEN CLARK
(Retired Park Ranger Supervisor)

> Steven: *I brought a friend of my brothers into the mansion for a quick tour. We are here in the hallway and I'm showing her the silverware safe*

in the hall—and while we're talking, behind me she sees a lady down at the end of the hall, coming up from the basement into the servants' dining room. She tells me, "Hey, there's someone down there." I mean, she thought it was a real person. So I actually walk down there just to make sure there was no one there because, back then, as you know, that was the servants' dining room and it was accessible and there was just a bunch of shit in it. So why would anybody walk in there? So I walk back and that's when my brother's friend is standing here just shaking, and I'm like, "Are you okay?" I mean, she's shaking and she says, "Oh my God! You can't see her!?" And I'm like, "See what?!" Because apparently the woman was now right next to her and she's like, "Look at my hair!" And her hair was filled with static electricity. I mean, it was starting to lift up. And she says, "Look at my hair! She's touching my hair!" And her hair is, in fact, completely filled with static electricity.

I suggested that it might be like when you rub a balloon on fabric to give it a negative charge, it will then stick to a neutral surface and create all that static electricity. Steve agrees.

Steven: *Yes, and it was starting to lift up. And then she starts screaming, "She's hitting me! She's hitting me!!" And I honestly didn't know what to do. I was like, "Uhhhhhhhhh!" So I said, "Hey, we gotta get outta here!" We both run out to the porte-cochere[1] that opens into the courtyard. And she was in tears. I mean, she really felt she was being attacked. She originally came in because she said she was sensitive to feeling and connecting with spirits, but she didn't even make it through the first part of the house. She didn't want to come back inside. And I'm like, "Well, you only saw the first half of the first floor." But that was more than enough for her and she left. And my brother called me later and he's like, "Dude, what the fuck happened!?" And I said, "I don't know!" Apparently, later she described the woman who attacked her as a housekeeper that didn't want her in that part of the house. I mean, when she was freaking out saying, "Oh my God, she's hitting me! She's hitting me!!" she was actually bending over with her head down, trying to dodge the swats! I guess the woman just started swatting her upside the head. Then that's when we ran out because we were so scared!! I think I had only two times where I had to run out of the house. That was one of them. The other was the basement. But when this happened, I was scared and confused, and it was early on before I really got a grasp on what was going on in this house!*

1 Porte-cochere, also known as a coach gate or carriage porch, is a large covered area located at the entrance to a building for vehicles to pass through, allowing passengers to disembark while being protected from the weather. Typically, this area opens into a courtyard.

Chapter 13

Basement

I was sort of feeling like I was letting Satan out of hell.
— Brehnen Knight
   Retired Greystone Park Ranger

Photo: Chris Keith

At this location in the basement were state-of-the-art, large Norwood Cascade and Monex washing machines, complemented by a huge Chicago Dryer Company dryer that housed pull-out compartments with racks where you would hang wet clothes, shut the compartments, and voilà—dry clothes minutes later. Very modern.

There were workshop areas and a tool bench for the maintenance workers. In the boiler room, coal was stoked into a huge furnace to produce heat for the mansion. There were living quarters on the east end of the Basement for several male workers. These men were locked in at night behind a metal gate with a chain and padlock, preventing them from intimate contact with the female servants.

Back in 1999, when I began working for the City of Beverly Hills, areas in the mansion that the public couldn't see when peering through windows were pretty much in shambles. Only the rooms utilized for filming were renovated by the film companies themselves. All other areas were left untouched. And most every film company rented the mansion for its grandeur—the Grand Entry, Grand Hall, and Living Room. The foulest area was the Basement. It would have been Wes Craven's dream location. It was filled with rotting old lumber, rusting pipes, and ancient equipment from years past. It was creepy—and that was during the day! At night, it was a completely different story. I know. I was there. Late at night, I would venture down with Ranger Steve, and we would sit together in the long hallway trying to capture spirit voices and/or any sounds of movement with our trusty digital recorders. It was dark as hell; all we could see were the tiny red lights on our devices. We never did record any voices. Eventually the Basement was cleaned for the installation of a massive heating and air conditioning system. Even so, to go down there by yourself is at best, unnerving.

Greystone Historical Report

"There are places in the cellar, places in the basement where you could get inside the walls. I never did make a complete trip from the lowest to the highest point. I never got stuck, but I dreaded it, I really did. Nobody would hear you, and you would be a skeleton by the time you were found."

— Timothy Doheny

"Slimy, Cold, and Wet"

Greystone was the host of nearly a dozen Garden and Design Showcase houses starting in 2006. The year when the event was on hiatus, it was suggested we host Halloween tours at night. They sold out immediately. During one particular tour (I was not present), Rangers Steven Clark and Dan Hernandez handled the excited visitors. For Bridgetta Tomarchio, this was an extremely disturbing experience. When I contacted her to talk about what took place that night, she was willing to discuss it, but didn't want to come back to Greystone. When she finally gave in, her friend, Katie Whicker, who was also on the infamous tour, came along for support. Bridgetta appears to have the gift of sensing spirits, which begs the question: Is that why she was the target to what took place that night? Having Bridgetta come back to the mansion was one thing, but getting her to go back down into the Basement to relive her horrible moment was another—but that's what we did. Standing just outside the boiler room, Bridgetta takes a deep and very nervous breath before we move inside.

(Please note: When Bridgetta refers to "you guys," it's in reference to the two rangers who worked the tour. Also, that night she was wearing a baseball hat and a hoodie.)

BRIDGETTA TOMARCHIO & KATIE WHICKER
(Visitors)

> Bridgetta: *I didn't want to go in there. I was just kind of hanging back in the hallway. Ranger Dan said, "You have to come in." I was like, "Nah, I'm gonna stay right here." And that's when he said, "You've got to go in." I was like, "Damn it!" And so, I went in there and it was only a couple of us because the others were still in another room. But he made me go in there.*
>
> Katie: *That was just to protect us. There was one ranger in front of us and one behind us. They're looking out for us. And so I think that's part of why*

they didn't want you to be separated from the group. But we were asking for permission and for protection from our spiritual guides. So we felt as we entered the boiler room that we had been given permission.

Bridgetta turns to Katie—

Bridgetta: *The thing is how do you know? You may ask for permission, but do you know how crazy that actually sounds? I mean, not to you, but in general? And how do you know that it's really okay?*

We walk inside the boiler room. Bridgetta is incredibly hesitant as she slowly walks over to where her incident occurred.

Bridgetta: *It looks smaller than I remember. But I was here. I was standing right here in front of the boiler and I'm talking to the ranger and I said, "I don't like it over here. I feel something really weird, this heavy energy. I don't know why." And the ranger starts talking about some stuff* [she turns to Katie] *as you guys and the others were piling in the room.*

Bridgetta: *So I'm standing there and I say to Ranger Dan, "You're making me be in here and I'm really uncomfortable and I don't like it." And I could feel that energy that was in here, whatever it was. It was just so weird. Then suddenly I feel my hat moving and it felt like a cold, wet... I can't explain it. It grabbed my ear and it was so violating. It freaked me out and like almost lifted me up. I've never felt anything slimy, cold, and wet like that. It felt like a huge energy. I thought it was a male energy. And then my hat came off at some point.*

Katie interjects:

Katie: *You moved so fast. You got out of there so quick.*

Bridgetta: *Yeah, I didn't want to be there in the first place because I knew something was going to happen! It grabbed my ear! I was grabbed and pulled. It was cold, wet, and slimy. I have a snake and it was almost like my snake. Almost like that. But more wet. And it was like a whisper, too. I don't get that.*

Katie asks, "Like damp? Like a cold air dampness?" Bridgetta nods her head "yes." Then she remembers more and now her recollection is more anxious, more dramatic than before.

Bridgetta: *And I just remember thinking, "Oh my God, it's in my ears! It's in my ears! It's inside! Let me get out! He can't be in me!" I don't know what it was trying to do. And then this thing is like, "I know you can hear me—I know you know I'm here." And it wasn't like a child saying, "Hi! I'm here!" It wasn't loving. It was a very heavy, intense energy. Like mad and angry.*

Bridgetta takes a long pause and changes direction. She's more introspective.

Bridgetta: *You know, not everyone can see or hear them. Obviously, they try to get your attention. So if you can connect with spirits, and know that you can, they're going to mess with you. They need that communication. So imagine being that spirit on that side, "I got someone! I got someone! They know I'm here! I've got to get her attention!" Whether it's good or it's bad. But imagine you're the spirit trapped in this place. That's why I don't understand how any spirit likes it here. Luckily, I could just run out.*

We begin talking about spirits stuck in the mansion. We discuss the fact that several people say they've seen a little girl in the mansion. As I listen to this recording while I'm transcribing this interview, I hear a voice whisper! Here is the actual conversation:

Bridgetta: *But imagine you're the spirit trapped in this place. That's why I don't understand how any spirit likes it here. That's interesting.*

Clete: *Maybe she has friends here. I've also been told of a little boy who has been seen on the stairs.*

Bridgetta: *Okay. And she feels it's safe. There's different levels too. So maybe they're not all on the same...*

Whisper Voice: Yeah.

Bridgetta: ...*plane.*

The voice whisper is very clear.[1] This means that a spirit was down in that Basement with us during the day. Who that spirit is, I have no idea. But it's moments like these that astound me and open the door to the possibility of spirit communication.

I found Bridgetta's compassion for the spirits so interesting. Back to the night in question: even though I didn't work the tour, I helped open the mansion and then locked up after the tour. Curious to see what the rangers say about this location, I decided to leave my phone in the Basement to video record the group as they came into the boiler room. And little did I anticipate that I would capture the moment when Bridgetta was grabbed by this spirit.[2] At the end of Bridgetta's and Katie's return visit, I show them the footage on my phone. They both got major chills as they watched and relived this disturbing incident. Little did I know we were sharing this moment with an unknown spirit.

1 Audio recording exists in author's collection.
2 Video recording exists in author's collection.

"Flipped"

A friend of mine who works for the City asked me if I would give his two daughters, Samantha and Alix, and their two friends, Ben and Kris, a tour of the mansion. I had no clue that this would turn out to be one of the strangest tours I've ever given. This group, all in their early twenties, were strangely quiet and introspective. At least that's what I thought. I told them, as I tell everyone at the beginning of a tour, "If something happens that scares or bothers you, please let me know, and if you feel the need to leave, then we all walk outside together." Little did I know, things were happening to them separately that were freaking them out, but they didn't say anything to me, or to each other. They were extremely quiet on the tour and didn't react to anything, not even to my great comedic one-liners!

Several days after the tour, their father called me and said, "Clete, what the hell happened that night?" I had no idea what he was talking about. He said, "On the tour? All the things that happened." And I said, "What things!? They didn't mention anything." He said, "Please, you've got to call them."

I was able to get them back to Greystone to talk about that night. This time, instead of being quiet, they were laughing, joking, and animated. I said to them halfway through the interview, "Who the hell are you people?! You're totally different!"

I escorted them down to the electrical throw switch panel so I could demonstrate how the old switches worked in the past. As I demonstrated the timeworn panel, my back was to the group. I had no idea a strange paranormal incident was taking place only a few feet away from me. When I contacted Samantha, one of the visitors, about a year later, she decided to fill me in. She admitted she didn't want to talk about what happened on that night because she was so freaked out. I convinced Samantha to revisit the Basement so she could show me what and where this incident happened.

Photo: Chris Keith

SAMANTHA GORMAN

(Visitor)

Samantha: *So we are all standing in front of this electrical panel, right here, and Mark, my friend who's also on the tour, was about here, several steps behind me. And my hair was down past my shoulders. You were explaining about the switch panel and my hair, like a chunk of it, just lifted up and moved to the other side. I freaked out a little bit, but I moved it back in place. Then that same section of hair moved back over again. So I turn around and I look at Mark, and he is far enough away and his hands were at his side. So I flipped it back again. Then it happened one more time and I just left it, because I wasn't messing with it anymore. But it was just lifted, really delicately, over to one side. And there's no draft in here. There's nothing. So that was really freaky. But I just said to myself, "Okay, you're here, cool. Stay calm." But I was freaked out. That's why I said I would never come back.*

"Gates of Hell"

This incident took place on July 2, 1989. Until the modern electrical upgrade to the mansion in 2008, once you turned off the power switches in the Basement, the only light in the mansion available to you would be your flashlight. Brehnen mentions that this experience was "like a typical horror movie."

BREHNEN KNIGHT
(Retired Park Ranger)

> Brehnen: *I'm locking everything up for the night after an event and I walk down those first-floor stairs from the servants' wing to those stairs that lead down to the basement, and there's a black metal gate, right? That gate is always locked and it's a separate key to open the lock that's probably the same key for thirty or forty years. So this is really creepy because the gate is wide open. The people running the event have no reason to be down there—plus they have no key. Eventually they all left the mansion and everybody is gone, so I lock the gate. I'm on my way out, back where the kitchen is in the servants' wing, and then, like a typical horror movie, I hear a chain rattling. That really scared me. I slowly walk back to the basement gate—it's unlocked and the gates are wide open again! And I'm like, "Come on. Really?!"*

This is seemingly impossible. It's a two-sided gate that swings together and is secured with a heavy chain and a keyed lock. How is it possible that the gate was again unlocked only moments after Brehnen securely locked it? In fact, only the rangers have the key to open that lock—and on top of that, the gates are swung wide open? Brehnen continues here to describe the strong feeling that came over him regarding the spirit.

Photo: Chris Keith

149

Brehnen: *The thing that stands out in my mind, and I just got chills thinking about it, was that it was not a nice person or a nice ghost. It was definitely angry. Bad energy. I mean, bad energy. And I was like, "I don't know if I really want to lock that gate again!" It's not part of the alarm system. "Okay, just man up and lock the damn thing!" Right? But, literally, it took everything I had to go down those few stairs, turn the corner, and lock it again. And of course, just like in the movies, it's not locking properly and I'm trying to get out. I finally get it locked and get back up the stairs and man I was done. There was clearly a bad energy. This was when a famous actor got married there. There were so many people who were being disrespectful to the house during that party. I just knew something would happen and I think what took place down at the basement, that really bad feeling I had locking that gate was part of that. I was sort of feeling like I was letting Satan out of hell. I mean, it was really dark. Not a good feeling. For some reason there's an entity down there. But that bad evil basement feeling was not Ned Doheny or Hugh Plunkett. I mean, in my experience at the mansion, I'm convinced that the gates of hell are right there.*

In subsequent interviews and conversations with Brehnen, he felt he had a real feel for certain energies in the mansion. I've also had rangers and visitors say that they too could literally feel a certain spirit's energy to the point where they could differentiate between a benevolent entity and one that was clearly wicked. It's also interesting in Brehnen Knight's case that he made a point to say he didn't believe the bad energy he experienced was coming from Doheny or Plunkett.

"RATTLING CHAINS"

When I interviewed Brooke, a realization came to me: the vast majority of the stories I've investigated start out very normal, just regular run-of-the-mill perfunctory life stuff…employees going about their daily routine or visitors enjoying the grandeur of the mansion or the manicured grounds.

Rarely do folks walk around looking for paranormal activity—unless of course, they're looking for paranormal activity. But when it comes to folks simply going through their day, something triggers a twist—a sound, a glimpse—and then the situation turns odd, possibly strange and abnormal, or downright spine-chilling. The unraveling of "normal" into "paranormal" is an intriguing transformation.

This next incident took place during the day in the summer of 1991. Greystone Park was open, but the mansion was closed and locked to the public. Inside were Brooke Picone and two rangers: Barry and Brehnen.

BROOKE PICONE
(Former Beverly Hills Camp Counselor)

> Brooke: *The three of us were standing right here in the middle of the grand hall, and all of a sudden, we hear a noise that's coming from the east hall. It sounds like chains banging against a gate. Almost like someone is trying to break free from these chains. Or trying to open up the gate. It startled all of us, I mean, we all heard it. So both rangers run over to see what it was. I'm running with them and Brehnen says to me, "No, stay here, just in case we run into somebody and I have to fight!" And I said, "No, I'm coming with you!" And I followed right behind them. We're running down the hallway and when we got to the basement, there was nothing. It was just total silence. But the gate that leads down into the boiler room has a thick chain wrapped around it with a lock. It sounded like that was the chain we heard, and it sounded as if somebody was trying to break through that chain and the gate. But no one was there. Nothing. It was pretty scary.*

"Rattling Back and Forth"

MARTIN J. PEREZ
(Janitorial Services)

> Martin: *My shift ended around one in the afternoon. So I turn off these hallway lights, and as I'm walking this way down the hallway behind the kitchen I see the basement door is open. I can see the gate now because the door is wide open. So as I start down the first step to close the door, I hear the gate being pushed back and it is rattling back and forth. I got so scared and I just stopped and thought, "Man, it's so dark in here!" I quickly grabbed my cellphone and I flashed a picture.[3] And I saw this white orb just hovering—it was right here in front of the gate. I can honestly say that I felt a very negative vibe when I was down there. There's no one there and I hear the gate rattling? Not to mention with the lighting really dim, that makes it even more scary. So I hurried and got out as fast as I could.*

"Denim Jeans"

When Charlie told me this story, I literally asked him to repeat what he just said. Even then, I broke down his sentence to specifics, "Wait. All three of you walk down the Basement stairs. You get to the bottom and describe again what you saw."

CHARLIE ACKERMAN
(Retired Building Maintenance Supervisor)

> Charlie: *Down in that basement area is where a lot of activity that I've heard about, or have actually seen, has taken place. One visit included George Chavez* [current Beverly Hills City Manager], *myself, and Tina, who at the time was Director of General Services. The three of us went down to the basement. We walked down the stairs, opened the door, unlocked the gate, and went down the stairs into the basement area. We got*

3 Photo is non-existent.

down to the bottom of the steps. Tina was in front of us and George and I were standing behind her. Suddenly we both heard something move. We turned around and looked at the top of the stairs and a pair of jeans just walked by! All you could see, basically, from the ankles to the waist, because of the angle of the stairs, were jeans walking by. And we were like, "What the hell? Who was that?" We thought, "Oh God, who's in the building?" So we quickly went back up the stairs. There was nobody. We searched that whole area up there in the old laundry room. There was nobody there.

At this point, I asked Charlie to describe the jeans a bit more.

Charlie: *They were a bit transparent but George and I immediately recognized them as blue jeans. We looked at each other and said, "Did you just see what I saw!?"* [he laughs.]  *It's like you couldn't see any feet and you couldn't see above the waist… it was just from the waist down. George actually got interviewed by the Los Angeles Times[4] about this experience. Oh God, that's got to be twenty years ago, maybe more, maybe 1995. I had forgotten about it really until George mentioned it. He goes, "Do you remember when we were in the basement at Greystone with Tina?" And I went, "Oh my God! I'd forgotten! It happened so long ago. That's right!" A pair of walking denim jeans! And we all saw it together—so, I'm not crazy, right?!*

I'm not sure about you, but if I ever witnessed a pair of blue jeans walking by—just a pair of jeans, no head, torso, or feet—there's a damn good chance I'd never forget that. Ever! But maybe that's just me.

And no, Charlie, you're not crazy.

4 Anna Marie Stolley, "Haunted House," Los Angeles Times Westside Weekly, November 17, 1995, 1, 13.

Greystone Historical Report

"The basement was all concrete. We used to pile empty cardboard boxes up, in what we used to call the shop—a workbench and tool shop. At the end of one large room, there was a slippery floor. We'd pile empty boxes up there and come flying down from the foot of the stairs, all the way down the hall on the concrete and down a slope into this pile of boxes, going about forty miles an hour."

—Timothy Doheny

"CLOSED DOOR"

CHAE YI
(Lead Park Ranger)

Chae: *I was working my first wedding reception and it was the first time that I stayed late. Ranger Steve went home and he left me in charge for the rental pickups. At that time, the kitchen setup was outside at the AFI lot and we had to turn the light on by going down in the basement. And I hate, hate, hated going down in the basement. And I always carry two flashlights. I still do. So it was about ten-thirty in the evening and I had to turn off the main switch at the electrical panel. I really didn't want to go down there by myself. That was my first time ever going down in the basement alone. So I asked the rental guys, "Can any one of you come with me to the basement to turn the switch off?" But none of them volunteered. I begged one of the guys, "Can you please come with me? I have an extra flashlight." Then he finally said okay.*

Even now, after years have passed since Chae experienced this event, he sounds nervous, like it's happening again as we speak.

Chae: *So we go down to the basement door. It's a wooden door. And then there's an iron gate. So I opened the wooden door and unlocked the iron gate. I was in front of the guy and I had a flashlight leading the way. We start down the stairs into the basement and he says, "Man, this place is creepy." I go, "Yeah, tell me about it. I told you so." So we get to the main switch and we turn the power off. No problem. We're walking back and he's in front of me. We go up the staircase and he comes to a halt at the doorway and I'm like, "What are you doing?" He turns to me and says, "No, I'm not going first. Why is this door closed? The wooden door?" I go, "I don't know. I went in first. You were behind me." He goes, "I didn't close that door." I said, "Well, if I didn't, and you didn't, then who did?" And he goes, "How am I supposed to know!"*

When I interviewed Ranger Chae, we went down to the Basement to see if the door could swing shut by itself. It can't. We investigated the possibility of a breeze being the culprit. There wasn't a breeze, a draft, or any noticeable portal for air movement that would cause the door to swing shut.

Chae: *We were both so scared to leave the basement because the door closed behind us! I can't explain how it happened. I didn't close that door and he didn't close it. And we didn't hear it close. And we're frozen there because we didn't want to go through that door—who knows what's on the other side.*

So finally, I turned the doorknob and kicked the door open thinking maybe somebody behind it was playing a joke on us. But nobody was there.

You know, I've heard some sounds down there too when I first started working here and ever since then, it just gives me very bad vibes when I'm down in the basement. Even after twelve years on the job. Even with the flashlight, with the lights, and everything on, I hate, hate, hate going down in that basement!

"Not Ready to Arm"

DANIEL HERNANDEZ

(Park Ranger Supervisor)

Daniel: This was early in 2003. It was a quiet Sunday and we didn't have much going on here. The calendar was empty. The mansion is always armed, always, with an electronic security system. That's the way we were trained. This is probably eleven in the morning. I was outside the house and the police dispatch calls me on the radio because our alarm company was directly connected to the police department. "Greystone Ranger come in." And I responded. They said, "The alarm is going off." So I said, "10-4, I'll check it out." So I enter the front door, shut off the alarm, and look at the alarm panel and it shows the zone that triggered is the boiler door. That's the basement door. So I walk down to the basement door, and it is, in fact, ajar. But the point is the mansion could not have been armed by the ranger the night before with this door open. The alarm panel would say "Not Ready to Arm." At the time, I didn't think anything of it. I close the door and go to the alarm panel, reactivate the alarm, and walk out. Now I'm in the park patrolling on foot and about a half hour later police dispatch calls me again: "Greystone Ranger, the alarm's going off, do you need assistance?" I said, "No, I'll just go check it out again." I open the front door and the alarm is going off. I shut it off and look at the zone that is activated—boiler door. So again, I walk down to the basement door, it's ajar like six inches wide—and remember this is after I just closed it. And there's no wind down there or air conditioning units that were running that could blow it open because it's like a closet door, it latches shut. And I made sure it latched shut when I closed it. Impossible.

Impossible indeed—and the experience opened the eyes of a self-professed skeptic.

Daniel: That was my first experience here. I heard stories from the other rangers at training when I started in 2000, that there's some activity going on here. But I'm a skeptic. I didn't think about it, but that Sunday morning changed my mind as to whether this place is haunted.

"CLAW MARK"

Jeff Bowler is a film producer and a good friend of mine for more than twenty years. He's always had a keen interest in Greystone. Jeff's visited the grounds many times and when his son, Jeo, was in town from back east, he mentioned it would be great for them to visit the mansion together. Jeo, a sharp guy in his early twenties, is "gifted"—he's experienced paranormal events his entire life. So imagine my surprise when the incident that took place in the Basement didn't happen to Jeo!

JEFF BOWLER
(Visitor)

> Jeff: *As we were touring the mansion, my son, Jeo, who is very sensitive to this type of thing, said he had been feeling pressure the entire tour. At one point, he said that he wanted to cry. But when we walked down into the basement he felt, what he called "heavy pressure" where the electrical switches are and then again in the boiler room. And he kept feeling this pressure and finally we left. I didn't really feel very much of anything. We left Greystone and went to get a sandwich and some gas. I was at the gas station down on Sunset Boulevard for maybe ten minutes and I go to get out of the car—Jeo's in the passenger side—and he goes, "Holy shit, Dad! Look at your neck!" I'm like, "What are you talking about?" And then he took a picture and I have a big three-inch red claw mark. Not a typical, like, I'm just itching my head, but a nice claw mark right down the back of my neck.*

I asked Jeff if he had any recollection whatsoever when this happened. I asked if it was possible that something happened earlier in the day before he arrived at Greystone.

Jeff: *Not beforehand. No. And at the mansion, I never felt anything at all. And then after Jeo showed me, it started slowly burning for the next two days. And then, after two days, it was gone. And the basement was the last place we were. So after the basement—no, wait, it wasn't the last place. We also went downstairs to the bowling alley—and then we left. So it could have been in the basement or the bowling alley, but it happened here on the property for sure. No question.*

For the record, the bowling alley is not the paranormal hub of the house. Nothing aggressive has ever happened there, at least that's what I've observed. That's why I think Jeff's scratch happened in the Basement. Plus, Jeo was very uncomfortable and very much on edge in the Basement, but not nearly as on edge in the bowling alley.

Photo: Jeo Colon Bowler

Jeff: *The scratch was fresh and still red when we saw it a few minutes later. So it wasn't from days past. But it burned for two days and I would put lotion on it and it would get worse. I just kept it clean but it was still burning at night and then it was just gone. Like overnight.*

I asked Jeff if he experienced any emotional unbalance over the two days.

Jeff: *No, I didn't feel any difference at all as far as emotionally, but my son sure did! He had residual effects for days. Oh, God, he wouldn't stop talking about it. He felt depressed. He felt like he wanted to cry, and he just kept talking about it. That was probably a good ten days after. At least once or twice a day he would mention it.*

I'm aware of situations like this where the strong emotions being felt by an individual who was in close proximity to the paranormal event were caused by a spirit attachment. It is the belief of many in the paranormal field that when you have the so-called "gift" of being able to sense spirits, they will gravitate to you and try to communicate. Was this the case with Jeo? Of course, I'm not sure, but there's no doubt that he was affected and/or influenced by something or someone outside of himself when he visited Greystone.

"THREE KNOCKS"

My sister, Kacey, and her husband, Jon, were in town to visit. I asked Ranger Steve if he would mind giving them a tour of Greystone and I would join them when my meeting was over. He agreed and walked them through the mansion. By the time I met them, they were already in the Basement. I was told they heard a loud crashing sound prior to my arrival. I dismissed it as probably a common occurrence at Greystone—inquisitive visitors often lift this large metal cover in the inner courtyard that protects the pump station controls for the water fountain, and then they drop it back down. It makes an extremely loud noise in the Basement so I wasn't concerned about Kacey being "terrified." It's what happened next that still haunts me today. And as it turns out — the following experience is the one and only real physical encounter that has ever happened to me at Greystone.

KACEY DALY & JON DALY
(Visitors)

THIS IS OUR CONVERSATION:

> Kacey: *I remember being down there and being absolutely terrified. And I shouldn't have been terrified because it was just a noise we heard, but I was. For some reason, I was absolutely terrified and I just wanted out. I wanted out of that basement. I remember that.*

Jon: [nods in agreement]. *Right. It was very loud.*

Clete: *When I showed up to meet you in the boiler room, Steve began to talk specifics about how the boiler and the huge swamp cooler were used back in the 1930s, when suddenly, behind me, on the wall, there were three loud knocks.*

Jon: *Yeah. It was three knocks.*

Kacey: *Yes, yes—and we grabbed each other!*

Clete: [embarrassed]. *As much as it's painful for me to say, being the investigator that I am, I ran and hid behind you.*

Kacey: [laughing]. *That's right! You grabbed me and hid behind me, and I was like, my brother is hiding behind me! Holy Sheba! What the heck!*

Back then, 2005 or so, I wasn't into investigating, let alone thinking I would one day write a book about the paranormal. Up until that moment, in all my years working at Greystone and being in the mansion, nothing ever happened to me. I was (as they say) uninitiated in the strange occurrences at Greystone. So when those three knocks boomed behind me, I freaked out.

Clete: *I said, "Holy shit!" And I ran away from the wall where I had heard the knocks and bolted over to you, Kacey. I grabbed you and held you out as bait! But truth be told, it really scared me. I gathered myself, having lost all my dignity, and said to Steve, "What the hell was that?!" And he said, "I don't know!" Then I said, "Who is that?" And he says, "Clete, you've always wanted something to happen to you. Here we are down in the basement, it happens, and now you're acting like you don't believe that it happened!" Then I said, "I think it's Ranger Dan. Get him on the radio." So Steve got Dan on the radio.*

Kacey: *And he was nowhere near the place.*

Clete: *He was at Roxbury Park, which is on the other side of town. So I knew it wasn't Dan, but I was really confused as to how it could be that loud because behind me was a cement wall. There was a cabinet that was wood, but when I knocked on it to try and recreate the sound it was too hollow. It wasn't close to sounding the same. But it scared me to the point that the next thing I know I'm grabbing you* [Kacey] *and holding you out for sacrifice! Giving you up to the spirits!*

Jon: [holding back his laughter]. *I remember the fear in you and I was stunned by the fact that the first thing you did was hide behind her.*

Clete: *Let's not focus on my lack of manhood.*

Kacey: *All I really remember was I wanted out of that basement so badly. But I was frozen. I was literally frozen. It was like I couldn't think. So terrified that I just froze.*

Jon: *I'm still not clear as to what would make that sound. I remember the knocks. It was obvious that it wasn't some sort of wind.*

Kacey: *Absolutely. And they all sounded equally as strong. No, it wasn't hollow, that's for sure. I just wanted out of that place. It just gave me the creeps!*

"BANGS AND SCRAPES"

Mario is a decorated U.S. Iraq War veteran. He was awarded the Purple Heart and the Silver Star. He's a private guy who keeps very much to himself. With all that he's been through serving in the U.S. military, I'm sure the least of his worries was working at the mansion in Greystone Park—until this day.

MARIO ATRIAN, JR.

(Facility Maintenance Mechanic)

Mario: *We get a call to go check a panel at the bottom basement area. There's these iron gates and they had a big padlock on it. You open it up and you walk down and hang a right and see this huge hallway. Then hang another right to where the old panel is in the electrical room. And this is the old panel before that whole area got renovated, back in 2007-2008. So we get in there and turn the light on and Felix, who has since retired, starts checking a panel and all of a sudden, on the far, far end of the basement, we hear this big bang. And so we stopped and we look at each other and Felix is like, "What the hell was that?" I say, "You know, it might be a rat or something. Just go ahead and keep doing what you're doing."*

Mario had worked long enough with the City of Beverly Hills to know that Greystone is haunted. When Felix asked him about the "big bang," Mario suggested rats. (With that kind of bang, I don't know if I really want to see that rat!) So Mario was either trying to calm Felix's fears, or justify a strange sound down there knowing no one else was in the Basement.

Mario: *So Felix keeps checking the circuits, and we hear another bang, which is now closer to us this time. And then it intensifies: we hear a scrape on the wall—like a claw scrape.*

And Felix is like, "You know what, that just sounds off! That sounds freaky, man. Let's get out of here!" I was like, "You're almost done. Just go ahead and finish up!" So he keeps working at the panel. We're there for another maybe two minutes or so when, right directly behind the wall panel where we're standing, a loud bang shakes the wall.

And then there's another huge scrape right down the wall. I mean, all these walls are old stucco or brick style, so what we heard were like claws scraping on that wall. So we fucking jump, look at each other, and we're like, "Okay, now it's time to go!"

Remember, this is a combat veteran with a Purple Heart and a Silver Star.

Mario: *I mean, the first bang, you know, I figured was probably something moving around like a rat, maybe something fell. The second bang with the scrape, I knew that was a little off. But then the third time, right behind where we were standing with that long scrape on the wall, I knew that was totally off! But Felix, he was an old facilities mechanic. He was freaked out. He was so freaked out! He was literally shaking… So I said, "Grab your shit and let's get out of here!" And we just boogied out of there as fast as we could!*

"LOST AND FOUND"

I've known Steve Clark for a long time. He's an absolute straight shooter. A real professional. Very analytical. He doesn't deal in "BS."

STEVEN CLARK
(Retired Park Ranger Supervisor)

Steven: *I think it was probably 2001. The alarm in the mansion went off, and back then, the alarm was pretty good. If one window was open, it would register. So the police called. I looked on the alarm panel and it says "Basement Door." I go down to the entrance of the basement and the wood door is open, but the gate is locked. So I walk into the basement and find nothing else is open. None of the other windows or doors, and that's at the time when the basement was full of shit. You could hardly walk through there, there was so much stuff.*

I remember well. It was an absolute catastrophe down there, cluttered beyond belief.

Steven: *Outside the electrical room, at the far end, I see this crate. It has been opened up. I mean, these crates have never been opened. Somebody* [he laughs], *or something... And that's when I called Brad, our manager at that time. And I took him down there to show him. And what's just sitting there on the floor? Pieces of marble for the living room fireplace! They were laid out in front of the crate, actually unwrapped from the protective paper. And I think Brad was the one who figured out that it was probably the old living room fireplace mantel. The fake fireplace was installed for the movie* The Bodyguard.

At this point, I reminded Steve about the keys back in 2001—something he mentioned to me earlier and a really important aspect to this story.

Steven: *That's right. And the weird thing about this, as you know, is back in 2001, we didn't have master keys like all the rangers have now. What we used to do is check one key ring out at a time. We'd go up and get the key ring in the ranger office, check it out, and then we would hang the keys back in the office when we were done. So there was only one key to that basement lock and chain. Nobody else had a key to the basement. So that's weird since no one checked a key out. And it was just one crate that had been opened up. There were about six pieces of marble, laid out and unwrapped with paper from the 1960s. We think AFI* [American Film Institute 1969-1982 at Greystone] *may have disassembled the fireplace and packed it up in the crate. We assumed that they stole the fireplace. We didn't know that they actually stored it.* [Sorry, AFI!] *But it was laid out in a little row of two or three pieces. The crate top had been opened, so we could see that it had come out of that crate. And it had not been laid out prior to that, and we would have noticed because that's where we turn on the electrical for the house. There was just a lot of stuff happening down there back then. I started correlating that things, possibly paranormal things, are starting to happen here. Which turned out to be true!*

"Creeper Sweeper"

March 26, 2020. It was early morning. I arrived at work and saw Joe Segura completing his final check on the renovation of the theatre. He told me he heard a story from a woman working at the mansion that took place in the Basement. After hearing this story, Joe said that the woman was hoping I wasn't there because she didn't want to talk to me. She told Joe she was afraid she might get fired for taking time during her work day to tell me her story. I'm not sure that's the case, because I tried to contact her after her work hours, as well as on the weekend, and she would not return my calls. As short as this story is, it's truly paranormally impactful. This is the story that was told to Joe.

JOE SEGURA
(Contractor Superintendent)

> Joe: *We scheduled the cleaning company down in the basement because we'd been working down there close to the electrical room and it needed cleaning. This lady—let's call her Rosie—was hard at work. Her co-worker thought Rosie was sweeping, but as she walked by, she noticed that Rosie was frozen in shock, just gaping in disbelief. When she looked to see what Rosie was staring at, it was the broom sweeping back and forth—by itself! When Rosie told me this, I was like, "Oh my God, Rosie, don't tell me anymore!"*

"White Jacket, White Hair"

The first time this police officer ventured down into the Basement was on a night tour with a fellow officer (we'll call "Bob") and Ranger Steve. This is the same anonymous police officer who had difficulty breathing and understanding the energy in the Murder Room. He had a similar, if not the exact same reaction, going down into the Basement. For my interview, the officer was willing to go back down, but I could see his

165

demeanor change as I opened the door, unlocked the chain, and opened the metal gates. Truth be told, it's not my favorite place either, having had my own daunting experience down there with the phantom knocks on a wall next to me. But I kept my focus on the police officer. I could see he was struggling to relive his experience from several years ago. The event obviously had an effect on him as he took a deep breath—then we crossed the threshold into the Basement. We chat as we walk the long hallway and pass several rooms on the left.

ANONYMOUS

(City of Beverly Hills Police Officer)

Police Officer: *There are spots in this house that are downright scary, like this basement. Down here, I felt like someone was sitting on my chest. You just feel pressure.* [Waves his arms] *This whole area gives me the creeps. Okay, when we came down here, Bob and Steve were a little bit ahead of me. I'm walking past these rooms and it was maybe a half second, but in my peripheral, I was like, "Whoa!" And I look... Gone!*

We stop at a door that is now a storage room. For a very long moment, he stares into the room with disbelief. I could see that thoughts and memories were flashing in his mind.

Police Officer: *This is the room, right here. There was a person that was in here, but when I double checked and looked again, he was gone. So over there in the far corner was what appeared to be a floating torso of, I don't know, an elderly man or at least a man with white hair and a white jacket. He looked solid to me. Not transparent. He looked like a person. I couldn't see his face because he was facing away to the wall, which was weird. I couldn't see any legs. It was nighttime, so I might have missed them, or they might've been dark pants, but all that I really saw was the torso and the arms. And like I said, it was definitely a white jacket. It was not a white shirt. It was a white jacket, white hair. And that's based on the back of his head. So no face. I couldn't see anything else other than just that—white jacket, white hair. And I got the chills. I told Steve and Bob about what I'd seen. They were both shocked. Steve told me about an old server or butler guy that he had seen in the recreation wing.*

The officer stops for another long moment. He surveys the room, which is packed with storage items. He gathers his thoughts. I can tell he wants to be precise.

Police Officer: *But bottom-line, there's an energy in this basement. The minute I stepped foot down here, my skin was crawling. Specific spots will give me a lot more energy coming through—even now my skin's crawling. And most of this clutter was here. And that's why he stood out, because it was a human being. And as soon as he was gone, I got that freaky goose bump feeling. I don't know why he was there. I don't know what caused him to take on a shape. I don't know if this was his room back in the late 1920s. All I know is what I saw—an older guy, or who I believe was an older guy, in a white coat with white hair. I don't know if the help back then wore white coats. I have no idea.*

Suddenly, the officer and I hear a noise. A loud bang. We look at each other and stay quiet for a long moment. "I heard that," he says. I offer us a so-called "normal" explanation. "They're doing a lot of work upstairs, so that's probably what that was." We stay silent and listen for another sound. It's quiet. "Okay, we'll go with that," he says nervously. I jump back into our conversation. "Your description of the servant worker almost matches Steve Clark's description of the spirit he saw coming down the stairs. It was a white coat with blue piping." I glance behind the officer to see if I can see anyone or anything that might have made that sound. Nothing.

Police Officer: *I think the coolest part about this place is that nobody really shares their story—they just kind of hold on to it. I had no idea Steve actually saw an apparition coming down the stairs, which might match what I saw. Like I said, I didn't see the front of this guy. I have no idea if there could be blue piping. He looked almost like kitchen staff. It was tailored, so it fit nice.*

Suddenly we hear another bang! It rattles us. "Okay. Seriously, that sounds like it's down here." He's right. The sound came from the other end of the basement. I look at him, "Okay, let's go see. I have no idea what it could be." We walk toward where we heard the noise. He's frustrated, "I didn't bring my flashlight." We keep walking through the basement. I'm nervous, but try to play it off that it's something we'll be able to explain. We walk into the boiler room. "Oh God," he says, clearly uncomfortable. This room will freak you out with or without spirit energy, but the fact we've heard two loud thumps, it feels like something is drawing us in. The room is dark. The huge, intimidating boiler dates back to the late 1920s. You can almost feel the flames and see the workers laboring inside this dungeon, stoking the fire. A multitude of pipes crisscross throughout the room. A huge, metal swamp cooler and all of its associated housing still stands next to the boiler. We stand there and listen. It's quiet, which makes it all the more unnerving. We're waiting for the next bang. I see he's anxious. "Are you okay?" He nods and we finally exit. We're both relieved to be out of there. We walk back over to the room where he saw the apparition. He points to the corner of the room.

Police Officer: *But I get this feeling down here, it's not a feeling of dread, it's like I'm not alone. So even though you and I are here, it feels like there's something else here with us. I don't know if I told you this story, but the reason Bob brought me here, initially, was to get a feeling from me.*

I need to clarify his statement to make sure I know what he means. "You think he wanted to see how you would respond in a paranormal location knowing that you have what many call 'the gift?'" He nods, yes.

Police Officer: *I'm thoroughly convinced of that because he knew of my paranormal stories even as far back as my childhood. And we started talking and he told me a couple of his own paranormal experiences and that's when he said, "Let's go to Greystone and see if you feel anything there." I had no prepping, no stories, no nothing.*

Once again, it becomes clear that the officer is very uncomfortable. I can see that he's had enough.

Police Officer: *Can we step outside?*

We walk out of the basement and then out the servants' quarters door. We step outside to the east courtyard as he takes a deep breath. The officer stands there trying to shake off the feelings and bad energy. It's abundantly clear he's happy to be out of the mansion, under a blue and bright Southern California sky. He shares his final sigh of relief.

Police Officer: *Oooooohhh weeeee.*

I never did figure out what the noises were that we encountered. I didn't want the officer to know that it really did scare me, because after all, he was hesitant to go down in the Basement in the first place. So I played it off like it was no big thing. Now, if it were Kacey, my sister, down there with me instead of the police officer, I'd finally have the opportunity to redeem myself, but I'd probably still shove her to the floor and run screaming, "Take her, she's wounded!"

"PARALYZED WITH FEAR"

No matter how many times I read or hear this story it's chilling. Whenever I talked to Steve about his stories, it is the Basement narrative that is his most riveting. And as I've said throughout the book, unless you're inside the mansion at night, and in Steve's case, down at the Basement door—at night, alone, and with only a flashlight—you will never comprehend how out-and-out fear can suddenly grip you, and all you have to protect yourself are your mental faculties. This certainly was the case with Steve. Standing with him at the Basement door and getting ready to discuss the evening in question, you can easily feel and plainly see that this was an event that haunts him to this very day.

STEVEN CLARK
(Retired Park Ranger Supervisor)

> Steven: *As you know, Mary Nichols is a professional photographer, and she was shooting here like she always does. It's the 2007 Design Show and it's around nine in the evening. She was just finishing up. I told her, "I'm going down to the basement to turn the lights off." It was dark and I only had my flashlight. I get down to the basement door and I'm standing right here, reaching for my keys, when I hear this growl. It was this awful, painful-sounding growl. No idea what it was. I'd never heard anything like it. I was so scared that I was literally paralyzed with fear. I couldn't move. Every hair on my body was standing straight up. I couldn't even breathe. I'm not sure why I didn't wet myself. I just remember standing here, my brain is trying to process, "What the fuck was that?!" It was loud and it was dark and I was afraid. I'm standing right here, just outside this metal cage that leads into the basement. And now I'm thinking something's going to come around the corner and grab me through the bars. Slowly, I back away from the gate to about here, about five feet away, and then my brain starts to reengage and I'm remembering what Rob Wlodarski* [well known paranormal investigator] *told us: "Verify. Always always verify."*

What Steve, and by extension, what Rob Wlodarski is submitting is this: remember, it may not be paranormal, it might be something explainable like the wind blowing through an open door or a window. Indeed, verify. It might be paranormal or it might be just a sound or noise because this is an old mansion.

Steven: *So I just said, out loud, "If there's something here with me tonight, can you make that sound again?" And this thing immediately growls out louder and stronger. Very similar to those recordings that we got.*

I've recorded extremely disturbing sounds in the mansion we call the "Screams and Wails."[5]

Steven: *You know, it's got that guttural sound* [he tries to mimic something awful]. *I can't even describe how weird a sound it was. But it sounded animalistic, it also sounded human. I never heard anything like it. So when it did it the second time, and it was actually bigger, stronger, and louder, it scared the shit out of me. I'm like, "Oh fuck!" My first instinct was to run! So I ran down the hallway. Mary Nichols was there in the card room with her assistant setting up and I'm just screaming, "Get out of the house! Get out of the house! There's something in the basement!" And I ran out. I was shaking. I mean, I was just a mess. Mary was like, "I'm out of here." She told me that all her batteries died that night. Every one of them was dead and she had just charged them. I mean, she came with full charged batteries and she's like, "I can't do anything, so I'm getting out of here." She was scared, too, because I was a fucking mess. So she packed up and left. I then called you to come and lock up the house with me because I didn't want to go back inside by myself. And I was so scared to go down there by myself for probably a year.*

Of course, I interviewed the photographer, Mary Nichols, as well. Here's an excerpt of her recollection of this night in the mansion with Steve.

MARY E. NICHOLS INTERVIEW

Mary: *All of a sudden here comes Steve from the other end. And you know how he gets so intense on the job. He's out of breath, "Were either one of you just down there in the basement?" And we're looking at him and we said, "We've been right here doing exposures." And he said, now in an*

---

5 Audio recording exists in author's collection.

aggressive tone, "So neither one of you were down there for anything? To adjust a light or do anything?" And we're like, "No." And he says, "Well, something's down there! And I hope it's a ghost rather than a real person!" He says he heard something make what sounded like a growling noise down there next to him. And it really scared him, and that's when he came up the stairs. He said it didn't sound like a human sound. It was almost an animalistic sound. It was very seldom, if at all, that I'd seen him panic, but he definitely was. I mean, he was vibrating, do you know what I mean? How you are when you're really that afraid? At that point, we just wanted to leave.

BACK TO STEVEN'S INTERVIEW

I reminded Steve what happened after I got his call and I showed up that night. "I said, 'Let's go down there.'" And you said, "NO!" And I said, "I'll go with you. Let's go down there." So we did. And we stood right here, right outside this door. And I said to whatever the hell was here, "You scared my friend, why don't you scare me? Come on, you scared my friend, scare me." And nothing happened and you said, "I swear I heard this horrible growl!" And I said, "You don't have to try and convince me. I can see it in your face." In fact, I've never seen his face so filled with fear as it was that night. Steve is now staring at the Basement door. Memories are drifting back to him.

> Steven: *I just remember that painful crying, growl. It was just an awful sound. I've heard nothing like it before or ever since. Until we got that recording. That was the closest to what I heard down here.*

The disturbing recordings I mentioned above are the same ones to which Steve is referring. I've left my recorder running inside the mansion on many occasions. There have been what sounds like gunshots; they echo as if a gun is firing inside the mansion. I've recorded bangs, thumps, random movement, voices, but the most horrifying was the "Screams and Wails" recording. It's a little girl off in the distance sounding very scared, along with a deep, chilling voice that yells and screams. I tell Steve that when the renowned psychic and medium, Chris Fleming, heard that recording, he said it was a demon and that it travels between the Attic and the Basement. Steve agrees.

> Steven: *I hate to use that word evil but the growls I heard sounded tortured, which is exactly what you recorded. And when it starts that guttural thing, I was like, "What the fuck is that?!" And that's what that moment was. It was a "What the fuck is that thing?!" But you know something is going on and you're like* [Justification Alert!], *"This has to be something else! It can't be paranormal! There has to be an explanation!"*

Steve shakes his head, still not believing what happened to him that night.

> Steven: *Yeah, that was a bad night. And you know, even now, when other rangers tell me their paranormal stories, I'm still skeptical. I mean, when people want to know what things have happened to me here, I tell them, and you can see in their eyes that they don't believe me. And I just say, until it happens to you, you won't believe it.*

Chapter 14

New Kitchen

*No, no, no, no, no, no, no. There's no one here. I know they spook here.
I can feel it! This is weird.*

— MANUEL
JANITORIAL SERVICES

Photo: Chris Keith

In 2011 and 2012, five servant's rooms were demolished in the servants' quarters to make way for a new modern catering kitchen. I can only imagine how the spirits felt about that demolition project. Just how helpless they must have felt to see their rooms being destroyed. Until recently, 2019, I hadn't heard anything about sightings or paranormal activity in this location... then all of that changed.

"Watching From the Window"

Andrea had information about a co-worker she wanted to share with me. To protect his privacy, I have not included his last name. He, along with several other witnesses of the paranormal, didn't want to talk about his experience, let alone come back to where his sighting took place. It can sometimes be like returning to the scene of the crime. Andrea Flores tells his story.

ANDREA FLORES
(Janitorial Services)

Andrea: *His name is Manuel. He took over for me on the weekends to clean the Greystone restrooms when the park is closed at night. He's Mexican and doesn't speak English at all. I talked to him when he called me on the Sunday night of the Oscars in 2019 and he asked me, "Do you know if there are ghosts at Greystone? Do you know if they spook at Greystone?" And I was like, "No, you're crazy. Why?" I said that because I didn't want him to quit. I knew that if I told him the truth, he would quit immediately because he sure sounded spooked. So I asked him, "Why, what's going on?" And he said, "Well, it's not the first time, but I saw someone looking at me from the catering kitchen window inside the mansion." So I asked him what was going on. Fill me in. And he said, "Well, it was already dark and someone had a flashlight and they were flashing it at me. They pointed the light at me, on and off for about five minutes. And I said to him, "Were you able to look inside the window?" And he said, "No, I only saw the light." So he moved into the firehouse restrooms to clean and someone, or something, kept flashing this light at him from the mansion. You can easily see the kitchen window from the lady's restroom. So he started cleaning the lady's restroom and every time he would come out, someone would be flashing at him, trying to get his attention. And when he finished, they were still flashing at him. That's when he called me and I told him, "No, don't be silly. It was probably the rangers flashing you. It's the Oscars night. They play a lot of pranks because of the Oscars. They're just fooling around." Manuel was very sure of this, "No, Andrea, it's not the rangers, they are all gone. The parking lot is empty, there are no cars. There's no one here," he says, "There's no one on the property. I know when the rangers are here." And I said, "No, Manuel, there's got to be a ranger inside." I knew what I was telling him was a lie, but I didn't want to tell him the truth because I didn't want him to quit!*

I asked Andrea how sure Manuel was that there was no one on the property. (Postscript: I checked the records—there were no rangers logged in as being at Greystone the night of the Academy Awards, February 24, 2019.)

Andrea: *His response to my telling him that there must be a ranger inside the mansion was, "No, no, no, no, no, no, no. There's no one here. I know they spook here. I can feel it. This is weird." I think after that night, Manuel asked my floor care crew guys who have worked at Greystone if they've ever been spooked. They told Manuel, "Andrea's lying. She has been spooked as well!" But I kept saying, "No, Manuel, you're crazy." Anyway, I know he didn't believe me and three weeks later he quit. I feel bad, I didn't want to lie to him or have him quit, but I know he was really, really spooked and he didn't buy my ranger explanation.*

Andrea also mentions an employee named Ernesto who told her about his experiences. I asked her what she knows about Ernesto.

Andrea: *Right… Ernesto is another guy from this floor care crew who feels very attracted to that same window that Manuel talked about. Ernesto would fill in for Elva, the daytime janitor, every once in a while, or he would even fill in for Manuel when I wasn't available. Ernesto told me on three or four occasions, "Hey, I feel someone watching me and making me look at that same window." And I was like, "Did you ever see someone?"*

He told me, "No," but it just draws his attention. He says it feels like a magnet. He looks but sees nothing. But I know he gets scared as well.

"FEAR INSIDE"

I started hearing that many of the janitorial service workers who come up to Greystone were starting to talk amongst themselves about the spirits. They are all Hispanic, and Catholic I'm told, and quite religious. The paranormal and organized religion are like oil and water. But they have a job to do, and when paranormal activity gets in the way, they are bound to quit or ask for a new location. So Andrea and Vilma (Andrea's co-worker) told me that all of her workers meet at City Hall, gather the supplies needed, and head out to their specific job locations. I asked her if she would mind if I met with some of the workers who say they've had paranormal experiences. She said that was fine, so I met with several of them. Some of the interviews were through interpreters. Their stories are spread throughout the book. I caught up with Ernesto before he was to start one of his shifts.

ERNESTO CELIS-ZARATE
(Janitorial Services)

> Ernesto: *Every time I clean the female restrooms, something makes me look to the window in the kitchen. The big new kitchen window by the servants' wing entrance. I know there's nothing there because I've been there during the day and I've never seen anything. But something just makes me look at it. Like something is calling me, and I just stare at it. It's not a voice, but a feeling, like something comes to me. I feel weird. I get a fear inside me. That's what I feel. But every time I'm coming out from the woman's restroom, something makes me look into the window on that side of the kitchen. I don't want to, but it's just making me look. Like I said, it's weird. I know there's something there, I just can't see it. There are a few*

windows that I look at, and I don't see anything. I have never experienced anything like this anywhere else. Ever.

Chapter 15

Servants' Wing Staircase

I do remember yelling because I should have been the only one in the mansion. Then I stopped and I thought, "Shit, maybe I didn't see a little kid here. Maybe it was just my imagination."

— RANGER MIKE
  FORMER GREYSTONE PARK RANGER

Photo: Chris Keith

The Puppet Masters starring the venerable Donald Sutherland and featuring Yaphet Kotto was lensed on this staircase.

Walking in through the servants' door you see the new kitchen on the left, and a few steps away, on the right, is the entrance that leads to the upper Servants' Wing. This winding staircase has a handmade iron railing and there are two small windows that offer a view out to the beauty of the inner courtyard and a large water fountain. Looking downward from this staircase you can see past two floors to the basement door.

"VANISHED"

The interviewee has asked that his identity remain anonymous—we'll refer to him as Ranger Mike. I really like "Mike." He is truly an independent individual. We were friends when he worked at Greystone. He left the job about fifteen years ago. I touched base with Mike and he agreed to come back to the mansion and be interviewed inside. I'm glad he did because as we chatted where his experience took place—it helped to stir his memory regarding the incident. I've never forgotten Mike's story; it is etched in my mind. We walked into the mansion through the servants' door.

RANGER MIKE

(Former Park Ranger)

> Mike: *I recall as I walk in here, I didn't directly look to my right, but I knew something was there. I not only sensed it, but what I believe I saw out of the corner of my eye, as I almost passed the stairway, was a child. A little boy. He was on the staircase at the handrail looking at me as I walked by. When I glanced back, the boy was gone. So as I walked right past here, these steps leading upstairs, I even said, "Who's that?" Then I stopped and listened, and I thought I heard the footsteps. And I remember believing, hearing, thinking, that the boy took off running and went into the upstairs hallway. It's funny because coming back to this location, I'm recalling that one moment vividly.*

As we walk up the winding staircase, I asked Mike if he tried to make contact with the boy.

> Mike: *So I ran up the stairs and I think I said something like, "Hey, the mansion is closed! Come back!" I looked down the hallway and I stopped. I was trying to figure out where did this kid go? It bothered me because I realized there was someone in the mansion and the servants' entrance door was supposed to be closed. If I remember one thing from back then, it was that the interior was closed off to the public. So we wouldn't have allowed*

anybody in here. There was a design show at the time, so it also bothered me because that's even worse with all the expensive furnishings that were in here.

I asked Mike how long he searched.

Mike: *I spent at least ten to fifteen minutes looking for this kid. I remember I had to get something for my boss, Steve Clark, which is why I was going down to the kitchen in the first place. But I was bothered by the fact that now there was somebody in the mansion—or at least I thought someone was in the mansion. But after listening and trying to look for this child and not finding him, it occurred to me that maybe I didn't see anyone. Maybe it was just my imagination. Maybe it was just in my mind.*

As you can see, this is a reoccurring theme. For the "victims" of the paranormal, they invariably attempt to rationalize or justify what they've experienced. "It doesn't make any sense to me, so it must be my imagination."

Mike: *But I remember it bothered me because I was kind of fearful to tell Steve, "Hey, I screwed up. The door was open. I let somebody in." Now, I wasn't sure if what I saw was real. It felt real. I thought for certain there was a kid that came in and was hiding from me, but afterwards I wasn't totally sure.*

And I think when I first told you this story, I was like, "Hey, Clete, I had something weird happen to me!" And it's so odd coming back here after thirteen years and reliving it, because it's all now coming back to me and I remember thinking, "Oh shit, I screwed up. I let somebody in the mansion!"

Or was that not real? Was that a ghost or was that just all in my mind? But it was so real that I had to look for somebody. That's how real it was. I didn't hear anything else. I didn't see anything else. I looked down the halls and I started going through the doors saying, "Hey, the mansion is closed. The mansion is closed! Where are your parents? Who's in here? You need to come out now! This is the ranger!" I do remember yelling because I should have been the only one in the mansion. Then I stopped and I thought, "Shit, maybe I didn't see a little kid here. Maybe it was just my imagination."

Months later, I walked downstairs into the doll room and the Greystone historic group put up a whole display that showed the history of Greystone mansion—it was during a design showcase. And I'm looking at all these different black and white pictures, and I remember seeing one photo with a lot of little children. There must have been four or five kids in that photo. And I brought you into the room and pointed out, "Hey, the child in dark clothing, that's the kid that was on the stairwell!" I recognized that kid without a doubt. I mean, how crazy is that, dude?

Mike did indeed ask me to check out the historical display with him and he pointed out the child in the photo. If he thought his mind was playing tricks on him when he first saw this apparition, how could he have been so sure in making such a positive identification of that child? To say you may have seen a spirit is different than pointing out that apparition in a photo like you're identifying someone in a police line-up. Again, I was almost taken aback at how sure Mike was that this was the boy he saw on the stairs. I often think back to that picture in hopes to one day find that photo, identify the child, and delve into why he is still in the mansion.

Chapter 16

Breakroom (Servants' Wing)

I just ran out! I flew off the steps and I was gone!
— CHANH HANG
    GREYSTONE LEAD PARK RANGER

Photo: Chris Keith

What Greystone employees call our Breakroom is actually one of the bedrooms upstairs in the servants' wing that overlooks the inner courtyard. The story passed down from years ago, long before I started, was that a female servant hanged herself in this room. Lisa Williams, the famous psychic and medium, filmed a segment of her television show *Life Among the Dead* at Greystone in 2009. Regarding the female servant hanging story, Lisa told me that she was seeing a woman waving frantically at her from that room. I didn't see her, but I'm not psychic.

Regardless, there has been substantial paranormal activity in this room to suggest that a horrible triggering event may have indeed taken place.

"Footsteps"

When I received an urgent text from Dan, saying—"I'm freaking out!"—I knew he wasn't kidding. He said he was freaked out by what had just taken place. I told him to wait right there, I'd come up and see what was going on. When I arrived and saw his face, I knew something really unnerved him. We went into the Breakroom for this interview.

DANIEL HERNANDEZ
(Park Ranger Supervisor)

> Daniel: *I came into the breakroom around three in the afternoon to make some coffee. Sara* [Greystone's Venue Coordinator] *is in her office over in the firehouse, and Chae* [Lead Park Ranger] *just left for lunch in the ranger's office in the upper parking lot. I make my coffee and I'm sitting down to relax in the corner of the room. I can look out the door from this vantage point, so I can see that no one else is around. I'm on my phone wasting time on the Internet and I hear footsteps. And again, I know for a fact, no one is in the house, but it sounds like someone is coming up the stairwell to the second floor—and the footsteps are very light, gentle. So I get up and I peek through this little window here that overlooks the stairs—but I don't see anybody. But I for sure heard these footsteps that were very, very light. Like it was a small person. A child? We've been in this breakroom before and we've heard people come up the stairs, so we know what footsteps sound like. We hear it all the time. But nothing was there.*

This is the same stairwell where Ranger "Mike" saw a small child looking through the railing at him.

Daniel: *I stayed in the breakroom for at least another minute or so, and I had to leave, even though my break wasn't over. It really frightened me.*

We've all heard what we thought were footsteps, and depending on where and when we heard them, unknown-origin footsteps may have scared us. But for Dan, knowing the history of this room as well as the staircase featuring Mike's story of the little boy, among many other stories, highlights the fact that this area is active. Dan doesn't scare easily, so I trust he heard footsteps. Even in the daytime, there remains a certain creep factor inside the mansion. I tried recreating the footsteps for Dan and eventually I was able to make the same sound he heard by gently touching the steps as I made my way up the stairs.

"STRANGE FEELING"

When I interviewed Chanh, it was obvious that he had no idea about the paranormal history of our Breakroom. He never heard any of the various stories. But it turns out he knew something wasn't quite right before anyone had to fill him in about the activity in this area.

CHANH HANG
(Lead Park Ranger)

Chanh: *Steve Clark* [Retired Park Ranger Supervisor] *told me that we had this new breakroom for the rangers upstairs in the servants' quarters. He said, "There is a table, a fridge, and a coffee machine. Feel free to go up there, enjoy your lunch and hang out. There's a window in the breakroom so you can look out over the main courtyard, just to keep an eye on things." So I started eating my lunch up there whenever I was working up at the mansion. It's very quiet. I liked it. One afternoon, I'm eating lunch and I could hear someone coming... someone was walking up the stairs. So I thought it might be Steve, since I saw him downstairs. No one else was in the house. So I continue eating, looking out the window... And then I realize that Steve didn't come in and it felt like something prompted me to look at the door again... nothing. And I'm thinking "Where did the footsteps go?" I take another bite, but something keeps urging me to check out the door. Why? So this time I turned my whole body and faced the door and I never took my eyes off the door. I had a strange feeling, like somebody is watching me eat. And then I thought maybe Steve is screwing around. And I go, "Steve?" No answer. I stood up, walked toward the door, leaned out and didn't see anybody, but I still felt weird. So I wrapped up my sandwich and walked out.*

"You told me you ran into Steve Clark afterward," I remind Chanh.

Chanh: *Exactly, I see Steve in the courtyard and he says, "You finished your lunch already?" And I'm like, "I'll go up to the old ranger's office." And Steve wonders, "What happened?" I say, "I'll tell you later, but someone's watching me up there." And Steve tells me, "Oh, didn't you know? A servant hung herself in there?" And I turned around to Steve and said, "Now you tell me!"*

"SLAM!"

When I interviewed Ivan, I found out that he had the ability to connect with the other side. It's strange and probably a statistical anomaly how many people that work or have worked at Greystone have the gift to see, feel, and/or sense spirits. Ivan, who was new to the Ranger Program, is no exception. Throughout his life, he has seen and felt energy and spirits before. I heard from another ranger that Ivan already experienced activity inside the mansion, but he wasn't keen on announcing it publicly and was also a bit overwhelmed by what happened to him on his training tour at Greystone. The spirits don't waste any time, do they?

IVAN MARTINEZ
(Park Ranger)

> Ivan: *I was in the breakroom, and I heard footsteps coming up the stairs from the basement, so I go check it out. I didn't see anybody and the footsteps just sort of stopped. So I thought, "Okay, I'm just scaring myself." As I go to walk back in the breakroom, I was about two feet away and the door slams in my face! I stopped right before it slammed. So I'm thinking, there's no wind in here, no windows are open. It's just me. So at that point, I was like, alright, I'm gonna walk out of here, and I left right away. I just walked away. I can't explain it. I didn't know what to think of it. I was looking around to see if someone opened a different door and the air pressure just closed this one. But no one was in there. So I just decided to get out.*

"YES"

CLETE KEITH

With all the recurring stories of employees feeling like there was someone or something inside our Breakroom, I decided to go in there by myself one morning. I wanted to try and connect with whatever spirit was in the room, if indeed there was a spirit. So I turned on my phone recorder and said, "Is there anything you want to say? You can talk to me. Anything you want to say? Why are you still here? Why didn't you go to the light? Were you afraid of what you might find there?" I didn't hear any sound or voice after I asked these questions. But when reviewing the recording,[1] after I asked— "Were you afraid of what you might find there?"—the recorder offered a clear male voice that answers, "Yes." Who was this? Ned? Hugh? A servant? And why? Why are they afraid to move on from this realm to the next? Is it because of religious ramifications when it comes to suicide?

---

1 Audio recording exists in author's collection.

Is it guilt? If it is Ned or Hugh, is this answer with regard to the murder? Or again, suicide? Is this spirit afraid of what is to meet him or her should they move on from this physical plane? Obviously, I don't have answers. Only questions.

"Were you afraid of what you might find there?"
"Yes."

"THUMP, CRASH, AND SMASH"

For Chanh, this story was quite traumatic. He called me in a panic—just as I was pulling into Greystone. I immediately drove to meet him in the upper parking lot. He was very nervous and talking fast. He was saying that he wouldn't go back into our Breakroom. He said a framed poster—on its own—flew off a bookcase and crashed to the floor. It terrified him to the point where he flat-out said he won't go back in. I told him I would check out the situation.

I entered the mansion through the servants' door and turned on my phone's video recorder. I walked up the staircase with, I must admit, some trepidation. Upstairs, I walked toward the closed door of the Breakroom. I turned the doorknob slowly and opened the door. There on the floor, as Chanh described, was the smashed glass and the poster still in the picture frame. As I documented the scene with my phone, nothing in the way of paranormal activity happened to me. I went back outside to talk with Chanh, who was still unsettled and anxious. I finally persuaded him to return to the Breakroom with me and detail exactly what happened. Please note: The only electrical socket in the Breakroom is in the closet, so that's where we have the coffee maker and refrigerator.

CHANH HANG
(Lead Park Ranger)

Chanh starts to act out exactly what happened. He holds up his coffee tumbler.

> Chanh: *Okay, my coffee tumbler was here, it was filled, I was done and ready to go. I reached over and turned the coffeemaker off. Then I stepped out of the closet and thought, "Oh, I forgot the top to my tumbler," which was on the refrigerator. I grabbed the top and I screwed the cap on. I stepped out, grabbed the closet door here with my right hand and I closed it. I walked toward the light switch here by the entrance door, and with my left hand, I switched off the light. As soon as the light went off, I heard like a thump in the room. I look back and that's when I see this picture in the frame fly off like this.*

Chanh demonstrates exactly how the picture frame flew off the cabinet.

> Chanh: *So I just ran out! I flew off the steps and I was gone! But I remember I turned the light off with my left hand. Was the light off when you came into the room? Because I shut the light off when I flew out of here.*

I checked my video footage and see that the room light was on when I walked inside. I show him the footage. He sees that the light is on. He's dumbfounded.

> Chanh: *I know I was about to grab the door and the light was off, and that's when the picture in the frame went crashing—bang! And we've had that up here on the cabinet for two or three years and it's never fallen. Plus, it didn't fall, it flew off.*

I show him the footage and it's freaking him out. He wants more clarity.

Chanh: *So when you came up here to check this out, was the door opened or closed?*

I remember it clearly being closed and I have the recording[2] to prove it. I asked Chanh, "Did you close this door when you left?" And he's adamant about exactly how he left the room.

Chanh: *I took off running! I'm not going to stop, run back and close the door, and run away again! No. I'm gone. I'm out of here!*

I understand what Chanh is saying and I understand his frustration, but that's not what's on the video. I show him the footage again for clarity—and I'm glad I recorded video because it documents the reality of when I walked up. But I keep thinking about the "thump" sound Chanh described just before the picture frame went airborne—that's very curious. "Chanh, what do you think that thump noise was?" He shakes his head.

Chanh: *I don't know. My back was turned as I was walking out. The thump got me to turn back around. Next thing I know, I'm out in the hallway. I ran so quick out of the servants' wing and I was like, what just happened!?*

---

2 Video recording exists in author's collection.

Chapter 17

Servants' Wing — Second Floor

It was a dark silhouette, no eyes, but it was facing toward her.
— ANDREA FLORES
   JANITORIAL SERVICES

Photo: Chris Keith

The Puppet Masters, starring Emmy and Golden Globe-winning actor Donald Sutherland, was filmed in the Servants' Wing.

The upper floor of the service wing contains a linen room, a sewing room, four maid's rooms, and a gift room. Walking up the spiral staircase and entering the Servants' Wing hallway at night fosters a foreboding feeling. It's a long, dark hallway with windows looking out to the inner courtyard. Most of us who have worked at the mansion have a habit of stepping into the hallway from the stairs and first looking to the right. Why? Because the stories of activity are well known in this location and our instincts are to check to see if anyone or anything is present and waiting.

Greystone Historical Report

Re: the gift room: "My mother used to wrap presents which she gave copiously at Christmastime to everybody in the family, to the near family and whatever." —Timothy Doheny

---

"COLD CHILL"

The Klondike is a large, expansive region of the Yukon Territory in northwest Canada, just east of Alaska. Another large, expansive region is the intimidating presence of Klondike Nelson. Standing six foot three inches tall and weighing three hundred and fifty pounds, Klondike looks like a guy that nothing could ever come close to shaking his foundation. But when he took a tour of the mansion, Greystone rocked his world.

KLONDIKE NELSON
(Reprographics Assistant)

> Klondike: *Man, that was a while ago, maybe ten-twelve years. Some friends were in town and I wanted to show them some great LA sites. I thought Greystone would be perfect. Park Ranger Steve* [Clark] *was our tour guide.*

I asked Klondike exactly where his incident took place. He tells me at the freezer. I inform him it's actually called the meat locker.

> Klondike: *So we're going through the mansion and Steve's telling us about all the stories and all the drama that went on there with the Doheny's and the son and his secretary. And he did tell us a little bit about the ghost stories. So I don't know, maybe it was a subliminal thing, but frankly, looking back, I don't think so because what happened was so powerful and so real. So as he's talking about the servants that died there, we're by that meat locker. I felt like this cold chill that hit me here, right in the center of my chest, and it went through me and right out my back.*

And it wasn't like it hung inside of me or anything. It just, whew—right through me. It wasn't a gust of wind, because I'd feel it on my sides and all over. I'm a big guy so a ghost could shoot through me pretty easily without hitting the whole body. So now I'm really freaked out. I wasn't super scared, because it's daytime, right? I don't know that nighttime has any bearing on anything with ghosts, but they're more powerful at night and they could really do something. But I definitely felt it and it was pertinent because we were talking about the ghosts and about some of the maids passing away. It was ice cold. Probably even colder than a refrigerator or like when you open a freezer.

I interrupt Klondike to remind him that the meat locker is non-operational and has been for decades.

Klondike: *Yeah, right. I didn't think so. But it was definitely a cold that I couldn't manifest on my own, even with subliminal thoughts of ghosts or whatever. I wasn't even thinking, "Oh, I'm going to feel a ghost," or I wasn't scared of ghosts at the time when I was walking through there. But definitely, it coincided with everything I'd heard on the tour and it just felt so real. It was real. It was definitely an experience. I didn't tell Steve. I didn't want to freak everybody out because I was with a girlfriend of mine and she was already freaked out by the whole ghost thing, and the creepy mansion, and she didn't want to hear about it. So I didn't think it was a good time to bring it up [he laughs]. But it definitely had like an energy presence to it. It wasn't super negative, but it felt like a, "Get out of here," type of thing. I didn't hear anything and it didn't hurt me, but it was weird. How do you explain something like that that doesn't ever happen? I didn't believe ghosts were in the mansion. And I have got to admit, I'd hear people talk about their experience or ghost stories and go, "That's B.S.!" But after going through that, I definitely do believe in ghosts now. I mean, it was that impactful.*

"Don't"

Luz, her fourteen-year-old daughter, and I walked through the Servants' Wing hallway and we stopped right outside the ranger's Breakroom. I'm listening intently and Luz appears ready to cry. During this conversation we have an unexpected guest.

LUZ RODRIGUEZ
(Retired Park Ranger)

> Luz: *There's a lot of energy in here. I can feel it. This feeling... If I get teary-eyed...*

When I was home transcribing this audio recording of our interview for the book, something remarkable was also captured. Right after Luz says, "If I get teary-eyed," I hear a female spirit voice say, "Don't."[1] I was stunned. This voice was not heard by either one of us during our live interview. The voice is so clear and present, I thought, "Was there someone with us?" But again, it was just Luz, her daughter, and myself. The voice is definitely a mature female. The clarity of this voice is what is known as a "Class A EVP." It's considered the best you can record—totally clear and easy to understand. You may ask why a recorder can capture the spirit voice that we didn't hear. The theory is that the recorder captures the voice, which is at a frequency or volume in which the human ear is not tuned. Nevertheless, it was an intelligent response to Luz stating her emotions. As I continued listening to the interview, Luz talks about what she's feeling at that moment.

> Luz: *It's just the energy. So if I start having trouble breathing, it's...*

Here again, amazingly, the same female spirit voice speaks—this time a full sentence, possibly commenting on Luz and her emotions. This blew

---

1 Audio recording exists in author's collection.

my mind! Except this time, I can't make out what the spirit is saying. In fact, to me, it almost sounds like a different language.

This is how it sounds phonetically: *Hen ess ouse brit.*

Could she be saying: "In this house it's…" or any variation of that? I don't know, but it's recorded[2] and the three of us never heard it during our interview. Luz continued…

> Luz: *It's just the energy. There's a lot of overwhelming feelings. There's sorrow, there's anger, there's moments of happiness, but it's mostly that people were not happy here. They were not happy living up here. That's what I'm feeling. I'm picking up on sorrow. Just this deep sadness.*

The three of us begin to walk out of the Servants' Wing and Luz is shaking her head. I ask her if she is okay? She nods "yes."

> Luz: *Whoa. I could sure feel it today.*

Clearly, it seems a spirit joined us that afternoon and Luz picked up on her energy and emotions. And my digital recorder, with its ones and zeros bouncing around, captured a conversation from across the ghostly veil.

"SAD FEELING"

Think horror movie in a perfect setting. Even during the day, the rooms upstairs in the Servants' Wing can be unnerving. But when the sun goes down and the mansion is empty, it's a totally different vibe. During my time at Greystone, before and during the investigation that has birthed this book, I've heard and continue to hear ongoing stories that emanate from inside the walls of these rooms. So when Vilma and Andrea asked

---

2 Audio recording exists in author's collection.

to talk to me, I could sense that something serious went down. Vilma and Andrea are Elva's work supervisors and both women are extremely kind and compassionate. As I've said, Andrea feels she has the "gift" and this book is a testament to her many personal stories at Greystone. Vilma, on the other hand, wants nothing to do with spirits.

There is never a day when I'm in the mansion on the upper floor in the Servants' Wing that I don't think about this next story. It is in two segments. First, from Elva's perspective, and then the story from Vilma and Andrea.

ELVA
(Janitorial Services)

> Elva: *Andrea arrived with Vilma because we were supposed to clean up the first and second floors. So when we went up to the second floor, where the servants' rooms are, I'm working and I start to feel really sad, out of nowhere. I mean, really sad. All day I was feeling normal and was in a good mood. So when Andrea came into the room I was cleaning and I told her what happened, that I'm feeling sad, kind of depressed, and she suddenly starts singing Gospel music because I think she felt there was some kind of energy in the room. She says to me, "I feel the same thing you do." And she didn't say anything else to me because she knows how I am about ghosts inside the mansion. So that's how everything happened. And you can ask Andrea if you want. She will explain it better than I do. So I start praying and I keep praying until I leave the room.*

Many stories that I've heard over the years include a "heavy" depression overcoming many people in the mansion, as if they are psychologically in sync with the lamentation of the spirits, who seem to be yearning for an emotional rescue.

"Please Don't Leave Me Alone"

Vilma is a quiet, soft-spoken woman who helps run the janitorial company that services Greystone. She wants nothing to do with the paranormal. Andrea is her co-worker and there have been nights when Andrea has called Vilma to meet her up at Greystone because of the paranormal activity. Other times Vilma will come along during the day to help with all the cleaning in the mansion. This was one of those times.

I met Vilma and Andrea outside the mansion on the grounds. They are willing to talk about what happened recently to Elva.

VILMA R. LOPEZ & ANDREA FLORES
(Janitorial Services)

Vilma: *It was three weeks ago around eleven in the morning. Elva had to go clean the second level of the mansion and she does not like going alone. So Andrea and I both went with her. We were helping her dust and get rid of cobwebs in the area where the servants used to live. I was in the linen room that has all the shelves where they folded laundry. Andrea went with Elva to the room next to where I was cleaning. Andrea was vacuuming and I hear Elva plead with her in Spanish, "Please don't leave me. Please don't leave me alone!"*

Andrea: *When Elva and I walked into the room, to my left, I saw a black shadow looking straight at her. She had no idea. She didn't see it. And this shadow was behind the door, in the corner, and its attention was straight on Elva. It was a dark silhouette, no eyes, facing toward her. Elva was clearly feeling something in the room but she didn't see it. That's when she just yelled, "Please don't leave me alone!"*

Vilma: *Because later I asked Andrea, "What was that all about?" And she said when she walked in, there was a black shadow facing directly at Elva, who must have felt something that made her start to yell.*

Andrea: *I didn't know what to do, and I don't know why, but I just started singing this religious song I learned a long time ago. I thought Elva must know this song. As soon as I start singing, she starts singing with me.*

Vilma: *It was kind of amazing. Elva naturally followed along because I could hear them next door while I was still cleaning.*

Andrea: *But I don't know if you could hear that my voice was kind of shaking? It was hard for me to remember the words. I was thinking, "Please, please, please. I need to remember the words." But I didn't want to see the dark shadow again. I could feel it, but I didn't want to see it. I didn't even finish vacuuming. I just made sure when Elva went out, I blocked her view so that she didn't see it. And we both got out.*

This conversation is unnerving to Vilma.

Vilma: *When she talks about it... [a huge sigh] I don't want to feel it. I don't want to see it. I just don't want to.*

"I totally understand," I say to Vilma. "I think it was a good idea not to panic and tell Elva. She would probably quit and never come back." Andrea nods in agreement.

Vilma: *Yeah. That's why we didn't. We didn't tell her anything about this. We're never going to tell her anything about this day.*

As they get back in their van, I walked up to the driver's side, to Andrea, and asked her, "When you were getting Elva out of the room, did you glance over behind the door to see if the shadow was still there?" She turned from me and was now staring out the front windshield, as if to recall the incident. Then Andrea looked at me—"It was still behind the door watching her as we left."

————⟨∾⟩————

"HELP ME!"

IVAN MARTINEZ
(Park Ranger)

> Ivan: *On the very first day of training as a ranger at Greystone, I was already seeing things going on in the rooms. I saw shadows running from room to room on the second-floor servants' area. From the breakroom, down the whole hallway, I would see dark shadows coming in and out of the rooms. They didn't have a face, just really dark shadows. I didn't know what to think of it.*

"Is this the first time you've ever seen anything paranormal?" I ask.

> Ivan: *I've seen things before. I don't know honestly if I have the so-called "gift," but I see things. I've seen family members at funerals who have passed away. I've actually seen them. But, at Greystone I see stuff. As I'm walking through the hallway up here, all the doors are open to the rooms and I can feel someone staring at me the entire time—in every single room as I'm walking by. I can just feel someone looking at me.*

At one point, Ivan mentioned something about a dream he had regarding Greystone. I asked him if he had this dream after his training.

> Ivan: *Yes. After the training, I didn't go to Greystone for maybe another two or three months. But then I had a dream about the spirit girl. This was maybe two-three days prior to working a wedding at Greystone. I actually saw her face. I've never actually seen her, but I saw her face in the dream. I don't remember what she looks like, but I remember dirty blonde hair. Two ponytails and a white dress, white leggings, and again, maybe white shoes. And in the dream, she said, "Help me." But in the dream, there was furniture but as you know the mansion has no furniture. Oh, and rangers Chanh and Chae were there. They were sitting down right outside of Lucy's room* [daughter Lucy] *and Emily comes out from that*

room and says, "Help me." Chae and Chanh ran away in my dream and they disappeared by the stairs. But it's creeping me out because Patrick [another Park Ranger] told me that there's like a portal there. And it's funny because as soon as Chae and Chanh ran through the portal, they just disappeared. And the girl said, "Help me" again. And I didn't know how to respond. I was just stuck in my dream and I was like, "I can't help you." And then, as soon as I said that, she had a very demonic voice and she just scared me off and I ran out of there.

I interject, "Okay, that was your dream. Did anything else happen?"

Ivan: *Yes, then I'm at Greystone working a wedding and I see the spirit girl on the second floor. I was by myself. I was turning off all the lights. But I didn't see her face. She was walking into Lucy's room and I didn't know what to think of it. I just thought maybe I was seeing things, you know? But I did see the back of her head, and it was like I said in my dream, two pigtails, white dress, white leggings, and white shoes. But this time there was no furniture or chairs out there. But I saw her face in my dream. And I've never seen her before. Maybe my imagination just put a face to her face. But I've never interacted with her. I honestly have no idea how to explain this.*

On a side note: is it possible that Ivan was seeing Emily? His story fits her description and we know she has been seen mostly on the second floor. What do you think?

"GLIMPSE OF SOMEONE SMALL"

JUAN ANDRADE
(Park Ranger Supervisor)

Juan: *In the morning, around nine o'clock, before we open to the public, I go upstairs with Ranger Patrick. One of the habits I have when I get to the top of the stairs to the second-floor servants' quarters, is to always look to my right and then to my left to make sure no one's there. But that morning, I don't know, I saw a glimpse of someone small. It looked like a child. I couldn't tell if it was a little girl, or a little boy. It was like it was waiting for me to get to the top step, and once I reached it, it just ran away towards the meat locker on the other end of the hall.*

It was there and then all of a sudden, it's not. I don't want to say a shadow person, because it wasn't. It was white, almost translucent, and I can distinctly see that it was a small person. It was all in white and it looked like the arm was moving forward as it ran away. I mean, is what I'm seeing real? It could be someone alive, or not alive. I'm not sure.

Isn't this last statement interesting? Once again, as with others I've interviewed, it's so hard to comprehend what has taken place. To Juan, he's seen something "almost translucent," which, you would think, would be a dead giveaway (excuse the pun) that it was an apparition, not someone real. But your logical mind steps in and tries to help justify. Juan then questions himself, "It could be someone alive, or not alive. I'm not sure." I find that fascinating.

"FREEZING!"

The Friends of Greystone is a non-profit volunteer organization founded in 2001. Their mission is to raise funds to restore, preserve, and protect the Greystone Estate and mansion. They have an office/storage room in the mansion.

SUSAN ROSEN
(President, "Friends of Greystone")

Susan: *It was a warm day outside. I was all alone in the mansion and I was just walking down the second-floor hallway of the servants' quarters to go to our office. All of a sudden, I get this frozen feeling. It was so cold. It was like being out in the snow. It was just so chilling. It's like I stepped into a frozen ice patch, because I remember walking and it was warm and normal, and then all of a sudden stepping into like, "Ooh!" And then stepping out. It was such a huge difference in temperature. Huge. It's like opening a door and being out in a snow blizzard. It was so drastic. I just kept walking, and then when I was out of it, I thought, "That's so odd. It must be the spirits." I mean, there was nothing else to explain it, because this building doesn't have freezing air conditioning and it doesn't have heat [at that time]. So what else could it be? And I said it wasn't my imagination. Nothing else has ever happened to me, but at that time I didn't feel fear. I was just so cold. And I just went about my way. I never went screaming to anybody. I guess every time I've been in this house, I always feel a happy, pleasant feeling. I'm not afraid to be in here. So I just figured it was somebody saying hello to me. It's the only thing I could think of—I didn't go back to test and feel it. I'm not that brave!*

I asked Susan if anything has ever happened to her before this event in this area or any other area of the mansion.

Susan: *No…as many more times as I've walked down this hall, I keep waiting for it to happen again and it's never happened. And I'm up here a lot and I've walked this hall many times. It's just dark and I go to put my key in the door and there's nothing. I swear to God, so far, nothing. It's so weird! I'm telling you, I come up here at night and when I'm up here, the cell phone sometimes doesn't work, but also, nobody can hear you. I should wear a nice cross!*

"TRYING TO GET OUT"

I'll never forget this moment with Luz. On our walk through the mansion, we stopped outside the meat locker, which is in the east end of the hallway of the Servants' Wing upstairs. Her personal experience here still puzzles her after all these years. In our conversation, I filled in the missing pieces of her puzzle regarding what took place at this location. The look on her face was one of being stunned, saddened, and reflective. Then, to top it off, she experiences a visitation. Here is how it unfolded.

MY DISCUSSION WITH LUZ RODRIGUEZ
(Retired Park Ranger)

Luz leads me to the meat locker in the upstairs hallway. Her teenage daughter is also with us. "This thing, the meat locker, you could hear the knob. The latch." I said, "This almost looks like a shower inside, but it's really for the hanging of…" Luz finishes my sentence. "The meat." I open the door to the meat locker. "So that handle would shake sometimes, you could hear it," she recalls. "I was downstairs the very first time I heard it. I couldn't place that sound. And I was like, 'Where's that coming from?' And I went all through the house and I couldn't figure out where that sound was coming from. And then I heard it again. So again, I went all through the house and still couldn't figure out where it's coming from. One day I was in the small upstairs kitchen, just off the servants' hallway, and I heard it again. And it was really close. So I just stepped out of that kitchen and realized it was coming straight from the meat locker. Almost like someone was inside or someone was trying to open it. Something was going on, you could hear it rattling, and I was like, 'OK, you guys stop.'

Interestingly, she thinks it might have been Ned Doheny or Hugh Plunkett playing a joke on her. I ask Luz, "You know what the story is here, don't you?" She looks at me and I can tell she doesn't know the true story of the meat locker. "No, I don't know anything about it. Other than it being the meat locker." It's at this point I tell Luz the truth. "A servant killed herself inside there. She slit her wrists." Luz and her daughter are stunned—they just stare at the meat locker. Luz asks, "In the?" I nod, "Yes… inside the meat locker." Luz pauses and thinks about the new information she's trying to absorb. "That makes sense." Luz tells me she now understands why she felt the emotions that she has in the past. I tell her the rest of the story. "There's a drain inside, so all her friends wouldn't have to clean up the blood." Luz is quiet. She's taking in the new angle. "I didn't know that story. That just gave me chills. That would explain why there's so much up here. Like I couldn't hold it in. It was like... emotional."

Suddenly Luz looks to her left. "I just got touched." This takes me by surprise. "What? Really?" She laughs nervously. "I just felt it. But that's what I was trying to tell you!" Clearly, spirits have been trying to communicate with Luz all the years she's worked here, and they still are by touching her. Luz continues, "Because I would always hear (she makes a whispering sound)... like a rush. It's like a rush. It was like them saying, 'Let me tell you my story!' And it's all at once. It just sounds like you're in a room filled with people and there's conversations going on, but you can't make out what anybody's saying. That's what it sounds like. Wow. Yeah. It always sounded like someone was in there trying to get out. So now I understand."

Luz's experience is the classic example of spirit energy trying to communicate with the living.

"OPEN AGAIN"

The first paranormal story I ever heard from anyone working at Greystone was from Ranger Steven Clark. We became friends immediately, and at some point, he told me what had happened to him. I couldn't believe it. But knowing Steve, he isn't the type of person to tell anyone a joke regarding the paranormal and the mansion.

STEVEN CLARK
(Retired Park Ranger Supervisor)

Steven: *The first paranormal experience for me was the window in the breakroom in the servant's wing. I saw it open like that.*

We're standing in the courtyard below and he points up to a half-opened window.

Steven: *And back then, there was nothing up there. It was just garbage. None of those rooms were being used before it underwent a remodel in 2007 by the UCLA students in that design show. But I was here in the courtyard and I saw it was open—and back then it was a big deal if there was a window or a door open because nothing was ever opened. So I went in and I closed the window, and when I came back out, it was open again* [he looks back up at the window], *like that. I didn't know what to think. I was scared, so I didn't go back in and close it again* [he laughs]. *I just left it open! It doesn't seem like a big deal now, but back then it was, because my bosses were adamant that nothing is ever opened and everything remains sealed tight. Nobody goes into the mansion period. Even the rangers weren't supposed to go in unless you had a reason.*

"Don't Mess With Me"
MARIA THORPE
(Former Park Ranger / Camp Director)

Maria: *When I was a park ranger, I remember there was one late afternoon where it was raining really hard. It was pouring. It was coming down all day. So I get a call at around four p.m. that we need to let the movie crew inside the mansion, and I'm like, "Oh great." I was hoping I'd get away without having to open up on a really dark rainy day. Just the scenario you want to be in. A dark, rainy day, by yourself, walking through the mansion! So I let them inside and when they were finished, I went to turn on the alarm and it says that there was a window open* [the alarm isolates the location of the open window]. *I went to check it out and it wasn't open and I was like, "Oh great." Because someone had told me a story where they've done this. They opened up and when they're ready to leave they set the alarm, and when they go to check, the window is actually open and they were like, "That's weird. I thought I closed it."*

I asked Maria where in the mansion did the alarm system identify the open window.

Maria: *The window, if I remember correctly, was in the servants' quarters. So I'm thinking to myself, "Oh my God, please do not mess with me." I remember walking through the mansion looking around and checking windows going, "Please, do not mess with me."* [she laughs] *I was actually saying it out loud and I was being very nice. I was saying, "Oh, please don't mess with me. I'm just a poor girl here. I've left you alone all day long." I got back, checked the alarm, it showed the window was closed, so I hurried and set the alarm and I got the heck out of there!*

"FAULT"

TONY GARDELLO
(Facility Maintenance Mechanic)

Tony: *I was in the house and it was past the park's closing time. We have an alarm we have to set then we close and secure the house with that alarm. So you have a push pad and it reads, "Ready to Alarm." I pushed the keypad to lock up the mansion for the night. And then it said "window ajar—second floor bedroom." So I went outside and I looked up, and sure enough, the window was open. So I went upstairs inside the mansion, cranked the window shut, physically locked the window, and came back down to the alarm pad. I repeated the keypad operations and it said "Ready to Alarm," then suddenly it said "Fault—second floor bedroom window." That's the same window I just closed. It was the same exact window and it's now open again?! It was the second floor where the girl... you know...*

As the story goes, a maid hung herself in that location, which is now the ranger's Breakroom.

"THE ROCKING CHAIR"

This conversation confused me. The specific chair to which Ivan is referring is a chair I placed inside the room because it's old and a true antique item from the late nineteenth century. I thought it would fit the look of the room. This chair has very small, carved wooden wheels so that, back in the day, it could roll on the floor. Keep this in mind: it is not a rocking chair.

IVAN MARTINEZ
(Park Ranger)

Ivan: *When you go up to the second-floor breakroom in the servants' wing, you make that right, and there's a room on the left. I remember going to take my break and there was a chair there. I'm not sure if it's still there.*

Photo: Chris Keith

There was a rocking chair [this chair is not a rocking chair]. *Is it still there? Or was there ever a rocking chair there? Because that day, I saw that chair moving like someone it was rocking. I didn't see anybody in the chair but there was something—it was dark… it was a dark mist and the chair was just rocking back and forth. I didn't think much of it. So I just went into the breakroom. I didn't want to overthink it, you know? I was alone, but I saw something was rocking and I'm like, you know what, it's probably nothing.*

"Didn't think much of it!? Didn't want to overthink it?! Probably nothing?!" It had to be something!! I know Ivan quite well. I'm pretty sure he has the ability to sense spirits. But come on, what's to "overthink"?! Is it just me?! I mean, if I saw a dark mist rocking in an antique chair that isn't a rocking chair, I don't think I could say to myself, "Let me see, I'm alone, there's a dark mist rocking back and forth in a chair that shouldn't rock? Ah, let's not overthink it. I think I'll eat my burrito."

Ivan: *So I went to the breakroom and that was it. But I looked again after my break was over and I noticed the dark shadow wasn't there. It was like I was just seeing things.*

"SHE RAN OUT!"

Ranger Chae contacted me and he was adamant that I had to hear his story. His tone made it sound like, "You're not going to believe this!" He was almost giddy and couldn't believe what had happened—especially to one of his relatives.

CHAE YI
(Lead Park Ranger)

Chae: *My nephew and his girlfriend were visiting me on a Saturday afternoon around five-thirty. We were inside the mansion and I was pointing out different rooms inside the servants' quarters upstairs. At that first room, the yellow room on the left, as you come straight up the staircase, I turned back towards them and I was surprised to see her hair all standing up. I said, "What's wrong with your hair?" She's like, "What are you talking about?" I said, "Your hair is all standing up. Like static." All the hair at the top of her head was standing straight up.*

I asked Chae if he ever witnessed anything like this before.

Chae: *In my fourteen years I've been here, I've never seen anything like this ever happen to anybody. And so she got really frightened and scared and she ran out of the servants' quarters! She said she felt something like energy or something, but she just got really frightened and she ran out! When she got away from the servants' wing, her hair came back down. My hair wasn't standing up, just hers. She's Asian, so she has very straight hair and she had her hair in a ponytail. But this section* [circles the top of his head] *was, like, loose and it was just straight up. Her boyfriend, Brian, he got scared, too. In fact, both of them ran out. I was just so surprised at what I saw!*

Chapter 18

Second-Floor Landing and Hallway

I'm freaking out completely. You know, like the tears started coming!
— Patrick Ferris
  Greystone Lead Park Ranger

Photo: Chris Keith

Town & Country, starring Academy Award-winning icon Warren Beatty, as well as Carl Reiner's *All of Me,* was filmed on the Second-Floor Landing and Hallway.

Back in 1928, this Second-Floor Landing, like the Grand Hall below it, occupied the full length of the living area upstairs in the mansion. Lined with antique carpets throughout the hallway, the landing was adorned with 17th-century furniture. Later in 1945, an evocation of Chinese motifs, known as Chinoiserie, decorated colorful tables, along with Venetian-style furniture. At the far eastern end of the hallway is the Gun Room as well as the second-floor kitchen.

This location is one of the most active paranormal areas in the mansion. A reason for this could be that most all the bedrooms are connected to this hallway and landing. Are there spirits still connected to their bedrooms? Read this chapter and you be the judge.

"SHADOWS AND WINDOWS"

Luz and I walk upstairs to the landing and take a stroll down haunted memory lane. Interesting note: Luz mentions that when this story took place there wasn't any electricity in the mansion. Indeed she's right. It was later upgraded in 2008 with ten miles of new wire.

LUZ RODRIGUEZ
(Retired Park Ranger)

Luz: *Has anyone else seen the shadow people? Or the shadow man? I don't know if it's Ned* [Doheny], *but there's a full body. It's in the shape of a man, and whenever I would see him it creeped me out. He's just black. Solid black. The first time I saw him, Sumner* [a fellow ranger] *and I were working here together. It was getting late. We are waiting for a set dressing truck for a film shoot to arrive. We're outside talking to the security guard and Sumner says, "I'm going to go to the restroom." At this point in history, there was still no power in the house. So we had flood lighting and it was all being run by the generator outside. So there were some lights on here at the landing when Sumner goes inside. But I felt like he was gone a long time, so I walk over to the entrance, the doors are open, and I call out, "Sumner?" No response. And so again, I call out, "Sumner?" When I look up, I see a shadow coming out from the master bedroom area in the west hallway. And as he walks, or the shadow walks, it was like he is floating. It wasn't like walking. He is floating across this hallway in the middle of the second-floor landing and into the next hallway toward the gun room. And I can see him cross behind each pillar. There was no bobbing of the head like when you walk. It was just a float. Floating. And when I first saw him, I said, "Sumner, what are you doing up there?" because we would only go through the house together in the dark. Neither one of us would go alone. And so when I saw him, I was like, "Sumner!?" But there was no reaction. He didn't turn. He just kept walking. Then I said again, "Sumner, what are you doing up there?" And as I'm focused in on this shadow, I hear Sumner's voice outside the mansion. I think the color must have rushed from my face, because I was so scared at this point. And I said, "Sumner, what the heck? I thought I saw you upstairs!" And he's like, "No, I'm here." I am still shaken, "Clearly you're outside, but I could've sworn I just saw you upstairs." But it was a shadow. And I think Sumner spooks easily, so he was like, "Oh, stop it. We have to go check the windows."*

A quick reminder about the mansion alarm system at the time of this story: it was notoriously difficult to set because it would detect a window or door ajar and it wouldn't allow you to set the alarm.

Luz: *Whenever there were film crews in here, it was a given that they would open the windows. So we'd have to go in the dark with our flashlight and close all the windows. So on this night, after we closed the window in the daughter's room* [Lucy Doheny's room, just off the landing], *the alarm system pad keeps saying there is an open window. But Sumner and I had closed it. Now Sumner was outside dealing with some trucks and it still kept saying that the window was open. But I know we closed it. So then I said to Gary—the policeman assigned to the film shoot—"Can you come with me to close this window, please?" And he's like, "Why can't you go?" And I said, "I already went and it keeps saying it's open. Plus, my flashlight is getting dim." So he comes with me and we close the window. When we come back down the alarm pad says that window is open and one of the windows or the doors in the gun room is also now open! He looks at me and says, "Let's go." And as we're coming up here to the second-floor landing, his flashlight also starts to dim. And I was like, "Gary, you said you had fresh batteries! Now it's gonna get dark!" He says, "C'mon, let's hurry!" So we're running through to the room and we see that the window is open! And it's open all the way! But it is like someone just hit the latch and it popped.*

I said to Luz, "Wow, it's like they weren't going to let you out of here."

Luz: Exactly... And it seemed like they ["spirits"] *kept opening the windows! So we ended up force arming the alarm system—just bypassing the regular procedure to set the alarm. But they kept playing games with us and you start to feel like you're losing your mind because you're like, "Wait a minute! I closed that and I latched it!"*

Also note that these windows are opened and closed by cranking the knob, which brings the window close enough to where you can take the latch and secure it. It's a two-step process.

Luz: So when Officer Gary was with me and both of our flashlights are going dim, by the time we make it to the window, we would close it, lock it, make it back down here to the front entrance and the alarm would say "Window Open." And he's like, "Are you kidding me?" And I said, "See, this is why I needed you to come with me!" And we didn't go back up. I said "I'm just gonna force arm it and leave a note for Bill [her boss] *to let him know that we had to force arm because there's an issue with the windows."*

"CONNECTION"

Patrick became a ranger in 2015 and I find him to be a very smart guy. And when he gets excited and passionate, he talks a mile a minute. Through our many conversations it became clear that he has a real fascination with the paranormal, especially at Greystone. I also discovered that his girlfriend, Raeha, shares his same paranormal interests. In fact, I've conducted several late-night investigations in the mansion with Patrick using flashlights to connect with the spirits. One night Patrick contacted me during his own investigation. This incident at night involved an Internet camera placed in the center of the Second-Floor Landing, allowing me to observe and talk through a speaker on that camera from my home miles away. When Patrick refers to "the thing," he's referring to the Internet camera. Another reminder, "Emily" is the name given to a young girl by a visitor (see Chapter Two – Grand Hall - "My Name is Emily") who died on the property.

PATRICK FERRIS
(Park Ranger)

Patrick: *So I laid out the red and blue colored maglites* [small flashlights with a twist on and off light]. *There is a mansion event going on, so I'm going to be there late until about ten o'clock. So Clete, your recording device was set up there on the landing because you wanted to try that out. You told me to give you a call when they're set up and then you'll hop on and join me on the Internet camera. So I put down on the floor the flashlights that I set up to be on the verge of turning on* [the idea being, you twist them on and then slowly twist them until they barely blink off; now they're set for a spirit to manipulate the light back on] *and the theory is you ask a question.*

In Patrick's case, he had two different colored, small Maglites. How this, in theory, would work is that you say out loud to the spirits, "Turn the red flashlight on for "yes," and turn the blue flashlight on for "no." Sound nuts? I thought so too—until it worked!

Patrick: *The spirits can now make the connection with the flashlight and communicate with you. So I wait about a minute and neither light turn on. I have a recorder in my hand. I push it once, thinking that's all I had to do to turn it on. So I'm like, "Okay, well, here I am, I'm going to start doing this." I wasn't planning on standing there for very long to wait and watch the flashlights. I didn't believe in the light thing anyway because I thought it'd be easy for it to accidentally turn on. So I asked out loud, "Is*

217

Emily here with me? Or does anyone want to talk?" And then the red one turned on as soon as I said that. It was creepy. I remember it being creepy because right as the question left my lips, "Does anyone want to talk?"— boom, it just immediately turned on! And because it's pitch black in there, I'm like, "Alright, cool." Then I remember you telling me, if the flashlight came on, to ask them to turn it off. So I wait, and it is on, not flickering or anything, and I'm thinking, okay, it's a little bit of a coincidence. And I'm like, "Can you turn that off?" And then immediately right after leaving my lips again, it turns off. I'm like, "Oh shit! That's two for two!" And then my third question I think was just more general, like, "Is it okay that I'm here?" Again, as soon as it leaves my lips, my flashlight turns on! Then, again, I asked it to turn off again and it shuts off!

I'm mesmerized as Patrick chronicles his story, I asked him, "What are you thinking at this point?"

Patrick: *By this time, I'm completely freaking out. You know, the tears are coming, I'm like, "This is really happening!" So I remember talking into the recorder, like therapy or something, "This is what's going on! It just turned on! It's off!" And I think this is the point when I called you and told you, "Hey, get on the camera immediately! You don't even know what's going on right now!" So you said, "Yeah, okay, I'll get on!" So I hang up with you and I remember that taking forever, because I wanted someone to be there to at least see it, see what I'm seeing! Also, I'm thinking, "What if this is still a coincidence? I'm just gonna wait here and then if it doesn't turn on or anything..." And I remember asking, "Okay, well, is it Emily?" Nothing. And then I start going through the list of names. Still no response. I'm like, "C'mon, is someone here with me?" Again, nothing. And then, "Is some thing here with me?" And the light immediately pops on! And at that point I was like, "Okay, Clete needs to get on this thing so I can get outta here, because I'm kind of over this!" And I remember between the questions, I would wait. I didn't want it to be like too rapid fire, like, if I ask enough questions eventually, one of the lights will accidentally turn on during one of my questions, or during the middle of it and I'll take that as a sign. So I remember between questions, I wait and I wait, but it always happened right after I finished the question. Right after it. Eventually you hop on the camera and then you are asking questions remotely through the camera. I went down and was waiting by the front door and could hear your conversation. It was getting kind of late and I'm like, "I just have to go. You take it from here." And then I headed out. But that was an intense one. So that's how I now believe in the flashlight communication thing. And then I found out later that the recorder needs to be pushed twice, so I didn't record the event!*

"OPENING DOORS"

What stands out to me in this following segment is just how calm, cool, and collected Martin remains throughout his experience.

MARTIN J. PEREZ

(Janitorial Services)

Martin: *Sometimes when I work, some of the doors keep on opening. When I clean a room, I close the door behind me, because then I know that it's been cleaned. There are times I would come back to that same room and the door would be wide open. And I remember this one time, I was in the gun room, and as I went into clean Patrick's room* [third youngest Doheny boy], *which is right next to it, I closed and locked the door that leads between both rooms. As I turned around to put my gloves on to clean the windows, the door behind me unlocks and opens slowly. And it does this weird, creaking sound. I honestly thought it was like one of the rangers in the house who was trying to scare me. But I ran to the other side of the door to the gun room, to see if someone was there, and there was no one. But I could hear footsteps as if someone's coming or is walking up there. But there was no one. So I said to myself, "All right, I'll leave it open. I guess you don't like it closed."*

"Creepy Male Voice"

JOHN HUYBRECHT
(Former Park Ranger)

> John: *I was kind of jonesin' to quit my job and move away. Just give up on L.A., and in my head, I was thinking, "This could be my last day. Maybe I should just say goodbye." And I was actually talking to the ghost in my head like saying, "See you later ghost, I'm out of here," because I wanted to be back in Wisconsin. Right after I said, "This could be my last day," I heard a voice, it was a male voice, and it sounded just like, "JJJJJooohhhhnnn." Almost like in a creepy way you would expect it to sound in a horror movie. I stopped dead in my tracks and just froze for a second. I was so freaked out because I'd heard about this happening to Ranger Patrick like about a year ago. I immediately felt very distressed and got out quickly. I think I even said, "Please don't say my name!"*

John finally did leave the job and moved back home to Wisconsin to pursue his love of, believe it or not, shooting horror films. Greystone offered him great life experience!

"My Evening With Emily?"

CLETE KEITH

My story in Chapter Two—"My Name is Emily"—is based upon having met a woman who said she interacted with a young spirit girl named "Emily." From that moment on, whenever I enter the mansion, I say hello to Emily. Obviously, I don't know if she is actually in the mansion with me, but if she is present, I want her to understand that I know she's there and I know her name. Emily has been seen many times by rangers, camp counselors, and the visiting public. In fact, a man giving a tour to a group of people told one of the rangers when he looked in the front door (just like Ranger Chanh, Chapter Three, "Ghostly Girl") he saw a little girl standing in the hallway. His description matched that of Emily.

I purchased an Internet camera with the idea of putting it in the mansion on the Second-Floor Landing. The camera can pan left to right, tilt up and down, has infrared capabilities to record in the dark, and I can speak through it—all remotely from my phone. I wanted the ability to monitor the area from any remote location. I needed to set this up with approval and get an Internet connection through the City of Beverly Hills. I met with the IT Department, camera in hand, and the conversation went something like this

I.T. *What do you want?*
Clete *I'd like to set a camera up in the mansion with access to view it remotely.*
I.T. *What for?*
Clete *Well… to monitor what is going on at night.*
I.T. *What goes on at night?*
Clete *Ghosts.*
I.T. *Seriously, what goes on at night?*
Clete *Seriously… ghosts.*

Long, awkward silence.

Clete *Hey, check out this cool camera!*

One of the IT guys starts scrutinizing it. He sees what it can do.

I.T.   *This is actually kind of cool.*

Clete   *Right? If we could set it up in the mansion, that would be great.*

They kept the camera for a few days. By the time I went back to see them, they were more interested in the camera than the ghosts. They agreed and arranged for me to have access via the Internet.

I arrived at the mansion one evening around 9:30 with the goal of connecting with Emily. I brought my new camera along with several ghost hunting devices, two different types of EMF meters, and a Maglite flashlight. I placed the camera on an existing pedestal in the middle of the Second-Floor Landing and faced the camera toward a corner where we've been told there is a portal. Standing alone in this very dark mansion, holding the devices, I said this out loud:

> *Emily, I know you're here. I can't see you, but I know you're here. I brought you some things to play with tonight. If you come close to these two meters, they light up.*

I put my hand next to them to light them up.

> *See? Just get close to them and you'll see all the colored lights shine. This last thing is a flashlight. You make it come on by turning it. See how I turn it and it comes on? Easy. So I'm going to leave these here for you.*

I turned the Maglite barely to the off position. Any touch or manipulation of the device will turn on the light. I placed all three of them on the floor in the corner in the portal.

> *You have a great night, honey. Have fun playing with these, Emily, and I'll be back in the morning.*

I left the mansion and drove home not thinking that I had actually talked to the ghost of a little girl or any ghost, for that matter. I was sure nothing was going to happen. When I got home, I used my iPad to access the camera. I logged on and a few minutes later, to my absolute astonishment, I see the Maglite turn on! I'm thinking, "Is this just because of the way I set it?" It was barely on the edge of turning on and maybe it just came on and will stay on for the rest of the night until the batteries run out. And then… I see the light shut off. I grabbed my phone, turned on the video, and recorded my conversation on my iPad just as the light comes on again! I continue my conversation with Emily, now remotely through the camera:

Okay, you turned the light on. Now, turn it off on the count of three: One, two, three.

The light starts flickering.

Go ahead, turn it off. [Light shuts off] *Excellent. That's you, isn't it, Emily?*

Sixteen seconds go by and the light comes back on and then off twenty-two seconds later. I'm still thinking this could be a coincidence. So I ask:

Emily, turn it on one more time please?

Two seconds after I ask her that question, the light turns on.

Thank you!

Suddenly, what appears to be a bright white light or orb flies out of the light. I'm not sure what that was. A ball of energy? A bug? Whatever it was, it shot up from the floor and flew right out of frame toward the ceiling.

This is so much fun.

The light turns off. I want to see if she'll turn on one of the other devices.

Can you touch one of those other devices?

The Maglite comes back on at the same time as one of the other devices.

Turn it off, Emily, turn it off.

The light shuts off. I ask her a few more questions.

Do you want to stay in this house?

No light.

Do you want to leave?

The light comes on. The light then goes off.

Do you want me to find someone to help you get out? If yes, turn the light on... if no, leave the light off.

I wait a little longer before I speak again, in hopes the light will come on and she wants help to get out. It doesn't come on.

Do you have friends in the house?

The light comes on immediately. This to me was amazing in that I waited for a response on my last question and nothing happened. I ask this question and boom, the light comes right on. I kept thinking to myself, "Is this really happening?"

Oh, good. Let's turn that off. You can turn that off, Emily.

The light goes off.

Excellent. Are you scared in the house?

The light stays off.

Good. Do you like the rangers? Do you like Clete?

The light stays off.

Do you like Ranger Clark?

The light comes on. Damn you, Steve Clark! I was hoping she liked me!

Good. He likes you, too. You can turn the light off.

The light turns off. Somewhere during this conversation, I FaceTimed my sister, Kacey, in Hawaii. I told her not to talk because her voice would be transferred through the camera into the mansion. She watched as I asked Emily the following question:

Emily, how old are you? Are you… eight?… Nine?… Ten?… Eleven?

Suddenly the light comes on. We thought she was around eleven or twelve because of the descriptions of her sightings.

Oh, okay.

The light turns off.[1] I quietly say goodbye to Kacey. I ask Emily if she's still there. Silence. I wait and ask again. No light. She's not responding. I feel a little panicky inside. I don't want this to end. I want more information. I want to continue connecting. In a way it has become so personal— so unbelievably intimate and special that I am reaching a soul who, for whatever reason, has chosen to remain just out of reach on the other side of the veil.

1 Video/audio recording exists in author's collection.

I ask again if she is still with me. More silence. A wave of sorrow envelops me. I need to say goodnight to Emily—to let her know that I care about her and I want to help her move on if, indeed, she wants to move on and get out of the mansion. I want her to know that I'll find someone to help her. But she's still not responding. It now appears my interaction with her is over. I'm feeling emotional because it felt so real. It was real. This little girl in the mansion was actually communicating with me. Maybe she's scared to leave. Maybe she doesn't trust me. I wondered if our conversation gave her any comfort? I hope it did. But knowing this little girl died a tragic death (by falling from Lucy's window or possibly a different location) and doesn't know how to continue her journey to the other side makes it hard for me to let go of her. It's now late and I need to be up at the crack of dawn. As I put my head to the pillow and I pour over and over our conversation, I can't pinpoint just what it is that's bothering me. Just as the whirlwind of thoughts in my mind begin to settle down and I'm about to fall asleep, I suddenly realize the reason for my angst—I never asked the most important question: "Is your name, Emily?"

"Pssssst!"

On September 10, 2019, I received a call from Kristin Buhagiar, the Recreation Services Manager at Greystone. Several new employees were recently hired to work out of the Greystone gatehouse—the small building at the south end of the property—to help with city recreation events. Kristin gave up her office in the gatehouse to the new employees. She asked me if there was any other office space on the property that she could use. I told her the only space available was inside the mansion.

I know what you're thinking—if the mansion is so haunted, why would I suggest that to her? Am I that demented that I would do anything for my book? The answer is… yes.

Honestly, that was the only place left on the property that an office could be set up with WiFi, a phone system, and printer. Did I think she would be safe inside the mansion? Absolutely. Did I think that anything ghostly would ever happen to her? Well, as you can see, the more time you spend inside the mansion, the greater the odds that something or someone will try and make contact with you. She even said to me that she was worried with winter approaching there would be less daylight and she would be working in her office while it's dark outside. She asked me what I thought about that. I told her that it didn't affect me because I'd be leaving before it got dark! She laughed and called me an idiot. I laughed as well, but I did have my reservations about having her in the mansion, alone, especially at night. But I also took into consideration that her schedule was such that she was off site in meetings most days, and the time inside her office and mansion would be limited.

Finally, at my suggestion—Kristin moved in to a small room just off the Second-Floor Landing. On her first day there, I went into her office to check on her. She looked at me and said, "Something doesn't feel right." She was touching the top of her chest up by her throat, almost as if she couldn't swallow very well. I asked her, "What is it you're feeling? She said, "It's just… I just can't explain it. It's just not right." She kept touching near her throat. I told her, "This is your first day in the mansion. Maybe all the stories you've heard are playing into what you're feeling." She nodded. As for me, I didn't feel anything odd or any weird vibe whatsoever. I said, "Why not give it a day and see how you feel tomorrow?" She agreed.

I checked in with her the next day hoping all was well. She turned to me and said, "That feeling is still here." I asked her to try and describe exactly what she was feeling. "It's just, kind of…" and she touched near her throat again. "Do you feel sick?" I asked. "No. It's not like that. I can't describe the feeling." I said to her, "I tell you what, give it one more day to see if

227

that feeling goes away. If it doesn't, I'll start thinking of another place for you to work. Maybe you can have my office in the Firehouse." She agreed. I didn't know for a fact that what she was going through was paranormal. She was having a feeling. A feeling that she couldn't describe. It was real to her. I could see she was very concerned. All I could do was hope that it would go away after one more day.

The next day when I walked into her office, she looked at me and said, "I don't feel it!" I was totally relieved. But truth be told, in the back of my mind, I was thinking it was a possibility that what she was feeling was something or someone that was trying to connect with the new person in the mansion. I was hoping I was wrong. But it was now day three and she was happy and that's all that mattered. I told her, "See? There you go! Awesome!" We talked about the view she had of the inner courtyard and how, when opening up the window, she could hear the sound of the fountain. Very calming and pleasant. She agreed. As I walked out, I was just hoping she wouldn't encounter any kind of paranormal activity.

One week later, I received a phone call from Kristin. She was unnerved and scared. I met her in the mansion to get all the details.

KRISTIN BUHAGIAR

(Recreation Services Manager)

Kristin: *It was during the day and it was really dark and gloomy in here. I had this chandelier on that's right outside my office. The main chandelier on the landing was off, but I turned it on before I went downstairs. There were no other lights on because I was just walking downstairs to the restroom. So it was actually pretty dark once I headed down the staircase. On my way back from the restroom, I walked back up the stairs and when I turned the corner and walked down the hallway toward my office, from the room on the right, I heard a loud, "Psssssst!"*

It freaked me out! I jumped and looked to the side and both of those doors

228

were open [to Lucy's room and her dressing room]. *I just looked for a second. I wasn't looking to see whatever made that sound because I didn't want to know! And then I just got so scared that I walked back to my office. It was so loud that I literally jumped, which, that's the only thing that makes me believe that it's real, because if it was in my head, you don't react like that if it's in your head.*

Again, our ongoing theme of folks trying to justify what has taken place because what just happened seems impossible.

Kristin: *And I know the sounds of this place from being in here now, so I know it wasn't the alarm system. I know what that sounds like. This was loud and it definitely came from this direction—Lucy's room—because I immediately looked that way. And there was no echo to it. It was like, "PSSSST!!" That loud! Loud enough to make me jump. Like, genuinely jump. And the sound didn't come from outside, because I wasn't near any windows or anything. It came from the right side, where the rooms are. I think it was from inside one of these rooms. Has something like this ever happened? Have people heard noises like that?*

I have to pick and choose my words carefully. Kristin is new to all of this and I don't want her to freak out, although I think I'm a little late in calming her. I try to allay her fears, "We've had sounds before, absolutely, not that specific sound, but I think you're okay." Not the best explanation but, hey, I gave it a shot! Kristin and I have talked before about Emily on several occasions. It kind of sounds like it could be her because the interaction was playful, but who knows. She wasn't trying to scare Kristin. She finally has a female to play with who is in the mansion every day. Without scaring her, I turn to Kristin and quietly say, "If you get freaked out by hearing another, 'Pssssst,' just say, 'Emily, what do you want? I heard you. Tell me what you want.' Then maybe if she knows you know it's her, she might calm down and not do anything like that again to get your attention." Kristin is clearly unnerved.

Kristin: *It was just so loud to be a little girl. I don't know.*

Based on my experience and research, I suggest to her that sound versus size doesn't necessarily correlate in the spirit world. "I think that would depend on the spirit's energy. Emily's been here a long time. If she's learned how to build up her energy, maybe she could do that." Some researchers and investigators have observed that spirits can pull energy from sources like batteries, electricity, or human beings to try and manifest, or to move an object, or to make a sound. Kristin and I walk back over to just outside her office door.

Kristin: *When I'm in my office with the window open, I feel like I'm connected to the outside world. I hear people and it's totally fine. It's just when I come out here to the second-floor landing and I either have to go down the hallway or down there toward the grand entry that I'm like, "It's just so big." This place really does have a foreboding feel to it.*

I understand how she feels. The mansion's size, its hollowness or concavity can be intimidating.

Kristin: *I'm fine right now, but it's starting to get dark. And as we get into the winter, it's going to get darker earlier, and I'm scared of that.*

We walk into her office and sit. I come up with an idea. "I know it's scary in here, but you know what we'll do? I'll turn on all the lights in the hallway because they won't want to come out in the light. You just keep the lights on whenever you're here in your office. And I would suggest you get another lamp for inside your office to make it even brighter (we got her another lamp). You can leave your hall light on right outside your door and even the chandelier on the second floor. And let's also keep the large chandelier above the Grand Entry stairs on as well. We'll keep all those on and I guarantee that's going to help." Kristin smiles. She is very appreciative. "Okay. Okay. No worries. Thank you very much."

But as I walk away you can tell she's still on edge—and who wouldn't be? Do lights being on help curtail paranormal activity? I don't know. I tend to believe the answer is no. If spirits are there and they want to make themselves known, they will. I don't know the percentages at Greystone as far as how many incidents have happened in the day as opposed to the night, but I'm guessing there are more in the day than at night just because more people are on the grounds and in the mansion during the day, so the odds are more in favor that something paranormal might happen during the day. Then again, many stories happen during the night time events.

I went back into the mansion alone when Kristin wasn't at work. The "Pssssst!" she heard sounded innocent and playful as opposed to a growl. My thoughts are unchanged. I believe it was Emily. I stood outside Lucy's room upstairs and said, "Emily, I don't know if you're here, but you can't scare my friend. I know it's a new girl and you want to play and have fun, and she's really nice, but because we can't see you, it scares us. Please don't do that to her again or else we'll have to move her out of the mansion and you won't be able to have a friend inside here. Do you understand? You can't scare her, honey. Thank you."

As of this writing, it's been nine months and Kristin hasn't had any other paranormal incidents. On a side note, because of the COVID-19 pandemic, most of the city employees are working from home. Kristin hasn't been back to her mansion office in at least six months.

"Poked"

At the time of this writing, Victoria is the new Senior Recreation Supervisor on our team at Greystone. She was so new that I didn't have time to talk to her about whether she has experienced any episodes with the paranormal, but it didn't take long to find out. Kristin Buhagiar, her Recreation Services Manager, asked Victoria to join her upstairs in the mansion in her new office to go over the upcoming recreation events. Victoria and Kristin know each other well having worked together for another city. I went inside the mansion to check up on them to make sure everything was okay. Since Victoria was new to the mansion, we chatted for a minute and then the three of us walked across the hall to show her Lucy's room—and that's when things got strange. After this incident, Victoria and I kept it to ourselves because we didn't want to scare Kristin.

I connected with Victoria later that day, and started by asking her if she felt any energy when we were walking through Lucy's room.

VICTORIA ELIZABETH CUSUMANO
(Senior Recreation Supervisor)

> Victoria: *You saw there was a spot that got cold—I actually got goose bumps!*

I remember Victoria held her arms out to me. At first, I had no idea what was going on. I watched her looking up for an air conditioning vent but I told her we didn't turn on the air conditioning. She looked at me very perplexed because her goose bumps weren't going away.

> Victoria: *I got light-headed when we were in the closet area in Lucy's dressing room. I opened the doors and I was looking at the drawers and then you guys went around to Lucy's bedroom, and as soon as I stepped foot in that room, I really started feeling kind of light-headed. I'm like, "I need to eat something." That was the first thing I thought, "Oh gosh, I need to eat something. I haven't eaten much today. My head is light."*

As she explained her uneasiness, I had a feeling that something was affecting her.

Victoria: *Then you suggested I should get out of the room. So we walked out and I got really hot in the hallway.*

Victoria suddenly looks like she is on the verge of breaking out in a sweat. I'm getting concerned. I recall standing there with her. "Feel my neck," she says. I do and it's very warm, so I suggest we go inside Kristin's office to get out of the second-floor hallway. Victoria is shaking her head, still dumbfounded by it all.

Victoria: *I was on fire! Like I had a fever. Then when we went into Kristin's office it was like, whoo! Nothing! It was gone. I thought I was going to start to break a bad sweat and then suddenly it all just went away. Now, I'm not going to lie, I get hot flashes, but they don't go away like that. Like you break a sweat, it's two to three minutes. It's like a whole thing. It doesn't just go away like that.*

I agree with her that it was very odd and perplexing.

Victoria: *Kristin said she had to go to the restroom and asked if we would walk with her downstairs because she was nervous. So we did—we walked toward the ladies lounge—and I was right at the top of the stairs following you and Kristin.*

During this walk with Kristin and Victoria, I glanced back up at Victoria. I saw her grimace and rub the upper left side of her chest. I asked her if she was okay.

Victoria: *That was when I felt the pain, when I was about four or five steps down. You happened to look back at me at that exact time when I felt the pain. I was like, "Ohhh!" And then maybe a few more steps down, it went away. We got to the bottom of those steps and that's when I looked at you because I thought you poked me in the back of my arm.*

I didn't.

Victoria: *It was very quick. That's why I looked at you. But I don't even know if the two are related—the pain in the chest and pokes in the arm. I don't know. I really don't know. And right now, I almost don't believe myself. And that's weird because I told you, I've seen something before— not at Greystone—and I really don't tell people unless they tell me they've seen something. I don't tell stories unless others are going to believe, because they'll think I'm crazy. But as we got to the bottom of the steps, and I passed in front of you, I turned back because I thought you poked me when I walked by. I looked at you and you said, "What?" Then Kristin went in the restroom. You said, "What?" And I said, I felt someone poke me. Then I thought, "Okay, if it wasn't you, am I imagining this?" I don't know. I'm baffled right now. I'm a little thrown. I'm like, "What the hell happened today?!" But the pain was like in my heart. Is that weird? And it was such a strong emotion! What was it? I don't know how to explain it. Maybe I'm doubting myself. Like, is it in my head? Did I just imagine that?*

Justification Alert!

Victoria: *I'm a visual person, so I can be like, "Okay, that doesn't feel great, but I'm going to get out of here soon and I'll feel better." But an actual interaction? That's different for me. Completely different. It was weird. It was like a dull ache in my heart. I felt like, what is that? It was like a pain. An ache... a very odd feeling.*

You can hear how Victoria is struggling to figure out what just happened to her. First the goose bumps. Then feeling light-headed. Then the sweats. Then she felt the pokes—and she felt the emotional strain from the pokes. And lastly, she tries to justify the who, what, why, and how all of this is even possible.

Victoria: *I'm just more nervous now—what if there is a connection? I have this weird feeling. It's not that I'm scared. It's more like this weird, anxious feeling. Like anxiety. I was feeling very light-headed and I've never experienced that. I seriously don't know how to deal with it. You know what I'm saying? Someone seeing something and being like, "Oh yeah, I've seen it." But when it's happening to you, and it's unseen, I don't know, I'm thrown right now.*

This isn't the first time I've interviewed someone who was completely lost as to how or why a paranormal incident happened to them. But in Victoria's case, the number of incidences in a condensed amount of time was overwhelming. She was definitely struggling with her emotions.

Victoria: *Like I have this nervous feeling, this nervous, anxious feeling. Like anxiety. I'm trying to be a strong and positive person for Kristin. But right now, I don't think I could be as calm as I normally am. And that's very odd for me because I've always felt like I'm comfortable with the paranormal. I've seen a spirit walk by. My Dad leaves a light on* [she says her dad turned on a light in her house after he passed]. *It's all good. You know, it's love. But I don't know what this is! And maybe it's because it's not someone I know? I talk in my sleep. I'm doing it more so lately. And if you ask my husband, I've been doing it more since I started working here. I was nervous last night about coming to work. And when I got to work, I felt fine. Why did you turn to look at me when we were on the stairs? I feel like you definitely have that connection, because every single time you looked at me, it was when something was happening. I thought that was the most bizarre thing. I felt like saying out loud* [to the spirits], *"Don't mess with me! Are you trying to scare me?!"*

"Shadow Man"

As short as the next experience is, think about how you would react if the same incident happened to you in a cavernous mansion all by yourself. Could you remain calm? Would you freak out? Maybe more importantly, would you dare to venture back inside the mansion?

LUZ RODRIGUEZ
(Retired Park Ranger)

> Luz: *This is the only place up here where I would see that dark shadow. Not downstairs, just up here. I've only seen him up here and maybe he's the one who slammed the door.*

Luz is referring to the door slamming while she was in the Minstrels' Gallery.

> Luz: *I don't know if he's coming out of there* [she points to the stairwell leading to the attic, just off the second-floor landing], *but I've walked out of the gun room and I've seen him in the hallway. And it's just a dark, solid, perfect silhouette of a man. I don't know if there's any validity to this, but I've always heard shadow people are not good. They don't have good intentions. But other than seeing him up here, I've never felt threatened. But with him, there was always this feeling of a threat.*

"HELLO"
ELVA
(Janitorial Services)

> Elva: *I was working with the vacuum, the one you wear like a backpack, and I heard something say "Hello." But I thought it was the vacuum 'cause sometimes it makes a funny noise. I kept thinking about it and it was just like a boy saying, "Hello." This was where the marble thing is in the middle* [a marble pedestal is positioned in the middle of the second-floor landing].

I tell Elva that Ranger Juan heard a male voice go "Whooooo" inside the mansion and he was trying to figure out where that sound or voice came from.

> Elva: *That's what Juan told me. He called me after I was outside the mansion. He said, "Well, for me, that was my first time* [hearing a voice] *and I'm just telling you because I don't really care. I'm not afraid."*

But we can bet she put a lot of prayers in after that "Hello."

"Hidden Clues"

Throughout the years, we've had many psychics and mediums visit the mansion. Some were great and detailed in their communication, others not so great, and some, quite frankly, not good at all. It's such a grey area because many times they can confirm specific information that no one knows except those of us who have worked at Greystone. Other times it's all in generalities. Nothing really specific; it's their feelings as to what is or has taken place. So far, Chris Fleming, Peter James, and Lisa Williams were the best at giving us pertinent information. Both Steve Clark and I spent quality time in the mansion with Lisa Williams. I've spent quality time in the mansion with Chris Fleming… as well, Steve has spent quality time in the mansion with Peter James.

> *I've long been fascinated by the paranormal and have a very open mind. Our bodies give off 2 kilowatts of energy every day, and I'm sure some of that energy must remain behind, trapped in the walls, floors, ceilings of buildings we have been in. Having lived in two haunted houses, I am one hundred percent certain that ghosts exist.*
> Peter James
> Bestselling Author, Filmmaker, Student of the Paranormal

Here is Steve's story of his time with Peter James.

STEVEN CLARK

(Retired Park Ranger Supervisor)

Steven: *Early on, Peter James, the psychic, was here. Our boss at the time, Michelle, was worried. She was afraid he and his friends would sneak in a camera and illegally film footage of him inside the mansion. So I stayed close by our walk through the mansion. Back then, the upstairs was carpeted and that's when Peter said something happened right here* [upstairs landing near Lucy's room] *and that there's something under the floor here that proves that. In fact, two years later they pulled the carpet up for filming on* Garfield 2 *and there were all these marks and it looked like someone was trying to draw something in the floor and then it kind of dragged off a little bit. It was a good marking. But it was exactly where he said, "There's something under the floor here about another death in the house."*

Photo: Steve Clark

Steven: *Peter specifically said that it was about "a death in the house" and that there was something under the carpet. And we suggest, "Well, what? Like a bloodstain?" He goes, "I don't know, but there's something right here." And it was about three or four feet from the wall. When he left, we tried to pull the carpet up, but we couldn't because it just started crumbling and we didn't want to get in trouble. We would have to pull up five feet of carpet to get to where he said. But when they pulled the carpet up for* Garfield 2, *and before they sanded the floors, exactly where he said, was where we found that thing scraped into the floor. Peter also affirmed what others have said about there being a portal here at the top of the stairs.*

"SLAMS"

CLETE KEITH

When I recount these stories in this chapter, I can't help but remember the night after an event when Ranger Steve and I decided to go into the mansion. With all the lights off, we walked up to the Second-Floor Landing and sat on the floor against the south wall between Lucy's entrance door and the door to her dressing room. We sat in silence and eventually began discussing what took place at Greystone that day. It was around eleven that evening when in the middle of our conversation, we suddenly heard a door slam downstairs. It gave me chills and I think it was the same for Steve. We looked at each other and I said, "Servants' Wing." We stayed quiet to see if anything else would happen. Minutes later we continued our conversation and another door slammed from what sounded like the same location. I have to reiterate, the experience is completely different when the events happen to you. It's one thing to watch it on television, or hear someone explain what happened to them, but it's quite a different story when it happens to you sitting in the dark.

Steve and I stayed completely still. He then whispered, "Let's sit in the Grand Hall." We crept down the stairs to the middle of the hallway and sat on the marble. Within minutes the door slammed again. We could now be relatively sure that it was coming from the kitchen/hallway area. We stayed perfectly still. I had goose bumps. I'm not sure about Steve, but our senses were definitely heightened. And then again, the door slammed. Now it was near midnight. We had enough. We set the alarm and walked out of the mansion. This happened in the early 2000s. If it happened today, I would investigate further and try to find the source of the "slam," but back then, honestly, I was too frightened to walk into the Servants' Wing and face who or what was slamming doors to get our attention.

"SHE DISAPPEARED"

You have to marvel at the fact that Luz isn't in an institution taking her meds to stop the drooling and silence the mumbling: "Ghosts… Mansion… Lucy." Don't believe me? Her next story is a prime example. Be aware, it is one thing to read about her story in the safe confines of this book, but when you're in the mansion, by yourself, day or night, and this type of paranormal manifestation takes place, it's an entirely different story. Imagine how you would react.

LUZ RODRIGUEZ
(Retired Park Ranger)

> Luz: *When I walk past this area outside Mrs. Doheny's dressing room, I always get the chills. Has anyone ever reported seeing a woman up here? I have—and I think it's Lucy* [Ned's wife] *because of the way she wears her hair.*
>
> *It's kind of up and tucked in and I've seen pictures of her, and in the*

Photo: L.A. Times

majority of the pictures, her hair is up and tucked in. Same thing when I saw her up here. She was going toward her bedroom. I've seen her a couple of times. She was solid once and transparent the other time. So the first time I saw her I was coming out from the upstairs servants' wing. I was just walking through and as I came around the corner, I saw someone standing at the double doors to the master suites, facing away from me. I stopped and I looked because I thought someone came in the mansion. But as I started walking toward her, she turned, she looked at me, turned back away, and she started to walk into the bedroom area. And then she was gone. She disappeared. She physically faded away as she crossed the threshold into the rooms.

And again, I marvel at how composed and straightforward Luz is when she reports her experiences. She offers exacting details in a simple narrative. Calm, cool, and collected.

Another side note… a few years later I contacted Luz after finding the photo. I sent her this text: "Hi there, you mentioned in one of your stories that you would see Lucy with her tied hair up. Did it look like this?" Luz replied, "Yessssss!!! That's her."

"THE FALLING PRISM"
JOHN HUYBRECHT
(Former Park Ranger)

John: *So I'm with my friend Mallie, and her friend Corrine, and we're walking out of the servants' hallway here, right by the butcher's kitchen*

door, and I'm explaining what we tell visitors on tours about Jerry Lewis'
movie, The Disorderly Orderly, *and how they replaced a real wood panel*
on the door with a fake foam panel to soften the blow when Jerry hits
his hand on the door. Then, all of a sudden, I hear this noise, like a rock
just hit the floor by my feet. And at first, I'm thinking it's Ranger Chae
playing a joke. That is my initial reaction. He knew I was in the mansion,
so he's just messing with me. Then I look down and I see it's a prism, this
teardrop looking cut glass decoration from the light fixture hanging above
in the hallway. I looked closely at the light and saw how the wire holding
the prism was literally bent straight down! [the wire hangers on the
lighting fixture look like Christmas ornament hangers but much
stronger]. *How could that have just fallen off? The light is not historic.*
It's from a recent design show. But what are the odds of that falling off
right as I'm walking underneath it? And it's not heavy. There's no reason
why it would ever bend like that.

This detail was confusing to me because I remember having cleaned this
specific light fixture, and there wasn't a wire bent down to where it would
allow that prism decoration to fall. Besides, if the prism was hanging
precariously, I would have fixed it.

John: *How would that just fall off like that? Now, my friend Mallie, she's*
a little bit... What's it called? Clairvoyant? We did some ghost hunting
in college and weird stuff would happen when we were with her. But she
still thinks I was messing with her. She's like, "You made that fall, didn't
you?!" It's ten feet up. I can't reach that. I'm six-feet-four and it's still two
feet above me with my hands up. There's no wind or air blowing. Even if
there was, how's it going to make a prism fall off? What the hell? Right?
Crazy weird shit happens when I'm around Mallie. So when I saw that
Chae wasn't messing with me and it randomly fell, I wasn't shocked, or
like scared, but just, "Wow, that's unexplainable." It's probably the weirdest
thing that's ever happened to me.

"STOP DOING THAT!"

Mary's story relates back to Steven Clark's Basement door experience during the Design Show in 2007 (Chapter 13 – Basement). Prior to that incident, she was struggling with her equipment to shoot her photos of all the rooms. That night, up on the Second-Floor Landing, her frustration culminated with her having a conversation with a spirit.

MARY E. NICHOLS
(Professional Photographer)

Mary: *My batteries were being drained* [by the spirits], *but it was mainly that things just stopped working. I'd be standing there with my spotlights and they would shut off. And these spotlight switches don't turn off by themselves because it's a manual switch. I can understand if there's a problem with electricity and it just goes out. Or the plug is unplugged or whatever. But I would be there ready to shoot, and click, off it would go. And you could literally see the switch* [she mimics the switch clicking off], *and I use these lights all over the world. I mean, switches don't turn off unless you manually do it. But I would watch the switch turn off by itself! The way I was traveling all over the world, you couldn't have anything like that go wrong. I have backup lenses. I had the lights. I have backup everything. So there was no room for mistakes because often times you're in places where you can't get anything fixed. So the equipment must work.*

I've still got those lights that I used at Greystone. I think I have one of those exact spotlights. I'll show you how impossible it is to turn the switch off.

Mary retrieves a spotlight similar to the one she used. Plain and simple: it has a switch that must be pressed to turn the light on or off.

Photo: Chris Keith

Mary: *You just can't turn it off unless you manually do it. That's what's so great about it. But I would watch it turn off. I got so angry that I said out loud, "You've got to stop doing that! We're trying to get some people in here to make some money for the house so the electricity can be fixed. Otherwise, it's going to burn down and you're not going to have a place to live!" And then it stopped. But that's what was so annoying, I'd be standing there and I'd see the switch click right off. It's crazy. It was just crazy!*

We've all seen these switches on electrical appliances. They don't accidentally flip over from on to off. It takes a distinct action to press it and snap it over to the other side. The amount of energy it would take a ghost or spirit to do just that little feat is massive. A very strong entity, perhaps, was messing with her on this night.

"Crashing to the Floor"

Peter Devlin has been nominated for five Academy Awards for production sound mixing. His first gig at Greystone was working on *National Treasure: Book of Secrets* in 2007. Ten years later he was back, working with Patty Jenkins, who was directing her series, *I Am the Night*, in December of 2017. I caught up with him after a long shooting day to talk about that night in 2007 when he accidently recorded an astounding incident in the mansion on the Second-Floor Landing.

PETER J. DEVLIN
(Motion Picture Production Sound Mixer)

Peter: *We were here on the second-floor on* National Treasure 2. *I knew no history of the Doheny mansion. I'd never shot here before and I really hadn't gotten into conversation with any of the rangers here. I was with my boom operator, Kevin, and we both just got a sense that this is such an interesting house—how cool would it be to set a recorder up and record the sounds of the house at night? And it's not that we were ghost hunters or anything like that, or suspected anything, but I don't know what made me think, "Yeah, I'd like to do this." So we set up the microphones on that upper level* [near the portal at the top of the stairs, second-floor landing] *and because we now have hard disk recorders, we knew that we could basically leave a machine recording all night. It used to be if you had a quarter-inch tape* [the industry standard for decades to record sound prior to the advent of digital hard drives], *you could only run for thirty minutes, whereas these recorders can run for twenty-four hours. So that night we wrapped, I think it was nine-thirty, and we covered the cart because I think we were concerned that somebody will see the machinery was still on. So we covered it and put the microphone elevated above the recorder and left it running and we left. So the important thing was not telling the rangers. We didn't want them to know we were going to do that because I didn't want them to give me any insight into anything that was happening here.*

The next morning, I came in, I think our call time was like seven. So I went over to the machine and I started to play back the material from that moment we started recording, which was at ten the night before. You can double speed it and go really fast. So I'm listening and I'm hearing the crew leaving. I'm hearing the rangers making their rounds. I heard the water fountain get turned off. And then I heard the front door close and then the door opened again. I heard some park rangers say, "I think there's a light on. It looks like that equipment's on." And they said, "He must be charging something." And they were coming right close to my microphone. So they obviously saw there was a light on and they're like, "They must know about it." And then they left. And then there was absolute silence. So I was able to fast-forward through the silence and I could hear the sounds of like the city in the distance, an airplane, and just the silence of a house up here in this area. The recorder has a time code value so you can see what time it is. So I was going 10:00, 11:00, 12:00 and every so often I'd stop and play and there would be nothing. So I was going through and it was like one a.m. when I stopped and played it. And I heard this first little movement. But what was eerie was I could hear, because it was so quiet *in here, I could hear our hard-drive humming. So there's like a low level "hummmm." It was the hard drive spinning. So it was vibrating and the vibration is going up the pole to the microphone and you could hear that level. So I'm listening to that and then I hear this kind of movement and I'm like, "Whoa, what's that!?" And then I sensed a perspective change to the next noise, like something fell. And then there was another movement, then what sounded like layout board* [large sheets of cardboard used by movie crews to protect the floor] *sliding. So I'm like, "Okay." And that was followed by two loud movements or something crashing to the floor. And that's when the blood drained from my head and I was like, "Oh my God!" And then there was just quiet again. So I looked to my right at my boom operator and I said, "Kevin, you've got to hear this!" So I played it for Kevin and he's like, "Holy crap!" So we played it for our video assist guy and he's like, "Wow, you got to let everybody hear that!" A ranger* [me] *there heard it and said, "We've got to let Steve Clark hear that!" And then I think the ranger came back and said, "Steve doesn't want to hear it."* [Peter laughs].*

So I think it went around the crew. Nick Cage* [Academy Award-winning actor, Nicholas Cage] *thought it was gunshots. And by now I'm starting to hear the history of the house and I'm like, "Wow, okay." So Nick Cage thought those were gunshots, and Jon Voight* [Academy Award-winning actor] *was like, "Oh, you guys were just messing around." He just didn't believe it. He was a total skeptic. But I think we played it for absolutely everybody on that crew. So that's the only time I've ever done a recording in a house or left a machine running. And since then, I have read the history on the Dohenys and obviously that kind of gives me a little more of a sense of what this house is about and the fact that there is probably… whatever it is, an entity of some type, still here in this house. So yeah, it was just that initial sense of the blood draining from my face was* *something I will never forget!*

In fact, I was working the mansion when Peter came back to the set the next morning. The crew members filed in and it was back to work. Peter's sound cart was now moved into Mr. Doheny's Room or the Master Sitting Room. I walked into the room, obviously not knowing what Peter had captured on his recorder. I was watching the production crew set up. Peter, with his headphones on, suddenly turns to me with an, "Oh shit, something happened!" type of look. I knew there was a chance that something paranormal went down and he was going to question me. Peter asked, "Did you have security here last night?" And I said, "Yes—and the alarm was on." I didn't know Peter well at that time, so I said, "Just tell me. It's okay. Just tell me what happened." And he said, "At 12:58 a.m., here's what happened." He handed me his headphones, I listened, took them off and said, "Oh my God, you got it, you captured it. Awesome!"

The recording starts out quiet and then you hear what sounds like footsteps coming right toward the sound cart, which was set in the portal area. Then there's a small "bang." Then what sounds like layout board is being slid across the floor and it slams into the wall. Then what sounds like a camera case (there are many placed all over the floor on the layout board) is pushed over with another "bang!" And then another larger case is shoved over and it slams down several times—with great force. Then suddenly, it's quiet for the rest of the night. And there were no "footsteps" walking away from the cart/microphone.

Now without footsteps leaving the scene… in theory—when I opened up the mansion at 7 a.m., and walked inside - I should have seen someone standing upstairs by the cases, which were shoved over. But of course, there wasn't anyone there or anywhere in the mansion when I opened up. Unfortunately, we don't have security cameras so we can't check the video and confirm who or what caused this mayhem. The bottom line is this: it's the best recording of random noise we have ever captured in the mansion in my more than twenty years. We've recorded some other great sounds—gunshots, screaming, bangs, and voices—but Peter's recording[2] is the absolute best. Thanks, Peter!

2 Audio recording exists in author's collection.

Chapter 19

Kitchen — Second Floor

Something's wrong, I can feel it. There's someone looking at me.
— Peggy Ackerman
  Greystone Visitor

Photo: Chris Keith

The small upstairs kitchen is adjacent to the Gun Room. A small refrigerator is built into the south wall next to a line of cabinets. Just to the left of the entrance is a classic dumbwaiter, which delivered freshly shot animals to be sent up to this kitchen for butchering. A grooved drain board counter top is on either side of a steel sink. This counter was used for the butchering of meat, allowing the blood to easily drain into the sink.

"GET OUT OF HERE!"

CHARLIE ACKERMAN

(Retired Building Maintenance Supervisor)

> Charlie: *My wife, Peggy, and I had attended an afternoon tea on the terrace. We enjoyed the tea, and if you wanted, you could also tour the first floor of the mansion. Ranger Steve was there and says, "You guys want to go upstairs?" Peggy had never been up there, so we ventured down towards Mr. and Mrs. Doheny's area. And we walked through the kids' rooms [Patrick, Timothy, and Lucy], and I told Peggy all the details I could remember. We went to the gun room and checked out the little upstairs kitchen there. And as we're standing there in the hallway entrance to the kitchen, my wife goes, "I gotta get out of here." I asked her, "What's wrong?" She says, "I don't know. Something's wrong, I can feel it. There's someone looking at me." I'm looking around, and she just took off towards the staircase and I thought, "Okay, what the hell was that?"*

I commented to Charlie that, "Wow, that was sudden. She must have really sensed something." Charlie agrees wholeheartedly.

> Charlie: *Well, she has a high school friend who has psychic abilities. And she contacted her friend Mary afterward and said, "We went to Greystone and I had this really strange feeling. I don't know what it was." And using her psychic abilities, Mary tells her, "Well, you didn't see him?" And Peggy says, "See who?" Mary tells her, "There was a guy standing there at the sink in slacks and a white shirt holding a knife with blood on it and he was looking at you like you better get out of here!" I don't think Peggy's ever been back in the building. That completely freaked her out, I mean, it scared her to the point that she had to leave. She felt it, no doubt, and she just freaked. But she didn't tell Mary any of the details, just that she felt kind of creepy. She didn't tell her that she was in the kitchen and Mary tells her, "Well, he was standing at the sink in front of you." And Peggy wondered, "How*

did you know he was at a sink? I didn't tell you I was in a kitchen." I guess Mary saw the whole thing. And I, of course, saw and felt none of it!

Chapter 20

Gun Room

When the spirit finally did step out of her body, she collapsed.
— Luz Rodriguez
 Retired Greystone Park Ranger

Photo: Chris Keith

You may recognize this room from the movie *Guilty by Suspicion,* starring Robert DeNiro and Annette Bening. The movie, filmed in 1991, dramatized the Hollywood blacklisting scandal of the 1950s.

In 1928, the Gun Room was known as the sitting room and playroom. All the toys for the four boys were kept inside a large closet. In later years, when the boys were grown, the room was converted into an office and used by their stepfather, Leigh Battson. He remodeled the closet as a display cabinet for his gun collection.

Greystone Historical Report

"We used to sail gliders and stuff off this porch. They would sail all the way down into Beverly Hills." —Timothy Doheny

---

"INCREDIBLE FORCE"

On the east side of the room, the windows open to a small balcony. When summoned, the animal handlers would release deer and other animals for the men to shoot from this balcony.

CHAD NELSON
(Retired Park Ranger)

> Chad: *I've experienced doors slamming shut in the house. One time, it almost took off my fingers when one of the big heavy doors upstairs from the gun room just slammed on me. There were no windows open, upstairs, downstairs, or anywhere in house. There was no draft. The door was wide open and just went—WHAM!!! It slammed with incredible force. I mean it slammed! If it* [the spirit] *could slam a door with that much force, it must have had major psychokinetic energy.[1] He sure could move things! It wasn't like it just creeped shut. It was like a bodybuilder, using all of their strength, slammed it shut. It was amazing how fast that door moved and shut.*

---

1 Psychokinetic energy refers to spirits having enough influence to move physical objects without the use of a physical body.

Greystone Historical Report

"Battson put in the gun case for shotguns, probably in the forties right after the war or in the fifties. This used to be a big closet where everybody put his own stuff."

—Timothy Doheny

Chapter 21

Patrick's Bedroom

I want out! I really don't want to do this anymore!
— Krizza Elisabeth
Greystone Visitor

Photo: Chris Keith

In 1928, this bedroom was sparsely dressed with two small beds and two nightstands for Patrick, who was five years old. When the mansion was remodeled in 1945, the majority of the room's furnishings were decorated with red fabric. It was then referred to as the "cherry guest room."

"BAD, BAD EXPERIENCE"

STEVEN CLARK

(Retired Park Ranger Supervisor)

> Steven: *A film crew was at the mansion and literally went through three generators that either broke down or malfunctioned. Two generators just went out that night and they were also having electrical problems.*

A friend of mine, who worked for the movie studios in transportation for almost forty years, told me that generators would occasionally break down, but three in one night? According to my buddy, Frank, "That does not happen."

> Steven: *This was the same day that the apple box* [a wooden box used on movie sets] *slid across the floor upstairs right in front of a grip, who came running downstairs, all worked up. That was a bad, bad experience. It kind of felt like the house was protecting itself, you know?*

"DISRESPECT"

CLETE KEITH

Steve Clark's story jogged my memory of that day. When I began working on a regular basis up at Greystone (about 2000) that production company was filming a Sprite commercial. It was my first chance to see a film crew up at the mansion. It was a large crew (crews on a major production average anywhere from sixty to two hundred people). The crew was running around frantically—a film set is always controlled chaos—or just chaos, and it was one of Steve Clark's first jobs as a ranger to oversee a film shoot. He was frazzled because nobody was listening to his instructions. Film crews are notorious for invading a location and doing what they want, how they want, and whenever they want. I understand they have a job to do in a finite amount of time (and time is money!), but they invariably push rules of a location aside to complete their job. So here's Steve—a new ranger trying to figure out the process of film production and all the ramifications that come with it—and he sees that the crew is out of control and disrespecting the mansion. He was trying to tell them to be careful—don't drop things on the floor, be respectful of the estate, this is a historic landmark—but it was falling on deaf ears.

As I came up the west courtyard, this guy came running out of the mansion yelling, "I'm not going back in there! Fuck this place!" Everybody working on the commercial was wondering what the hell happened. What's wrong with him? We found out he was upstairs in Patrick's room, with some of the grip equipment. He was on the floor putting cables away, when one of the crates moved by itself across the room right in front of him. That's when he freaked and ran out of the mansion yelling he'd never go back inside. It seems like the spirits probably had had enough of the disrespect of the mansion and decided to let him know who was in charge! It certainly wasn't the first, nor last time, an incident like that has happened.

"Where the Devils Play"

If you ask most folks, "Where do the Devils play?" they will probably tell you on the ice at The Prudential Center in Newark, New Jersey. But according to Andrea Flores' mother, she'll tell you they play in the sunshine of Beverly Hills, California, at a place called Greystone Mansion.

ANDREA FLORES
(Janitorial Services)

> Andrea: *This happened on a Saturday, and I was filling in for Elva who normally cleans that day. I was on my way to Greystone and I was on the phone with my mom. It was around seven in the morning. I told her I was coming to work to fill in for a co-worker. I never told her where I was going*

[Andrea works at several locations]. *When I got here on the property and went into the mansion, we kept talking when all of a sudden, I could hear a child playing and laughing. I heard it and I didn't say anything. Then my mom asked me, "Where are you at?" I told her I was at work. In the background on the phone she also heard the child laughing and playing. So I looked around because the park was closed and didn't open until ten. There was no one outside and we could still hear the child, who sounded very, very young, maybe five or six years old. I can't say if it was a boy or a girl, but the child was happy. But then my mom freaks out and asks me, "Where are you at? Are you at that mansion, where the devils play?" She got mad at me because I didn't want to leave the mansion. I kept doing my job, working until I finished. I was on the second floor inside the restroom with the fishes painted on the wall* [Patrick and Timothy's connecting bathroom] *and I went across the hall to the window to see if maybe it was someone in the courtyard. There was no one, but we both could still hear them. The laughter was there for a while, like three minutes or more. Because at first, I wasn't paying attention, I just thought that someone was there, maybe people were coming in early. Or maybe some children snuck inside. That has happened before. But now it sounded like the child was inside the house. At first, I thought it was outside, because I was talking with my mom on my earphones. But when I took one earphone out, I could tell the laughter and playing was inside because there was an echo to it. I never did find the child. What or where it was I still don't know.*

"HIDE AND SEEK"

This is a continuation of the tour I gave Krizza and her friend, Tonje (Chapter One - Grand Entry and Chapter Five - Murder Room). As you may recall, Krizza felt energy at the Grand Entry right when we walked in, and she also felt footsteps approach her in the Murder Room—and her purse was pulled. Here is the third experience on the tour: We're walking up on the Second-Floor Landing, going west from the Gun

Room. I was walking ahead of Krizza, talking to Tonje about stories of the mansion and pointing out who in the family had lived in the rooms. Krizza walked by Patrick's room and all of a sudden, our tour came to an abrupt end. This interview was months after the incident. I'm talking on the phone to Krizza in Norway, and I could hear her anxiety level rise as she relived this moment. She still finds it hard to believe.

KRISSA ELIZABETH
(Visitor)

> Krizza: *Oh my God. I remember you pointed to the left saying people lived here and blah, blah, blah* [shows how impactful my tours are!], *and then I saw something from the other side of the hall—on the left. I slowly turned and I saw someone. I don't know if she was playing hide and seek with me, but she, or that thing, was just... I mean, I don't know. I saw something. I don't know what age. It just looked like someone playing hide and seek with me. I was looking that way and she peeked out. Then she hid again. She came out again, and then she was just gone. And that's when I wanted out. I don't know exactly what it looked like. It was kind of blurry, but it was also something white. It looked like a girl when I looked at it, but kind of not. Do you understand what I mean? And her hair was to the shoulders. And she was really cute, but maybe not, because it was scary. I think her hair was, I'm not sure, but in my head, I want to say blonde, or light brown. I didn't want to look at it, but my eyes were just drawn that way. It was so friendly, but I still didn't want to stay anymore. But I was really drawn to look at it. And then you said something, and I jumped and said, "I want out! I really don't want to do this anymore!" And then you told me about this girl* [Chapter Two – "My Name is Emily"], *and then she was just gone. All the energy was gone, too. And I felt exhausted. I was so exhausted. I just wanted to go. It felt like I'd run 10,000 miles and did 100 pushups because I was so exhausted. When we went out of the building, I was so tired, and when you drove us home, I don't remember anything because I was so tired. I think I fell asleep when we got home. It drained my energy. It really did.*

This is not the first time I've heard about the exhaustion and the draining of someone's energy. In fact, it's very common. Those who have researched this phenomenon have theorized that in order for the spirits to manifest or interact with living beings, they need energy to do so. That energy can be amassed from batteries, electrical equipment, or in this case, the spirit felt that Krizza has the ability to connect with spirits on the other side, so she used Krizza's energy to physically show herself and try to communicate. And the spirit did that in a playful way, although it turned out to be more than Krizza could handle.

> Krizza: *It was so much energy. But I think it's a good spirit. I don't think she would do anything bad, unless you did something bad. I was with Tonje last night and we were saying that we have to go to L.A. again and she was like, "Yeah, because we have to go back to Greystone Mansion." And I was like, no, I really don't want to!*

Chapter 22

Lucy's Bedroom

I felt like hands rubbing against my thighs and my knee area. I stood still and the chills just started going up through my body.
— RAUL ESPINOZA
    GREYSTONE TOUR DOCENT

Photo: Chris Keith

In 2001, the movie *Town & Country*, starring Warren Beatty and Diane Keaton, used this room for Andie MacDowell's childhood bedroom.

The Dohenys had four boys and one girl. The daughter's name was Lucy Estelle Doheny. Her name proved to be a mouthful for her youngest brother, Timothy, who couldn't pronounce Lucy Estelle. The best he could say was "Dickie Dell," and the nickname stuck. In 1929, when Dickie Dell was thirteen, the Doheny family moved into Greystone Mansion. Her combination bedroom, dressing room, and bath were located in the center of the Second-Floor Landing. She married in April of 1937, and by 1945, her bedroom was turned into a guest room.

The majority of experiences involving Lucy's room are really almost childlike energy. Now, that's not to say that if you are in this room alone at night, or even during the day when the lights are off, that it can't look or feel creepy, haunted mansion-ish. That's certainly how Martin felt.

"REALLY SCARED"

MARTIN J. PEREZ

(Janitorial Services)

> Martin: *Ranger Dan told me, "Hey, Martin, I need you to go upstairs and clean all the rooms on the second floor." I said, "Okay, not a problem." As I was cleaning, I passed by the middle room* [Lucy's], *and there was nothing in there. A few hours later I passed by again and I noticed a chair. It was sitting in the center of the room. And I was like, "That's really odd. Where'd that come from?" And it really creeped me out. It honestly felt like someone was sitting there. I asked Dan, "Did you put the chair in here?" Dan was clear, "No, I haven't stepped foot in the house until now." So I'm not sure who would have placed it in there since no one was in the house. It really scared me.*

"Find the Light"

It was June of 2019 and I was working the Friends of Greystone's (FOG) Open House event, where the public pays a fee to tour the mansion both upstairs and downstairs and that money goes toward the restoration of the mansion. Docents are in all the rooms to answer questions and keep a watchful eye on things. The Servants' Wing, the Attic, and Basement are off limits. On this day, one of the FOG members told me I should take advantage of the gathering and talk to some docents who've experienced the paranormal here at Greystone. She gave me several names.

I approached Raul and asked him if he wouldn't mind telling me what happened to him. Little did I know, it had just taken place! So he was still rather stunned and overwhelmed.

RAUL ESPINOZA
(Tour Docent)

> Raul: *I'm standing in Lucy's dressing room area in front of the bay window, talking with one of the guests who was asking me how to use her new iPhone. She was an older lady. All of a sudden, I felt like hands rubbing against my thighs and my knee area. I stood still and the chills just started going up through my body. You should know, I'm really sensitive to this kind of energy—but the lady was totally unaware of what was happening. So I'm thinking to myself, if I'm feeling her why isn't the lady feeling her? Because I was standing very close to this woman. Actually, right next to her and she felt nothing. And then the sensation went away. The lady with the phone said, "Thanks for helping me," and continued on her way. And then the sensation came back again! I started praying and I couldn't move. Then the anxiety started coming over me, but I just started breathing deeply because I was frightened.*

I asked Raul if he had heard any stories about Greystone.

Raul: *I had heard some things about what happened in the home, but that wasn't in my thoughts at all. But at one point, a tour guest was at the door and I guess they saw me speaking to myself. I was saying* [to the spirit], *"You're welcome here, but please find the light. It's time for you to go. If you're restless, let's pray that you find the light and that you find comfort and joy in the other world in the name of the Lord." I'm sure that person was wondering who I was talking to. Then there was silence and it didn't feel scary or anything. But there was no gust of wind going through the hallways, nothing. It was clearly a playful touching of my knees to my thighs. I just stood still like, I didn't want to freak out! But I did feel a buzz—an energy from that entity. Like a vibration. Very small, and it felt like I was connected to a generator! I'm getting chills just telling you this!*

I'm wondering if you picked this up in Raul's interview. I realized a very important detail when I was listening to the recording. Here it is again:

Raul: *You should know, I'm really sensitive to this kind of energy—but the lady was totally unaware of what was happening. So I'm thinking to myself, if I'm feeling her, why isn't the lady feeling her?*

"Her." Raul offered a subtle but monumental detail—a casual and natural gender to the entity. Her? And the entity was rubbing his thigh and knee area. Obviously, a low touch on Raul's body. A child? Her? A little girl? It seems to point to Emily, but who can say it was her for sure.

"Tug"

Every person is different, right? Some folks freak out and simply cannot fathom what just happened to them in the paranormal realm. And that's cool, it's happened to me. Others, like Eleanor in the upcoming story, just roll with the punches. But notice how seamlessly Eleanor absorbs what happened, accepts it, and then positions the emotional impact it has on her as if it all happened in the "normal" physical world.

ELEANOR SCHRADER

(Tour Guest)

> Eleanor: *I was on a Halloween tour of the mansion a few years ago, and I was standing in Lucy's, room, and I felt a tug on my ear. And it was a good, substantial tug. But I sensed a very playful tug, and there was no one else around me. I didn't want to freak anybody out who was on the tour with me or scream or anything like that, so I went to one of the docents and said, "I just felt a little tug on my ear." And he said, "Yeah," as if he meant, "We hear this a lot." But it was just a tug. A playful tug. Like a someone saying, "I'm here! I'm here!"*

"SLIPPED"

Psychic and medium, Chris Fleming, known for his television and public appearances, claims he's been having psychic and paranormal experiences since the age of four. He is currently a renowned and sought-after public speaker at various events, colleges, and universities about wide-ranging paranormal topics. On this day, Chris, three of his friends and I entered Lucy's room. He stood silent for a moment and then walked over to the bay window and sat down. Chris was suddenly overwhelmed with emotion. He bent over and held his head in his hands as if he were distraught. I observed him quietly until he suddenly looked up directly at me.

CHRIS FLEMING

(Psychic / Medium)

> Chris: *Something happened here. What happened here? I'm either extremely depressed or I'm really sad. I'm seeing people walk past this door* [to the second-floor hallway and landing], *but I'm not sure what happened here. Did something happen here?*

I told Chris, from what we understand, Lucy was playing with one of her friends. We don't know the friend's name, although, you may recall I was told her name was "Emily" by the woman who approached me in the Grand Hall. The story that's been told down through the years is that Lucy's friend somehow fell out of the bay window and down to the slate terrace below and died. We don't know how or why she fell. The rumor, which I have never believed, was that she had been pushed out the window by Lucy. Chris Fleming then transitions into a meditative state.

> Chris: *Are you there? Are you around us?* [pause] *There you are. I feel you. What happened to you? How did you fall? Oh. Okay.*

Chris finished the conversation with her silently and then looked back over to me.

> Chris: *She and Lucy were playing 'who could lean out the window the furthest.' Her hand slipped and she fell to the ground below.*

Was this real? Did Chris really connect with the little girl? Who can really say for sure, but his track record speaks volumes. And I must say, what transpired with Chris in Lucy's room really affected my outlook on the paranormal and will always stay with me.

Here's what we know: Lucy's friend died at the mansion and the belief is her spirit has been seen in the mansion and on the surrounding grounds at least five times since I've been working at Greystone. Did she die falling out the window of this room? As I mentioned, this story has been passed down to us over the years. But others have different stories to tell...

Chapter 23

Master Sitting Room

I'm having difficulty breathing. My chest is getting heavy.
— Anonymous Beverly Hills Police Officer

Photo: Chris Keith

In Carl Reiner's 1984 movie, *All of Me,* starring Steve Martin and Lily Tomlin, the criminal break-in scene was filmed in this room.

This room is often called Mr. Doheny's room. It wasn't a bedroom, but in the short time he was living at Greystone before his death, it was his sitting room. Some have suggested that it was his office as well. The dark, olive-colored, swirled marble fireplace matches the motif in his master bath.

When Mrs. Doheny redecorated the mansion in 1945, she turned this sitting room into a display room for her carved crystal and porcelain figurines.

"TEMPERATURE CHANGE"

This is my favorite room in the mansion. The wood inlay pattern on the floor is extraordinary—it's beautifully crafted. The window on the southwest corner of the room is my go-to spot. The view is amazing—you can see from the skyline of downtown Los Angeles to the Pacific Ocean. I can only imagine the magnificent view back in 1928 when the tall pine trees on the front lawn were small, freshly planted and the downtown Beverly Hills buildings were sparse. I walked inside this room with Brooke to have our conversation.

BROOKE PICONE
(Former Camp Counselor)

> Brooke: *This incident happened somewhere between nine and ten at night way before the new heating and air condition was put in the mansion. We* [Brooke and Ranger Brehnen Knight] *were in the house casually walking in and out of rooms, just talking. I was wearing sweatpants, a sweatshirt, and a heavy army jacket, like a bomber jacket. So I was dressed warm. We walked in here and we're talking and it's room temperature, just like it is now, mid-sixties, and then we walked out and went down the hallway toward the second-floor hallway landing. About five to ten minutes later, we walked back into this room and I'm literally standing right here in the middle of the room and I said, "God, it's freezing in here." I just described to you what I was wearing. There was no reason to be freezing, right? It literally felt as if we stepped into a walk-in freezer. I mean, it felt like it dropped to forty degrees or something and I mentioned that to Brehnen and he said, "Well, they say that's usually when there's a*

spirit in the room." And the reason it was so pronounced to me is because we were just in here ten minutes before and it was totally comfortable—and then to walk back in here ten minutes later and it's absolutely freezing? I'd never heard that about spirits in the room. It was just so drastic.

"THREE TIMES!"

Barbara is one of my favorite people. We've been friends for more than twenty years. She worked at Greystone for many years prior to my working for the City of Beverly Hills. She was working there when Greystone first allowed weddings on the property. This is a story of her night during the first wedding ever held inside Greystone Mansion.

BARBARA ROSENMAN
(Retired Recreation Specialist)

Barbara: *On July 2, 1989, actor James Woods was married at Greystone. Among those attending the ceremony were fellow actors James Garner, Robert Downey Jr., Sarah Jessica Parker, director Jonathan Kaplan and rock stars Don Henley and Bob Seger. At the end of the evening when it came to cleaning up and locking the house, the rangers went through and made sure all the windows were locked and everything was secured. We're standing in the west court and we looked up at Mr. Doheny's room and one of the bay windows was open. They're two windows up there and one window was open. The rangers looked at one another, and one said, "Well, someone must have left it open." They went in, closed the window, came back down, looked up, and the window was open again! And they did that three times. Finally, their attitude was, "Okay, you know what? Something's going on. Someone doesn't want that window closed." And they locked the house up and left.*

At times like this, when a window remains open and the alarm cannot be set, they have to override the system and force arm the alarm. That way the alarm will be set even though the damn window won't stay closed! But I love the rangers' final attitude—sometimes, you have to say, "If you can't beat 'em, join 'em."

"MURDER ROOM BELOW"

ANONYMOUS

(Beverly Hills Police Officer)

Police Officer: *My first time ever inside the house I'd been on the force maybe all of two years, and having no idea of any of the history, I was standing in a room upstairs and my chest was feeling pressure. It felt like someone sitting on my chest. Now, unbeknownst to me, the murder room was right below me. I had no idea. When I walked in, I was like, "Whoa!" And at this time, it was with Ranger Danny. He had taken "Bob", another officer, [not his real name] and I in the house and Bob says, "Oh, have you ever been in here?" And I said, "No." And he's like, "Do you know anything about the house?" I was like, "No. No idea. I have no clue." So we're walking through and I just started breathing deep. I'm like, "Man." And Danny wonders if I'm okay, and I said, "I dunno. Just tough to breathe. I mean, maybe it's just an old house or whatever." So we walk upstairs and go in the kitchen and there's no problem. I go everywhere else and we get to Mr. Doheny's room, which again, I know nothing about. No history of anything, and we walk in here and Danny's telling us about the movies shot here, all very G-rated things. Nothing about the killings. But I think Bob had set Dan up to see my reaction.*

Our police officer is referring here to the fact that "Bob" knew that he's very keen when sensing the paranormal and told Dan Hernandez ahead of time.

Police Officer: *And I'm on the top floor having a tough time, "Oh man, I don't know what it is, but man, it's my... I'm having difficulty breathing. My chest is getting really heavy." And they're like, "Do you get any weird vibes in here?" And I said, "No, I'm just... like... it's really hard to breathe." But like I said, I didn't know the murder room was directly below us!*

Was the officer feeling a spirit in that room? Was he feeling the energy from the Murder Room below? Or was it the energy of the spirits in the mansion? People who are sensitive are said to be able to pick up on many different aspects, such as temperature fluctuations, energy shifts, and the presence of spirits in a haunted location. This officer was convinced that the cause of the pressure in his chest was the energy from the room below. He very well might be right.

Chapter 24

Massage Room

She made eye contact and then she disappeared.

— Luz Rodriguez
   Retired Greystone Park Ranger

Photo: Chris Keith

The Massage Room is located between Mr. Doheny's bathroom and the Master Bedroom. Originally, in 1928, this was Mr. Doheny's dressing room. Concealed behind a panel on the wall is a massage table that unfolds into place. Years later, in 1945, when Mrs. Doheny refurbished the mansion, a chest of drawers—decorated with two small lamps and framed hunting scenes—was added to this room against the west wall.

"Protect Him"

On my tour with psychic/medium Chris Fleming and several of his friends, we entered the Massage Room just before noon. Chris pulled out his spirit box, the same device Ranger Dan and I used in the Living Room to connect with Ned Doheny and Hugh Plunkett. As a reminder, this device uses radio frequency sweeps to generate white noise through which, researchers say, spirits may communicate. The visit to the Massage Room was midway through our overall tour and Chris immediately sat on the window sill. He took out the device, turned it on, and asked, "How many spirits are in the mansion?" Through the box we heard, "Seven."[1]

I conducted this brief interview on the phone with Chris who lives in Chicago.

CHRIS FLEMING
(Psychic / Medium)

I asked Chris, in the course of his communication with the spirits, with the spirit box running, if he remembered mentioning me.

> Chris: *Yes, I said something like, "Well, you must know, Clete? He's been here quite some time. Do you know, Clete?" Then they said your name twice. I remember saying to you, "See, they know you."*

I remember it blew my mind. My name is an odd name at best. Certainly not a regular name, and it came through the spirit box twice. It's nice to be recognized!

> Chris: *They're showing you respect is my interpretation. And then I said, "You understand he works here? Just be friends with him. Don't do anything to him. Protect this place. Protect him." But I heard your name twice.*

---

1 Audio recording is non-existent.

This, to me, was verification that, if indeed, there are spirits here at Greystone, they're aware I'm here, and hopefully aware that I'm here to help protect the mansion. And to know that both Ned and Hugh communicated through the spirit box (Chapter Four - Living Room and Minstrels' Gallery), and now my name came through, is astounding. At this point, I thought, "What a cool experience." Little did I know that things would change drastically on this day with Chris when we ventured into the attic.

"DID YOU SEE HER?!"

This is one of my favorite stories of Greystone. It's just so crazy and funny, but must have been so frightening at the same time. Luz remembered exactly how it went down.

LUZ RODRIGUEZ
(Retired Park Ranger)

> Luz: *It was between one and two in the afternoon. I was here with a film production guy. They had accidently stained the white carpet in here with what looked like red wine so he came back to clean it. He is here in the center of the room on his hands and knees scrubbing it off. I walk into Mrs. Doheny's room to look around while he is working. When I walk back in to check on him, he is pale white, staring right at me. Then out of the corner of my eye I can see someone else in the doorway. It is a see-through apparition. You can see right through her to the hallway. It's the same woman I've seen before.*

I confirmed with Luz that this was the same woman/apparition she witnessed on the Second-Floor Landing detailed in Chapter 18.

Luz: *Exactly… and she looks over right at me. Once she makes eye contact with me, she simply disappears. She was wearing a dress. It's a light-colored dress. Maybe the pattern was floral? It may have even been polka dots. She had pearls, a pearl necklace and pearl earrings, and her hair was up and tucked in. It's almost like her attitude with the production guy is "What are you doing?" But then, when she saw me, she was like, "Oh, okay." And she left. It was just that strange. But the guy was pale white! He just stood up suddenly and said, "Is this good enough?" I said, "No, I'm sorry, you have to get it all out." And he was like, "Okay, but can I take a break?" He went outside and smoked a cigarette and then came back inside to finish the job. I mean, I wasn't gonna let him leave until the job was done!* [she laughs].

Now imagine you're cleaning the carpet and you glance over and there's a translucent woman staring you down. What would you have done? Knowing me, I'd have to scrub out a new stain on the carpet. And I love the fact that Luz told him to stay and continue cleaning. What a great Park Ranger! Imagine what was going through this poor chap's mind when he came back, got on his knees, and started scrubbing again. You can bet his back wasn't to the door. Luz continues.

Luz: *When he came back in, he asked me, "Did you see that woman? Did you see her?!" And I said, "Yeah, I saw her." He said, "Good, I just want to make sure it wasn't just me." And I said, "No, I saw her. I'm not sure who she is, but she may have been Lucy Doheny."*

How many of us, like the man cleaning the carpet, would probably have been thinking, "Lucy, who?! Oh, who gives a shit! There was a ghost standing in the doorway looking straight at me! Get me the hell out of here!"

Chapter 25

Master Bedroom

Excuse me, did any of you just hear someone yell out my name?
— Michelle W.
Former Greystone Recreation Supervisor

Photo: Chris Keith

This was Pat and Richard Nixon's bedroom in the Oliver Stone film, *Nixon*, starring Joan Allen and Anthony Hopkins.

In 1928, this bedroom had what appeared to be a full-sized bed—not the larger-size bed one would expect for such a large room. With two small nightstands on either side, and a princess canopy, it was decorated with a moderately feminine touch. This set-up was replaced in 1945 with two large dressers and a hand-carved Louis XVI bed. On the wall behind the bed was a hand-painted Chinoiserie decoration.

The reason Lucy Doheny selected this room as the Master Bedroom was so she could keep a close eye on who was coming up the drive. Any visitors would enter through the 501 Doheny Drive gate, and drive up the hill by the south lawn, winding up to the west courtyard, which is right outside her windows. This also allowed her to see the children coming home after school. It was the perfect lookout.

"THE BUTLER?"

CLETE KEITH

I was relatively new at Greystone. The year was 2003. At that time, we hardly let anyone into the mansion. I was walking through the west courtyard when I saw a young couple looking up at Mrs. Doheny's Room. They looked at me and said, "Excuse me, do you know how we can get a tour inside the house?" I explained that we don't offer tours inside the house unless it's an event or it's been scheduled with the rangers in advance. And they said, "Oh, okay, because we saw the person inside there and we thought it was a period piece kind of tour where you walked from room to room through the mansion." I told them that I wasn't sure what they were talking about. And they reiterated, "Well, we just looked up at the window (Mrs. Doheny's bedroom window that overlooks the west courtyard), and we saw a man standing there, so we thought he was part of the tour." Obviously, they piqued my interest, "You saw a man standing there in the window?" Their response was detailed, "We did… and he looked like he was dressed almost like a butler in an old, like twenties or thirties suit, with a tie. And he was staring down at us." I'm sure they must have seen my surprise. Had I known then that years later I'd be writing a book on the paranormal at Greystone, I would have grilled them on all the physical aspects relating to the so-called "Butler." When they walked away, I kept thinking, there's no one in the mansion. Who could they have seen in that window? I physically checked through the entire mansion, especially in Mrs. Doheny's room, and there was nobody to be found.

"Warning"

Michelle agreed to visit Greystone to chat about her story when she was employed by the City of Beverly Hills. She was a recreation supervisor at the park in the early 2000s. And again, back during this time, no one was allowed inside the mansion unless it was sanctioned for filming or an event. Along with overseeing Greystone Park, Michelle was also involved in the park's restoration and upgrades. I don't recall speaking to Michelle back then about paranormal activity inside the mansion— either in general, or of any personal experiences. Regardless, I'm not sure she would have believed anything I offered in the way of spirits roaming the mansion. She's a straight shooter and all business, so what happened to her must have really awakened her to the possibility of the paranormal at Greystone.

MICHELLE W.

(Former Recreation Supervisor)

> Michelle: *I was standing in Mrs. Doheny's bedroom with former ranger, Chris W, Charles Ackerman* [Building Maintenance Supervisor], *and Ann, who was a historic liaison helping us to refinish the bedroom floor back to what it was initially. The mansion was closed to the public. I locked up very carefully behind me when we came in. We were standing in a circle inside the room when I hear, right next to me, "Michelle… Michelle!" twice. But it was a hollow sounding "Michelle." Kind of like you might hear when your hairdryer is on and you hear someone call your name. The others just kept chatting away and I said, "Excuse me, did any of you just hear someone yell out my name?" And they said they didn't hear anything.*

So I said, "You know, I heard something, so I'm just going to go walk around and see." So I go out into the hallway and there's actually a person in there. And I said, "Oh, I'm sorry, the mansion's closed to the public." And he said, "Oh, I didn't know. I got in through the front door." And I said, "Are you by yourself?" He was and I said, "Have you said anything out loud?" He said, "No." So I escorted him outside. But I always felt like it was someone warning me like "Hey, someone's in our house." I never did find out how he got inside, since I had closed and locked the door. But I always felt welcomed here. Like there was a weird feeling of, thank you for taking care of this house. Thank you for caring about this house. I felt such a connection to it. Such a warmth. So that just sort of solidified what I was already thinking. Like they appreciated me being here.

"I Am Lucy"

CLETE KEITH

Hearing voices from Mrs. Doheny's room always reminds me of bringing Chris Fleming into the mansion. We were on the Second-Floor Landing, and as we began to walk into her bedroom, Chris stopped and had a very visceral reaction. I stood back. I rarely said anything about spirits to him during our entire day of investigation. I allowed him to experience the situation and verbalize what he felt was taking place without me interjecting anything. I didn't want to lead him in any direction or suggest any details.

Once we walked inside the Master Bedroom, Chris said, "We have someone here with us." Chris believed it was the woman he saw in the window of the Boys' Wing when he first arrived. He pulls out his recorder and says, "I know you're here with us. And so now that you know that I know you're here, would you tell me who you are? Could you tell me what is your name?" We stood there for a short moment in silence. He shut off the recorder and played it back. We listened and a female voice responded. Chris turned to me and said, "I am Darcy? Is her name Darcy?" When I listened to it, I knew exactly what she was saying. I said, "No, what she's saying is, 'I am Lucy.' That was Mrs. Doheny first name and this is her bedroom." So Chris said, "Lucy, it's so nice to meet you and thank you for allowing us to be in your home. You have such a beautiful house. Thank you for letting us be here."

At the beginning of this tour with Chris Fleming, I kept thinking that until I get some kind of an actual response on these recorders, it's hard to believe what is being said. Just because you say you're talking to spirits doesn't make it true. I've already mentioned that we've had a long line of "psychic mediums" at the mansion and many were not accurate at all. But with Chris, it was an entirely different story. When you actually hear a voice out of a recorder,[1] trying to communicate with you in real time, your overall perception changes completely. I wouldn't have believed it if I hadn't heard it myself. It was truly amazing.

---

1 Audio recording is non-existent.

Chapter 26

Master Dressing Room

I mean a freakin' female's voice coming out of nowhere? I can't explain it and it would be wrong to rationalize it, rather than just accept that something insane happened.

— PATRICK FERRIS
 GREYSTONE PARK RANGER

Photo: Chris Keith

This location served as the dressing room for Joan Allen, portraying Pat Nixon, in the Oliver Stone-directed film, *Nixon*, also starring Anthony Hopkins and Ed Harris.

Throughout the years, this room was furnished with a dressing table and two small lamps that rested in front of a mirror. They were replaced with different styles by Mrs. Doheny several times. A large bank of built-in shelves with mirrored doors lines the one wall of the room. Another wall ushers you to a large closet with mirrored doors.

Both of these locations still have the original wallpaper hangings from 1927. Having worked here long enough, one is bound to hear rumors of secret hiding places. With that in mind, several rangers were exploring this room and tapping on the wall panels with the hope of finding mysterious and obscure hiding places. To their amazement, the wall near the entrance to her walk-in closet sounded hollow. Using a utility knife, the rangers carefully cut around the molding—and in fact, after all the years of renovation and many coats of paint—they discovered that a seam had been sealed. Once the paint was removed, they found a door to a hidden wall panel. When the panel was opened, they uncovered a jewelry safe with a combination lock.

For those who might be curious—like all of us—the safe was unlocked and… drum roll… it was empty.

Upon entering the walk-in closet, this area is also decorated with the original 1927 pink wallpaper. Straight ahead is a large walk-in safe, where Mrs. Doheny kept her fur coats.

Photo: Clete Keith

"YOU MISSED ONE"

Before I even thought about writing this book, Patrick told me this story and it was fascinating. To see Patrick freaking out about what happened to him was alarming. It was inconceivable to him, as it was to me. As I questioned him for specifics, I could see he was experiencing a type of

Post-Traumatic Stress with what had taken place. We all handle stress in different ways. In Patrick's case, it appears there was a period of time after this incident where he went into a state of denial as to what he encountered. He buried it in the recesses of his mind as if it never happened. When Patrick opened up to me about the incident, I asked him to join me in the mansion and spend some time in the Master Dressing Room with the hope that it would help Patrick recall and recreate the events. He agreed.

PATRICK FERRIS
(Park Ranger)

Patrick: *It was dusk. Every night, if there's an event inside, there are always lights to turn off. My ritual is to start on the bottom floor, the right-hand side, which is the living room, doll room, murder room, and all that. I wind back, check the restrooms, continue down the hallway through the card room, library, and so forth. Then I wrap around and go up to the second floor to check on the servants' wing and I head back through to the second-floor landing and go to the master wing. And on this evening, everything is normal. I don't remember feeling anything unusual. You know, every once in a while, very rarely, I'll feel something and get creeped out at night—especially at dusk. But this time I wasn't feeling anything. I already checked all the bedrooms and I knew the boys' wing had no one in there all day. So I normally don't check that. If there's a light, you're going to see it on the way out. So I'm heading through the master wing and the last room is Mrs. Doheny's dressing room. So pretty simple. There's a couple of lights on. There's the bathroom and these lights inside the shelving units. So I'm turning the lights off and I remember exactly where I'm standing, it was right here in the center of the room facing the door that opens to the hallway, and I was about four feet away from the door right here. You know how you can kind of gauge where a voice is coming from? In my left ear, I suddenly hear, and it wasn't like a whisper, it was a middle-aged female's voice, no inflection or anything, a normal voice say in my left ear, "You missed..." It wasn't creepy and I'm facing right here thinking about*

287

the second word, "missed"—"You missed," but there's no one there. And in your brain...

Patrick is struggling to find the right words. Sentences are started with a thought and then he stops abruptly—he can't find a way to express a feeling that he's never experienced.

Patrick: *I remember crouching a little bit, like this* [like a protection stance], *and I did a little swivel turn on my left foot, right to where the voice came from. My arms are out like this in a defensive maneuver, because you're freaked out, you know? Imagine not seeing something, but hearing it, and nothing is there. Nothing. Now I don't remember thinking anything really, just staring, freaking out. My brain was in overdrive— I'm trying to process. "Okay, you just heard a voice... No, you didn't, there's nothing there... but you heard a voice... no you didn't... there's nothing there. So probably for a half a minute, I'm just staring trying to not freak out as I'm freaking out. But when she said, "You missed..." and I'm just kind of freaking out, because by then it's already registered that there's no one there." The voice then finishes the sentence by saying, "One." And I start thinking, what the hell did I just hear? "You missed one?" I'm turning off lights and I hear what!? That "I missed one?!" And then on top of all of that, no one has died in here, so I'm thinking, "What? Why here in this room?"*

I had to interrupt here once again because the fact that Patrick says, "no one has died in here" doesn't mean that souls or spirits from other locations within or outside the mansion can't drop in and say hello. For example, it was told to me by several rangers and a city worker, all who have since retired, that the ghost of Gypsy Rose Lee, a famous American burlesque entertainer known for her striptease act in the 1930s and 1940s, was said to have been seen wandering the grounds of Greystone. You can still see her house directly above the upper parking lot. Point being, it's not mandatory for spirits to only remain in the location in which they've died.

Patrick: *I immediately think no way that just happened. I'm going to go through, turn off lights, and I'm going to be calm. But at the same time I'm thinking I need to go through the whole house again—"You missed one"— but I normally don't miss turning off the lights. I'm pretty good about it. Okay, my brain is pretty frazzled. So I go through the master wing, here, the massage room, this room and everything is turned off. It's dusk, so it's actually becoming more and more dark as I head back into Lucy's dressing room. I check her dressing room shelves; they're cracked open a little and I can see a light on the inside! And then I start freaking out more—"You missed one!" I turn it off and I head straight down and out. Then my head starts really spinning. It starts becoming more real as I leave the park.*

I asked Patrick, "Did you talk about it with anyone afterwards?"

Patrick: *I go home and tell my girlfriend, Raeha, "You're not going to believe what I just heard. I heard this voice!" Now we listen to podcasts about some pretty strange things and I know of this thing called the "Third Man Effect," which is where you hear an outside voice that could be trying to help you out, but that's usually if you're in a dire situation, like you're gonna die or something. This wasn't that. Besides, no one's died in that dressing room, so it couldn't have happened in there. So I don't talk about it for about three months. I don't tell anyone. I'm thinking, "I'm just going to ride this one out." And then I'm with Raeha having a beer, rehashing all of the strange things that happen here at Greystone, and I was like, "Well, that was a bunch of crazy shit, right?" And she's surprised, "Well, what about the voice?" And I just stared at her, "What voice? What are you talking about?" She says, "The woman's voice, 'You missed one.'" And then it was so weird because all of a sudden it all starts coming back to me, "Holy shit, I think I repressed the whole thing!" How could I forget something like that? Is this what repression is?! That's when I started freaking out, like on a whole other level!*

I remembered that Patrick talked with fellow ranger, Chanh, about the event.

Patrick: *Right. The next day or two, I'm working with Chanh and I'm telling him the story, like, "Isn't it kinda crazy I completely forgot about it, but, you know, no one died in there. So maybe it's just me. Maybe it's my head." And he's like, "Well, dude, it was Mrs. Doheny." And I start freaking out again, "Oh shit, that's her room! And that was her daughter's room!" And Chanh says, "Patrick, that's her freaking perfume, that's been smelled many times in her room." I started freaking out again, like on a third level! I'm like, "Oh shit, there's no way getting around it anymore! That makes too much sense!"*

I didn't expect Patrick to go where he went next—it's an unusual take, and frankly, a personal reflection on these experiences that is very evolved.

Patrick: *When you're in the moment, you don't want anything to happen, but when you reflect on it, it's actually awesome when things happen because you're experiencing things most people never have a chance to. So reflecting on it, it's really cool, but still, whenever something happens to me, in that moment, I'm freaked out, but it was really interesting. Like I said, how many people get to do that? So I always appreciate it, but in the moment, I don't—I mean a freakin' female's voice coming out of nowhere? I can't explain it and it would be wrong to rationalize it, rather than just accept that something insane happened.*

According to Friends of Greystone Historian Emeritus, Katherine Timme: "One of the many scents Mrs. Lucy Doheny Batson used in her collections, was Tabu and Chanel No. 5." Susan Rosen, President of Friends of Greystone, revealed that her daughter, Lucy "Dickie Dell" Doheny, also wore Chanel No. 5.

Chanel No. 5 was the first perfume launched by French couturier Gabrielle "Coco" Chanel in 1921. Tabu by Dana is a women's fragrance created by French perfumer Jean Carles (the House of Dana was a perfumery established in 1932).

Attic

You've got a demon in here. And I hardly ever say that. But you've got a demon in here.

— Chris Fleming
   Psychic and Medium

Photo: Clete Keith

At the time, Hoover Dam was the largest dam in the world and was conceived to trumpet man's dominance over the forces of nature. In envisioning the architectural presentation of the dam, its designers wanted to make an impression of technological supremacy. To accomplish this task, they turned to a Southern California architect of English descent named Gordon Kaufmann—also the architect of Ned Doheny's Greystone Mansion.

Greystone Historical Report

Some of the mansion's most practical features were the network of catwalks which crisscrossed the attic and the passageways which ran between the walls from the basement to the attic so that workmen could repair the plumbing and electrical systems without ripping open the walls in the rooms. But little did architect Gordon Kaufmann realize that these passageways provided some of the Doheny children and their friends with hours of fun.

To get to the Attic, you climb a small set of stairs just off Lucy's dressing room. When you reach the landing, that carpeted area was once the gym. From there you climb several steps that lead up into what was actually the Attic. In the center of this area is a hand crank wench to raise and lower the Grand Entry chandelier, which allows the servants a realistic way to clean this ornate light fixture. There are two entries to catwalks in the gym along with several other catwalk entrances in other parts of the Attic. After aviation hero Charles Lindbergh's twenty-month-old baby was kidnapped and found dead in March of 1932, each Doheny child was assigned a security guard, protecting the children wherever they went. The kids hated these guards because they kept an eye on their every move. The boys—Edward, William, Patrick, and Timothy—would often sneak up into the Attic to get away from their full-time protectors. The catwalks were one of the very few places where they could hide.

Inside the catwalks, wooden planks are suspended by thick cable creating walkways (or "catwalks") that allowed workers access to anything in need of repair. Flash-forward to 2009 when a new heating/ventilation and air conditioning system was installed in the mansion. This technological upgrade necessitated massive changes—and the Attic required considerable modifications to accommodate these large equipment units. It was an immense and difficult undertaking. Ramps and cables were added to help reinforce areas for the installation of these units, along with new cables, ducting, and electrical lines. All of which meant the original appearance of the catwalks would be forever changed.

"STOP PUSHING ME!"

BARBARA ROSENMAN

(Retired Recreation Specialist)

Barbara: *We are closing up the mansion. It is in the evening and Ranger Paula* [a former ranger who we could not contact] *has gone upstairs to the exercise room in the attic. She has to turn the lights off. So I'm waiting for her at the foot of the stairs that lead up to the attic, and all of a sudden, she says, "Stop pushing me!" I look up and she is at the top of the stairs. As she starts to take a step down, she begins to fall, and no one else is near her! She is able to catch herself by holding onto the railing. But she felt that there was someone pushing her. She didn't know who. Evidently, she had an experience before because Paula worked the shifts when filming was done here. Well back in those days, that's all we really did in the mansion anyway. Filming would go to eleven or midnight and she would lock up. So you know, this attic thing wasn't her first time. So she just turned around and said, "Stop pushing me!" I just stood there. I was sort of dumbfounded. And I just said, "Paula, let's get outta here!"*

Greystone Historical Report

"There's a winch in the ceiling above the chandelier. By turning it, you could lower the chandelier to change the bulbs or polish the glass." —Timothy Doheny

"SOMEONE IS WATCHING"

CHANH HANG

(Lead Park Ranger)

> Chanh: *I was here with Steve Clark and he is showing me how to lower down this historic chandelier at the main entrance so you could reach up and check out each individual light bulb. I didn't hear or know any stories about the attic at that time. I said, "Okay, I can do it, Steve. I know how to crank it and lower it, so just radio me when you think that it's low enough." So I went up there by myself, opened the panel, put the...*

When I was doing the transcription of this interview with Chanh, which was recorded in the Attic, immediately after he says, "put the..."—a whisper not heard during the actual face-to-face interview, but only on the recording,[1] says, "Go ahead. Get out." I was stunned. If I played it once, I played it twenty times. I texted it to Chanh. He agreed, something or someone didn't want us up there. In the story following this one, Chris Fleming might have discovered the answer to just who or what communicated this threat to Chanh and myself.

> Chanh: *So I go up there, by myself, opened the panel, put the crank handle in and I start to crank the chandelier down slowly because this whole system is old and fragile. As I'm cranking it down, my feeling is that someone or something is watching me. It was there. I felt a presence. But it is toward my left side to that one catwalk door. At the other two catwalks in that*

---

1 Audio recording exists in author's collection.

area I didn't feel or sense anything. I continued cranking down and then a second later something is telling me, someone is there. So I keep looking at that same catwalk. I take my flashlight out, turn it on and I point it toward that one door opened to the catwalk. I then physically turn my body so I can focus straight toward that door while at the same time, I'm still cranking down. But my eyes are looking toward that catwalk door. It was just an odd, weird feeling, like if you walk at night by yourself and look over your shoulder because you feel someone's there. But when you look, no one is there. It's that feeling. So I have my flashlight on as I finish lowering down the light. Steve begins changing the light bulbs. It takes him like a minute or two to change out five light bulbs. Boy, when he said, "Okay, Chanh, crank it back up," I cranked it back up, took out the lever, covered it up, and walked off. I actually ran down. I get goose bumps all the time in there. My hair was standing up. Like when you walk into a room, you'll feel a presence, that odd feeling? Or when you're by yourself in the dark and you feel something's there, but you can't see it, but you know someone is looking at you? It's that kind of feeling. That's what I felt.

"A LOT OF JUICE"

CHAD NELSON
(Retired Park Ranger)

Chad: *I did have a spiritual event that was very scary. It was a day where nothing much was going on. I went upstairs as high in the house as you can go, to the attic. You can see the roof line, the beams, and the girders. I was up there and suddenly, for some reason, and this was like one or two in the afternoon, I got really, really sleepy. I mean, oddly drowsy and I thought I should lay down for a minute. So I laid down on the carpet. I had my radio on next to me, but I felt like something was trying to make me go to sleep. It was the weirdest thing. Like, "Go to sleep," you know? Almost like audio hypnosis. So I just closed my eyes, just briefly, and I felt this heaviness, like I'd been sedated, and then I felt this presence try to push itself down on top of me. Very violently. Very intensely. Like it was trying to get into me or something. And with all of my effort and all of my might, I forced myself to wake up. I opened my eyes. I was doing my best to try and sit up. Finally, I pushed myself up and got the hell out of there. Whatever it was, it's got a lot of juice; a lot of energy if it can try and push itself into me. Yeah, that was really scary!*

Greystone Historical Report

"I remember one of the places we used to start at was in the gym, which was off the upper hallway. The gym was at one level, and then there were two or three steps and then it became the attic. There were a couple of doors up there where you could slip into the walls. There were some little ladders and things like that. I never got stuck, but I dreaded it, I really did. Nobody would hear you, and you would be a skeleton by the time you were found." —Timothy Doheny

---

"DEMON"

This following segment covers my "Attic" tour with psychic and medium Chris Fleming and his entourage.

Before we ventured up into the Attic, we were sitting in Lucy Doheny's bedroom (the Doheny daughter). Chris asked what was above the bedroom. I told him the Attic. Chris immediately asked, "Can we go up there now?" Ranger Steve Clark entered the room and joined us as we moved up to the Gym/Attic.

OUR EXPERIENCE IN "THE ATTIC" with CHRIS FLEMING
(Psychic / Medium)

As soon as we arrive Chris points to one of the several catwalks in the gym and says, "Can we go in there?" I open the small door that leads inside as we all crouch down and move in. Chris reacts instantly—he looks at the woman psychic in his group and asks her, "Do you feel that!?" She nods, "I do. I do." He looks around in the catwalks. "We have something here with us." He suddenly reacts as if something flew past him and out the catwalk door and blurts out, "It just left!" We hurry out of the catwalk. Chris points up to another door inside the attic. "What's in there? Can we go inside there?" It's as if he's on a mission. It's clear—he thinks whatever passed us at the first catwalk is now on the other side of that door. We walk up into the attic and open the door. Chris takes one step inside, stops, and quickly steps back out. He turns to me, "You've got a demon in here… and I hardly ever say that, but you have a demon in here." After hearing that, I keep saying to myself: "Until you see it, don't believe it." It keeps me balanced when things are supposedly happening that can't be proven, even though this was coming from Chris Fleming, who has a lifetime of experiences and is a seasoned investigator. I stay calm. Chris steps inside the catwalk with the idea of confronting what he felt was a demon. With a slight hesitation, I follow him inside.

Quick sidebar: Follow him inside?! What was I thinking? Sorry, I just had to get that out. Back to the action!

I'm standing next to Chris. He takes out his digital recorder and turns it on. "I know you're in here. And not only do I know that you're in here, but I know that you're the bad spirit that is scaring all the good spirits in this house. But guess what? You don't scare me. What do you think of that?" He pauses. It was quiet. Unnervingly quiet. Chris continues, "What are you? Are you half human? What do you feed off of? You're not human, are you?" He turns off his recorder and plays it back. On the recording, right after Chris finished his comments, whatever the hell was in that catwalk screams, "ASSHOLE!" The look on Chris' face scared me as much as the damn demon screaming "ASSHOLE!" I didn't want any part of it. After all, I have to work here and I don't want any attachments, especially with this malevolent thing. Many researchers believe that spirits can attach themselves to a human, who unwittingly takes it home with them like a virus. I told them that was enough and that it was time to leave. As I start to wrangle them out of the Attic, the woman psychic in the group pulls out her recorder and turns it on. She talks aggressively toward the demon, "Then you must take Jesus Christ as your Lord and Savior!" I didn't like her provoking the demon. Bad idea. "Let's go," I tell them. She plays back her recorder and you could clearly hear the demon scream, "FUCK!" At that moment, I wanted out and I told them, "That's enough! Let's go! Everybody out!" I not only hustled everyone out of the Attic, but out of the mansion. I said my goodbyes and stood there trying to comprehend what had just taken place.

Bottom line, something was in that mansion and it sounded evil. I didn't see it and I didn't feel it, but I sure as hell heard it.[2] In fact, I stayed out of the mansion for a while. This was several years before I even thought about publishing these stories. It still resonates with me when I'm inside the mansion, especially if I must go up into the Attic which I avoid at all costs. So far, I haven't been confronted by any demon as of this writing. And hopefully I never will.

---

2 Audio recording of "FUCK" is non-existent; audio recording of "ASSHOLE" exists in author's collection.

When Ranger Steven Clark first heard the Screams and Wails recording, he asked me to turn it off. He couldn't listen to it. The sound of the scream/growl on the recording is the same sound he heard down in the basement in 2007. When I played this for Chris Fleming, he said that scream or growl is the same demon he confronted in the Attic.

Chapter 28

Boys' Wing

He said, "The lights in the kids' room were on." I said, "That's impossible. There's no power to the house. The entire house has no power!"

— Luz Rodriguez
Retired Greystone Park Ranger

The comedy *Austin Powers in Goldmember* starring Mike Myers and Beyoncé was filmed in the Boys' Wing.

Photo: Chris Keith

This wing in the mansion has a long hallway with several sconces lighting the way. A beautiful hardwood floor leads you past two bedrooms, which share a bathroom. At the far end of the hallway, there is the library and study with glass doors opening out to the terrace. A bridge from this terrace connects this wing to the northern gardens. On the eastern side of this hallway are several windows overlooking the iconic inner courtyard. Early morning sunlight streams into the hallway. At the far northern end of the hallway is a door that leads to the Recreation Wing.

Greystone Historical Report

The boys "wing extended in a northwesterly direction over the entrance loggia and driveway, perpendicular to the main body of the mansion. This wing contained two more boy's bedrooms (first E. L. III's—or Larry's, then William's,) and another sitting room which was used as a library."

"Some Kind of Blur"

This story occurred on the evening tour that I gave for the daughters of a fellow City worker, Samantha and Alixan Gorman, and their friends, Ben Lowrie and Kris Huayta. They had another story included in the Basement chapter. But this incident may have been the most bizarre of the night. As we neared the end of the tour, we made our way to the Boys' Wing and from there to the Recreation Wing. We completed the tour and we were all standing on the landing just outside the theatre. I left the group and went downstairs to turn off the theatre lights, which are controlled on a panel behind the bar just off the billiard room. Little did I know what type of paranormal activity was about to take place.

MY DISCUSSION WITH BEN LOWRIE (Visitor)
We all walk inside to the Spiral Staircase landing to recount Ben's story. He looks up to the door above that leads to the Boys' Wing.

> Ben: *"Basically, I know what I saw. But there's two things that kept me from saying anything. One was ridicule, and I don't mean to put you on the spot."* He looks at his friend Kris. *"But you were nearly like, 'Fuck you! You didn't see shit!' Be honest."* Kris is laughing and defends himself. *"I did*

not say that!" Ben looks at me. "I didn't want to be ridiculed for something that I know that I saw." Alixan joins in. "We were all at the bottom of the stairs looking up. All five of us. The door [up the stairs to the Boys' Wing] *was opening slowly. We're looking up and we're all watching it open. And then Ben ran back up there to shut the door."*

Ben nods in agreement and says:

Ben: *They're all kind of freaked out that the door opened, so I went back up to close the door, like nonchalant, and I saw some kind of blur. Like a motion blur. Like if you see someone run? To me it looked like the height and size of a kid running down the hallway. I just barely caught a glimpse, but it seemed to be wearing some kind of nightgown. It looked to me like it was a girl. It was sunset. So I remember the light was kind of pink. I don't know if it was a pink gown or white with the pink light shining off of it. Like it was just really quick, but that's what I saw.*

Here, Ben shifts gears a bit and becomes more introspective.

Ben: *Then I really started questioning what was it? Like that is crazy and we're the only people here in the mansion. I'm skeptical of what I saw, and I've thought a lot about it. But it happened, you know what I mean? But I'm thinking, dude, you just heard all these terrifying haunted stories on the tour. I'm alone up there and, shit I don't know, "Let's go see the bowling alley." I wanted just to get away.*

I asked Ben to explain further his thoughts and feelings when he saw what he thought was a young girl running away down the hallway.

Ben: *I wouldn't even say that it was a terrifying feeling that I had; it was one of just surprise. I felt very calm actually seeing it happen. It wasn't like, "Fuck!!" you know what I mean? It was, "Did I just see that?" And I also didn't want to have to explain it. I didn't want to get played up too much because it was something that I considered maybe potentially special and I didn't want to be ridiculed for something that I saw. I don't quite recall if I told anybody, but I must've told someone because the word got out.*

We continue on, walking up to the door that leads into the Boys' Wing from the spiral staircase. The door is locked, and I don't have that key, so Ben looks in the keyhole. "I can see at the end of this hallway there's a staircase and a door. And that's exactly where I saw whatever I saw go from that door to the stairway." At this point, I can clearly see that Ben is being affected by something. He appears to be getting warm. "Is it really hot up here? Seriously. Don't fuck with me." He starts laughing, but he appears nervous. "I'm burning up right here. Let's go downstairs."

We walked outside of the Recreation Wing, back into the Grand Entry, and then back up to the Boys' Wing. Ben stands at the north end of the hallway looking south. His point of view is now exactly from where he opened the door and saw the blur of a child.

You can tell that he's seeing it again in his mind. "Like I said, it looked like it ran from out of that door to there." Ben points to William's bedroom and then points to the small stairs that lead out of the hallway to the Second-Floor Landing. "I don't know what it was," Ben continues, "but it was a gown with someone about this tall." He holds his hand at a level that indicates roughly four feet tall. "It must've been a girl because it looked like girls' clothing and it seemed to have some kind of trim, like white ruffles around the edge, something kind of frilled." Ben takes a long moment as he scans his memory banks. "That was pretty clear to me. It looked like someone playing or something like that. It was someone running. So weird."

It dawns on me on what might have taken place and I suggest, "Maybe she didn't run out of a room, but down the hallway away from you as you walked up to check the door?" Ben considers my logic and says, "That would make a little bit more sense because the motion was going towards the stairs leading down, so yeah, that would make more sense. And remember, all I saw was the equivalent of this." Ben fills in his pause as he runs in place for a couple of seconds. "It was just the last second or so. I just assumed that it came out of the bedroom. But, you're right, it would make more sense if it was running away. Wow. Interesting." Ben looks uncomfortable. I asked him if he was doing okay—he reluctantly, almost apologetically, tells me he has something else to add to what happened after his visit.

Ben: *There's another part to this story I'm not real proud about. The next day was crazy, and this is hard to talk about. But after that day, I was in a very strange state of mind for about a day or two. Like very stressed out. At my wit's end. Not feeling myself. I went to work and my boss had been joking for a few months, it sounds crazy, but he'd say, "You punch Phil* [his very close friend] *in the face or if Phil punches you in the face, I'll give you guys a thousand dollars. Because he knew both me and Phil are very pleasant people. We'd never get violent. But that day, man, I thought about how Phil could use the money too. I punched that motherfucker in the face. I mean, this is a forty-something year old man. I knocked him to the ground with a big old lump on his head. He was stunned, "Why did you do that?!" And I'm like, "I shouldn't have done that." I apologized. We made peace, you know, it's good. We're still friends. But, yeah, I almost lost my job actually because my boss was like, "You think I'm serious?!" I'm like, "Yeah, I thought you were serious." I'm not saying that I justified what happened, but I felt like I lost my mind for a few days after being here.*

By the way, Ben's boss never paid up.

I wonder if Ben has figured out why he acted the way he did. I ask everyone. "Do you think there might have been a spirit attachment to him from his visit at the mansion?"

Alixan responded immediately. "I do. To me the most remarkable thing about the whole trip was that he was really not in a good place after that." Samantha agrees. "Yeah, I remember talking to Alix the next day and she was talking about Ben and how he's been weird since the mansion. Then after work, she was like, he punched somebody in the face today. That's so very unlike him. And he was like that for a few days too. When you reached out a couple of weeks ago, we were talking about this and I started to remind Alix of our stories and she said the most significant thing was that Ben punched a good friend of his the next day. And he would never do that." Ben nods, recalling how he felt. "No doubt... I feel like it took some time to go away. There was a lot of chaos after the Phil thing. It felt generally like a turbulent time after that moment for a few weeks." Samantha is compelled to agree, "Oh yeah, we could see the change." Ben sighs a bit and shrugs. "The business that I was working for at that time went under shortly afterwards. I did feel after being here that I had very bad luck and brought bad luck with me. But I didn't connect it to this. I just felt like I was having a bad couple of years." I notice that Ben is looking anxious and unnerved again. Something is definitely going on with him during this interview as we stand in the Boys' Wing hallway. He looks at me. "I feel like I'm totally not right. Now I'm really hot. I feel angry. I'm sweating right now. It's crazy."

I can see that the mansion is affecting him again. I joke to break the tension.

"Ben, I'll give you a thousand dollars if you punch my brother, Chris, who's recording this interview." Ben lightens up and laughs. "Watch out, Chris!" Chris smiles and joins in. "I'll take the money!" I ask Ben if he's okay. "Talking about it gets me worked up. But since the Phil thing, I definitely have not gotten violent with anybody. People have their ups and downs, and stuff like that, but that was a particularly strange feeling. One that I think I purposely stopped thinking about because I felt guilty about what happened to Phil." Ben seems calmer now, more like himself.

"Actually, thank you very much for letting me come back, because it's giving me a lot of relief and closure on this. I don't feel as crazy about what happened. I'm not the type of person who really wants to talk about this sort of thing. I was worried about what everyone would think, you know?"

At this point, it's obvious that Ben has had enough. "We all were on edge. I was very tense coming back in that front door, specifically. It was a little stressful. I think it's time to go."

"SHAKING DOOR"

For this interview, Dan Hernandez and I went inside the mansion and up to the Boys' Wing so he could show me exactly what he experienced. Each time Dan demonstrated what happened, he looked at me with a "How is that possible?" look. Then he would do it again and give me the same look. It was comical, but at the same time, so impossible that we would just stare at the door and shake our heads.

DANIEL HERNANDEZ
(Park Ranger Supervisor)

> Daniel: *Ranger Steve Clark and I are preparing to start a tour. I'm turning lights on and getting things ready. It's a morning tour. And so I'm walking through the house, turning on lights, and I get to the door on the north side of the boys' wing that leads to the spiral staircase in the recreation wing. It separates the north wing and the recreation wing. So this door here gets stuck, meaning you kind of have to turn the knob and shake the door to open it. And that's exactly what I did. I turn the knob and I shake it to see if it is locked. It's locked. So as I'm reaching for my keys, the door shakes, like I just shook it. I thought someone was on the other side, mocking me. I reach for my keys and open up the door really fast, because I thought it's Ranger Steve on the other side—and nobody is there. I knew*

309

Steve was in our office when I was turning on lights and getting the house ready. But hey, you know, sometimes we kind of joke around scaring each other every now and then. But not now. So bizarre—when I reach for my keys, the door shakes really hard just like this [Dan grabs the doorknob and gives it a good hard shake]. *When I open it, no one was there. I thought, Okay, the spirits are definitely getting my attention!*

"WHO CALLED ME?"

DALILA PEREZ

(Janitorial Services)

Dalila: *This happened a few years ago, when I first started working here. The first room I cleaned was this one* [William's]. *I dusted and did everything, and I closed the door because there are doors between rooms. So I close that door. Then the front door that goes to the hallway in the second room, just shuts! It closed hard! By itself! And I say, "Wait a minute!" Then I heard a voice call my name and I thought it was one of my co-workers. So in Spanish, I ask, "Que paso?"* [What's up?] *And they didn't answer me. So I walk to here* [near the boys' wing that looks down at the grand entry] *and they were right there at the bottom of the stairs, and I said, "Anna, did you call me?" They said, "No, go back to work." I told her, "I don't want to go inside no more. I don't want to do it." She was confused, "Why not?" And I said, "Because I don't know who was is in there. Somebody closed the door on me and called my name." And the voice that I heard was close. That's why I thought the girls I work with were getting close to me. And they say, "No, you're crazy. Go finish!" But I didn't go back to clean it until Anna went with me. She tells me, "You're a chicken!" I say, "I'm not a chicken, I just don't want to be here by myself!" So both of us, we finished cleaning fast and I haven't gone in there since. It is crazy.*

"A Muffled Scream"

I received a text from Ranger Juan Andrade: "Ivan and someone from the rental company heard a woman's scream from inside the boys' wing window facing the courtyard." I immediately contacted Ivan and he agreed to meet me to talk about what happened. This was a first for Ivan as far as hearing a spirit. As you have read, he has had sightings inside the mansion, but this was different. This time, as he was overseeing the cleanup after a wedding, he was with an employee from a rental company who also experienced this incident. Ivan didn't get his name, so I couldn't locate him for an interview. As with Ivan, most people I interview recall the event, and by the end of our conversation, having relived that incident again, are confounded by what they experienced and are still searching for a logical and not a paranormal explanation.

IVAN MARTINEZ
(Park Ranger)

> Ivan: *It's about ten or so in the evening. There was a gentleman from a rental company who is helping me out. I'm standing in the inner courtyard about to scrub spilled wine off the slate. As this gentleman's coming my way, we hear a scream that comes from the second floor. It sounds like a girl, and the scream sounded muffled. So we're both standing across from each other, I'd say about fifteen feet apart and we look up at the boys' wing 'cause we think, "Shit, where's the bird?" But there's no bird. And I asked him, "You heard that, right?" He goes, "Yeah, what was it?" And I go, "I don't know. That's why I looked up. I thought it was a bird." We both thought it came from inside and upstairs. But it sounded muffled. And so I looked up in the room and shined my flashlight in there. Nothing. And then Ranger Juan comes by and I tell him, "Hey, we just heard a woman screaming on the second floor. "He goes, "Nah, it's probably just an Egret." And I was like, "I know the difference." Then I Googled the sound an Egret makes, and it was nothing like that. And even the guy, he goes, "No, that's not what we heard." And we didn't see a bird fly over. It sounded like a*

311

woman screaming. Like when a girl gets scared, you know? And it was pretty loud, even though it was muffled, like it was coming from inside. And it was above me where the hallway connects the second-floor landing to the recreation wing. There's a window there and it was right over me.

I asked Ivan if he went inside to check it out.

Ivan: *I didn't go inside the house to check it out because we had already locked up. The kitchen was all cleared. All of the catering staff was gone. The coordinators left. Everyone was out. So we know for a fact that no one was in the mansion.*

Ivan takes a moment and I can sense he's searching for a "logical" explanation.

Ivan: *I want to think it was a bird! Really... but in reality, I know that it wasn't a bird, because it was too high pitched. The only thing we hear at nighttime are owls. We have a lot of owls up at Greystone. Then that guy asked me, "Is there any funny stuff that happens around here?" And I go, "Yeah, a lot of funny stuff happens, but I don't know what to tell you. I don't know what it is." He wasn't scared, he was just kinda confused. Like what's going on? I told him stuff does happen here. We hear things. But me, obviously, I already know the history of the home and I'm thinking, "Oh, something's happening." I got the chills right away when I looked up and I didn't see the bird.* [long pause] *Anyway, I didn't want to check it out. So I didn't go back in the mansion.*

"MYSTERY LIGHT"

When I spoke to Lydie on the phone, I could hear the astonishment in her voice even though it's been more than twenty years since her paranormal experiences have taken place. But it's clear: her recall is strong—in fact, she remembers the incidents in great detail and exactly how things unfolded. And she wasn't the only ranger who talked to Ned!

LYDIE GUTFELD
(Retired Park Ranger / Camp Counselor)

Lydie: *I was pretty much responsible for most of filming at Greystone. I closed the house down every single night, and as you know, there was no electricity in the house back then, but we had the generator system down in the basement that would work and we had the alarm system. The alarm system was connected to and based off the doors and windows. And so if my recollection is correct, I think the total number was eighty-four alarmed connections. And so you have fifty-five rooms in the house with doors, and then there were windows as well. You would have to go every single night, shut every door and every window, and then you would get to the main door, alarm the system, and then you would have thirty seconds to get out of the house, close the front door, and lock it. But you couldn't alarm the system if any windows or doors were open. And so it wouldn't even let you walk out of the house. That's how the system worked. And so I turned it on. It said, "System On." Okay. So I walk out of the house and I made a right. And when you go under that tunnel [porte-cochere], and look up, that's where the little playroom was in the boys' wing—and there was a light on in there. There's no electricity in the house! How can there be a fucking light working?! It made no sense! So I'm there, I'm by myself, and I'm like, "Well, this is interesting." The other ranger was up at the top ranger station, so I radio him and say, "Hey, there's a light on in the house and I'm going to go in and check it out." So this was during a movie shoot, and we figured, "Alright, they left a light in there. Right?" So I walked into the house, and anytime you walk in the house you have to engage the alarm pad to "System Off" and it would literally tell you if there was something wrong in one of the rooms. Nothing. Nothing was wrong. So I walked upstairs, but now there's no light, but the window is open! I couldn't have set the system on if the window was open like that! It wouldn't have happened!*

313

Even over the phone, and across all these years, I can tell Lydie is trying to calm herself down because it just doesn't make any sense.

Lydie: *So then I was like "Okay, rely on your training" because as a park ranger you're trained that if something goes wrong, like this, you have to start talking to Ned, like right away.*

Are you reading this?! Back then, the protocol amongst the rangers, probably born out of self-mental preservation, was to have a conversation with Ned Doheny (remember, he's been dead since the Great Depression) about whatever was causing the problem. Fill Ned in on the situation and hope for his blessing. Sounds preposterous, right? But it must have worked (or at least was taken as a serious option) because Lydie isn't the only ranger I've interviewed who kept Ned in the loop with what was taking place in the mansion.

Lydie: *As for me, I was always having conversations with Ned inside the house—like this one when locking up that evening:*

"Ned, I don't know what's going on here. I don't know if the film crew changed something in your house, but I really need to get home. I'm going to close the window, set the alarm, and I'm going to walk away and everything's going to be good tonight." I closed the last window and I make sure to see if maybe a mirror caught the moonlight. Like I'm thinking what could have made a light go on, you know? Then I went back downstairs. I set the alarm system and walked out of the house, thinking everything's fine. I walked up to the Ranger Station and from there I literally saw four lights on in the mansion! So the other ranger on duty and I walked back down—and by the time we opened up the house, you could feel this weird, freaky, cold.

Researchers believe this is usually a sign of the spirits dramatically affecting the environment or manifesting themselves by drawing in the heat for energy.

Lydie: *And so I'm like, "What's going on?!" Needless to say, we didn't step foot into the house! We said, "Screw it! We're not going back in there!" And we left.*

"ILLUMINATIONS"
LUZ RODRIGUEZ
(Retired Park Ranger)

Luz: *When I left working for the City of Beverly Hills, my husband had a security company that the City would hire on occasion. My brother worked for us and there were a couple of times when he had to stay here at Greystone overnight. And this is before we had electricity working in this place. He told me he had his car parked right out here in the west courtyard and he saw that the lights in the boys' wing, the rooms, would illuminate. Like there were lights being turned on. And he said he didn't understand where the lights were coming from. After that first night it happened, we got here in the morning to check with him, he said, "Hey, someone left the lights on last night." And I said, "What are you talking about?" He said, "The lights in the kid's room, in this wing, [the Boys' Wing] they were on." I said, "That's impossible. There's no power in the house. The entire house has no electricity!" And he's very matter of fact, "Oh, well, they were on. The lights would also come on in Mrs. Doheny's room [Master Bedroom]. Like bright. Like a bright light in that room, too." But there's no power. And I mean, everything was locked up. And the production companies were not allowed to go down in the basement. They weren't allowed to touch or tamper with any of the old electrical boxes in there. So it was kept locked at all times.*

315

It's always so interesting—and this happens with so many interviewees: even though Luz is recounting a story well after the fact, her emotions start to rise with events that seem incomprehensible when you factor in the practical reality. I asked Luz to tell me about her brother's second experience—the one possibly involving Gypsy Rose Lee, the famous burlesque entertainer, who once owned the house above the upper parking lot.

> Luz: *Yeah, he also said there was a woman dressed in white that he saw on the grounds. At first when he and his partner saw this woman, they were like, "Wait, the park's closed. No one's supposed to be in here!" So they went after her, but she disappeared. Like they don't know where she went—there weren't any cars. All the gates were locked. He told me, "I don't know where she went or where she came from, but she just disappeared!" He said they saw her a few nights in a row. And I said, "Well, you know, there's stories of a woman in white here. Some people would say they think it was Gypsy Rose Lee. Maybe it was her. I don't know."*

There are many examples cited in this book of "energy fields" manifesting in the form of extreme cold spots, sudden goose bumps, or a pins and needles feeling in the extremities. I've heard a number of theories regarding lights, electrical equipment turning on and off, and batteries being excessively and strangely drained. From having experienced this myself and talking to others in the paranormal field, as well as those not in the paranormal field, energy can be drained from electrical equipment, appliances, and oddly enough, even people. Yes, people are often drained of their energy, left exhausted, and the spirit/ghost/entity can gather strength from this newfound energy. Remember Chad Nelson in the Attic chapter? And with that energy, they're able to affect their surroundings such as electrical devices, equipment, and living breathing people. Symptoms people may feel include nausea, headaches, and vomiting. When I interviewed Lydie and Luz, they both reported there were lights on in the Boys' Wing when power wasn't running through the mansion. It surprises and even confounds me—but it's not out of the realm of possibilities since two straight shooters seriously stated their own absolute realities that the lights were on.

Now, as for the woman in white… your guess is as good as mine!

Chapter 29

Recreation Wing

He had no legs. He was just a torso. He floated down the staircase to the bowling alley below.
— STEVEN CLARK
  RETIRED GREYSTONE PARK RANGER

Photo: Clete Keith

Star Trek Into Darkness was filmed in the Bowling Alley and the Billiard Room. *The Puppet Masters* was filmed on the staircase and *Spider-Man* was filmed in the bathroom. Other movies and television shows filmed here include: *The Wizards of Waverly Place*, *There Will Be Blood*, and *The Day Mars Invaded Earth*.

In this chapter, the locations are comprised of four separate sections: 1) Theatre Roof and Exterior, 2) Spiral Staircase, 3) Theatre, and 4) Bowling Alley and Billiard Room. The Recreation Wing is one of my favorite parts of the mansion. It's beautifully laid out with the turret staircase connecting all three floors. When I first started working at Greystone in 1999, the Bowling Alley was in shambles. The paint was peeling, the lanes were covered with red paint, plywood covered the gutters, and there were no ball returns. It was a square box with manually controlled pin setters that are original from 1927. In fact, in the entire world, there are only a few of these original pin setters still in working order.

When scouting the location for the movie *There Will Be Blood,* director Paul Thomas Anderson saw the pin setters and told Paramount this was the place to film his ending scene. Interesting coincidence: *There Will Be Blood* was based on the novel *Oil,* the classic tale of greed and corruption written by Upton Sinclair, which is said to be based on Edward Laurence Doheny.

When I started writing this book, it was suggested I should contact Glenn Gregory. He worked at Greystone in the early 1990s. I was told his stories were fascinating. When he told me his accounts, I wasn't disappointed. During the interview, I was stunned to hear what he witnessed. He seemed as amazed today as if it had happened just yesterday—and with good reason. Because this next story is so unbelievable, literally, he often questioned himself as to the validity of what he actually experienced. The story in and of itself is mind-boggling, but even more astonishing is that someone else had a similar experience. That story follows Glenn's.

THEATRE ROOF AND EXTERIOR

Photo: Chris Keith

"FALLEN"

GLENN GREGORY

(Retired Park Ranger / Camp Director)

Glenn: *I used to get to the park early in the morning for the kids Catskills camp because I was the one who opened up. I'd drive my jeep and park right in front of the garage* [aka Firehouse]. *My summer camp offices were the two rooms above that garage. I'd unlock everything and go up to the top parking lot to meet the other counselors and the kids for the morning check in. One day I got out of my jeep, walked into the office, picked up a clipboard, and as I walked out of the office, out of the corner of my eye I saw a girl standing on the roof of the mansion next to the railing* [above the Theatre of the Recreation Wing]. *And I thought, "Wow, that's really odd. First of all, who dropped their kid off that early and just left them without signing in? And I know they didn't sign in because I am holding the clipboard in my hand. And then why did the kid walk down from the top parking lot to the roof? Okay, what's going on? I started walking down the stairs from the office to go over there, but because of the perspective as you're walking down, you can't see the roof clearly. And then I saw out of the corner of my eye, what I thought was the girl falling off the roof into the inner courtyard area. And I was like, "Oh my God!!" My heart was beating a hundred miles an hour! So I ran into the inner courtyard and there was no little girl. Nobody had fallen off. And I went around the back of the bowling alley area and the garage area to see if I could find the kid. There was nobody. I searched that entire part of the park. I even went up into the formal gardens, the pool area and then to the parents drop off area. I checked everywhere. And then the counselors started showing up a few minutes later and I was like, "Oh my God, I swear I saw a kid fall here off the roof!"*

"Did you run this past any other rangers after this happened?" I asked Glenn.

Glenn: *A couple weeks later I'm talking to Bob B.* [a ranger at that time; we were unable to locate him for an interview], *who was always obsessed with all the people who died at Greystone and all the macabre stories. He told me a story about a little girl who had, at one point in the thirties, fallen off that roof and died in the courtyard…*

I'm not sure where Bob heard this story, but could this have been Emily?

Glenn: *…and this was without me telling him anything about what I'd seen. "Oh my God, Bob, I can't believe you just said that because let me tell you what happened to me two weeks ago!" And I told him the whole story and he just kind of freaked out about it. I don't know why I assumed it was a girl. I think she was wearing a white dress or something like that. I'm almost sure it was a white dress.*

As Glenn relives this moment, it's so very apparent how this affected him, thinking he just witnessed a child falling off the roof.

> Glenn: *But when she went straight off the roof and into the courtyard, I remember the shock, "Oh my God, she just fell off the roof!" I panicked. And then I ran down to the courtyard and when she wasn't there, I immediately thought, "Oh, I just imagined that." It wasn't like, "Oh wow, I'm looking at a ghost!" I just thought she must've been running back off the roof and it just looked like she was falling off. I don't know… I'm kind of a skeptic, so my assumption is, it was early in the morning, I wasn't totally awake. I haven't had my coffee. I saw a flicker of light from a shadow being cast, or a bird jumping or something like that, and then I imagined all the rest. But who knows, maybe I really did see a ghost falling off a roof, recreating something that happened in the 1930s.*

As we've heard numerous times, folks witness something extraordinary, something of which they are absolutely sure, and then they transition into the denial mode, "Did I really see what I saw?" The Bob B. recollection, without being prompted, is an intriguing part of this story. Was this a residual image of Greystone—time stamp: a dark day in the 1930s? Or did Glenn just really need his morning coffee?

"SLIPPED DOWN"
LYDIE GUTFELD
(Retired Park Ranger / Camp Counselor)

> Lydie: *I was a Park Ranger in the late eighties and also a camp counselor, so my responsibilities were at Greystone. But during camp, the firehouse— which is directly across from the mansion—was what we called our art center. That's where we would bring the kids for their art projects. We would also have outside time on the little patio right there on the second story and they would see other kids. Well there's these two little girls, who*

one day started screaming bloody murder. Screaming to where we thought something had gone terribly wrong. We ran out there and they were pale as could be. I was a lifeguard before I was a Park Ranger, so I felt like, "Something bad happened to these girls!" They were screaming at first and then they just went silent, just staring over at the recreation roof. You could see so much fear and panic in their eyes. We sat them down and asked, "Girls, what happened?!" And they said, "There was a little girl on the roof and then she slipped down, and she just went away!"

And we're like, "What are you talking about?! Show us where it was. Show us what happened!" They pointed to the roof, but we found no signs of a little girl. As Park Rangers, we shared these stories whenever something happened, and that's when Glenn told us, "I saw her a couple mornings ago. And it was the same thing. She was on the roof and then it looked like she slipped off and then she was gone. There was nothing there!"

I asked Lydie what she thought when she found out the historical significance.

Lydie: *Well yeah, then we found out* [passed down from prior rangers] *that a little girl actually died falling off the roof! And so I just got the chills just now talking about it!* [she laughs] *And it's been twenty years! Wow, That's so wild.*

A side note regarding "Emily": Glenn and Lydie were working at Greystone many years before me. Their frame of reference as to what happened to Emily came most likely from the rangers that worked at Greystone prior to their being there. For me, and the rangers of my generation, we were told by the rangers that preceded us, that Emily fell out of Lucy's bay window, down to the terrace below, and died. We certainly believed what was told to us, but having talked to Glenn and Lydie, I'm not so sure she didn't fall off the Theatre roof. Was she showing them the way she died? Part of my journey with this story is to go through coroner documents to try and find out the truth. So far, the facts have been elusive. We know a little girl died at Greystone. That has been confirmed. There is a chance her name is Emily, or so I was told. How she died has yet to be determined. I have presented both scenarios, but which story is accurate? What we do know is there has been a little girl's spirit in and around the mansion. If it is indeed "Emily," let's hope she has found some sort of peace.

SPIRAL STAIRCASE

Photo: Chris Keith

Greystone Historical Report

"Edward Laurence Doheny, Jr. placed a silver saddle on the landing of the circular stairway near the theater." —Sam Schultz

"No Legs"

This incident happened on a Valentine's Day. Steve Clark contacted me right after this event. He was astounded, to say the least, as I was, after hearing him tell me this extraordinary story. It sounded impossible and nothing like any other ghost sightings reported at Greystone. But Steve told me he had a witness, Rob Wlodarski, a paranormal investigator who arranged a preliminary walkthrough with Steve prior to his organization conducting their investigation. But what I thought was a one-of-a-kind incident, turned out to be one of several amazing sightings that took place on the spiral staircase. Rob Wlodarski's account of this sighting follows Steve's.

STEVEN CLARK
(Retired Park Ranger Supervisor)

> Steven: *Rob Wlodarski and I were here, just outside the theatre door on this landing. As we were talking, we saw this apparition float down the staircase. A male servant. He had a chef jacket on. We could see color and we couldn't see through him, but he had no legs. He was just a torso. He floated down the staircase to the bowling alley below.*

"Did you and Rob compare notes?"

> Steven: *Yes, and we both saw the exact same thing. We were like, "Oh my God!" We were so shaken... and I'm like, "It was a male, right? He had a jacket and like a chef's coat on, right?!" And Rob's like, "Yeah! Let's go find him!" So we ran downstairs to the bowling alley expecting he'd be laying around or doing something down there and of course, there was nothing. But he was solid. We couldn't see through him. And like I described when I saw that guy lying on the stairs out there* [this story is detailed in Chapter 31], *he looked very similar because he had kind of sandy blonde hair. Not real well kept. It was a little long. Maybe in his early thirties. I mean, I saw the guy! He was moving pretty fast. He wasn't slow. And it was like*

a white coat, with blue piping. You know, kind of big and long and it came down past his waist with the blue seam right here along the center and all around the bottom. I mean, you could see it and it looked like a jacket that a servant would wear, like a busboy would wear. I used to wear them as a busboy when I worked at the casinos. And he just was like…floating. But like I tell people, your brain just can't assimilate that because it's trying to figure out what you just saw. But there wasn't a whole complete body. And your brain just kind of freezes up. You're like, "Ahhhhhhh!"

"From the Waist Up"

Rob Wlodarski is a well-known intuitive paranormal investigator who has authored dozens of books on his investigations. Since this incident, I've been on several investigations with Rob at Greystone, but this is my favorite story regarding his experiences—especially the way he weaves the narrative.

ROBERT J. WLODARSKI

(Investigator, International Paranormal Research Organization)

Rob: *As Ranger Steve Clark and I were leaving the theatre, we were engulfed in cold. I got the chills and an immediate sensation that we were being watched. We were looking up from the landing at the bottom of the wrought iron winding stairs before heading toward the bowling alley when we both caught a glimpse of a man from the waist up on the stairs. He was wearing blue and white clothing. My sense was that he knew we were there, but was in a hurry to get to another part of the building. We both saw him on the stairs at the same time, initially out of the corner of our eyes, then for a brief moment, as a distinct apparition as we faced him. My immediate sense was that he was the caretaker, or should I say, former caretaker, still making sure that things are all right; in working order, and attending to issues related to the house. For a moment he was very curious as to who we were and what we were doing inside, but it was apparent that he had another more important obligation to attend to. I suspect that others who have worked here have also seen this man before in various parts of the house and grounds. He was under six feet tall, with brownish hair and a chiseled, well-defined face. He was around forty to fifty years old, slim and very agile. He had that certain look, like "here we go again... what else was wrong?" He was wearing a ring on his left hand. There was a sense that he was from the 1940s or 50s. This caught us off-guard as we descended into the bowling alley and billiard room area on the bottom floor, looking around to see if the ghostly caretaker was still watching us... and the sense was, yes. He thought we were intruders and not members of the family, and we didn't belong!*

As you can see, Rob's attention to detail is that of an experienced and seasoned investigator. His recollection of the sighting is distinct and without hyperbole—what you might expect from a veteran detective surveying a crime scene. "He was wearing a ring on his left hand," left me speechless how that registered in his recall. The bottom-line: both Steve's and Rob's story line up in sync.

"Half Torso"

When Alex told me this story, I was laughing. The way he talked about what happened to himself and Felix was really funny. Of course, it's not comical when it's happening! I know Felix—he has a great sense of humor, but as it turned out, he also has a great sense of fear regarding Greystone Mansion.

ALEX CHOBANIAN
(Facilities Maintenance Mechanic)

Alex: *This was in the afternoon. Almost three o'clock. We're moving something downstairs in that area leading to the bowling alley. The guy*

who worked with me, Felix, is talking about, "Yeah, this place is haunted!"
and all this stuff. We're on the bottom steps and as he's saying these things,
all of a sudden, looking up, we see at the top steps, a half torso! Half of
a person, all in white, coming down the steps. So we freeze! We're both
looking, and suddenly it stops and looks at us. Could be a woman, I'm not
sure. And it is floating because it doesn't have a bottom part. No legs, just
upper torso. Hands. Head. And it seems like a female because it has a lot
of... like flowing stuff [he gestures like it was a gown]. *And Felix says, "I*
can't believe it! I can't fucking believe it!" He starts freaking out, jumping
around and just... freaking out! He wants to run, but he can't because she's
blocking his way out. So he's got nowhere to go. She suddenly stops and looks
directly at us, and that's when Felix is now really freaking out. I look at
him like, "Jesus, look at this guy jumping around." I look back to her and
she is still looking at us. Then my attention is drawn back to Felix who is
looking how to run and get out. When both of us look back, it's gone. It was
just gone. No sound. No nothing.

I suggested maybe Felix scared the spirit away!

Alex: *Felix kind of ruined it because I wanted to have my eyes on this*
thing. I didn't want to lose my attention. But the person or spirit did stop
and was enjoying Felix just jumping around really freaking out!

Alex is laughing as he remembers the Felix freak out. I asked Alex if he
could recall any other details.

Alex: *She had some kind of a... what do these people wear when they go*
to church...a veil thing or maybe a scarf. Yeah, like a white scarf thing.
Everything was white... bright, bright. It was almost like a light lit it
up... but you couldn't make out the facial stuff. I got goose bumps because
we were scared. We didn't know what was going on. But there's nothing
[energy] *going through us or anything like that.*

Alex takes a long pause, a moment to reflect.

> Alex: *I'm not making this up. I mean, we saw it once and that was it. Actually, I'm glad Felix was there because it stopped floating to watch all that jumping around, or else the person seemed like it was going to come visit and talk to us!*

"FLOATING"
LUZ RODRIGUEZ
(Retired Park Ranger)

> Luz: *We were at the door of the movie theatre and I looked up and saw someone coming down the spiral staircase. It appeared solid, but again, it was also like a shadow. And so I said, "I just saw someone coming down the staircase!" And he* [fellow ranger] *was like, "There's no one else in here." But this figure disappeared. Like it came around, it floated down, and then it was gone. So I said, "Well, it may have gone all the way downstairs or it may be in here with us, I don't know." But he didn't see it. The theatre always gives me that chill up my spine. But I just remember, I could see someone coming down the stairs. They were floating. It seems like they never walk.*

"BOOM AND STATIC"

In January of 2020, during the Theatre renovation, I learned that an incident happened to one of the main technicians, Del Flores, who was willing to talk with me. The location he describes is at the top of the stairs in the turret. At that landing, there is a door that leads into the Boys' Wing (the same door Ben opened to see the running apparition in Chapter 28 – Boys' Wing). The "offices" that he refers to are makeshift set-ups in the Boys' Wing library/study, which is located right when you enter the hallway. I was surprised when Del told me he had two stories, not one.

DEL FLORES
(Lead Audio / Visual Technician)

> Del: *My co-worker and I were talking at the top of the stairs, when all of a sudden the door leading into the offices up there just shuts right next to us. Boom! Just like that, totally closed. I mean, big time—BANG! There's no wind, no one else up there, nothing that could've done it. We just looked at each other and were like, "What just happened here?"*

I could see Del replaying the incident in his mind, still trying to grapple with it.

> Del: *Then this morning, we're talking to Joe* [Segura, contractor superintendent] *and we're telling him about that story and all of the sudden I hear a lot of static on my walkie talkie. I say, "Wait a minute, I don't remember having my radio on." So I take it out and look at it and I say, "Wow, that's weird, it's off." And Joe looks at it and goes, "Oh my God!" His radio was also off. Everybody's radio was off, but all three of us heard the static noise on my radio! There's no possibility for that. I think this is the first place in my life where I can actually attest that there are some forces beyond our comprehension at work. When the slamming of the door, that's when I believed there was something moving around in here. Because it shut that door, and then for that to happen with my walkie, it just totally proves to me that there has to be something.*

Del still needs to clarify the specifics as to what happened to him. I think it's also his way to justify in his mind the reason for both situations having taken place.

Del: *I've heard people talking about stuff and I was thinking, "Okay, sure, well maybe, they're imagining it and maybe that's what happened, who knows? But in our case, we're not even talking about that stuff, then the door shuts. I mean, it was totally out of nowhere. And then this morning, we were talking about the door episode and sure enough that happens to the radio. I don't know if it was a spirit. Obviously there are spirits in the spirit world. I do believe in that. So maybe he or she or whatever it is, heard the conversation and they were probably saying, "Hey pssst… I'm here." Just making sure that you won't think it was the wind that closed that door, or so you won't think it was a coincidence. Here you go! Boom! Pretty interesting way to start the day!*

"SPINNING VIOLENTLY"

Brooke's story by itself is quite compelling. She was very animated when recalling this incident as we stood on the landing outside the Theatre. It's hard to imagine, but she said it happened. What is so intriguing to me is that she wasn't the only witness to this event. As you will see, there are others that observed the same type of activity on several different occasions.

BROOKE PICONE
(Former Camp Counselor)

Brooke: *It was after a final performance for Catskills* [the children's performing camp held at Greystone]. *The counselors like to stay back and after everybody leaves, we lock the park and then move into the house. We're with a ranger at the time, Ilan, who was also a counselor, and our camp director, Glenn Gregory. There were ten of us in total. So we're in the house and we're playing hide and go seek games. We're about to pick the leader to play the next game and we're here on the landing* [right outside the Theatre] *on the spiral staircase. There are no windows, at least none that could be opened or that were opened. And here's the chandelier, right in the middle up above. We're all standing around the bannister discussing who was going to lead the next game when all of a sudden Glenn says, "Oh my God, look at that!" And he points up at the chandelier. And now this chandelier is not just swinging, okay? It's violently circling, like this.*

Brooke swings her arm overhead, illustrating how violent the chandelier was rotating.

Brooke: *I'm talking violently and we were all dead silent. All ten of us just stood there in complete silence until it slowed a bit and then right before our eyes it just… stopped. Just like that. It just stopped. It didn't like, slow down and continue to sway. It was spinning violently* [she gestures again]… *and then slowed but still spinning in a circle, and then the circle slowed down more and then… stop! That was it. The ten of us were all standing there, in complete silence, staring at it.*

At this point, Brooke is staring at me with her mouth agape almost as if it just happened again.

Brooke: *At that point we left the house. Now again, there's no window for any kind of wind. And wind wouldn't cause the chandelier to spin like this. There are no wires that are attached to it that anybody could pull as a prank. All ten of us were there, nobody left, and then all of a sudden—I mean, if it would've been swaying beforehand, we would've noticed it when we walked in. It's not that high up, because when you're on the top of the landing, it's like right there in front of you. But had I not seen it with my own eyes, I don't know if I would have believed it. I mean, I can't even think of an explanation. So that will always go down as the story I cannot explain at all, mainly because there were nine other people all looking at the same thing… and we all felt the same way afterwards.*

And I've always been comfortable in here, you know? But that night, I remember I was like, okay, I'm going to leave. Somebody doesn't want us to be here. We're going to leave.

"SWINGING BACK AND FORTH"

This next segment is Maria's version of Brooke's chandelier story.

MARIA THORPE
(Former Park Ranger / Camp Director)

Maria: *We walked into the spiral staircase and it was very musty because there were rarely people in there. You know, there are people in there for film shoots, but it wasn't open regularly. So one night, Brooke Picone and a bunch of us walked into the spiral staircase area, and the chandelier starts swinging back and forth. No one could lean over and actually push it. And it wasn't like a little breeze caused anything, because the chandelier was just really swinging. Someone would've had to stand on the actual railing to do it. And we were all together. There was no one ahead of us. We all came in together. You would really have to take the chandelier and throw it. So no, it wasn't someone who pushed it. It was very odd.*

"WHY IS THAT MOVING?"

LUZ RODRIGUEZ
(Retired Park Ranger)

Luz: *We had a new person, a guy named Tyrone, and I was showing him around. So I brought him up to the mansion and showed him the two boys' rooms and the boys' study in the boys' wing. I undid the padlock at the end of the hall and opened the door to the spiral staircase. You've seen that chandelier that hangs in the middle? It's like solid brass. That thing was swinging side to side. For sure, Tyrone and I were the only ones in the mansion. He was right there with me. There is no way that air... I mean, you can feel it if there's air blowing. And even if you open the door, it's not going to cause a burst of air to make that brass chandelier swing.*

I ask Luz if it was just barely swaying?

Luz: *No, it was swinging! My eyes were wide open, and when I turned to look at Tyrone, his eyes were just as wide! So I said to Tyrone, "Do you see what I see?" I just wanted to confirm. He said, "Of course. The chandelier is moving." I said, "Okay... we'll just come back later." Then I closed the door, placed the lock on the door and we walked back into the mansion. We didn't talk about it until a few days later. Then I was just like... I've never seen anything like that. That thing is so heavy and we're staring up, "Uh, why is that moving?" It was pretty scary. I figured "they" didn't want us in there at that moment. It was best to listen!*

"PHANTOM GUEST"

Brent is a hair stylist at a shop where his brother, Chris, cuts my hair. I was telling Chris about some of the stories I've compiled for this book and Brent joined in on the conversation. He seemed in tune with the topic. I had no idea that Brent experienced the paranormal in his past. He can feel energy and sense spirits. On the night Brent visited Greystone, I was giving the tour and we entered the spiral staircase. I looked over and saw Brent react to something further down on the staircase. As it turns out, Brent and three other people on the tour saw the same thing. One of the three, we'll call "April," refused to be interviewed.

BRENT JONES
(Visitor)

Brent: *I'm watching my co-workers walk down the staircase and pretty much the first one I saw is April. She is the tall girl with the big curly hair. Well there is someone walking next to her, but I couldn't see who it is. They're making their way downstairs and I'm still trying to see who it is—and then that person just sprinted downstairs. But it looked strange. I was like, "Who's fucking around?" It was too dark to see who it was, but the point is they were solid. Just like you and me. So it almost looked like a person was walking next to her, you know what I'm saying? It didn't look like a shadow. It looked like a real, solid person, who just ran downstairs, and I said, "Who ran downstairs?!" Then everybody's looking around and they're like, "No one." And that freaked me out. I said out loud, "Dude, I swear to God, I just saw someone running downstairs!" I wasn't kidding. And here's the deal: everybody's laughing about that, but when we got into the bowling alley, I found out Ausby* [another man on the tour] *saw a person go downstairs, too! But April was in front of the line going down. So I said to April, "Who was that person next to you?" And she told me, "Nobody. There was nobody!"*

"WHO'S DOWN THERE?!"

Ausby Larkin shared the same experience and corroborates Brent's recollection. Ausby reports that this was his first paranormal experience.

AUSBY LARKIN, Jr.
(Visitor)

Ausby: *We were all standing in the area where the staircase goes down into the bowling alley. I turned because I thought I saw people going down the stairs and I was thinking they're gonna miss what you were saying to us up here. When everybody else started to go downstairs, I said, "Wait a minute, didn't some people already go down there?" And they were like, "No, nobody's down here." At this point in time I didn't know Brent had seen the same thing I'd seen. I just figured people were already walking down the stairs. And then Brent says he had seen someone, and so I said to everyone, "Wait a minute, somebody's already down there, right?" And they all said, "No. We're the first ones going down there. There's nobody down there." I can tell you what I saw was about midway down the staircase. And that's when Brent brought up that he thought somebody was next to April. He and I hadn't talked yet about what I saw going down the stairs. But it shocked me when they all said, "Nobody's down there," because Brent said he saw someone and I know I saw someone or something go down those stairs!*

THEATRE

Photo: Marc Wanamaker / Bison Archives

337

As I'm writing this in December of 2019, the Theatre is under a total renovation. The entire inside of the Theatre has been gutted down to the poured concrete. Everything inside will be restored and/or replaced; the stage extended, a new ceiling, new seats, carpeting, state of the art projection and sound system, all new electrical and lighting, and complete ADA accessibility… you get the picture. And I can tell you that the spirits don't take kindly to physical changes in their environment. From what I've been told, the number one action that stirs up activity the most is renovation. And this Theatre is no exception. People have heard and witnessed banging, voices, movement, footsteps, orbs, and various shadows when the Theatre is empty. I always think of it this way: if it was your home and some strangers came in and started renovating, and they couldn't see you, how would you get them to stop? I'm guessing you'd make yourself known to them in ways that might get rid of them. The Theatre was completed mid-April of 2020.

"Who Turned on the Lights?!"

No doubt, this story as told by Ranger Ivan Martinez presents us with a real conundrum. Throw logic out the window. Cue the music, you know the tune:

> *You're traveling through another dimension,*
> *a dimension not only of sight and sound but of mind.*
> *A journey into a wondrous land whose boundaries are that of imagination.*
> *That's the signpost up ahead—your next stop, the Twilight Zone!*

IVAN MARTINEZ
(Park Ranger)

> Ivan: *One night in July, we had a tour for the Catskills* [the summer kids' camp] *counselors. We already turned off every single light in the mansion because it was supposed to be a "scary tour" and we wanted it to be dark. We*

start the tour and the murder room light is on. I turned it off. Could have sworn they were all off, but okay. Then Lucy's light is on in her room, even though we had turned that off! The tour was going great, and then toward the end, we are going down to the theatre and the construction lights, those portable standing lights for the renovation, are on in the theatre.

I ask Ivan if there was another ranger with him for the tour.

Ivan: *Earlier, Ranger Jesse is with me as well. The plan was for him to go down to the bar below ahead of us and hide to scare the counselors* [a time-honored tradition]. *So we're going down the stairs and I see the lights come on inside the theatre. The ones off to the side, the sconces, where you have to actually go down and hit the breaker* [behind the hidden bar on the circuit breaker panel] *to turn them on. So I assume Jesse is downstairs turning them on. I was like, all right, perfect, he's going to scare them. So we all go down below to the bowling alley and I told everyone to look for the hidden bar. They find it. So I pull up the sliding door to show the hidden bar and Jesse doesn't pop up from behind the bar. He isn't there. He is nowhere to be found. So I'm thinking to myself, "Okay, if Jesse's not here, who turned on the lights?" It turns out he had already left. He wasn't even at Greystone anymore. He is down at City Hall* [two miles away]. *So then who turned on the lights? It was just me alone with the Catskills group.*

Now remember, no one in the Catskills group knows there's a breaker behind by the bar. And when Ivan went back behind the bar to the circuit panel to turn off the Theatre lights, the Theatre switch was already in the "off" position. What?! Knowing the layout and old circuitry, here's the thing: I don't think the lights were ever "turned on" by a breathing, flesh-and-blood sentient being—either the panel light switch was turned on and shut off before Ivan got there and the lights didn't go off even though the switch was in the "off" position, or the electricity was manipulated by the spirits or whatever and the switch was never turned on. I know—none of this makes sense.

Ivan: *So for whatever reason, I don't know what happened or who was there, but I was freaking out. I just wanted to get out of there 'cause I had no idea what's going on. I mean, the lights were on in the murder room, and then on in Lucy's room where we had turned them off. I don't have an answer for that. And I'm thinking to myself, "What's going on? Did Jessie turn on the lights?" Because I texted him, "Hey, did you turn on the lights in the theatre?" He wrote back, "No, I took off. I was already gone at that point." So he was nowhere near the mansion. The thing is, it's kind of creepy that all the lights were on, on that side of the mansion. The bowling alley, the theatre room... the whole rec wing was lit, and I didn't turn the lights on. I have no idea who turned them on and probably never will.*

"ZIGGY-ZAGGY"

Christian was new to working at Greystone—one of many construction and electrical workers renovating the Theatre who have been interviewed for this chapter. As we walked inside the Theatre, he told me he had heard the mansion might have paranormal activity, but he wasn't convinced. He still might not be convinced, but he was at a loss for words to explain what he experienced.

CHRISTIAN MURGA
(Electrical Contractor)

Christian and I walked inside the Theatre and we were standing by the projection booth. He looks up at the booth and then back to me.

Christian: *I work as an electrical contractor. It was around noon time. None of these portable work lights are on in the theatre and the door to the courtyard is open. I'm looking at some of these panels* [in the projection booth area] *and it looks like someone just shined a laser right here* [next to him]. *And I'm like, "What the heck?" I didn't see it directly. I'm looking up here at the panels, but I see it in my peripheral vision to my right. And I don't know if it is just a trick in my eye or some weird thing. It doesn't seem bright enough to be a laser. It's real soft, but it's red for sure and it is a small dot, like an orb. That's the first thing that came to mind—a laser pointer. It floated here for a split second and I look over where it was, and it's just gone. And I thought, "Well that was weird."*

Something didn't make sense to me and I pointed it out to Christian. "But lasers are a straight line until it shines on an object. In other words, it wouldn't be a red ball floating in the air, it would be a line of light that would shine past you and be a visual on the wall." Christian agrees, "Right. That's why I couldn't figure it out." He has a puzzling look on his face. He's still trying to wrap his head around what he saw and then come up with a logical explanation.

Christian: *Usually if you think of a ghost, you think like a big spirit or a bright light or something, but this was very, very small. But I saw it. I definitely saw a red thing, but I don't know what it was. It did have movement, but it was so subtle. But like you point out, it really couldn't have been a laser, because the movement of it was like a squiggly line. It moved and floated around in a weird little ziggy-zaggy type of thing. That's what made me notice that it was moving. But I've seen a million red lasers. It definitely was not bright enough to be a laser. I was the only one in here. That's why I didn't say anything. If someone was in here with me, I would have said something. So if I were to try to make a logical explanation for it, I would say it was a refraction of light in my eyeball. But honestly, I don't know.*

I sincerely love to see and hear how people who've experienced something unexplainable go through mental gymnastics to try and then embrace what they perceive to be the logical explanation. During this conversation with Christian, I ask clarifying questions because it's important to flesh out and reach as truthful a conclusion as possible—it's not to be rude, but to distinguish what actually happened as opposed to what someone thinks might have happened.

I ask Christian, "Have you ever had a refraction of light in your eyeball before?" Christian thinks a moment, "No, I haven't. But you know, it's like if you get hit in the head and you see stars or something like that?" I tell him, "But you didn't get hit in the head, did you?" He shakes his head. "No, I didn't. But this was like red. I know it was red. I remember I saw the red. It's a pretty trippy thing." I want to let Christian know that he isn't the only one seeing this phenomenon. Hopefully, it will ease his mind. "Ranger Juan also saw what he thought was a red laser light" (Chapter One – Grand Entry). Christian is amazed. "The fact that you told me someone else has seen a laser pointer thing makes me even more tripped out!"

"ABOVE THE DOOR"

Scott Smith is on the same crew as Christian Murga. Once I found out about Christian's story, I asked him to keep on the lookout for activity with other workers because I believed there would be more. I was right. One morning Christian saw me in my office above the Firehouse and he said, "Hey Clete, you might want to talk to Scott." Everybody deals with the paranormal or what appears to be paranormal, differently. Scott seems like an easy-going guy; he sports a big beard and a great sense of humor. His attitude was one of being so dedicated to completing his job that what happened to him was not something that was going to stop him from working. I found that interesting and amusing. By the end of our chat, Scott finally admitted that what happened was indeed "peculiar."

SCOTT SMITH
(Electrical Apprentice)

Scott: *It's a Friday, middle of October. This is inside the theatre. We are demoing out some existing electrical. I'm cutting up some pipes and we have one light source, a small little Husky plug-in light about thirty feet behind me. And as I'm cutting up the pipe, right above the entrance to the theatre from the spiral staircase landing, on the wall, I see a shadow figure walk behind me. But when I turned completely around, there is nothing there. I knew I'm the only one in there and I am just to the right of the door up against the cement riser for the projection room. The light was behind me, so I had a visual above the doorway. The light shined right there. So whatever shadow there was had to have been between me and the light source that was coming from behind me. So that shadow was no more than thirty feet away. But I just kept working. When I saw it, I thought maybe someone had opened the door to come in through the back, but there wasn't anyone there. It is what it is. Work's gotta get done. It was just a shadow.*

I ask Scott to tell me what he was feeling at the time? What were his thoughts?

Scott: *It was definitely peculiar, I'll give you that. I mean, there's no rhyme or reason for it. But I didn't feel any energy, anything cold, nothing. No heavy feeling. Nothing like that. I figured that it's probably a ghost! It was definitely a shadow figure walking. You know, out of the corner of your eye it just looked like someone walking by. So if you're looking at the projection room, it went from right to left. I'm assuming it was some kind of spirit. But I don't care at all. The more the merrier* [he laughs].

I ask Scott if he experienced any other strange behavior in the mansion.

Scott: *I was down in the tunnel for two weeks* [these are catacombs in the basement] *and I loved every minute. I would sit there and whistle, turn the light off. I like all that stuff. It's interesting. And this is the first time I've ever seen anything like that in person. I mean, you always hear stories, but it's the first time and I was like, "Oh yeah, that was definitely something!" It was actually kinda cool. Doing the renovation has brought some stuff up. I believe it. I totally believe it. This is hands down the most interesting, coolest job site I've ever been on. But somebody was floating above that doorway!*

"BIG CRASH"

RANGER M.M.

(Park Ranger)

Ranger M.M.: *It is just a regular Sunday. There's nothing going on. Not even construction. It's around five in the evening. I'm locking up and turning off all the lights. There are lights on in Kristin's office on the second floor* [small room that looks out to the inner courtyard] *but she already left. So I turn off all the lights. I think I only found one more light after Kristin's and that was in Mrs. Doheny's closet. I get everything locked up. Then I go to the winding stairwell and I start walking up just to check the door. It was unlocked to get into the boys' wing. And I was like, "Oh, maybe they want it unlocked." So I left it unlocked. I start walking down the stairwell and I hear a big crash, like BOOM! Really, really loud. I know construction's set up there, so I don't want to turn on the lights in case of an electrical issue. So I have a flashlight that's really bright, almost looks like daylight. I turn my flashlight on to check all the areas. I don't see anything inside the theatre. I don't see anything broken or damaged. I walk through the whole theatre. I also walk upstairs. I go down into the bowling alley. I don't see anything. People are in the park on the outside, but no one's inside the mansion. And it sounded like it was coming from the theatre because I was walking up the stairwell that's right above the theatre, and I was not even halfway up the stairs and I hear, "Boom!" But I saw nothing. I mean, what if there's something on the roof? I even walk out to that little area and opened that lock on the top stairwell, right next to the boys' wing and I peer out. I looked on the top, I don't see anything that has fallen through. So I did my due diligence and I tried to see if anything was broken, because it sounded like something crashed. Something maybe in the roofing area. Maybe something that I can't visually see. But something crashed. Nothing could have made that noise outside—it had to come from inside. So I just assume it's the construction. But they weren't here, period. Kristin is gone, so it's just me, by myself, closing everything up. I didn't feel like I was in danger. I just thought, "Oh my gosh, what's that noise?" It just made me jump a little bit. So that's why I had no problem going everywhere and looking.*

I asked Ranger M.M. if any thoughts of the paranormal entered his thinking at the time.

Ranger M.M.: *I could think maybe it's a ghost thing if it was anywhere in the mansion, but it's where the construction is in the theatre* [the recreation wing is still part of the mansion… just saying!]. *I don't deal with construction, but that's the only thing I can think of—but I physically couldn't find anything. I called Ranger Dan and I said, "Just in case you see anything broken tomorrow, I heard a big crash—it wasn't like, 'Oh, a lamp fell over'—it was like, 'BOOM!'" I've never heard a crash that loud in person. You only hear a crash sound like that on TV. It sounded like the ceiling fell through. Other than that, I don't know. Maybe the place is haunted. Maybe they don't like that we're touching the theatre.*

On a side note: With this story in mind, I began setting my recorder in the Theatre at off hours to see if there was any evidence I might capture electronically. I recorded many sounds of knocks, bangs, and strange movement, but not the big crash that the ranger referred to—until one night when a crashing sound was so loud that the microphone on the recorder literally shut down. With the recorder set on "sensitive," the noise was so explosive that you can hear the beginning of the sound, but then the middle drops out because the sound wave was simply off the charts, too loud for the microphone to handle—and then you can hear the very end of the crash. This has never happened with the hundreds of recordings I've catalogued at the mansion. Was it the same crash the ranger heard that night? I can't jump to that conclusion. But from what I heard on that recording, it's a credible possibility.[1]

"VIBE"

I came into work and was notified by a construction crew member that another "ghost thing" happened to a fellow worker. As it turned out, Ralph is one of several contractors who was hired to work on the renovation of the Theatre who had no clue about the haunted history of Greystone. It didn't take long for him to be educated in the paranormal. In fact, it happened on his very first day.

RALPH FLORES
(Audio Visual Contractor)

> Ralph: *It was close to four in the afternoon on the very first day we came here. We cleared out after working all day in the theatre. When I got to the parking lot, I realized I forgot my blueprints. So this door* [the east side of the Theatre] *is open. When I go back inside, I was like, "Oh shit, man." It's kinda... I don't know, I got this little funny feeling. I just felt awkward, like is somebody watching me? It's an actual feeling. I got that vibe. I saw my blueprints all the way across the other side of the room and I was like, "What the fuck? I don't want to walk all the way over there." So I close the door and enter from the inner courtyard. I go in quickly and*

---

grab my prints, and hurry out. When I close the door, I hear something inside like, "Boom! Slam!" No way did I want to go in and check anything. I just left. The next morning, we're the first ones to come in, so I was going to pick up the ladder, and I was like, "Oh shit. Nothing fell." I thought that something would have been on the floor, but everything was just like we left it. I thought maybe a ladder fell or something else heavy or big, but everything was where it's supposed to be. I don't know what it was. Maybe it's just an old place, you know? I didn't know anything about it [possible haunting] *until after I started mentioning it. And then once I brought it up, everybody started saying, "Oh yeah, this place is haunted." I was like, "Oh shit!" Then I started hearing different stories. And this place just looks spooky. But I don't know what happened in the theatre.*

"SINGLE BANG"

Matt (did not want his last name revealed) and Joe Segura are the Theatre Project Engineer and Contractor Superintendent, respectively. As the renovation of the Greystone Mansion Theatre was underway, it was part of their job to keep the workers on schedule. They were given a room for an office inside the Boys' Wing of the mansion. This location put them next to the spiral staircase, which connects the Bowling Alley up to the Boys' Wing—positioning them one floor above the landing that leads into the Theatre. (Confused? Check our maps!) One of the rangers contacted me and said I should talk to Matt and Joe because they experienced something that they couldn't explain. Clearly, this became a theme as work continued on the Theatre. We met in their temporary office located in the boys' study.

A CONVERSATION WITH MATT & JOE SEGURA
(Theatre Renovation Project)

Joe laid the foundation: *"It was just a normal working day. The restoration company working inside the theatre had left, so the theatre's empty."* Matt *joins in.* "Yeah, they were the only ones here, so it was just me and Joe working here up in the boys' study. The hallway's empty. The exterior doors are closed. And about forty-five minutes after they left, we hear like a "bang!"... almost like someone pushed something over. Or something fell over. Not huge, but you know, like a box fell over." *Joe nods his head in agreement. Matt continues,* "It caught our attention. I went down there and for the moment I thought it was Ranger Patrick. So I called him and said, "Patrick, were you down there in the theatre room?" He says, "No, I was in the courtyard. Why?" I said, "Well, I just heard a loud bang in there."

Joe speculates. "For me, it could have been the wind. I don't know. But there was a loud bang. Also, there's a vent over by the actual stage on the Northeast corner, so anyone can basically tunnel through there." *What Joe is suggesting is that someone could climb in the vent and get inside. But there are rangers patrolling the park and Joe knows that is highly unlikely— and so do I.* "Tunnel through and do what?" *I ask an obvious question.* "Knock a ladder over? Is that what you're saying?" *Joe is a very smart and logical guy and he must know that his suggestion doesn't hold up. Clearly, he doesn't want to talk about the elephant in the room—the paranormal activity. Joe nods as if in agreement but offers,* "Maybe come in, grab some lumber or something. I don't know." *I understand where he is coming from. Matt jumps in:* "I mean, that's basically it... because we both heard it. We were both up here and we both heard it. Joe went down to look, and no one was in there. Patrick wasn't inside. And it was a City holiday [Veteran's Day], so Patrick was the only one who had access to the interior. I mean, you hear weird noises and stuff happens, but there was nothing. The moral of the story—nothing was really down there. And nothing looked like it fell over either." *Joe looks at me and agrees with Matt.* "Yeah, so nobody was there." *Matt clarifies the sound,* "And it was a single bang, just a single percussive. And I wouldn't say it was incredibly loud." *I look at Joe.* "It sounded like it was probably metal." *Matt nods in agreement.* "I either say it was metal or like a two by four falling flat. Something similar to that."

Joe then reveals his reluctance to delve into the true source of the sound. "I don't know. I guess the more you look into it, the more you'll probably find it. You know what I mean? My thing is to complete what I'm here to do, which is restore and rebuild the new theatre and then move on. Whatever's there is probably going to appreciate that I'm not disturbing it. You know what I mean? I'm Catholic. The way we find our comfort is we pray."

This is also a common theme in preternatural investigations: Religion and prayer equal protection from the paranormal.

I agree with Joe. "Well, this is a good place to start praying my friend." He nods and reaffirms his beliefs. "I guess we could say we know there's things out there, but if you look for it, it's gonna find you. So if you don't disturb them, then they won't disturb you."

Amen.

"Do You Need Help With That?"

By January of 2020, work on the renovation of the mansion's Theatre was several months along and this construction upheaval proved to be fertile ground for paranormal activity. Robert Tuiasosopo was working near a transformer in a very small confined space under the old projection room. When we met to talk about what had taken place, I had a feeling nothing of this sort had ever happened to Robert. I was right.

ROBERT TUIASOSOPO
(Electrical Apprentice)

Robert: *We had two guys standing on the outside working on some stuff for our next wire pull. I'm in there by myself struggling to get a fitting on, when all of a sudden, I feel someone next to me on my right—just like they were looking over my shoulder. I could feel it. And then I hear someone say,*

"Do you need help with that?" And I'm all, "What?" And I turn around, and no one is there. I say, "What?" so loud the guys outside ask, "Who are you talking to you?" I told them, "Dude, I could have sworn you guys were messing with me, or were in here with me, because I felt a presence in here." For a few minutes I was like, "Okay, cool. This has happened." [he laughs] *I told them, "Hey, I felt it!" They agreed, they're like, "Dude, we heard you, and you seem startled."*

I asked Robert for more details on the voice and the feeling he experienced.

Robert: *It was a male voice because I thought it might have been one of the guys. The first couple of minutes I didn't know what to feel, and I didn't know what to think. It tripped me out to be honest with you. It was like someone was looking over my shoulder, I could just feel it. 100%. We all know when someone is right there. Feeling the presence of it, physically right next to me, was like someone coming up close to you and you feel the warmth. I thought maybe the guys might have slipped in through the window without me paying attention, 'cause I was actually really, really struggling getting the wire through the connector. So I thought, okay, maybe they're in and out of here all the time. Maybe I wasn't paying attention. And then I said, "What?" so loud that they actually heard me. That's when I thought it was one of the ghosts. I mean, we hear stories and everyone says this place is haunted. There are upgrades happening in here, so maybe they wanted to help out, as weird as that sounds, or maybe it was them protecting the house. I was messing around with my buddies saying, "As long as they don't mess with my hand tools, I don't really care what happens." It's not like I'm not gonna come back to work here anymore. So I was like, "Okay there's probably spirits here." But when I heard, "Do you need help with that?" That's why I kind of tripped out—especially 'cause I'm actually facing the transformer, so there's no room in there to work, so how can anyone physically help me? I don't know how to explain it. Nothing like this has ever happened to me before. I've heard about stuff happening to people and they've had encounters, but not to me. I never really believed in these things.*

I asked him, "What about now?" It didn't take but a nanosecond—

Robert: *Now, I'm a believer.*

BOWLING ALLEY AND BILLIARD ROOM/BAR

Photo: Clete Keith

In 2007, Paramount Pictures selected the Bowling Alley to film the memorable last scene from Paul Thomas Anderson's film, *There Will Be Blood*, starring Daniel Day-Lewis, who won the Oscar® for Best Actor. The filmmakers pulled up all the old plywood, refinished the bowling lanes, gutters, and built the ball returns to match what they would look

351

like in the original era. They also cleaned up the pin setters along with stripping and repainting all the walls. Lights were hung above the alleys, and an "Innings" board to keep score was hung on the wall by the left lane ball return. Once completed, it looked as if you stepped back into the 1920s. Part of the deal that the City of Beverly Hills struck with Paramount was after the filming was complete, the studio had to leave everything the way it was refurbished. It still looks beautiful today.

Greystone Historical Report

The bar was hidden behind paneling that retracted into the ceiling at the push of a button. Notes Timothy Doheny: "We had a sign that said, 'We don't serve mom, but we have pop on ice.'"

Photo: Chris Keith

"KNOCK. KNOCK. KNOCK."

CHARLIE ACKERMAN

(Retired Building Maintenance Supervisor)

Charlie: *Disney was filming* Wizards of Waverly Place *in the billiard room. They turned it into a girl's dorm room inside a clock tower. It was kind of after the Harry Potter craze really took off. And supposedly it was about a female Harry Potter type. At one point,* [Ranger] *Steve Clark said, "Hey, you gotta see what they've done to the billiard room. You're not going to believe what it looks like." It was around lunchtime, so all the cast and crew were up on the main parking lot having lunch. There was nobody in the building. So Steve and I walked downstairs to the billiard room. And the way that area is set up, there was really only one way in and one way out. So we walked into the billiard room to find that they built a false wall between the billiard room and the bowling alley so you couldn't see the bowling alley. There's nobody else in the area except Steve and I and we're standing there looking at everything and talking. Suddenly there's three knocks on the other side of the false wall. Knock. Knock. Knock* [he laughs]. *And we're looking at each other like, what the hell was that? So I looked around the wall to the other side to see if somebody was playing a trick on us, and there's nobody there. So I just knocked on the wall—knock, knock, knock—and we just sat there kind of going, "Okay." There was nothing. And then we got out of the room. It was kind of wild. I remember Steve telling me like a week later that you guys* [my sister, brother-in-law, and myself; see Chapter 13 – Basement] *were down in the basement and heard the same type of knock, and you said, "I'm out of here!"*

"WHAT THE HELL WAS THAT?"

This is a follow-up chat I had with Steve regarding Charlie's interview above. Steve and I walked into the Billiard Room as he recalls what happened.

STEVEN CLARK
(Retired Park Ranger Supervisor)

Steven: *Disney was cleaning out the lead paint from the turret because they wanted to shoot in this room. They put partitions between the rooms. Charlie and I were standing on this side, in the billiard room and we heard three knocks. They were very distinct, and we just looked at each other, and I'm like, Ohhhhhh!* [he laughs]. *And we looked around the corner to the other side of the wall and we're like, "What the hell was that?!" And Charlie said, "Okay, I'm outta of here!" And he just left* [Steve laughs again]. *And it was so similar to when we were down in the basement with your sister where there was that knock. And you were scared! You jumped behind—*

I cut him off. "Yeah, yeah, yeah. I jumped behind my sister. I'm not proud of that. Can we let that go?" As we get ready to leave, Steve walks closer to the wall and knocks three times.

Steven: *That was the same sound like we experienced in the basement. It was just very distinct. And it wasn't like wood creaking either. It was...* [he knocks loudly three times on the wall] *I mean it was loud! It was like somebody was on the other side. Literally!"*

"It's a Boy!"

I was giving a site visit to an engaged couple and their friends. They were looking at Greystone as a possible location for their wedding. Ranger Dan was on the walk with me. With the visit nearly done, we stopped in the inner courtyard and I asked Dan if he would stay with the group while I ran up to my office to get some brochures. I hurried upstairs and as I headed back to the group, Joe Segura, the Contractor Superintendent overseeing the renovation of the Theatre, was standing in the east courtyard—he asked me if I had a minute. He was talking to

354

a construction worker, but needed to talk to me. He told me something just happened to one of the crew cleaning the Bowling Alley. "Something paranormal?" I asked. Joe nodded "Yes." I bid the wedding party good luck and walked into the Bowling Alley with Joe. He pointed out the woman who had the experience. He left as I said hello to Roxana. She was very sweet and approachable—and on the surface, seemingly unafraid by what had just taken place… only to find out that she has the gift.

ROXANA TOSCANO
(Cleaning Services Supervisor)

Roxana: *This was mid-morning and we're doing a rough clean on the bowling alley. I'm cleaning on the left side of the alley and there's all this dust. I have my other co-worker here; she's vacuuming and she's also down here on the left lane. So I turn around to see what my other co-workers are doing, and they were where the ladders are, near the entrance to the billiard room. But I see a shadow. It's a boy. A Caucasian, white boy, curly blondish hair, like between seven to nine years old. And his shirt has the kind of sleeve, like the Mayans wear? It goes to right here* [halfway down the wrist]. *There aren't any buttons. It is like a pullover shirt. It's a grayish, brown, potato sack color and he's playing with the dust.*

Dramatically, Roxana actually shows me how he was holding his hand away from his body and was rubbing his fingers while watching the "dust" fall to the floor.

Roxana: *My co-worker is not seeing him… but I do. And I don't tell them because they get afraid. But I know he isn't real because there's not a possibility that there's a kid here. No child should be in here. So I turn to look at my co-worker and when I turn back around, he is gone. So I start walking toward the billiard room because I want to tell my co-worker, but I thought no, I'm not going to scare her either because we still have a long day. So I go into the bathroom area and when I turn back around, he's standing right there, by the bowling chalk bowls. He's back again. So*

I say, "Hi." He doesn't say anything. So I walk away from him toward the bowling pins. I don't want to turn back and look because I got scared. I was laughing, but in a way, I was scared. I was like, "Whoa, what was it?" There are myths that say you don't talk to them; you don't ask them anything. So I got stiff and I walked away.

Roxana is literally shaking as she tells me the story.

Roxana: *I look back, and he is gone. I think it was a spirit, because there was actually the face and everything. I've seen them with nothing. No face. But this had the face. This was a kid. I don't recall the eyes or anything, but I know he was Caucasian and had the curly, blonde hair. I was face-to-face, but I didn't want to look at him. I did not feel scared at the beginning because I knew I'd seen him and I knew there was nothing wrong. It was no scary type thing. No monster. But as I turned around and said, "Hi," I felt something like, not cold, but it was just like a stiffness. That's why I walked straight away from him at first. I didn't even turn around. But you could see that the chalk in the bowl was moved because when I first came in that morning, I wiped the bowls clean, but later this bowl had chalk with finger marks.*

Roxana puts her finger in the bowl and shows me how smudged it was with finger marks when she started cleaning.

Roxana: *I know because I wiped them clean. But you could see later that it* [the chalk] *was moved all around!*

This story amazed me. When you're talking to someone and they've just had an experience, you can see it in their eyes. She was excited and articulate about the facts. She was smiling and almost making light of what had taken place minutes earlier, but at one point she showed me her goose bumps as she recalled the spirit. And as I'm recording her, I'm thinking she must have the ability to see spirits. She has a way about her that tells me she has seen apparitions before. I was right. But even after eighty plus interviews, I'm listening to her and I'm caught in my own Twilight Zone thinking: is this story real or not? It's real to her—she was convinced that this boy was present.

I know crazy things happen here. They've happened to me! But it's hard to wrap your head around the paranormal. The old adage, "Seeing is Believing," works for almost everything, but it doesn't always work in the paranormal field. I found that many witnesses "see" but still have a hard time "believing." As for me, if that kid appeared during the interview, I'd do what most great investigators would do—I'd hide behind Roxana, then shove her as bait toward creepy dust boy and make a run for it!

Chapter 30

Greystone Mansion:
Here, There, and Everywhere

As soon as I heard it, chills just shivered up my skin. I ran out the front door of the house. I was really scared. I'm like, damn, did I just hear that!?

— MARTIN J. PEREZ
JANITORIAL SERVICES

Photo: ©SWA / Tom Fox

Greystone Historical Report

"With the sole exception of Hearst Castle at San Simeon, Greystone is the grandest estate ever to have been created in California." On April 23, 1976, "The United States Department of the Interior recognized Greystone's architectural, landscape, and historical importance to California and the nation, when it placed the property on the National Register of Historic Places, which is the Federal Government's list of national landmarks."

During the hours of interviews for this book, there were many times when folks would discuss the mansion as a whole. Not specific locations, but more esoteric and general thoughts and feelings. They would talk about experiences when they felt a presence or heard noises and voices but couldn't pinpoint an exact location. There were also stories told about events happening in multiple rooms if not all over the mansion. This chapter is dedicated to those stories.

"REOPENED"
BREHNEN KNIGHT
(Retired Park Ranger)

> Brehnen: *Almost every time I closed up the mansion, I would go from one end of the house to the other and shut everything… and invariably I'd come back the other way and things were opened up again. And I know absolutely positively I'm the only person in there. How do I know? Because that's the first thing we're trained to do—make sure that there's nobody in the house. And then we sweep through to make sure everything's locked up. It's not just me: other rangers get done and still find doors opened or windows that are reopened. Talk to any ranger and they'll tell you that. And it happens on a regular basis. It's like part of the job. You just deal with it.*

"BANGING"
MARTIN J. PEREZ
(Janitorial Services)

> Martin: *Another thing—and I'm not sure what it was—but it seems everywhere I go there was always like* [he hits the wall with his hand] *banging. For instance, I finish a job somewhere, I walk away and there*

360

will be like "SNAP!" or like a loud "BANG!" It was always happening. I'm not sure if they were trying to scare me, but they sure did!

"HAIRS ON THE BACK OF YOUR NECK"
CHAD NELSON
(Retired Park Ranger)

> Chad: *Cold spots. Cold spots. You know, walking through the mansion and suddenly feeling a cold spot in the air—then it's gone! That happens periodically. A very distinct coldness. And then you hear weird clicks and pops that always had the hairs on the back of my neck going up!*

"CONVERSATIONS"
LYDIE GUTFELD
(Retired Park Ranger / Camp Counselor)

> Lydie: *It felt like it was Lucy downstairs having tea. I could hear clinking of her tea glass. And then I'd hear the spoon clinking on a teacup. It was wild. And I always heard women's conversations.*

I asked Lydie how she knew it was Lucy Doheny having tea.

> Lydie: *Of course, it was a feeling. It "felt" like Lucy. Also, I would explore and walk the catwalks upstairs and we'd hear echoes of voices in other rooms. Or sounds and things going on in other rooms when we knew that there was nobody in the house. And then this happened all the time—whenever something was pissing Ned off, and it was all the time, the alarm would go on… or I'd be with another ranger and we'd be walking back up to the ranger station and the alarm system would suddenly come on. We'd go back down to the mansion and find doors to rooms were open, windows were open, that kind of thing.*

Greystone Historical Report

The mansion's construction indeed was fortress-like. The gray Indiana limestone walls, which gave the 46,054 square foot residence its name, were merely a veneer for the three-foot-thick steel-framed concrete walls. Even the steeply pitched roof was steel-reinforced concrete, which had been covered with several-inch-thick pieces of slate. And architect Gordon Kaufmann made sure that these roof slates would never fall off. "When they poured the roof," Timothy Doheny declares, "they laid a wire mesh in the concrete. They drilled each slate with two holes, and then they wired those slates to the wire mesh."

"KNOCKING AND BANGING"

BREHNEN KNIGHT
(Retired Park Ranger)

Brehnen: *I've heard knocking and banging and things like that in places where I was never able to associate where it was coming from, other than it wasn't happening in the room where I was. I always had to go and try to find the source. And I just attributed these occurrences to the spirit of Ned messing with me. And of course, you would think, "There must be some reason for the noise." But remember, all the windows have to be closed in order for the alarm to work. And so this isn't like the wind blowing something or something hitting against something else. To have a consistent knocking and then you go to find that noise and there's nothing that could possibly even knock? So it's just like, "Come on, Ned, seriously?"*

"WHO'S THERE?"

The Beverly Hills police officer in the story below refused to speak with me about the incident, so I retrieved the information from a source close to him—his daughter.

ANONYMOUS
(Former Park Ranger)

> Anonymous: *My dad had a great story. He was a Beverly Hills police officer. And back years ago in his day* [1960s], *they actually did overnight security when there was filming because the mansion didn't have the alarm system like it does now. And the movie sets were all inside, so they hired the police for overnight security. I don't know if the alarm system was in or not, I can't remember.*

Ranger Steve told me, "I doubt the alarm system was installed as the house belonged to Henry Crown, and apparently the house was easy to break into in those days. When Greystone became the American Film Institute's campus in 1969, that's probably when the alarm was installed."

Also worth noting, there wasn't any heating or air conditioning inside the mansion until 2009.

> Anonymous: *I know they were filming* The Nutty Professor [1963, starring Jerry Lewis] *at the time, and my father remembers he was inside the mansion.*

Anonymous wasn't clear as to specifically what room the experience took place in, but the officer said it was upstairs.

> Anonymous: *He was sitting and the drapes on the windows started to blow inward toward him and he actually drew his gun. And he was like, "What the hell! Who's there?!" And when he checked, there was nothing*

behind the curtains. They were just blowing on their own. He was clear, "There were no windows or doors open." So he was just freaked out by that.

"Moving Furniture"

CLETE KEITH

I asked the security guard, "You're going to be here all night?" It was another film shoot. The film companies always have security guards to watch the location. I didn't want to freak him out, but we've had other overnight security guards who have heard, felt, and seen some strange things on their shift. He told me he would be there all night. I said, "Okay, well, good luck." And he said, "What does that mean?" I said, "Nothing, it's just going to be a long night."

I went home and came back early the next morning and the guard was standing in the west courtyard. I said, "Hey, how did it go last night?" I could tell by his face that something happened. He looked at me a long moment and then said, "Wow, this place is crazy!" And I said, "What do you mean by 'crazy?'" And he said, "Was there anybody in the mansion last night?" I said, "No, it was locked up. The alarm was on. Everyone was gone." He shook his head and again said, "This place is crazy." I asked him to explain. He said when he was walking around doing his patrol, he started hearing something inside the mansion by the front door. And I said, "What were you hearing?" He said, "Things were moving, scraping, and scratching, like something was being pulled across the floor. It sounded like the furniture inside the house was being rearranged." The mansion was set-dressed for filming, so there was furniture and props inside the house. But being "rearranged?" The security guard swore that things were moving.

He said he got on his radio and contacted his lead guard who was near the east courtyard of the mansion and said, "There's something going on over here." The lead guard said, "What are you talking about?" And he said, "I'm hearing things move." The lead guard said, "There's nothing going on in there. There's no one inside. Don't worry." So the guard decided not to let it bother him. If nothing is in there, then nothing is in there. But soon thereafter he heard the noises again. He got back on the radio and said, "Hey, I'm telling you, there's stuff inside moving around." The lead guard said, "Okay, I'm coming over." So they stood together and listened. Nothing. Then suddenly they heard the furniture moving inside. They both ran around to the terrace to look into the mansion through the windows of the card room doors. They couldn't see anything. They flashed their lights inside and still couldn't see anything—but they kept hearing things move. The lead guard looked at him and said, "Look, I don't know what's going on here, but you should just look at the ground for the rest of the night. Don't look up. Just look at the ground with your flashlight and do your rounds and never look up at the windows!" And to their credit, they stayed the night and that's when I found him in the morning.

When he told me this story, I could see he was really unnerved by what he called "an unbelievable experience." He asked me, "Is this place haunted?" I said, "I didn't want to scare you before I left yesterday, but there are those who believe it is. In fact, there are quite a few stories similar to yours." And he said, "You know what? I don't even want to know." And he walked away shaking his head.

A side note about the mansion: It was designed and built with four sets of chimneys made out of brick. Each set was crafted by a different artisan. Attached to the two sets of chimneys on the south side of the mansion were large spotlights. Back in the day, one light was aimed in the direction of the Beverly Hills Police Department and the other at the L.A. County

Sheriff's Department. If the family felt threatened - when Ned was alive, or after his passing - or if Lucy thought she was in danger—they would flip the switch, and the luminous rays of light would beam in the direction of law enforcement. This was the genesis of the famous "Batman light" used in comic strips and subsequent television shows and films. Mrs. Doheny would randomly take a pouch of money and have it run down to the estate guard at the 501 Doheny Road entrance gate. She would then flip the switch to the lights. The first policeman or sheriff to arrive would receive the bag of cash… and that trained the officers that when those lights lit up the sky, get to the Doheny residence ASAP!

"FREAKED OUT"

This story is one of my favorites. It sounds so frightening, so much like a horror movie, that I wouldn't have believed it unless I heard Chad tell this to me. He was very animated and detail specific. The account was told directly to him from the original source. This happened back in the late 1980s, and needless to say, someone or something wasn't happy when the police showed up to interrupt their party!

CHAD NELSON
(Retired Park Ranger)

> Chad: *Here's what the Beverly Hills cops told me in the eighties about an event that happened a few years before. It's the scariest thing, and this is something they completely hushed, hushed, hushed up in the department. A couple of the old veteran cops, the ones who actually witnessed it, told this to me. So apparently the alarm went off in the house, around two or three o'clock in the morning… and they responded. They opened the gate at 905 Loma Vista, and they drove in. And the thing that was odd was that all the lights in the house were on and they couldn't understand why.*

Back then, and it's still true today—at the end of the day or after an evening event, protocol is for all the lights to be turned off and for the mansion to be locked tight. Again, this is boilerplate normal protocol. But back in the 1980s when this took place, the power had to be turned on down in the basement by throwing the switches. So the question is: How did all these lights come on? They would all have to be set in the "on" position at each individual switch in order for the master panel switch to be thrown allowing them all to be on. But when the mansion is secured at the end of the day, all the switches are shut off. It just doesn't add up. Regardless…

Chad: *So they looked for signs of entry. They checked for broken windows, everything, but they couldn't find anything unusual. And then their hand-held radios—as well as their cars radios and their car engines—all started crackling and sputtering. Some officers had been sent down to the basement, others were upstairs… and some were outside. Suddenly out of the blue, all at once, all the lights in the house shut off! Then all their flashlights shut off. Then all their radios went dead. Their car headlights shut off. And then their car engines stopped!*

It sounds like an EMP[1] [electromagnetic pulse] *or something like that happened. And he says they completely freaked out! Remember, these are cops. And the most freaked out were the cops in the dark down in the basement. When they all finally raced out of the mansion, their cars suddenly started up again! They jumped inside their vehicles and peeled out—they just got the hell out of there! And he said he thinks they didn't even lock the front door. They just left it unlocked and got out!*

---

1 An EMP is a short burst (pulse) of electromagnetic energy which is often disruptive or damaging to electronic equipment.

Chapter 31

Courtyards

I definitely know that it was a man screaming in agony and pain.
— CHANH HANG
GREYSTONE LEAD PARK RANGER

Photo: Bryan Houser

Many Hollywood movies and network television shows have used the mansion Courtyards for filming locations. In 2008, *Superhero,* starring Tracy Morgan was filmed here. And back in 1964, the Jerry Lewis comedy *The Disorderly Orderly* was also filmed here. Two year later, in 1966, Debbie Reynolds graced the Inner Courtyard in *The Singing Nun. Above the Law,* starring Steven Seagal, was shot here in 1988, and then in 2007, *National Treasure: Book of Secrets,* starring Nicholas Cage, was also filmed in this location. Other films include: *Teenage Mutant Ninja Turtles* (2014), *Batman and Robin, Town & Country, Bird, X-Men, Stripes* starring Bill Murray and John Candy, *The Day Mars Invaded Earth, All of Me, Instant Trauma, Death Becomes Her,* and *America's Sweethearts* with Julia Roberts and John Cusack.

The Inner Courtyard is breathtaking. A beautiful fountain anchors the center of this location, complete with four spitters that add a whimsical touch. Vermont slate covers the circular driveway. If you stand in the middle of this courtyard, you're surrounded by the Servants' Wing (and living quarters), the Boys' Wing, the Recreation Wing, as well as the garage. The East and West Courtyards are located on either side of this central courtyard. Adjacent to the east courtyard is the Firehouse, which now contains offices above and public restrooms below.

Please note: I've combined the west, inner, and east courtyards in this chapter. They are all exterior areas that surround the mansion.

EAST COURTYARD

"DISAPPEARED"

STEVEN CLARK
(Retired Park Ranger Supervisor)

> Steven: *We were closing up and these two guys approached me, "We can't find our friend." And I said, "Well, we're closing up. Meet him in the upper parking lot." We started walking this way* [toward the east courtyard] *and it was at this staircase* [leading up to the back door of the theatre] *where I said, "What does he look like?" And I walk over here by the stairs and look over and I see a guy sitting on the stairs like this, his elbows up, just lounging here and I look away over to them and I say, "Oh, he's right here." And then I looked back at him and the guy's not there! When I looked, I actually saw this person. Then I started thinking about it, and my instincts kind of said that it was the same person or apparition that Rob Wlodarski and I saw going down the stairs—sandy blonde hair, early thirties, could have been late twenties. But I swear, we were looking for this guy and I look over and I'm like, "Oh, he's right here." And then there*

370

was nobody there when they turned around to look. They're looking at me like what the hell? I said, "I swear there was somebody just sitting here right now." He was solid. I saw his whole body. I mean, legs, the arms, he's just sitting there. But he looked like the same as the guy coming down the spiral staircase [Chapter 29 – Recreation Wing].

Inner Courtyard

Greystone Historical Report

"My sister Dickie got married in 1938. That was quite a big operation. They put a big canvas tarp over the central courtyard, but it caught fire the day before the wedding. They had to put another one up. That was where the reception was held." —Timothy Doheny

---

"Agony and Pain"
CHANH HANG
(Lead Park Ranger)

Chanh: *I came to Greystone at six-thirty in the morning* [June 29, 2018] *and pulled up the driveway to the west courtyard and parked my car there. In order to enter the inner courtyard from the west courtyard, you must pass through the "Richie Rich" gates which are designed out of metal and lock together with a heavy chain. Well this morning, it was a beautiful day. So before I open up, I backed up my car to take a picture of my car with the mansion in the background. While taking the pictures with my back turned towards the Richie Rich gates, I hear behind me in the inner courtyard, the loud sound of a man moaning in pain. I turned around and looked toward the courtyard to see if somebody was there. I unlocked the lock and chain on the Richie Rich gate, which makes a lot of rattling noise, but didn't open the gate yet. I thought I could still hear that same agony and pain of a man groaning. As I held the chain tight to keep it from making any noise, I caught a low-end sound of a "Uuggghhh!"* [he makes a groaning voice]. *And I'm like, "Nah, it can't be." So I opened the gates, unlocked the mansion, disarmed the alarm and stood inside at the front entrance. It's very quiet. I walked out to the courtyard toward the fountain to turn it on. Right when I pass the fountain, I thought I heard the same sound again* [he makes another groaning sound]. *And then I thought, "Okay. I definitely know that it was a man screaming in agony and pain." But it's like distant. It's far away. I don't know if I can pinpoint where it's coming from. The basement? In the mansion? Because it's like a bowl in the courtyard.*

The Inner Courtyard is surrounded by the cement and limestone structure of the building and sounds bounce everywhere. In fact, Chanh explains it perfectly when he calls it a "bowl" effect— there is a hollowness to the sounds and everything echoes.

Chanh: *So I stood there in silence for a minute, just to see if I could hear the sound again. Hopefully I can pinpoint the exact location. But nothing. So I continue to the east end of the courtyard and open up the double-wooden courtyard doors. They make a lot of noise and I thought I heard the sound again, but I'm not sure. Now I'm closest to the catering kitchen door and there it is—I hear it again. So I propped open the wooden doors and stood there. I caught a little bit of the end part; it's like this...* [Chanh makes another sound like a man yelling in pain] *and then it just fades. The sound reminds me of a recording from many years ago [we now call "The Screams and Wails"] that we play a lot on our tours. This was similar to the very same sound that's on that recording. But I never did pinpoint the exact location of the screams.*

West Courtyard

When Ranger Chanh told me this story, I had him accompany me out to the "Richie Rich" gates so he could physically show me exactly what happened. He kept reenacting the movement with the gate and looking at me like, "You tell me how this is possible?!" Then he would show me again. And after actually seeing what he experienced, I had to agree with him—how the hell was this possible?

"May the Force Be with You"

CHANH HANG

(Lead Park Ranger)

Chanh: *It was a Friday night* [Winter, 2017]. *I was working "The Manor," a play loosely based on the trials and tribulations of the Doheny family performed in the mansion. All the guests are leaving between eight-thirty and nine. I don't lock up the courtyard until all the cast members are gone. Once they are out, I make sure the mansion is empty, I lock the doors, and then I arm it. The last gate to be locked is the courtyard gate, which is a wrought iron gate made for the film* Richie Rich. *It's not solid at all. It's two gates with a chain that wraps around the gates and then is locked with a padlock. So that night when I close the two gates, I use my flashlight so I can see what I'm doing, it's dark… and I wrap the chain around the gate and I lock it. As soon as I pull the key out of the lock, it felt as if I locked someone inside a prison. It was like the person that I locked inside grabbed the gate and angrily shoved it towards me trying to get out. I physically felt the gate lunge toward me with force. The only thing that was holding the gate from hitting me was the chain and lock securing the gate together. I stepped back for a second with my flashlight shining on the gate. No wind. Nothing. The gates are not solid. See-through, wide-open wrought iron. Wind can't push this thing. A kid can stick their head through the gate between the openings.*

373

Officially, we do not condone children sticking their heads through the Richie Rich gates.

Chanh: *I thought to myself, "What the F just happened?!" I backed up slowly… backed up, backed up with my flashlight still pointing at the gate until I was maybe eight or ten feet away. I immediately turned around and walked toward my ranger truck, got in and left for the night. I mean, how could wind push that gate with such power? And there was no wind that night anyway! It had to be some kind of force.*

Chapter 32

Firehouse and Restrooms

I definitely got chills right when it happened. It shocked me throughout my body for the next five minutes. I was definitely shaken with chills to where I screamed pretty loud!

— VINICIO CASTRO
JANITORIAL SERVICES

Photo: Chris Keith

From 1912 to 1913, Edward L. Doheny completed the purchase of 429 acres of land in what became known as the "Doheny Ranch." With that amount of acreage, they needed a fire station to ensure they had the ability to get to a fire immediately to extinguish the flames. That building remains today and rests adjacent to the east courtyard, near the mansion. Currently, the two-story Firehouse has offices above and two of the three bays below have been turned into public restrooms.

This incident was very odd. I know. I was there.

There are stories in this book where two people are together and see the same thing, but they both have sensitive abilities. An example of this was when Steve Clark (Ranger) and Rob Wlodarski (medium/investigator) were present at the Spiral Staircase in the Recreation Wing chapter. They both have "the gift," they both saw a spirit coming down the staircase at the same time, and they both described its appearance the exact same way. Conversely, Alex and Felix (also in the Recreation Wing - Spiral Staircase chapter), as far as I know, don't have "the gift" and they both saw an apparition coming down the same staircase. I believe these examples, along with so many other contradictions, underscore the idea that there are no rules to seeing spirits. What happens, happens. Semi-controlled chaos.

This next incident happened to Ranger Juan and me up in our offices. It's important to note that between our offices is a non-functioning restroom separating the spaces. When sitting at his desk, Juan can see through the restroom area into my office with a view of the computer printer, as well as the desk of Greystone's Venue Coordinator. With a desk of my own, I share this office... so it surprised me when Juan walked through the restroom and into my office. I looked up from my computer and by the way he was looking at me, I knew something had happened. I grabbed my recorder and the following is our conversation.

"VISITOR BY THE PRINTER"

A CONVERSATION WITH JUAN ANDRADE
(Park Ranger Supervisor)

Juan looks at the sink and then back to me, "I thought it was you coming over here to get something." At this point, I had no idea what he was talking about. "What do you mean?" He is clearly dumbfounded when he tells me, "I just saw someone walk over to this sink near the printer." I can see Juan is on the edge of being unnerved when I try and be clear on what he just saw. "So you're in your office. I'm here in mine. And you looked over and what did you see?" Juan is shaking his head. He says, "A guy that I thought was you."

This is all new territory. We've never had something paranormal happen in our Firehouse offices. Now I'm dumbfounded. I need to know specifics.

"Was it just the movement of someone or could you see clothes?" He looks back at the sink and recalls the specifics. "It was dressed, I want to say, in white. He walked very, very slow. I thought it was you, but it wasn't. I got goose bumps. I almost wanted to cry." I can see he's still a little overwhelmed. "So how did you know it wasn't me?" I ask. "You're looking over and you saw somebody in white, but you're not looking straight on? Was it out of your peripheral?" He nods, "Yes—and as soon as I saw it, I had goose bumps, I wanted to cry. Something or someone walked right over here to the sink." I let him know my thoughts, "So Juan, this is a prime example of your "gift" because I'm here at my desk and I saw nothing. No white shirt, no goose bumps, no emotion, nothing. And you're feeling and seeing real energy."

We both take a moment to process. Then I asked Juan, "Do you think he was looking at you or was he just standing there?" Juan shakes his head. "No, it felt like he was doing his own thing. He was white, slender, maybe five foot nine." I push him to clarify, "And by 'white,' you mean a Caucasian? In other words, it wasn't an all-white shadow type figure. You actually saw his skin tone and he was Caucasian?" He answers immediately, "Yes. Also, I could clearly see some type of pants and a shirt. It was a male. His pants were gray with some type of white shirt." Juan sometimes gets a feeling as to the spirit's intentions. "Did you get any vibe as to whether he was good or bad? Positive or negative?" Juan thinks for a quick moment, "I want to say positive. I didn't feel any negative energy, but just the thought that I saw something pass by gave me chills. And when I saw it cross from my peripheral vision, it gave me a sense of emotion, strong emotion, like, my eyes got teary." I could tell this when Juan stepped into my room. "Was it solid or see-through?" He's certain as certain can be. "No, this one was solid. But it also had like a white glow to it. White shirt, long sleeves, like a dress shirt you would tuck in."

It's clear that the more Juan experiences Greystone, the sharper his abilities become. "How are you feeling, right now? What's going through your head? You're in your office, you're seeing these things. You must be tripped-out?" Juan shrugs. "I've never really felt too much up here. But I'm fine right now. No emotion. That only lasted from the time I got up out of my chair and came in here. As I began telling you what happened, it slowly went away." He seems to be calming down. "I could see it on your face that there was some type of emotion attached to what you just experienced." Juan agrees, "Yeah, there was. But that was… weird."

"Sigh"

In the fall of 2019, contractors galore were working on the renovation of the mansion's theatre. Several of those contractors are featured in this book. One of these contractors told me I should talk to his co-worker about a paranormal incident. At the time, he was setting up audio-visual equipment in the theatre. I immediately approached him, and he said he would talk about what happened. I conducted the interview right there. The next day he flagged me down and said he didn't want to be in the book. I've had this experience with several people. The idea of telling the world about your bizarre "ghost story" stands a good chance of having folks—even people you know and love—labeling you as:

crackpot • nutjob • losing your marbles • harebrained • half-baked
absurd • idiotic • off the wall • unbalanced • stark raving mad
loopy • looney tunes • just plain crazy

you name it, fill in the blank…

Or you'll be accused of simply "looking for attention."

For some, it just isn't worth it. And I get it. So I tried this: and if he wasn't comfortable with the idea, I would drop it—so I asked him if he would approve using the story if we used an alias instead of his actual name. He finally said I could use "G." So with that in mind, here is a strange story by G…

"G"
(Audio Visual Foreman)

> G: *We're the audio integration company doing the AV in the theatre. On the sixth of November, 2019, my second day here, we had to lay out the cable tray and the projection booth. And before leaving to go home, I use the restroom. Now I'm the only one in the restroom and the bathroom door is open. I can see the door from my peripheral. So I know no one walked in while I was in there. I remember on the way in, the three stall doors were swung wide open so I could tell there was no one in there as well. The stall to my left, which is the handicap one, was also open. So I know for sure no one else was in the bathroom. I'm standing at a urinal, and to my right, in my estimation, no more than four feet away, audibly, I hear* [he makes a loud sigh]. *It startled me because there's no one to my right. There's no one anywhere. I thought maybe someone walked in and they're in the stall. But based on my perception, the sound, this sigh was closer than the stall. But since there's no one there, it must be someone in the stall. So as I got done, I bent down to look underneath the stall to see if I could see some feet there, and there were no feet.*

Again, I always wait for and am tickled when I hear the rationalization or the justifying of what happened to those who have had an honest-to-god experience. At first, the narrative is told as real, because when the experience happened, it was real to them. In G's case, he heard something (and this is a trained audio professional), so when there isn't a rational explanation, he has to figure out some way of justifying that it was real… again, because it was real. And trust me, we all do the same. I have on numerous occasions. It's what separates us from the beasts: we have the ability to reason. And when it comes to the paranormal, we need to find a plausible reason.

> G: *So I thought there must be a child and they're standing on the toilet seat. I walked around and I looked at the door, and the door is still in the position that it was when I walked in. No one was there. In the other two stalls, no one was there. And now I'm like, "Am I hearing things?" So I still didn't believe because I'm like, there's no way. Maybe I'm tired. So I go outside and the ranger [Patrick] was sitting in his truck with the engine running getting ready to leave. I said, "Hey, tell me something. Is this place haunted?" And I was kind of kidding at that point. I wasn't serious because I'm thinking there's no way, and so the reaction I'm expecting from him is, "No, get outta here. Why would you say that?" And he turns his truck off and says, "Yes, it is."*

G pauses here remembering his reaction to an answer he wasn't expecting.

> G: *And I go, "Really?" And the ranger says, "Yeah, yeah, we've had stuff happen here." And I go, "No, dude, you're serious?" He goes, "Yeah." He gets out of his truck and asks me to show him where it happened. So we walk over to the restroom, and I said, "This restroom." And he goes, "This restroom?" And I said, "Yeah, why is that a big deal?" And he goes, "Just last week, one of the cleaning personnel, a female [Andrea Flores], she had her hair pulled in the female restroom next door." And so now I'm getting goose bumps all over. That was really an encounter I had, and I was like,*

"Wow." But I can't say I recall feeling any difference in the environment or any energy, chills or heat. I don't remember feeling anything. It sounded like a male. A deep, heavy sigh. Is it that he's tired or is it frustration?

G recreates the sound again, as if he needs to convince himself one more time.

G: *You know, I don't know what it was. I just know I heard a deep male tone. A deep sigh. A real heavy sigh. But it was an adult, it was not a child. I just thought maybe it's a child because only a child would stand on the toilet seat where I can't see their feet. Even though I'm in technology, I still don't know how half the things we do work, right? What happens inside the box that you can't see? But I know it works. I know if I connect the speaker to this amplifier and that person talks on the microphone, it works. When their diaphragm transmits energy into the microphone, the mic sends the sound to the speaker and we hear it. But beyond that, I can't tell you what else happens inside the box.*

What a great analogy to use in the process of trying to understand the paranormal. G then offers his philosophical take on the "seen and unseen" behavior at Greystone.

G: *So I use that as an example. I can't tell you how the non-living would be able to make audible sounds or make things move or make people hear things that are not there. Because I've heard, after mentioning this to other folks, I've heard that the night crew, when they go lock up inside the theatre, after walking away from the door they hear what sounds like the whole building collapse and when they open the door, everything is the same. I don't know how something that's not tangible, that's not there, can physically make things move and sound. I don't know. But I know what I heard. So that's one more event in the forty-seven years I've been alive to help maybe convince me that it is possible. So even if I was a non-believer before, now I believe a little bit more because I heard it. Firsthand.*

Someone didn't tell me—I experienced this for myself. And then adding up all the data that I've gathered from these stories that people have told me, their experiences, whether first or second hand, it has to be someone who lived here years ago and is very unhappy with all the activity. I don't know how many upgrades they've had here in the last several years. Maybe they're just not happy with the changes and so they're a little unsettled. I don't know if the things that we hear or experience, is just frustration with the goal to scare people away. Like, "Hey, leave us alone. Get away from here. Don't do that. Don't touch this!" It seems like someone, whoever it is, is unhappy with strangers meddling with their stuff.

Pretty great insight from someone who just hours ago was a non-believer until he stepped up to a urinal.

"THAT'S NOT THE WATER GUY!"

As you know by now, Andrea Flores is one of the stars of this book. She experienced this next incident just before Thanksgiving in 2019. It was approximately eight o'clock in the evening. Notice how amazingly detailed Andrea's descriptions are in this segment.

ANDREA FLORES
(Janitorial Services)

Andrea: *I was here to clean the restrooms at the firehouse. The service gate wasn't working, so I entered through the main gate* [905 Loma Vista]. *One of the water guys* [City worker who checks the reservoir and pump station in the park] *that I didn't know, was out there. So I talked to him and I said, "Hey, are you going to be here?" And he said, "I'm leaving in ten minutes." And I told him, "Okay, I'm just getting in. I'm with the janitorial company." And he said, "Oh, okay, don't worry, I'm going to leave the gate unlocked for you. When you leave, please just make sure to lock it, because if not, I'm going to be in trouble." And I told him not to worry. So I get to the mansion and sometimes they* [the City workers checking the pump station at night] *use the restrooms. So I'm in the family restroom storage area* [which is located just off the AFI parking lot, east side of the firehouse]. *I'm inside filling up a bucket with water, and I felt someone walking behind me outside the door and I thought, "Hey, the water guy is walking to the restroom, but I remember that door is locked because I haven't been in there yet. So I turn around and I see a guy with a long brown, beige, wool overcoat. The main color is beige, but there is also plaid in the brown, green, and burgundy. He is walking fast, and he suddenly turns towards me. I can't see his face. There is a light on outside—I can see him, the body, but I just can't see his face. Although I did see he has a pointy nose. I can't tell any other details. Also, he has on a fedora hat. He is a whole figure. Full body. But I can't see through him. He is solid. He looks at me, but he keeps walking and I thought, "That's not the water guy! The water guy had no hat and was wearing a blue jacket!" So I ran after him, but he was gone. And it obviously wasn't the water guy.*

Unless he did a wardrobe change!

Andrea: *This was not the usual shadow like I've seen in the past. When I saw this guy, I didn't feel bad. I didn't feel like anything was wrong. In fact, when I got out of here, I texted Vilma* [co-worker], *telling her what happened and she called me and said, "Are you okay?!" And I said, "Yeah, I'm fine." She said, "Why are you so calm?" And I said, "Because I didn't feel it was something bad. It was just a guy. And I didn't feel threatened. He looked at me and kept walking. So I cleaned the restrooms and left."*

For her to finish cleaning the restrooms after such a sighting is crazy. I feel like such a worm. I wouldn't have the nerve. I think you know what I'd do by now… hide behind my sister, Kacey!

"THE MAN IN THE MIRROR"

CLETE KEITH

I was working a film shoot. The crew and I were at the park late to complete their shots inside the mansion. Outside, in the west courtyard, is where they set up craft services (snacks, food, and drinks for the crew). I went over with one of the rangers to grab a cup of coffee when the conversation turned, as it frequently does in and around Greystone, to the topic of ghosts. The exchanges usually unfold like this:

Them: *Is this place haunted? Or, Are there ghosts in this mansion?*
Me: *I don't know. What do you think?*
Them: *No. I don't believe in ghosts.*
Me: *Okay.*
Them: *But have you ever seen anything? Is it scary?*
Me: *I thought you don't believe in ghosts.*
Them Again: *Right, I don't believe in that stuff. But it must be scary.*

I would engage them in conversation, but never try to convince them that the location has activity. For most people, they don't believe it unless they experience it themselves. And I understand that. I feel the same way.

Back at craft services… they all started laughing and kind of chatting with us and I told them, "If you're here long enough, you might end up believing." One of the guys came over to me and said, "Can I talk to you a minute?" We walk away from the others. He turns to me and says, "I really don't believe in this stuff. I never did." And I replied, "That's okay. I'm not asking anybody to believe anything." He lowers his voice and says, "No, no. The thing is… I've got to talk to you about what happened to me." We walk further away. As we stand facing each other, I can tell something happened that really shook him up and I say, "Tell me what's going on." He says, "On one of the breaks tonight, I go over to the restroom and I wash my hands. When I finish, I glance up in the mirror and behind me is a man standing there, staring at me." I ask, "He wasn't part of your crew?" He hesitated and finally said, "No. Absolutely not." I continue to question, "Are you sure he wasn't maybe an actor in the show?" He shakes his head. "No. He looked like he was from a different era. I looked away and then I look back and he is gone." I said, "Are you sure it wasn't maybe somebody just walking by?" He said, "No. No way." I asked him, "But you remember what he looked like?" He nods, "Yeah." I asked him if he had a couple of minutes to check something out.

We walk inside the mansion and I take him to the Servants' Wing—inside a small, makeshift storage area. I take out my flashlight and start pulling out posters and photos that relate to the mansion and its history. I hold up the first poster with people and faces: Edward L. Doheny and others of his era standing next to each other. I asked, "Do you recognize anyone here?" He said, "No." I pull out another poster that shows more people involved with, or friends of, the Doheny family. Again, "No." I show him several more photos and he still doesn't recognize anyone. I pull out another poster and show him.[1] The look on his face says it all. His eyes open wide as he stares at the poster. He finally utters, "That's him. That's the guy. Who is this guy?" And with a slight hesitation I say, "His name is Hugh Plunkett. He was Ned Doheny's secretary." He is stunned that he has seen a spirit from the past, but he isn't aware of the history of the family. I gave him a quick history lesson and ended with, "He died in the mansion in 1929. It was a murder-suicide with Ned." Now he's totally shocked: "No, no, no, no." He kept shaking his head in disbelief. We walk outside and he walked back into the crowd of crew members who are working on the film. I didn't see him again. I don't know if he finished out the night or left, but by the look on his face, I knew he was extremely unnerved. And now, I'm guessing, he is a true believer.

1 The poster at the time was the property of Friends of Greystone. No additional information available.

"ANGER, FEAR, AND NOISE"
ERNESTO CELIS-ZARATE
(Janitorial Services)

Ernesto: *Every time I go to clean the firehouse bathrooms, I'm just nervous. You know that little walkway from the men's restroom to the women's? There's something that makes me turn to look at the mansion. Something gets me nervous and I get so angry. I feel so mad. There was so much anger in me, and I don't know why. And then I got hot, and also a headache. When I went to Coldwater Park, the headache was still there. And by the time I got to Will Rogers* [another city park], *it was gone. I'm trying not to think about what is causing this because I still have to clean on Sundays! But it's that little walkway. Every time I'm walking back from the women's restroom, I feel something. It's always been there. Like someone's looking at me, I feel nervous. Like fear. I try not to pay attention to it and just try and get away from it.*

I ask Ernesto if he could give me a specific example.

Ernesto: *On another day it was windy. I was cleaning the women's restroom and I was changing the toilet paper. So I changed one, I locked the dispenser, and when I was in the next stall, I heard the noise of someone opening that dispenser. I heard the metal noise, just like someone had opened it, and when I looked back in that previous stall, I see nothing. Everything is locked. And I had the main door closed and locked while working.*

Justification Alert!

Ernesto: *And I'm thinking maybe the wind? Then there was another noise after that. It was the sound of a little metal door slam. Like the little metal door on the left wall when you walk in. So I want to say it was the wind,*

386

but there was no wind at all. So I just put myself in God's hands, and that's it. That's what I do, and I try not to think of it.

"Bump and Touch"

Juan and I have become good friends, in part, by bonding over these circumstances in which he finds himself interacting with the paranormal. He knows I don't judge him or think he's nuts or make light of these situations. I'm there to listen and help him figure out what has taken place and remind him that he has the ability to connect with the other side and the spirits are trying to connect with him. "Juan, think of it this way: it's an honor. They trust you." He smiles, "I hope so!" This next incident happened on a Saturday night in February of 2020—the day after Valentine's Day. Juan was working the annual Mother-Son Dance at the mansion. He called me on my cellphone right after it happened. He was unsettled by this event, but as we talked it out, he started to calm down.

JUAN ANDRADE
(Park Ranger Supervisor)

Juan: *We just finished the event and I came over here to my office to put away a check. I was putting a key in the closet and I heard a bump in your office. And I thought that was weird 'cause it was kinda loud. And then, as I was standing right in front of the closet in my office, I felt someone touch the top of my head and I got shivers and started getting very, very emotional. And that's when I called you. But it wasn't a stroke, it was a direct tap on my head. I could feel my hair being pressed down. It stayed with me, but I called you so I could get over it. But I'm pretty scared to go on your side of the office right now. The spirit felt playful, like someone fooling around, touching the very top of my head. After that, I grabbed my stuff, got out of the office and called you.*

"HARD YANK!"

Andrea experienced this activity in September of 2019.

ANDREA FLORES
(Janitorial Services)

> Andrea: *I was cleaning the men's restroom and I felt the energy. A weird energy all over the place. I could feel it inside and all over my body. It felt like I was having some kind of electricity running up and down all over my body, then all of a sudden it stopped. So I rushed into the lady's restroom to quickly clean and leave. I started cleaning the mirror and as I was looking in the mirror, there was no one behind me, and suddenly I felt my hair get pulled back. They just grabbed me by the hair and pulled it back. Hard. It didn't hurt, but it was hard like this.*

Andrea shows me. It was a hard yank, forcing her head back.

> Andrea: *It was as if it were calling at me and getting my attention like, "Hey!" So I turned around. I knew there was no one, but I turned around and I started talking to them. I said, "If you want to talk to me, just show yourself! I want to talk to you. Stop doing this to me!" But nothing. No response. Nothing at all. And I felt scared. Really scared. In fact, I left the trash. I never do that. I left the trash inside the storage room and I didn't even empty the bucket of water. I just thought, you know what, I'm done. I'll be here tomorrow morning. And I left. But when I left, I couldn't bear to look up at the bridge as I was driving down.*

She looks totally unnerved. I can tell it was overwhelming. At moments like this, I stop asking questions and let her talk and get it out.

Andrea: *I was scared, but every time I get in the car, I'm okay. But last night I was scared until I got off the property. So it's a third time in less than two weeks that they've touched my hair. They've touched me and they've touched my hair. But this time, they pulled it. The first two times they just kind of do this* [she shows me a caress]. *But this time they just pulled it. I don't know if it's a male or female… but I know they want my attention. This last time, they really wanted my attention. I didn't get any goose bumps, but I literally got the sweats when I left. But tonight, Louisa and her husband will be here cleaning. She's here Monday through Friday. She has never talked about it, but I think she has had things happen to her. I don't want to talk to her about it because I don't want to lose another janitor!*

"REALLY INTENSE"

When I heard about Vinicio from Andrea, this was the story I wanted to hear. Obviously, nothing about this location surprises me now that I've been here so long and have interviewed so many witnesses. But this story really intrigued me. Vinicio met me at Greystone and we walked up to the Firehouse restrooms. To watch him stand in the spot where on a pitch dark night, something happened that terrified him to the core, was chilling.

VINICIO CASTRO

(Janitorial Services)

Vinicio: *I was helping Andrea clean one night. When she walked away down the steps on the east side of the building, I took a break and stepped out of the men's restroom for a second. I walked over and stood right in front of the ramp against the fence and looked out into the night. Suddenly something grabbed my calf on my left leg! I tried to yank it away! That's how I knew something was holding my leg because besides being grabbed, I tried to move my foot and at first it didn't budge and that's when I went into panic mode. I felt a weird vibration. Like, I definitely got chills right when it happened. It shocked me throughout my body for the next five minutes. I was definitely shaken with chills to where I screamed pretty loud! Andrea heard me and hurried back up the steps. I explained to her what happened. I was straightforward. I told her it felt like a hand grabbed my leg. She stared at me, not knowing how to respond. Then she finally said, "That does happen here." It was really frightening because what I pictured at the moment in my head, like a quick picture, was someone was down here by the tree on the other side of the fence, reaching through the railing and grabbing my leg. It was aggressive, not like a light touch or tap—this held on for a good second. But I yanked my leg twice. The first time it didn't let go. The second time I kind of tumbled backwards. Not enough to fall, but at least like two steps and that's when I started screaming really loud, "Oh shit! Fuck! Fuck! Fuck!" This was around midnight, so obviously it's dark out here and I didn't see anything. It was really intense. I've heard stories before and I was pretty much a skeptic about this location. I didn't believe, so I thought maybe people were just scared here or their mind took over and a moment of fear happened. So I wasn't scared. And then it happened to me, it changed my whole perspective on this place.*

I've conducted many interviews for this book and the way Vinicio told me his story, I had a sense of what he may have been thinking. So I asked him, "Do you think that mentally you were, in essence, calling it out— maybe even daring it to come out—since you didn't believe this place was haunted?"

Vinicio: *I feel like at some point that night I might've thought, maybe subliminally, that it wasn't haunted. That stuff people said wasn't real. I'd only believe it if I saw it. And then I think it just manifested itself... but this was a bad kind of negative energy. It felt pretty awful.*

Chapter 33

Driveway and Loma Vista Gate

What I feel is, it's a devil. Something really, really bad. Someone who was really bad a long time ago, and is still here and that has transformed into something darker.

— ANDREA FLORES
  JANITORIAL SERVICES

Photo: Chris Keith

Driving up toward the mansion from the Loma Vista Gate, the road splits like a "Y." One part continues toward the West Courtyard, while the other bends around a huge pine tree and heads behind the Recreation Wing toward the Firehouse—which was equipped to fight fires. The original property was 429 acres, so if fire broke out, they needed to have their own "fire department." In fact, from 1929 through the sale in 1955, Greystone (originally named "Doheny Ranch") operated

393

almost like its own town or village complete with firefighters, mechanics, gatekeepers, and so forth.

Just off the Boys' Wing Study, above the Driveway, is an overpass that literally bridges the gap from the north side of the mansion to the walkways leading to the gardens above.

Greystone Historical Report

Emile Kuehl [lead designer] had followed Paul Thiene's [landscape architect] instructions and given the Doheny's "everything." The hillside behind the mansion had been transformed into terraces and a series of Italian Renaissance-inspired "garden rooms" containing a formal rose garden, cypress alley, swimming pool, and tennis courts, all linked by paths winding through dense stands of drought-resistant trees. For these terraces, fountains, and gardens, "no attempt was made to use cheaper materials," recalled Emile Kuehl almost fifty years later. [Kuehl continues] "The walks were all Vermont slate. The stone for walls was limestone shipped from Indiana. Ornamental lead pieces came from England. Sculptural stone details were all carved on the job."

Photo: Clete Keith

Several films used the driveway as a location, including Marvel's *X-Men*, with Hugh Jackman and Halle Berry, *All of Me*, *Rush Hour* with Jackie Chan, *Star Trek Into Darkness*, *Rock Star* with Mark Wahlberg and Jennifer Aniston, *Austin Powers in Goldmember*, *Stripes*, *The Loved One*, *The Prestige*, and *Teenage Mutant Ninja Turtles* with Megan Fox.

DRIVEWAY

"ZING!"

When Ranger Chae told me this story, his eyes said it all—fear. I was convinced that whatever he was about to tell me was true... or at least, he was totally convinced. When Chae described what happened, it was another first for me. I had compiled over one hundred stories by this time, but this one was markedly different. During our conversation, there were times even he felt it was impossible, that maybe it didn't happen. Again for Chae, like others, these experiences can be extremely hard to believe, let alone justify. We walked over to the driveway and stood where the incident took place. He was still uneasy and very demonstrative in relaying the story, which took place in November of 2016.

CHAE YI
(Lead Park Ranger)

Chae: *This was on a Saturday night around ten-thirty and I was getting off my shift. It was pretty cool that night and I had my windshield wipers going because of the condensation. Just as I got to this area where the bridge is* [about halfway down the driveway], *I came to a sudden complete stop because there was some type of silhouette or black smoke that appeared and floated across the front of my car. It was a mist or a silhouette of some kind. And it came out of this wall and crossed into this wall here, toward the movie theatre and bowling alley. I didn't know what it was. So I slammed on my brakes, gripped my wheel hard, and said to myself, "What the hell is that?!" Obviously, I had the headlights on and it was see-through. It looked almost like smoke and it was like a shadow of a figure. There was no indication that there was a human face or human body, it was just like a smoke figure moving across. Honestly, my first thought was, "Oh my God, what the fuck is that!?" As I kept driving* [through the path it crossed], *I got electrified! My whole body! Just energy, and I'm thinking, "What the hell is happening?!" I put the pedal to the floor and I just took off. I drove down to the service gate and just got out!*

I asked Chae to talk a bit more about the electricity and what it felt like as he drove through it.

Chae: *Honestly, it felt like I was being electrocuted. Like electricity running through my body. It was that intense. It wasn't a goose bump feeling, it was just zing! My whole body was electrified from head to toe. Like when you touch a live wire or a socket. It was that feeling through my whole entire body. I was like, "Oh God!" It didn't seem to affect my car, just my body. And when I drove off, the energy just went away. But I was stunned! I went out the service gate to Doheny Road and called* [Ranger] *Chanh. I said, "Chanh, you won't believe what just happened to me!" And I told him, and he said, "I told you! I told you there's something out there!" It was a crazy feeling. And I know that feeling because I hate electricity. I hate outlets. I don't touch anything electrical because I hate that feeling. But my whole body was electrocuted! This was really a ZING!!* [he mimics being zapped].

Chae takes a moment to compose himself—the memory of the electric "zing" really ramped him up.

Chae: *I was so surprised and couldn't believe what I saw and what happened to me! I was hoping it was a deer or some animal moving across the driveway, but that wouldn't give me the electricity feeling. Maybe I was just trying to psych myself into believing that it was something else. Maybe now it's roaming around inside the mansion! Who knows?*

Greystone Historical Report

Driving at Greystone presented an unexpected peril during winter rainstorms. Both sides of the driveway had a decorative inlaid brick border. The brick "became quite slippery when wet," says Sam Schultz, "and chauffeurs had to be careful about staying in the center of the driveway."

"ON THE BRIDGE"

I was fortunate because I interviewed Andrea the day after her experience. The event was still fresh in her mind.

ANDREA FLORES
(Janitorial Services)

> Andrea: *This was yesterday, the twenty-second of September, 2019. I got here around ten-ish at night. And as I made the turn on the driveway, I saw a figure standing on top of the bridge. Someone was there, but I couldn't look up because I was so scared. It was looking down at me. So today when it's bright out, I went up there to see if there was a plant or something on the bridge, because I thought there must be something that looks like a figure. No. There's nothing on the bridge. But it was kind of a white figure. I've never seen any white spirit before in my entire life.*

Did you tell Vilma?

> Andrea: *Yes, when I told Vilma, she was like, "I don't believe you. I don't believe you." I think she says that because it's not happening to her. And I hope it doesn't happen to her because I was so scared and I'm not sure how she would deal with it.*

On this same night, Andrea's hair was yanked in the women's bathroom (detailed in the Firehouse and Restrooms chapter). Was this the same spirit watching her arrive and then attacking her in the restroom?

Greystone Historical Report

East of the mansion was the estate's single most extravagant landscape feature: a waterfall that tumbled down an eighty-foot-high hillside of boulders before it fell into the upper lake, that emptied into the lower lake in a four-foot waterfall. While it ran from early morning until late at night, the cascade used 500 gallons of water a minute. But all this flow was continuously recycled by a thirty-horsepower pump that returned all the water from the lower lake to the top of the cascade.

LOMA VISTA GATE

Photo: Chris Keith

Edward Laurence Doheny purchased multiple land parcels in what is now known as Beverly Hills. The "Doheny Ranch" totaled 429 acres. He then gave his son, Ned, a 12.58 parcel at the far eastern end of the ranch. It is within this area today that the east entrance into Greystone Park is now located. Two large iron gates connect to secure the location. Next to that entrance is a small "guard shack." Twenty yards west of that is a small pump house station for the water department. Back when the property was constructed, there was a waterfall on this side of the mansion.

Greystone Historical Report

"We really used that property. I'll never forget the time I bought a new bass plug [hard-bodied fishing lure]. I went down to the pond at the bottom of the cascade to see how it looked in the water, and I caught a bass on the first cast. I caught fourteen bass and then put them all back. George Maile [Greystone assistant field superintendent] told me that the lake at one of our farms had gone dry. He had dumped the fish in the pond. I had no idea of that. Was I surprised when I threw the hook in and wham!"
—Timothy Doheny

"GOOSE BUMPS AND HEAVINESS"

Apparently, humans are not the exclusive vehicle of manifestation for spirits. Horses can even get in on the act. Retired Park Ranger Luz Rodriguez told me she spoke to overnight security guards who report they heard a horse's hooves clacking on the driveway and under the bridge by the Recreation Wing. The security guards told Luz that they looked for the source of this iconic sound but found and saw nothing. I've worked at Greystone for more than twenty years and I've never seen a horse in this neighborhood. There are no stables in the area except next to the car garages, and they've been dormant for at least eighty-five years.

Then in 2016, I heard that another overnight security guard had an experience while working on the Netflix show *OA* that was filming at Greystone. What she witnessed was beyond her scope of comprehension. When I heard her story, it was way beyond my comprehension as well. The following interview was conducted using an interpreter, as Ms. Cañas only speaks Spanish. She agreed to come back to Greystone and talk to me at the exact location of her paranormal interaction.

ISABEL CAÑAS
(Security Guard)

Isabel: *I was security by myself near the guard shack inside the park grounds. What I saw was quite a distance away and it was difficult to see because it was pitch dark. I heard a horse approaching because I could hear the hooves on the pavement. When he reached this pipe* [a large water pipe near the pump station, which is halfway down the driveway toward her location at the guard shack], *I shined my flashlight on him. I only saw part of him. He was wearing a white shirt and a very beautiful, big straw hat, like the type some gardeners wear; unfortunately, it covered his face. He was sitting on a horse, so his pants were covered by the saddle. The horse was so elegant, you have no idea. Grey and white. I've never seen a horse like that. But I could not tell that he was a ghost. He appeared natural. Solid. I couldn't see through him. I thought he would come closer, but he turned and went down the pathway here to the left* [south]. *When I tried using my flashlight to see him, it stopped working. I felt it was not natural when the light turned off. I thought maybe it was the batteries, but as he started going down the pathway, and I hurried up to see him, the light started working again. It was the first time I had worked here as a guard. I saw many people working on the property and thought maybe it was someone working at night. But then I started to think, they* [park employees] *know the gate is locked, if it was a park ranger, someone watching the grounds, why would they come down this way knowing it's locked? I'm not easily scared, but I have to admit, I did feel something strange when he headed down the hill away from me and my flashlight wouldn't come back on. That's when I got goose bumps. I thought maybe I was cold, but I felt my skin* [she nods "No"—her skin wasn't cold] *but my legs felt heavy. Stiff. Goose bumps and heaviness.*

As Isabel tells her story, it's unmistakable that she remembers the physical feelings vividly.

Isabel: *Right after this happened, I went up to talk to the two other security guards* [in the AFI lot], *and they were asleep* [she laughs]. *I thought to myself, "Keep sleeping." So I went up the hill and around the mansion looking for the horse and rider, but I saw nothing. I only heard the sounds of nature and what sounded like a coyote.*

Isabel is correct. There are coyotes that wander down from the canyons. For the nation's second largest metropolis—including the 'island' of Beverly Hills—Los Angeles has robust wildlife.

Isabel: *The next day I asked a gardener who worked here if anyone stays overnight on the grounds, and he told me "no." I have seen spirits at other jobs. Different apparitions. But this is the first time I've seen a man on a horse. No one has told me I have the gift, but I feel that I have the ability. I don't know why. Maybe it's because I'm not easily scared of things? I have these feelings, I don't know if it's God helping me, or if he gives me these feelings or premonitions, I don't know exactly what it is. I don't know if I came back here if he would appear again.*

Clearly, Isabel has the ability and "the gift." I wanted to know more. I asked her if she had any other feelings she can remember about the horse and its rider.

Isabel: *I think that vision of the man on the horse is a soul in pain. He wants to talk, but I don't know what about. My idea was to speak with him. To ask him about his sorrow. What does he need? What does he want with this place? This location? That was my idea, to ask him because I thought this is not normal. Nobody stays here overnight. Why would my light stop working? It must be someone in pain. Poor thing, I do feel that the spirit has unresolved sorrow or grief. If he got closer, I was going to talk to him and ask him why he's here. At first, I was very afraid. I felt my legs, my shins, they felt very heavy. But that went away. I did feel that it was something to do with the supernatural. It wasn't anything normal. I am scared to be here at night. Not because of the ghosts, but because of the animals I know that are here at night. The ghost isn't going to hurt me. I told the other security guards what happened, and they responded with "Ahhh! No way would I return if I saw something like that!"*

I found Isabel to be a remarkably strong individual. She faced a paranormal phenomenon and broke it down with ease and compassion. She admitted to being scared, but tossed that aside for a greater understanding. It's obvious she is a woman with great faith in herself and her beliefs. I only wish she had the encounter with the "soul in pain" that she wanted. He may have been able to ride off, leaving his pain behind.

"HARM"

This next incident took place the night after Andrea Flores saw the white figure staring down at her as she drove under the bridge on the driveway behind the Recreation Wing (documented earlier in this chapter). On the next night when Andrea arrives at work, she would usually enter through the service gate that has a keypad—but the keypad was out of service, so she has to enter through the Loma Vista Gate, which isn't an automatic gate. I don't know how this woman manages the strength to continue her night trek to Greystone to clean the restrooms, usually by herself, knowing at every turn she may be subjected to bizarre, spine-chilling paranormal activity. Would you have the nerve to enter this location in the dark of night having had as many terrifying events happen to you? Not knowing what might happen next? I've been up there at night, several times alone, and my answer is an easy and emphatic NO!

ANDREA FLORES
(Janitorial Services)

> Andrea: *It was a little before nine-thirty on a Saturday night* [November 23, 2019]. *I came in my personal truck with Vilma* [her co-worker], *and as soon as I got out of my truck at the 905 Loma Vista Gate, I started feeling the chills… and it was bad. I told Vilma, "Stay in the truck. If something happens to me, just drive away and call for help." But she got mad at me because she didn't know what was going on and she wanted to get out and help me with the gate. I said, "No, just stay in the truck. If something happens leave." I open the gate, drive the truck inside, stop, get out, close the gate, and I notice that one of the locks on the other side of the gate is unlocked. So I thought, okay, I'm gonna leave that one unlocked* [dummy locked] *and I'm gonna lock this one, so when I come to the gate later on my way out, I don't have to bring the keys to open it—I'll just move it to the side and drive out.*

Andrea sighs. I ask her if she felt anything strange once inside the gate.

> Andrea: *No. We clean the restrooms. Everything is okay. Vilma asked me if I am feeling anything weird and I said, "No, nothing. I'm feeling good." But Vilma seems a little bit shaky. And I say, "Do you feel anything?" And she says, "No, I'm just nervous." After cleaning, we get back to the gate. I get out of the truck and I tell her the same thing again, "If you see anything, if something happens, just drive away. Go for help." She says "You're crazy." And I tell her, "No, I'm not crazy. I'm just letting you know, if something happens do that." Now, when I get out, both the locks are now locked! And I'm sure—positive—that I left one unlocked. I'm totally sure because I consciously thought, "Hey, I'm going to leave it unlocked and I won't need the keys." So now both of them are locked—either the water guys came* [to check the pump station] *and locked them, which I'm not sure, 'cause I got*

403

here around nine-twenty and we left maybe twenty minutes later, which was fast. So we don't know if it was them. But then this isn't over because when I look toward that little house [small guard shack], *there's a black shadow looking straight at me. I can't see the face or anything, but I know that it is looking right at me. When I see this, I hurry into the truck and just drive away. And when we are almost in front of the Gatehouse, I tell Vilma, "I saw a black shadow." And she was like, "Get out of here!" And I say, "No, there was a dark, black shadow." So the feeling I had when I first got out, was from that black shadow.*

As she tells me this, I remember her experience with Elva (documented in Chapter 17 – Servants' Wing Second Floor). But before I can say anything—

Andrea: *And it was the same feeling that I had with Elva. I felt the same. But this time the shadow was looking at me. With Elva, the shadow was not looking at me, it was looking at her and I still didn't feel good. This time I felt like I was going to get physically harmed. That's what I felt. It was really bad. I could immediately feel that energy when I got out of my truck at the gate. What I feel is, it's a devil. Something really, really bad. Someone who was really bad a long time ago, and is still here and that has transformed into something darker. It's really dark and I feel almost as if it's not human. Even if you're dead, you're still human. This thing is something different. And the way I felt was so small. Helpless. I'm not anxious every time I show up here. When I get here my head is filled with all this work-related stuff or personal stuff. I don't get here thinking, "Oh, what's going to happen tonight?" I don't do that because if I do that, I will go crazy because then it's me provoking and creating this stuff. And I don't want that. Not now. Not ever!*

Chapter 34

Willow Pond
(at the AFI Lot)

It was tough knowing that I had to come back again for one more night... I'll never go inside. It was terrible. I'll never forget that.
— JD
SECURITY GUARD

Photo: Chris Keith

When entering the park, you drive up a hill and on the immediate left is a small parking lot—the AFI Lot—which is adjacent to a small pond. Named the "Willow Pond," this peaceful spot is not original to the property. There is a stream that's not natural. It's generated by a water pump, that feeds into the pond containing many koi fish and dozens of Red Eared Slider turtles. The parking lot was named after the American Film Institute (AFI), which established the AFI Conservatory for Advanced Film Studies at Greystone from 1969 to 1982. It was, and still is, often used to park generator trucks and trailers for various film and television productions.

Just when you think you've heard it all, Andrea tells me this story. It reminds me of Ranger Gabe's story (Chapter 12 – Servants Wing – First Floor), only this happened to Andrea in the winter, hence, her experience is more festive!

"I Hear Music"

ANDREA FLORES
(Janitorial Services)

> Andrea: *This one Saturday night during Christmastime, I was there by myself. It was around nine o'clock. I was walking close to the Willow Pond, by the old restrooms, talking to Vilma* [co-worker] *on the phone. Suddenly I could hear Christmas music. It was a female singer and I recognized the song and it was the old version. Not the new versions that come up every year, it was an older version.*

After this interview, I asked Andrea if she could listen to some Christmas songs and try to determine which song she heard. Success—she identified the song as "Winter Wonderland," written in 1934 by Felix Bernard and Richard Bernhard Smith. Dozens of artists have recorded this song, including Dean Martin and Johnny Mathis, but Andrea said the version she heard was recorded by then pop singer, Jo Stafford, in 1955.

> Andrea: *So I was telling Vilma there's some kind of party here, but it's hard for me to know where. When they do have parties, I can hear the music loud and clear everywhere. You can be close to the mansion, or inside the mansion, and you can hear the music from the parties and people yelling, having fun, and laughing. I could only hear the music close to the willow*

pond. When I would walk away to the road coming up from the entrance, I couldn't hear it. Nothing. Also, if I walked over to the firehouse, I could not hear the music. When I walked toward the trash bins [east end of the AFI parking lot] *I couldn't hear the music either, and that's not that far away* [20 yards]. *It's just in that one spot that I could hear the music. I have no idea where it was coming from. Artemio* [co-worker] *heard the same thing on a different day.*

"I HEAR MUSIC, TWO"

ARTEMIO RODAS

(Janitorial Services)

Artemio: *When I finished cleaning the bathrooms, I go to throw the trash in the bins, and on my way, I can hear music very low, and I'm thinking, "What is it? Maybe it's the neighbors." But if there's a party, I can hear the neighbor's music all over, no problem. But this music, it's not from the neighbors. I don't know what song it is, but I can hear and recognize that it's music. And it only gets a little louder near the pond. You can walk away over to the trash cans and you cannot hear it anymore. Maybe it's somebody listening to music with their iPhone, but there's nobody there at the mansion. I don't know if anyone else hears the music or just me. But that just doesn't make sense.*

"STRANGER ON THE BENCH"

Anthony Lennon's audio company has worked for years providing the City of Beverly Hills sound equipment on many events. He was at Greystone setting up his gear in the pool area near the top parking lot. It was the final show of the 2003 summer season for Catskills performing camp. On this infamous day, a doctor—distraught and riddled with cancer—sat on a bench at the Willow Pond and committed suicide by shooting himself in the head. I arrived not long after the shooting when the Beverly Hills Police were working the crime scene and Clark Fogg (see Foreword) was the crime scene investigator. The man left his suicide note in a Ziplock bag so it wouldn't get bloody, ensuring its readability. The aftermath of this tragedy was extremely sad and a brutal scene to witness.

On a bizarre note, a woman was driving up to the top parking lot to drop off her child for the Catskills Camp. She witnessed the shooting as she drove by. She continued up the driveway and told the camp counselors that a man just shot himself in the head by Willow Pond. She then said she was late for work, dropped off her child, and drove away. Hopefully, by now, she's altered her work ethic and has her priorities in order—"Have a great day, honey! Tell your counselor there's a dead man by the pond. Oh, and I hope you get the lead in Pippin! Bye!"

ANTHONY J. LENNON
(Audio Equipment Vendor)

Anthony: *I remember that we were doing Catskills and there were a couple of rangers at the gate* [park entrance off of Loma Vista]. *I could tell by the look on their faces that there was something up, something wrong. Nobody was really saying anything. So we set up everything in the pool area, off the top parking lot, for the Catskills show. Now, back then, when you went to the restroom, you had to come down from up top* [to the AFI lot] *because the new restrooms weren't built yet. So I walked down the hill and I remember passing the willow pond where the turtles are, and I see this older gentleman on the bench. Just sitting there. I just thought he was feeding the turtles. I went to the restroom and when I came back out, Steve Clark is standing near the exit and he tells me it's been a difficult morning. "We had an elderly gentleman shoot himself over by the pond." And I said, "I just saw somebody sitting on the bench." And Steve says that's impossible because the bench was just moved back and we cordoned it off. And I was like, "What? I just saw this guy sitting on the bench." Steve also told me the man's body had already been taken away. But the area was still cordoned off to the public* [to wash away the blood]. *I said again, "Steve... I just saw somebody, an older gentleman, sitting there at the bench." And I remember he looked like he was maybe in his fifties... maybe sixtyish. He had on like a tweed jacket. I don't know about his pants. But to me he resembled an older gentleman that was maybe out for his morning walk and he was sitting there feeding the turtles.*

In fact, the man who committed suicide was in his fifties. He was wearing a dark colored jogging suit, according to Clark Fogg, the crime scene investigator.

Anthony: *I didn't see anything cordoned off when I first walked past it. But when Steve mentioned it, I looked over at the bench and there were now orange cones to keep people out. The time it took between when I saw him, when I talked to Steve, and looked back to see if he was still there, was like 10-15 seconds. Impossible for somebody to get up and be out of that area in that amount of time. We would have seen him. It was just weird. Very weird. I know I'm not crazy. I know what I saw.*

AFI Lot

Photo: Clete Keith

"Calling Me"

Andrea's next experience happened on a summer evening between seven and seven-thirty.

ANDREA FLORES
(Janitorial Services)

> Andrea: *It was still daytime out. I was going to start cleaning the public restrooms when I noticed the old restrooms, the ones that are by the willow pond, had the storage double door open. It's never open, and it wasn't open when I got there. I swear it was closed when I was parking. I'm always checking everything around me. And the rangers are not here because the park is already closed. So the door is open, and the light is on. I go into the small restroom where we have our supplies stored. When I come out, I can*

410

see someone is sneaking out that storage unit door. I see something, but I can't see the face or anything like that. It's just like a shade. Like a shadow person. And I start feeling the chills. The energy. I think it's showing itself to me because I'm there. It scares me at first, but then I don't feel that it is something bad. I just wasn't expecting that because for a while everything [the activity in that area] was okay. And I am by myself and that's mostly when these things happen—I'm either by myself or with my cousin, who helps me sometimes. I didn't feel like it is a bad spirit. I don't know how else to call it. I didn't feel any bad vibes... but it drew my attention. There are no words, nothing, but he is calling me. I have to look. So I see the shadow peeking out, but I can't see a face. When I see it, I get scared and I look away. When I look back, it is gone. I didn't go back in that storage area to see if it was still there. I must be honest, it was the first time that I really got scared.

"BACK IN THE 1920S"

What really intrigued me about Roy's story was the fact that he was so specific and detailed as to what he saw. He was adamant that his experience was real, and he was very cavalier about the incident. It turns out that Roy has a personal history of paranormal activity since he was a child. So, again, it begs the question: Are spirits more apt to reveal themselves to those with "abilities?" And are those with these "abilities" able to see what those without abilities cannot?

ROY ESQUEDA
(Facilities Maintenance Mechanic)

Roy: It was during the daytime before lunch. I have a van that has a rearview camera and I was parking in reverse by the firehouse in the lot [AFI Lot]. As I was looking at the camera, it showed a lady dressed in what I would call 1920s attire. I was thinking it was probably someone getting married.

A very good assumption on Roy's part since he knows we have weddings and wedding photo shoots nearly every week of the year.

Roy: *So I ignored it, and turned off the engine. When I got out of the van and looked behind me, I saw a tree. There's no lady anywhere in sight. But while I was backing up, the whole time I was looking at the camera, the lady was there. She looked like she was from the 1920s. She was wearing a hat they used to wear like you'd normally see during that time. And the hat was black, which is weird because usually you'd see a white hat, for a wedding, right? She had on a dark coat; kind of a navy bluish, dark blue. She was wearing a dress, a lighter color than the jacket. And she just stared at the van as if I was trying to hit her backing up. But she just kept staring right at my camera. But honestly, I one hundred percent guarantee it was a woman. To the point where, when I got out of the van, I expected to see a woman, not a tree. So I just continued with my work. I ignored it. I grew up with demons all over me. I'm used to having doors opening, spirits touching me, whispering in my ears, grabbing my neck. The thing is, I know that if you play around with it, you will find it.*

"BUMPED AND SCRATCHED"

I usually meet every workday morning with Ranger Dan. We get together around six to six-thirty in the morning to catch up on what to expect that day before opening the park, as well as talk Lakers basketball. On this morning, when I rolled up to the AFI Lot, Dan was standing there with a strange look on his face—he seemed stunned. He was clearly agitated and anxious. I asked him what happened. When he started to explain, I began recording.

DANIEL HERNANDEZ
(Park Ranger Supervisor)

> Daniel: *It was my normal routine. I drive up the driveway and back my vehicle into a parking space in the AFI lot. And this time is the only time that I backed into the handicap spot. My first time ever. I usually park right next to the handicap spot.*

Justification Alert!

> Daniel: *So I don't know if this has anything to do with it. But I park and I'm on my phone looking at YouTube videos. This is about five-forty-five in the morning and it's still dark. All of a sudden I hear, and I feel, this scratching on my car. It's towards the trunk and the back window. I pause the video and I look in all of my mirrors—I don't see anything. I'm frozen... looking. My eyes are darting back and forth at each mirror to see if I see anything. The scratching was over by then. It happened so fast, but there was a little delay to it because while I was watching the videos, it was happening for probably a good three seconds. And along with scratching, my car is bumped. It felt like it was actually moved. I stay in my car because I'm freaked out. And then I finally get out. I don't see anything or notice any scratches on the car. I don't feel anything either when I get out of the vehicle. And it wasn't a bird scratching. I don't know what it was. I know the stories that have been going around that there's some type of entity near the AFI lot and in the restrooms here, so it must be something like that. But the nearby bushes weren't touching my car. I wasn't parked that close, so nothing like that could have rubbed or scratched it. It wasn't windy. But yeah, my car shook! And that's why I stopped my video right away. I'm like, this is not happening right now. But it was happening!*

"Bam! Bam! Bam! Bam!"

This final story in the chapter happened in 2006 while 20th Century Fox was shooting the film, *Garfield: A Tail of Two Kitties*. The production used many locations at Greystone and brought in a massive amount of equipment. When a film or television production company films for several days, the production company hires security to guard the mansion as well as their generator, equipment trucks, wardrobe, props, make up trailers, etc. JD was one of those security guards hired for several nights of the shoot. It was suggested to me by another security guard, that I contact him to hear his story. JD and I met at Greystone. When he told me his story, I must admit, I was flabbergasted—to the point where I would ask him to repeat what he just told me. I've worked at Greystone for a long time and thought I was well versed on the paranormal activity in the mansion and on the grounds. I was aware that the AFI Lot was active, but JD took it to a whole new level.

JD
(Security Guard)

> JD: *I'm in my truck and I'm parked right here in the marked spots. It's probably around eleven-thirty at night. There's nobody—just me. I'm the only guard, four nights in a row. But the first night, before the crew leaves, everybody keeps asking, "Who's going to stay the night?" And everybody keeps on smiling and laughing at me because I'm scheduled to stay. I keep on asking, "So what's going on? How come you guys are laughing?" And they just keep laughing. Nobody tells me anything. Nobody else wants to stay because most of the guards already know about this place. I didn't know anything. I was new back then. So they all knew, but they didn't want to tell me. And if I knew this place was haunted, I wouldn't have stayed either. So everybody leaves. They close and lock the gates and I'm the only one here. The first night is fine. Nothing happens.*

The way JD shifted his body and his overall demeanor, I had a feeling the story was going dark.

JD: *The second night is when I start feeling like something is outside my driver's side window. Like somebody is actually there, right close to my window just staring at me. And I can feel it. You know how you feel when there's a presence or something? Like someone's there? When I start feeling that, I get scared and my hairs are standing up. I start getting goose bumps. And since I'm scared, I take my jacket, because I feel like someone's looking at me, and I put it up to cover my window. And I stay just like that. Just holding my jacket up with my hand. But I still feel like someone's there, you know, just standing right outside, staring at me. And so that is what I do the whole second night.*

Honestly, the thought went through my mind: You're a security guard with responsibilities of guarding the mansion—if you think someone's out there, shouldn't you get out of the car? Maybe look around? But then again, I'm not the one feeling like someone is right outside my window staring at me.

JD: *I had to come back a third night. And again, I feel like someone is out there, outside my truck, all night. It's so creepy. But then something happens. At around one o'clock that night, I'm in the same spot, inside my truck, still feeling like someone's out there, still staring at me, when suddenly, right where I'm sitting, the top of my cab is hit four times really hard. It's like a hand banging four times—Bam! Bam! Bam! Bam! I mean, slammed it! But I never feel or see anybody physically get on top of my truck. So when that happens, I'm thinking, "Okay, should I look?!" I mean, I've got mirrors, but should I look?! But if I look and I see something... maybe not, maybe I shouldn't. No, I'm going to look!... my mind starts playing games with me. So I... have to look. I check the mirrors and I see nothing. I get out of the truck...and there's nobody anywhere. Nothing! So who hit the top of my cab?!*

415

I asked JD if he still felt a presence nearby.

JD: *I do. I still have that feeling that someone's there. So I jump back in the truck and drive down to the front gate. I'm thinking, "That's it. I can't stay here!" I open the gate, drive outside, and I park right outside the gate. I couldn't take it. I was like, "I'm not going in there anymore." So I stayed outside the gate, and in the morning one of those water truck guys* [Beverly Hills Water Department] *in the white trucks with the light on top, he sees me and he's like, "Hey, so who's been staying here all these nights?" And I'm like, "It's me." And the water guy says, "Have you seen anything? Anything happen?" And I tell him, "I have no idea what's going on because nobody told me this damn place is haunted!" I told him what happened with the bangs on my roof and then he's got stories about the paranormal activity in the mansion. I was like, "Oh my God, I can't believe I stayed here!" Then it dawns on me—the others didn't want to tell me because had I known, I wouldn't have stayed. It would have played games with my mind, so it would've been worse. And being all by myself and knowing about this place, I'm not sure how I would have felt.*

Of course, I asked him, "What happened when you saw your fellow guards?

JD: *I tell everybody about it, and they were just, "Ahhhh, yeah right!" You know, nobody believes you. They think you're just making it up. Or you fell asleep and you dreamed it. Even though they know it's haunted. That's what happened to me. Slam on the roof four times—and hard! Four times!* [long pause] *As soon as that happened, I had a headache for four straight days. It was so bad.*

I tell JD that I've heard other stories about people being sick or having a headache after being around dark force entities.

JD: *Yeah? Well, it was tough knowing that I had to come back again for one more night, so I stayed outside that gate again and never went inside. It was terrible. I'll never forget that. Ever.*

Chapter 35

Upper Parking Lot

I clearly saw half of their body, but I didn't feel any energy, nothing.
In the past, there have been times I barely catch the sight of the leg or
the torso, but this shadow person was moving.

— JUAN ANDRADE
   GREYSTONE PARK RANGER SUPERVISOR

Photo: Bryan Houser

Among the many movies filmed in this specific area are
The Disorderly Orderly, starring Jerry Lewis (1964), and
The Day Mars Invaded Earth (1963). Both films will give
you a glimpse of what this area looked like nearly thirty-
five years after it was constructed.

Oddly enough, the main reason the City of Beverly Hills purchased
Greystone Estate in 1955 from Henry Crown—at the time the
owner of the Empire State Building—wasn't for the magnificently
impressive mansion and gardens, but because the City wanted to
construct a 19.4-million-gallon water reserve at the far north end of the
property, which today, is underneath the upper parking lot. But when
the property began its construction in 1927, that upper area consisted

of waterfalls, lakes, a small pavilion, a kennel-potting-and-lath house, a picnic shelter, a tennis court, a pergola, and a playhouse for daughter Lucy, aka "Dickie Dell." But once the City purchased the property, the hill was excavated and leveled, the dollhouse and other buildings were destroyed and replaced with the water reserve. In doing so, this location was lowered nearly ten feet.

Below, the Greystone Historical Report refers to Chester Place, which was one of the first gated communities in Los Angeles. Located near the University of Southern California, Edward L. Doheny and his wife Estelle, purchased the 24,000-square-foot home at 8 Chester Place for $120,000 cash—the equivalent in 2020 is almost $3.7 million. The Dohenys moved into the house in October of 1901 (just days before the first woman—Anna Taylor—went over Niagara Falls in a barrel!).

Greystone Historical Report

When Edward Laurence Doheny, Jr. (the elder Doheny's only child) married Lucy Smith of Pasadena in 1914, the young man and his bride moved into the mansion at No. 10 Chester Place, a gift from his father who lived next door. Just two days before Ned's June 10, 1914 wedding, Edward Laurence Doheny Sr. completed another significant real estate transaction: He purchased the last large portion of his 429-acre Beverly Hills ranch. This 12.58 acre parcel later was the site of the Greystone estate.

The Doheny's had moved daughter Dickie Dell's playhouse from their Chester Place residence to Greystone late in 1927 or early in 1928. Installed on a hillside behind the mansion, this was not an ordinary playhouse. Boasting a steeply pitched roof and awning-shaded entrance porch, it looked much like the middle class bungalows that lined

---

street after street in the Hollywood flats and the eastern reaches of Beverly Hills south of Santa Monica Boulevard. "It was completely furnished," recalls George Maile, whose father became Doheny Ranch superintendent in 1943. "It was very livable, except that all the furnishings and all the appliances, including the baby grand piano, were approximately two thirds scale. They were all child sized. It was not too apparent, walking into the house, because everything was scaled down. But when one tried to sit, you were a little closer to the floor."

"Oh, Dickie went out to her playhouse once in a while. I set off a booby trap one time. I set off a bunch of cherry bombs tied together. That really rocked the house."
—Timothy Doheny

"SHADOW TORSO"

It was the end of February 2020 when Juan called me about what just happened. He sounded baffled. I headed over immediately and met him in the Ranger Office in the upper parking lot. He was ready and drew a diagram to illustrate specifically what he just witnessed outside the back door.

JUAN ANDRADE
(Park Ranger Supervisor)

Juan: *It was about eight-thirty this morning and I'm sitting at the desk doing my timecard. Behind me there's the back door that leads to the upper parking lot, right? Earlier when I came in, I checked the door and it was open, and I told myself I'm going to make a sign for the rest of the rangers to not leave this door open. So I'm working on the computer and I know Pedro* [park service employee] *is in the area doing some work. There are contractors still parking in the upper lot, but something caught my attention. I see a shadow walk by the back door towards the parking lot. I managed to see half his torso and half his leg.*

Juan begins drawing what he saw.

Juan: *It's walking past the back window and when I turned around and I saw it, I thought, "Oh, it's probably Pedro." But I wanted to make sure. So I went out the back door and I see Pedro all the way across the parking lot sitting in his Gator. So I thought, "Can't be him… maybe there are contractors looking for the bathroom." I walked completely around the building but there's nobody. You know, I thought I might find some guy peeing in the bushes* [yes, it happens, and it's caught on security cameras!]. *But I don't see anybody. I know someone was back there. I clearly saw half of their body, but I don't feel any energy, nothing. In the past, there have been times I barely catch sight of the leg or the torso, but this shadow person was moving.*

I ask Juan to expand on the details of what he saw and what he might have felt.

Juan: *It was completely black and it was solid. But I didn't feel any energy from it, nothing weird. I just felt like he was watching me, and then he walked away. I couldn't see any detail at all. It was completely black. It was a full body apparition from head to toe, but I only saw half of it because its view was cut off by the window. It is light outside, so that's why I didn't really get scared.*

I question him as to whether he has ever seen a shadow figure during the day.

Juan: *I've never seen a shadow person that early in the day. I've always seen them in the evening or at night, but never that early. But I clearly saw it move past the window. It wasn't peripheral. I clearly saw the leg, the waist, and the left arm as it was walking by. I even saw the head, but no detail. It was solid black.*

I ask Juan if this might have happened because it's near the date of the murder.

Juan: *Yeah. We just passed the anniversary and I think every year around this time, spirit activity picks up.*

The "anniversary" that Juan references is the infamous February 16 (1929) deaths of Ned Doheny and Hugh Plunkett. Do spirits celebrate anniversaries?

"PLAYING A PRANK?"

CHANH HANG
(Lead Park Ranger)

Chanh: *I was here in the upper parking lot Ranger Office and it's like nine at night. I'm doing my report and then I'm going to leave. As you know, it's a small office with glass windows all around, including the front door. I'm typing my report and I hear a knocking sound on the window. I know that everybody is out of the park and the gate is locked. But I hear this knock, sounds like...* [he knocks three times]. *I'm thinking there's someone still in the park and I locked them in because they didn't have a car, or they were just wandering around when I closed up. So I open the door and look around—nobody. I go back to my report—a knock on the glass door again. I'm like, "Who could this be? Is this one of the rangers playing a prank on me?" Now, I'm outside with my flashlight on. I go around the side of the building and I turn my flashlight off and stand there waiting for the ranger to move around in the dry leaves. I don't hear a sound. I wait like two or three minutes. Okay. Fine. He's not here. So I go back inside and give Chae a call.*

Ranger Chae, who was at Greystone earlier with Chanh, was currently on a shift at a different city park.

Chanh: *He picks up his phone and I say, "Chae, are you still here?" He goes, "At Greystone? No, I'm not. I'm at LCP* [La Cienega Park]. *" I asked him what he's doing there, and he says he's watching a movie. "You're sure you're not here?" I think he's joking. He goes, "No." So I believe him. I tell myself, maybe it's a bird or a twig or something hitting the glass. So back to my report. Two or three minutes later, for a third time...* [he knocks again three times]. *So this time I'm like, "Alright, what's going on?" I turn the office light off, now it's dark inside, and the parking lot still has the security lights on, so it's brighter outside than inside. So I'm standing in the dark for maybe three to five minutes and I have a clear view of the outside. I don't see anyone moving, or any sounds, nothing. It doesn't look like anyone is playing a prank on me. So I convince myself it's a twig or it's a bird or something. Maybe it's the rats in the ceiling. Fine. I can deal with rats. I sit back down for the fourth time. Start typing my report and maybe five minutes later, all of a sudden...* [he knocks three times again]. *This is the fourth time! Now I say, "Okay, that's it! I'm out of here!" I didn't finish my report. I ran to my car and drove straight to La Cienega, thinking that Chae's been playing a prank on me. I want to get down there before he does. I quickly arrive to LCP, run to the office, swing open the door and rush inside. Sure enough, I see Chae sitting there. I knew then that it wasn't him playing a prank on me. So I ask him, "Chae, have you ever experienced any weird stuff in the upper parking lot office with a noise that sounds like someone knocking on the window?" He tells me, "Oh, it's the rats." I say, "Have you experienced this before?" He goes, "Yeah, I believe it's the rats." He's convinced himself it's rats. I say, "That's not how rats sound. They sound like this—"*

Chanh makes a scurrying sound on the desk with his fingers. And then he's demonstratively clear.

Chanh: *Not like this.* [Chanh makes his rhythmic knocking sound.] *That's the true sound. He says, "No, Chanh, it's rats" I think that's what he wants to believe. But he did experience it. And still to this day, I don't know what was knocking three times on the door. But what I do know is it wasn't rats!*

"A Different Vision"

This next story, albeit short, is actually very significant. Back in 1927, the area now known as the "Upper Parking Lot," as mentioned above, was higher in elevation than it is today. Everything—all structures and many feet of topsoil—was removed and trucked off site in order to construct the water reservoir. This story, to which Chad is referring, happened in the 1980s.

CHAD NELSON
(Retired Park Ranger)

Chad: *Another ranger told me what he experienced: he was walking up the stairs* [to the Upper Parking Lot] *and he suddenly had this vision in his head of the parking lot not being there. Instead, it was all lawn. But he said the lawn was literally higher up, maybe four to six feet higher than the current parking lot. And he saw a girl, he said it could have been the ghost of a girl, running across the lawn. And then the vision of the lawn, along with the little girl running, just suddenly disappeared. He said that really tripped him out! He had no explanation of just how that was possible.*

This experience is captivating for one dramatic and extraordinary reason: a 1980s living and breathing human being was offered a vision courtesy of the 1930s—making this moment transcendental. Rewind the tape… the past became present. Absolutely fascinating.

"A Vision"

After the previous experience, a different type of "vision" happened to Juan on the upper lot as well—and I was with him when it happened. We were checking in cars that were parking for construction in the local area. These nearby construction sites contact the City of Beverly Hills, pay for parking, and then shuttle their workers to and from Greystone to the specific sites. On this day, most of the cars were parked and I was chatting with Juan, who suddenly looked past me to the large hill on the east side of the driveway. He stared at the hill and then looked back to me with an absolutely stunned demeanor. Matter-of-factly, Juan says, "Someone was just walking out toward us from the hill, but the hill was up higher." I had no idea what he was talking about. "From inside the hill?" I asked him. He tried to explain what he had just witnessed. I took down some notes and then a year later, in April of 2020, as I'm working on this chapter, I remembered Juan's story. I interviewed him so I could flesh it out—and hopefully he could elaborate on just what this vision might have been.

JUAN ANDRADE
(Park Ranger Supervisor)

> Juan: *As I remember, it was around eight in the morning. We were there standing at the entrance to the top parking lot. We're talking and I looked past you to the hill and I remember seeing what looked like a small house. I couldn't even tell the dimensions, but it was the front entrance of a small wooden house with a wooden roof—and it wasn't at our ground level. It was maybe, eight or nine feet higher and I clearly saw someone walking out of a door right toward us. He took a few of steps and then disappeared. I've seen what Lucy's dollhouse looked like and it didn't look like that. The vision only lasted a couple of seconds, but long enough for me to see that person come out of the house and disappear. I don't even know how else to explain it. It was like, what am I seeing? Is this really what I'm seeing or is it just my eyes? It was like a different place. I mean, how do you process seeing something like that?*

After Juan described this vision, I told him that I would send him some photos of historic Greystone. I sent him a text of an image of the picnic grounds and the pavilion from 1927. He said that wasn't what he saw. I sent him a photo of Lucy's Playhouse from 1928. Again, he was emphatic: "Definitely not Lucy's doll house. It had a large open door." Then I sent him a photo from 1932 of the kennel, potting house, and lath house combined structure, which was also located where the top parking lot currently sits. "Yep, that's it! I've never seen that photo."

Once again, the past became present.

KENNEL, POTTING HOUSE AND LATH HOUSE
1932

Photo: Friends of Greystone

"A GREEN ONE"

This phone interview happened immediately following the incident, which took place in October of 2018. It was at eleven o'clock in the evening. Both Juan and Chanh were anxious and dumbfounded as to what they just witnessed. I begin the interview with Juan. Chanh eventually joins the conversation.

JUAN ANDRADE (Park Ranger Supervisor) & CHANH HANG (Lead Park Ranger)
INTERVIEW

Juan: *We had a wedding here today and throughout the event we never saw any lights on in the servants' quarters. We would have noticed that because everything out in the courtyard was ambient light. So when the wedding was over, and everyone was clearing out, Chanh looked at me and said, "Did you turn those lights on?" I told him I wasn't up there all afternoon and that the house was secured all day. So we both don't remember turning them on. And we don't remember seeing them on during the wedding when they were dancing on that side. We asked the catering staff if they remembered those lights on, and they said, "No." So just before I went inside to shut the lights off and secure the mansion, I heard a bang! I called Chanh on the radio and asked if he was inside—he didn't respond.*

Chanh joins us in the conversation, "That's right, my radio was dead from being on all day."

Juan continues—

Juan: *So I turned off the lights, armed the mansion alarm, and walked out on the driveway to go up and meet Chanh in the upper lot Ranger Office. But for some reason I kept looking back because I felt like something was behind me. But when I got up to the office, I didn't feel anything. I felt normal. Then Chanh came out and he was maybe four feet to my right, when all of a sudden, he stops and says, "What the hell was that!?" I had no idea what he was talking about. He then says, "I just saw an orb next to your car going back and forth!" It really freaked him out.*

It's obvious that Chanh is still excited by the way he explains exactly what happened when he and Juan stepped out of the Ranger Office and walked toward their cars.

Chanh: *I saw this green orb hovering right behind Juan's car. Then it zoomed from the left taillight on Juan's car to his driver-side window, then to the right passenger window and then right back to the rear taillight— and then it disappeared. But it was a green round light. Like the size of a grapefruit and it was zig-zagging, by itself, close to the ground. There was no reflection. After it zig-zagged it just vanished. I know what orbs look like. I mean, I was maybe ten feet away.*

Juan: *I've been seeing orbs the whole time since I've worked here. All different sizes. Small, big, but I've never seen a green one.*

Then Chanh offers a very detailed breakdown of the "green."

Chanh: *It's not really green, it's like a mixture of green. It's not a full green when you look at it. The front end looks like a darker green than the back. The back-end kind of gets lighter. It wasn't a full solid green when I was looking at it. Actually, the back end was kind of see-through.*

Juan: *I don't know if something followed me up there. I mean, there's always that chance. Maybe it did. I don't know…*

You can hear in Juan's voice that he remains baffled by the incident, and even concerned that there may have been the possibility he was followed from the mansion.

Chapter 36

Entering the Grounds

I was feeling goose bumps. Not from what she told me—I was feeling the energy like never, ever before. I can feel it right now, just remembering it.

— ANDREA FLORES
JANITORIAL SERVICES

Photo: Marc Wanamaker / Bison Archives

Filmed here in 1963 was *The Disorderly Orderly* starring Jerry Lewis. While some moviegoers embraced the screwball comedy, others like Howard Thompson of The New York Times said the Paramount film played "like a juiceless watermelon." Other Hollywood films shot on the Greystone Grounds include *The Day Mars Invaded Earth, All of Me, The Loved One* with Jonathan Winters and Milton Berle, and *National Treasure: Book of Secrets* starring Nicolas Cage.

"GRRRR! GRRRRR!!"

When Andrea contacted me about this incident, I interviewed her and thought it was interesting, but it could have been just a technical problem—wires got crossed, that sort of thing. But when it happened to her more than once, and someone else had the same experience, I started leaning toward the fact that it might involve the paranormal.

ANDREA FLORES

(Janitorial Services)

> Andrea: *I was coming in at night to clean the restrooms and I was on the phone with my mother who's in Costa Rica. She only speaks Spanish. She knew I was coming to work but she had no idea where* [Andrea works at several locations]. *I've talked to her about this place, but she had no idea I was driving to Greystone. We were having a family conversation and my head was totally immersed in what we were talking about that had nothing to do with Greystone. I was feeling at ease. Peaceful. Nothing was shaking me at all. As soon as I went through the gate into Greystone, around nine o'clock, I felt goose bumps. Then she was like, "Where are you at?" "I'm at work." She pressed me, "But where are you at?" I told her again—at work. She asks me, "Why are people arguing?" I was driving up the hill on the driveway leading up to the mansion. "No, mother, there's no one here with me." She says again, "There's people arguing." I have no idea what she is talking about. "Mom, there's no one here. What are they saying?" She says, "I don't know. It's English. I can't understand." I told her again that I was driving and that I'm by myself. She was certain, "No, I hear someone." Then my mom's voice started shaking. I was feeling goose bumps. Not from what she told me—I was feeling the energy like never, ever before. I can feel it right now, just remembering it.*

Andrea took a brief moment to gather her thoughts.

> Andrea: *So I drove up towards the restrooms* [at the AFI parking lot] *and she was still like, "They're arguing and there's someone growling." I said, "Mom, growling?! How?" She makes the sound, "Grrrrr. Grrrrr." "Mom, don't joke with me." Then suddenly she's really scared for me, "Get out of there! Just get out of there! Please get out of there!" She was panicked. And I was like, "Mom, I'm okay." She says, "Tell me you are with someone else." I said, "Is this a joke, momma? I'm by myself." She said, "You are at that place that you told me about, right?" I told her I was, and not to worry.*

She says scared, "Please get out of there!" I asked her, "Mom, do you still hear the people?" And she's like, "Yes, they're arguing. They're growling!"

I asked her, "Did you contemplate just leaving? How did you deal with this?"

Andrea: *When I got all the way up there [to the AFI lot], it's the first time that I didn't even put on my cleaning gloves. I just opened the family restroom, took out as much toilet paper and supplies as I could and stocked the restrooms. I didn't even mop or sweep. I did the minimum and I said, "Mom, don't worry, stay with me! Stay with me!" She was still hearing the arguing and growling as I was cleaning. I took the trash and I didn't even go to the dumpster. I was so freaked out. I didn't want to look anywhere.*

"So at this point did you just get the hell out of there?"

Andrea: *Actually, at this point, I hear two growls on the phone. That's the only thing I got to hear, two growls.*

"So that proved your mom was actually hearing growls."

Andrea: *Yes. I was just so panicked with everything my mom was telling me. I got back into the car and I was going under the over bridge and there was a small coyote standing there, just looking at me. And I was like, "No, I don't want to see you, move!" I just drove, and as soon as I got out of the gate, my mom stopped hearing everything. But I was still freaked out for a long time.*

"Too Many People"

Artemio is a very quiet young man who mostly speaks Spanish. When Andrea contacted me about his story and how it was so similar to hers, I asked her to see if he would allow me to interview him. He agreed and I met him near City Hall as he was getting ready for his night shift.

ARTEMIO RODAS
(Janitorial Services)

Artemio: *When I go there, I open the gate and then when I'm driving up, I make a call to my wife, she hears some people talking around me and it sounds like somebody is having a party or something. And she says, "Where are you?" I say, "I'm working at Greystone." She said, "There's too many people there around you." I say, "No. There's no people. Nobody is here. Are you sure?" She says, "Yeah, there's so many people talking around you." I say, "No, there's nobody here. I can't see anyone. It's just me." I don't know why that happened. And then when I heard Andrea talking about the same thing, I say, "What? That happened to me too!" And to this moment, I still don't know why. I don't know what happened, or why it happened, but it never happened again.*

"TOO MUCH NOISE"

I conducted this interview with Andrea Flores and Vilma Lopez together. When Andrea experienced this event, she texted Vilma to tell her, which resulted in them discussing it over the phone.

A CONVERSATION WITH ANDREA FLORES & VILMA R. LOPEZ (Janitorial Services)

Andrea: *So I was on the phone with an employee who doesn't work at Greystone. She knows our other sites where we clean but not about Greystone. We were discussing work-related stuff for about twenty minutes. As soon as I arrived through the gate on Doheny Road, she was like, "Where are you?" I told her I just got to work. She says, "Yeah, yeah, I know you're working, but, where are you? There are so many people talking. I can't hear you." I was driving and I said, "No, I'm by myself." And then she says, "You're at that place, but there's people there. They're really loud." The crazy thing is that she has no idea about this place. She doesn't know my mom at all. And the worst part is they both don't know English. I wanted to call Vilma.*

Vilma joins our conversation.

Vilma: *Andrea sends me a text message and it says, "Please call me when you're free." And it was almost nine that night, because I had texted you just before…*

Vilma reads the texts:

Vilma: *"Are you at Greystone already?"*

Andrea: *"Yes, I'm doing the restrooms. Don't come help me."*

Andrea recalls what happened after she texted Vilma.

Andrea: *My conversation on the phone with the other employee ended by that time. I was worried, but Vilma was busy and I didn't want her to stop doing what she was doing. What can she do? She's so far away. She would have to drive here. It's nonsense. I needed to finish cleaning the restrooms. They were disgusting. Really, really bad, like never before. So I had to clean properly. I couldn't leave those restrooms like the first time with my mom on the phone.*

Vilma finds Andrea's text on her phone and reads it out loud.

Vilma: *"No need to call me. I'm out at Greystone." I found that text very weird and I'm like, "Then what the hell is she texting me this for?" So I thought something must have happened. So I called her right away and I'm like, "Where are you?" She says, "I'm right here getting to Coldwater"* [another Beverly Hills park nearby]. *And I can tell she's not okay, so I was persistent, "What happened?" And she says, "I don't want to talk about it." But I was persistent, like "What happened?" And that's when she told me that she was on the phone with another employee, and she tells me it was the same thing that happened with her mom, just happened to this other woman, that she heard voices and said it was too much noise. Then the woman says, "I can't talk to you now," and she just hung up on Andrea. She didn't even say goodbye. And she's Christian. She's really, really religious.*

Vilma looks at Andrea who nods in agreement.

Vilma: *She was freaked out. So I came to work with her the next time and when I saw how freaked out she was when we got there, I told her the mansion is getting to you. You're trying to be strong, but you have that ability to feel and to see certain things.*

Vilma looks at me, then quite seriously—

Vilma: *She does not want to come here alone anymore. It's getting to her mentally.*

Andrea: *I feel scared if I'm by myself. That's when I feel bad, because when I'm with Elva [daytime co-worker] I wasn't feeling scared because I knew that Vilma was there as well, and I felt no fear when we're together. When I felt really bad fear was when I was by myself. When I'm with the others, they could tell me this is not in my imagination. That things I've seen are not my imagination.*

I can sense that Andrea is frustrated and freaked about these bizarre phone calls—her mom, her co-worker, and Artemio, all experiencing the same inexplicable thing. Party lines were a thing of the past... and when was the last time you were on your cell phone picking up voices in a cacophony of conversations? And, lest we forget, these phone "interruptions" happened at more or less the same general location at Greystone.

436

Andrea: *But why are they telling me about the voices on the phone if they don't know anything about Greystone?*

Vilma: *I know you texted me to call you at that moment because you wanted me to see if I heard anything on the phone.* [Vilma looks to me] *Like I told her, I don't want to hear anything again. I really don't. I've never felt anything, and I've never seen anything. And if I do, I think it's going to mess me up mentally.*

Chapter 37

Surrounding Grounds

(Part One)

Tennis Pavilion | Cypress Lane | Pool Pavilion

Gives me the shivers! It walked over toward the front pool area, to the stairs… and then I saw it walk through that opening to the stairs—and suddenly it was gone.

— ERNEST DOMINGUEZ
  BEVERLY HILLS PARK SERVICES

Photo: Bryan Houser

The romantic comedy *What Women Want* starring Mel Gibson, Helen Hunt, and Marisa Tomei was filmed here along with *Flowers in the Attic*, *America's Sweethearts*, *Garfield: A Tail of Two Kitties*, and *Hanging Up* starring Diane Keaton and Meg Ryan—and also directed by Diane Keaton.

439

In its day, the beautiful grounds located in the upper area and the adjacent landscape were beyond compare. These four locations—the Tennis Pavilion, Cypress Lane, the Olive Garden, as well as the Pool Pavilion—closely resemble how they looked like back in 1929. But times have changed, and this property certainly has as well. The original Tennis Pavilion structure is there, but the tennis court is gone. The pool and its pavilion remain but the pool has been filled with cement and brick. Since it is now a public park, safety is the main concern. The Olive Garden doesn't have the same aesthetics it once had back in the day. Cypress Lane was originally named for the statuesque cypress trees that line this iconic and handsome walkway, but at one point, those trees were replaced with Eugenias.

Greystone Historical Report

For Greystone [Landscape Architect, Paul G.] Thiene's principal designer was Emile Kuehl, who spent "the better part of three-and-one-half years" on the project. Other than plant selections, Kuehl had a free hand concerning the design of the gardens. "The sky was the limit," he told David Streatfield [an expert in the history of California landscape architecture, who was professor of landscape architecture at the University of Washington at Seattle] in a 1974 interview. "I would ask Mr. Thiene what the client might want. 'Give them everything' was the reply."

TENNIS PAVILION
"GREY-WHITE SMOKE"

Ernie has retired since this interview. He was one of my favorite people up at Greystone. Look up "hard worker" in the dictionary and you'll see a picture of Ernie. He worked well into his later years and could be counted on to get the formal garden and other prime locations looking their best. I approached Ernie one day in February of 2018 and told him I was writing a book about all the paranormal activity at Greystone. He just smiled. I then asked him if he ever experienced anything strange or spooky during his years here. He mentioned that co-workers relayed some stories to him, but at this juncture I was more interested in any firsthand stories that he might have. I pushed, "Ernie, what about you?" He nodded in the affirmative. So we walked up to the Tennis Pavilion and began our conversation.

ERNEST DOMINGUEZ
(Park Services)

> Ernest: *It was a while ago, probably ten to twelve years ago. Somebody from that corner* [he points toward the back of the Tennis Pavilion] *was walking this way. My skin, you know, goose bumps on my arm! But I saw something. It looked like light-colored grey stuff. Kind of like a mist. Gives me the shivers! It walked over toward the front pool area, to the stairs… and then I saw it walk through that opening to the stairs—and suddenly it was gone. But that was one of those experiences I really had, you know? It looked like grey-white smoke. But when you see real people, you don't get goose bumps. This gave me goose bumps.*

This is yet another example, and we've had dozens throughout this book, where those who have come in contact with what they feel are ghosts or apparitions get immediate goose bumps. I always ask if the "goose bumps" are from being scared (which we've all felt), or from the energy radiating off these spirits? Some have agreed that it was the fright, but the majority have stated they're reacting to the energy radiating off the ghosts. Ernie then surprises me with his next story about Cypress Lane, which is just south of the formal garden.

Cypress Lane

Greystone Historical Report

For all their beautiful fountains and carefully crafted stonework, however, these Italian Renaissance-inspired gardens were not completely accurate in design. The so-called Cypress Lane (which was later replanted in eugenias, yet was still called Cypress Lane by the Dohenys up to the 1950's) had a lawn in the middle. "Lawn is simply not a feature found in Italian Renaissance gardens," notes David Streatfield. "But lawn was used at Greystone, because it could be used for outdoor entertaining. And so in this case, Thiene thought it desirable not to be completely authentic."

The renovation of the formal garden terraces and the areas surrounding the mansion, funded by the City of Beverly Hills, commenced in 2001 and was completed in 2004. During this period, the lollipop-shaped Eugenia trees were replaced by Italian Cypress, which was the species originally planted under the guidance of landscape architect Paul Thiene in the late 1920s.

"I'm Not a Chicken, but…"

After our first conversation about his incident at the Tennis Pavilion, Ernie leads me down to Cypress Lane to discuss his next sighting.

ERNEST DOMINGUEZ
(Park Services)

> Ernest: *I saw it* [the apparition] *again the next day at a different location. I think he walked this way, because when I'm in Cypress Lane, and I'm like* [he points to his arms to indicate goose bumps], *"Oh my God!" After that, I feel like I have to be careful around here. I'm not a chicken, but*

442

I got goose bumps from both of these [apparitions]. *Both of them were grey in color. Might have been the same one. I don't know. I'm a very religious guy. I was born in Mexico and somebody told me if I ever saw those spirits or ghosts or whatever you want to call them, I'm supposed to pray for them, because they're not resting in peace. So that's what I did. I prayed!*

Let's hope Ernie's prayers were answered.

Greystone Historical Report
"The grounds are intensively landscaped and are said to contain the largest sprinkler system in the world."
—Los Angeles Times, November 11, 1927

POOL PAVILION

"GET OUT!"

JUAN ANDRADE
(Park Ranger Supervisor)

Juan: *This was years ago. It was dark, late at night, maybe nine or ten. It was when I first started as a ranger. I forgot what event it was in that area of the pool house. Anyway, I was locking up all the doors, and back then you had a hard time closing some of the bathroom doors. So I would lock it from the inside and come outside through the other door. One night I was locking up and I heard a male voice say, "Get out!"—and this voice was very aggressive.*

Get ready, Juan is about to take a trip to the Hall of Justification!

Juan: *But I just thought it was in my mind and I was telling myself to get out. It didn't scare me because I didn't know what it was, and I wasn't here very often back then to know this place had paranormal activity.*

It's a truly unique experience to watch interviewees, within seconds, extricate themselves from their own hard testimony. Let's break this one down. In straightforward fashion, Juan states:

One night I was locking up and I heard a male voice say, "Get out…"

Juan could not have been any more distinct. There's no room for interpretation—locking up… male voice… "Get out." Then, Juan even describes the voice's attitude as "very aggressive." This sounds like courtroom testimony. And then here it comes, a nanosecond later—oh maybe I was just talking to myself!

Greystone Historical Report

"The property had its own water. There were seven caves, all dug out by old prospector friends of my grandfather with pick and shovel. Spring caves were then dug out, and the water was pumped into reservoirs. Some of the reservoirs were fed by two spring caves; others by one. Beautiful water." —Timothy Doheny

---

Chapter 38

Surrounding Grounds

(Part Two)

Front Lawn | Gatehouse | Car Garages | Trailer

I could feel the energy coming off of it. You could feel it and you could see it. There was what looked like a fluorescent, neon light coming from it!

— DAVID CARLTON GARRARD
  BEVERLY HILLS GENERAL PARK MAINTENANCE SUPERVISOR

Photo: Marc Wanamaker / Bison Archives

Greystone Estate 1935.
Mr. Atkins (mechanic) with (L-R) 1934 16-cyl. Limo Cadillac, 1934 16-cyl. Cadillac, 1935 five passenger (Mrs. Doheny's car) La Salle, and a 1935 Lincoln Zephyr

Films shot in these locations include the Steve Martin-Lily Tomlin comedy *All of Me*, as well as *Garfield: A Tail of Two Kitties*. Also filmed here was David Lynch's historic first feature film—the strange and curious *Eraserhead*.

445

Front Lawn

Greystone Historical Report

On the broad sloping hillside leading from the mansion down the Doheny Road, Thiene's office had planted a sweeping grass lawn, much like those of English country estates. In the center of this greensward, just west of the driveway that wound up the hill from the Doheny Road gate, Thiene sited a single large oak tree, which still stands today.

The oak tree mentioned above in the Greystone Historical Report began showing signs of dying after roots were accidentally compromised during an irrigation upgrade. On September 30, 2004, the tree was removed and replaced with another oak tree.

"Real Fear"

When Andrea Flores told me this story it really surprised me. It was the only incident of the nearly three hundred stories I've documented that took place on the front lawn of Greystone, just outside the Gatehouse. This large lawn sweeps up the hill that is on your left as you drive up toward the mansion from the service gate. It's a sprawling area lined with pine trees to the north. In the summer, because of the angle of the lawn on the hill, Catskills (the children's summer theatre camp) uses this location as a giant water slide. I've never thought of it as anything other than a beautiful part of the park... until now.

ANDREA FLORES

(Janitorial Services)

Andrea: *This happened in January, right after New Year's* [2020]. *When Vilma* [co-worker] *and I pulled up to the gate, I was feeling okay. We were talking about other stuff not related to our job or the house. As soon as I drove in the gate, I started feeling energy and chills. As I was driving, I could feel it. I was attracted to it. I looked up to the left on the big hill and there's this huge black shadow figure. It's not human. It's totally black and I could feel it. It was looking towards me and I didn't like it. I felt really, really scared. It was different than what I felt at the front gate* [see Chapter 33 – Driveway and Loma Vista Gate]. *That was black as well, but it was a different shape. Also, at the front gate I could feel that it was something bad, but I didn't feel as scared as with this one on the hill. With this one, I felt paralyzed. Like real fear.*

I asked Andrea if the fear stopped her from driving up the hill past the shadow?

Andrea: *No, I kept going. I didn't want to say anything to Vilma because I didn't want to scare her, because she gets really scared. But this time I got really, really, really scared. I knew that it wasn't good and when we got up to the firehouse, I don't know if it followed me or if it was just me having all that real fear, but I could still feel the energy. But Vilma could see that I was not looking so good. She was like, "I don't want to hear. I don't want to know." But finally, we talked about it and she told me, let's just drop off the supplies and leave. We didn't clean at all because I didn't feel like I could handle going into the restrooms. So we decided not to clean and we left. When we were driving out, I could feel the energy, I couldn't see anything, but I could feel the energy. And as soon as we got off the property, that feeling was gone.*

Greystone Historical Report

The field crew for Greystone usually totaled twenty, about half of whom were gardeners. And it is no wonder that ten were required. Just consider the job of lawn maintainence [sic] alone. "Totaled up, we had about five acres of grass," remembers George Maile, who became assistant field superintendent in 1952. "Now this meant every year a total renovation and re seeding and top dressing. This required approximately 100 to 150 pounds of grass and about 600 bags of manure." "Some of the lawn areas were quite difficult to care for, such as one section that required ropes at times on the power mower, just to keep it from sliding down the hill," continues George Maile. "And we had a crew that assisted the regular section gardeners with the lawn mowing, because that was a week—long event here. By the time we got through mowing the whole area, we had to start all over again."

GATEHOUSE

Located at the south end of the property, the Gatehouse was the original main entrance to the Doheny Estate. The two-bedroom, one-bath structure with a fireplace and kitchen was home to the security guard that met every visitor at the 501 Doheny Road gate before they were allowed to enter the property.

"SILHOUETTE"

One evening, I was getting ready to turn in and my phone rang—it's Ranger Ivan and my first thought is he butt dialed me. I wasn't going to answer but you never know. Ivan sounded frantic. First, I asked him if he was okay, and he was, but he was also clearly shaken by what just happened. He said he was at Greystone and that's all I needed to know. I asked Ivan, "Did something happen up there?" I can hear it in his voice: Ivan and his girlfriend experienced something bizarre.

On a side note: Ivan's girlfriend wouldn't talk to me about what happened. I asked Ivan to ask her numerous times, but she refused. Then I asked Ivan to talk to her for me. I gave him a list of questions that needed to be answered and reiterated that I wouldn't use her name in the book. I just wanted the story from her perspective. Ivan said she was very frightened and that she's had her own experiences in the past with the paranormal and this was a vivid and chilling reminder. As far as she was concerned, it happened and she'll never talk about it again. That's how real it was.

IVAN MARTINEZ
(Park Ranger)

Ivan: *After my shift, I came to Greystone to drop off my radio around ten-thirty that night. I told my girlfriend, "Hey, I'm going to FaceTime on the way up. So whatever I'm seeing, you're seeing. If anything pops up, we'll both see it." Okay, so the whole way we're FaceTiming. I have my phone pointing out, straight forward from the dashboard. I drop off my radio in the Ranger Office in the upper lot. I'm still FaceTiming her as I drive down the driveway, past the mansion, and towards the gatehouse to make that right turn on the driveway area. The phone is still facing forward out the front window. As I make that right turn, off to my left-hand side, I see a light come on inside the gatehouse. Like a computer screen comes on. So I see this, but it's not the first time I've seen a light come on in the gatehouse. It also happened to me another time during a wedding event. So as soon as I see the screen turn on, I go, "Oh, shit!" And she goes, "What happened?" She's thinking I saw what she saw. But apparently, I didn't. I just saw the light come on. So as soon as she hears me say, "What did you see?" she tells me she saw a man in a suit standing down towards the stable area. She said he was wearing a suit with slicked back hair. And it kind of seemed like the man owned the place. Like he knew it was his home. She had the sense that the way he handled himself was like a rich guy type of thing. To her, it looked like he was going to cross from one side of the driveway to the other, toward the mansion, but as soon as he saw the car, he just walked back behind the bushes. He didn't disappear or fade away or anything. So she tells me this and I immediately texted her a picture of Ned's dad* [Ned Doheny, Sr.]. *As soon as she saw the photo, she just kind of freaked out 'cause she's like, "That's who I saw!" In fact, since that time, she did a little research herself and she's now convinced it wasn't Doheny senior, it was Ned Doheny she saw.*

I asked Ivan if he remembers her saying whether the apparition was solid or transparent.

Ivan: *She said he was solid, not transparent. She couldn't see through him. And she didn't see the color of his suit. It was nighttime so it was too dark. But she did say he was kind of like a silhouette, type thing. She didn't see his face clearly, but she saw enough of him to see that his hair was combed over and slicked back. She didn't know what color his hair was, just the style of his hair.*

I discuss with Ivan why he thinks he didn't see this apparition.

Ivan: *I think that light in the gatehouse was a distraction to me, I wasn't looking anywhere else. But having the camera pointing straight forward, as I was FaceTiming, she ended up seeing that person crossing. We're looking in two different places. She wasn't sure what to think.*

Justification Alert!!

Ivan: *She was questioning as to whether she actually saw something or was it just her imagination playing games with her? But the way she described it to me, I was like, "Dude, that sounds like Ned Doheny."*

In a lot of these cases, witnesses often say that they felt an energy after seeing an apparition. I put that question to Ivan.

Ivan: *No, I honestly didn't. Maybe it's because I FaceTimed her. Usually when I'm in the mansion by myself, locking up, I FaceTime either my mom or someone else because honestly, I feel a little more at ease when I'm actually talking to someone. I tend to see things and I just don't want to say anything and sound crazy, you know? And I told my girlfriend that things appear up here out of nowhere. I guess she had an open mind about it and it ends up happening to her over FaceTime.*

CAR GARAGES

The rear area of the Car Garages was used as a location for *Garfield: A Tail of Two Kitties.* Also, in 1977, David Lynch filmed the classic *Eraserhead* in the Car Garages when he was enrolled at the American Film Institute—located at that time at Greystone.

Based out of Greystone, a lot of my time over the past two decades has been working down in the Car Garages. We all call it "the stables" because there are old horse stables adjacent to the Car Garages. But these garages, located on the lower southern portion of the estate, are where we keep our city equipment for our community services events. As of this writing, I'm in charge of maintaining all the equipment utilized for the Beverly Hills Art Shows and several other city events—and I've spent a lot of time in this location. It never dawned on me that this area might be, or is, haunted. Now granted, I am almost always down there during the day. My brother, Chris, and I used the garages years ago to store and wrap educational gifts for a non-profit foundation he founded to help underprivileged children. There were a few times when we were there at night, but we weren't thinking of ghosts. All we were worried about were the rats running along the rafters. Also, I would use the upstairs rooms above the garages to create my artwork on many occasions. But again, that was during the day. So imagine what I thought when I started lining up interviews for this book, and asking fellow City employees if they've had any experiences at Greystone, and immediately they said, "Yes, down by the stables!"

"Woman's Voice"

A historical note about the "kitchen" to which Robert refers in the upcoming segment: in one corner of the garages, a kitchen was built for the Doheny employees.

ROBERT RUSSELL

(Irrigation Specialist)

Robert: *It was a cold December holiday weekend and Greystone is quiet. This is about two-thirty in the afternoon. Not many people working. Nearby construction sites are closed down and I'm in the stable area just winding down my day. Suddenly I hear a woman's voice. It sounds like a one-sided conversation. Nobody is in the park. I am the only one there on staff. But I can hear a woman's voice come out of the stable's kitchen area. So I walk around that way, but I don't see anybody. And then I hear it again. Now it's freaking me out because I'm pretty damn sure there is nobody around here as well as at the construction site next door. I even double check and go over to look at the construction site, but like I thought, nobody's there. I walked back over behind the stables and this time, I hear a faint female's voice. I look in the window to that room where I think I'm hearing the voice, and nobody's in there. I know nobody was at Greystone. I'm sure of that. Nobody is in the park. It freaked the shit out of me.*

Greystone Historical Report

"The cars were 'porcelainized.' Each cost $10,000. The inventor came to Greystone from Denver to oversee the process. The mixture was rubbed into the finish, then polished with Freeman's piano cream. It took two men one and a half to two hours to do one car." —Sam Schultz

---

Back in the late 1970s and early 1980s, the gardeners had offices above the Car Garages. It wasn't unusual for them to sleep in the rooms if they worked long days and were required to be at work early the next day. But sadly, those areas are now dilapidated and unsafe, as the building has fallen into disrepair.

"Haunted Stairs"

TONY GARDELLO
(Facilities Maintenance Mechanic)

Tony: *We used to do events in and around the City that took all night to set up and then we'd have to come up here to Greystone and get all of our equipment, which we stored here. There is a second story in the stables above the garages with rooms where we could sleep, and one night I woke up because it sounded like somebody was walking up and down the stairs. A lot of walking, back and forth. I remember looking in the hallway because you could hear things going on, and I wouldn't see anyone. It literally sounded like somebody was there, but they weren't there.*

After talking to Tony, I decided I was going to place my digital recorder inside the building near the stairs leading up to the second floor— exactly where Tony said he heard the footsteps. If there's energy or spirit movement on the stairs or in that hallway, it will be captured moving around on audio. On March 25, 2018, I went inside the building, walked up the stairs, and found an old chair in an adjoining room. I placed the chair at the top of the stairs that lead to the hallway, set my recorder on the seat, turned it on, and left for the night. I went back the next morning and listened to see if any sounds were recorded. At 11:06 p.m., you can hear loud and clear footsteps going up and down the stairs as well as walking down the hallway.[1] Tony was right! So much for the garages not being haunted!

"A Night Vision... Vision"

Infrared or "night vision" detects infrared energy (heat) and then converts it into an electronic signal, which is then processed to produce a thermal

---

1 Audio recording exists in author's collection.

image on a video monitor. In other words, infrared light illuminates images in the dark. Our eyes can't see it or detect it, but infrared light is all around us. The binoculars Vinicio and Mike used in the segment below detected these "invisible" infrared wavelengths, which enable the binoculars to "see in the dark."

VINICIO CASTRO
(Janitorial Services)

> Vinicio: *It was around midnight. I was with Mike, my brother-in-law, my sister, and Andrea* [Flores], *who was cleaning the trailers. Mike brought his night vision binoculars, so he started looking up above the car garages. He didn't see anything at first, but as he looked up towards the middle window, he sees a figure standing on the left side of the window, like peeking out. He passed me the binoculars and I looked up at what I thought was a curtain. We checked again a couple of minutes later and there was nothing. He said it looked like a figure when he first saw it. I thought he was kidding because he has that joking personality. But then I looked again and I definitely saw something standing there. My sister also saw it. She was a little freaked out, but she didn't really think of it as a figure. She also thought that it was a curtain because it took up about three quarters of the window. It looked like it was peeking out, or kind of leaning out the window. It's just unexplainable to me how it was there one minute and then gone—and we couldn't see anything without the binoculars. That's the odd freaky thing about it. And it's hard to explain because there was no one inside the building.*

I asked Vinicio if he physically felt anything when seeing this vision.

> Vinicio: *At the moment, we didn't feel scared or weird at all. It was just like a strange feeling afterward when we figured out what was happening, what we saw, and that it had disappeared.*

"Locks and Knocks" – Part One

This story came my way in December of 2017. If you've ever visited, or know the Beverly Hills area, there is a park called, "Beverly Gardens Park." This park is famous for hosting the large "Beverly Hills" sign that sits above a reflection pond, just off Santa Monica Boulevard in the heart of Beverly Hills. I was there working an event and I saw two fellow City workers setting up chairs. One of the workers, Raphael, saw me and was anxious to talk. "I've been looking for you! I need to talk to you about something crazy that happened to Chris and me at the stables." Chris Hamilton is one of his co-workers. I was all ears. We arranged our schedules and Raphael met me at the stables. When he told me "something crazy" happened, that turned out to be an understatement.

RAPHAEL H. ZAPEDA
(Facilities Maintenance Mechanic)

Raphael: *It was a Saturday morning, right around seven. Nobody is here. Obviously, the park was closed. I was picking up some chairs from inside the stables. Chris Hamilton and I drove here in separate city trucks, and we call the ranger* [Ranger Chae], *who said he was at La Cienega Community Center and would drive over to open the stables. So we're sitting at the picnic table right over there* [just outside the stables] *and we start talking nonsense. Just bullshitting and joking around. Suddenly we hear a banging sound inside the stables.*

I wanted Raphael to meet me at "the stables" so he could show me exactly what happened. And again, when he refers to "the stables," he actually means the Car Garages.

Raphael: *But at first we didn't say anything. We just keep talking. Suddenly, not more than a few minutes later, we hear a second bang inside, just as loud as the first one. So Chris, says, "Hey, do you hear that?" I did, and I say, "Whatever." And we keep talking. Suddenly, we hear a third one—and this one is even louder. Like, "Bam!" Really loud. It was right in the corner.*

Raphael is certain and isolates the area: it's the last bay on the west side of the Car Garages. It seems as if his recall of this dramatic sound is etched in his memory.

Raphael: *At first Chris thinks it might be a Park Ranger inside playing a joke, like maybe he got here first, he's messing with us. So we walk around the trucks on our way to the door, which is the only access inside the stables, and I say to Chris, "Hey, look, the door's locked* [with a padlock]. *It's impossible for him to be inside!" So now I'm yelling out loud at the doors, "Bullshit! Whatever! You don't fucking scare me! Get the fuck out of here!" At that moment, the fucking padlock starts moving by itself! Like banging into the door frame, "Bam! Bam! Bam!" It's fucking moving by itself! Swinging. Like somebody was swinging it. Banging into the sides. We were shocked because we're trying to find a physical explanation. I mean, the padlock is heavy. The wind blowing is not going to move it. It's not gonna move unless somebody is moving it. And then Chris is like, "Do you see that Raph? You better not piss them off. Let's get outta here!" I was literally backing away, "Okay, okay! Holy shit! Alright, alright! I'm just kidding! I was just kidding! Sorry, I said that. I'm outta here!" And then suddenly it stopped! But as I turn to walk away from the door, I get a fucking weird sensation on my back. Like goose bumps. Like a bad energy behind me. I don't feel anybody touching me, but it's like somebody is standing close behind me that's going to get me. I don't want to lie to you. I just felt fucking bad energy right behind me.*

Raphael is now in that mindset that many interviewees get into: they're actually feeling what they felt when the experience was underway. He's mimicking the sensations.

Raphael: *Like all my body gets big goose bumps. Like ahhh! It was something like that. But I never look back. We both walk quickly over to the gate and just hang over there until Chae, the Park Ranger, shows up. And then I hear Chris mumbling. I don't know if he was praying or what he was doing because he's a Christian guy. He said later "I don't get scared." But I dunno. He has his own way to think when he sees things. I'm not that way. I just say, "Fuck it, I'm not scared of you!" And then I'm like, "Oh shit, what did I do? Maybe something is wrong!" It was a fucking weird experience, but it happened to me.*

Raphael takes a long moment to wind down and now looks back on the incident without the ramped-up emotion.

Raphael: *We never spoke about it again. I was very freaked out. I thought later about trying to find a physical explanation. Like what could have happened? But now I feel different. I feel like, okay, I know you're there and I won't try to bother you, whatever it is. But damn, all I remember seeing is the fucking padlock moving and banging the wall for like thirty seconds. It was crazy. And then we tell Chae what just happened and he's like, "Oh, that's normal, we feel so much shit here." Chae opened up the lock and we went inside and checked. Nothing. So I'm like trying to be calm, "Holy shit, let's just load the chairs and get the fuck outta here, dude!"*

Raphael is introspective here and meanders around a bit.

Raphael: *That day, maybe I went a little too far. But I'm not the first person to see or feel something here, so there must be something else in there. Chris says, "Oh, well, I didn't feel nothing much. We just saw the lock moving, and that's it." But that sensation that I felt on my back, he didn't feel it. I'm like, "Oh shit, you know what? This shit is not normal!" I don't know if it's good or bad. And I don't want to know. I'm good with it. I'll just respect that.*

"Locks and Knocks" – Part Two

Chris Hamilton is definitely not an individual who looks for the paranormal. If he's working at Greystone, it's to deliver and pick up tablecloths, furniture, and tables for events and then leave. He wants nothing to do with ghosts or spirits, doesn't want to talk about it and he's made that known to me. But clearly, I needed to get Chris' firsthand account on what happened that day. It was so compelling that I wanted to find out what he remembered and what he thought about it. He also agreed to meet me at the Car Garages and discuss the incident.

CHRIS HAMILTON
(General Repair)

> Chris: *So we are waiting here outside the garages for Chae to come down and unlock the door to let us in because this is where the chairs are that we're supposed to pick up. Suddenly we hear a knock* [he hits the stable door to make the sound], *like that, but from the inside. And we're like, "That's weird," you know, not thinking too much of it, but every minute or so, there would be another bang on the stable doors. And Raph said, "I don't believe in those stupid ghosts!" So we weren't even paying attention. And we start hearing the knock again. And then we hear another knock. I walk over here* [to the door with the lock] *and I'm like, "Raph! The lock is shaking back and forth." So I guess it could be paranormal because of the knocks and when the lock was moving right after it, we connected the two like, "Oh shit!" So anyway, Chae gets here and we tell him what is going on and he's like, "Well, maybe someone got in through the back." So he checks and everything is locked up. We go inside the garages and there's no one in there. So that was probably the weirdest part.*

I asked Chris if he knew that Raphael felt what he thought were two hands touching his back that gave him shivers and goose bumps as he walked away from the lock. Chris stares at me—clearly deep in thought about the question. It's obvious this information is new to him.

459

Chris: Wow, okay. No, I didn't know that. Yeah, you know, those inside knocks were kinda weird. It was kind of eerie.

Greystone Historical Report

In an incredible irony for a family that made most of its money from petroleum, one of the most difficult maintenance problems at Greystone was the oil that seeped (and still does) out of the ground, mostly in the low-lying southwestern portion of the estate near Doheny Road. Landscape architect Paul Thiene had built a below—surface tile and gravel drain system, but it plugged up often. "We would have to open them up, clean them out, to make sure that the oil would collect in the drain, and would flow down to a sump," where it would be pumped out, declares George Maile. "Our most difficult time with this oil seepage was during the hot periods when, regardless of how well the drains were operating, the oil still wanted to come to the surface and would naturally kill the grass and make a mess in general."

TRAILER

Greystone Historical Report

"I used to spend a lot of time down at the garage keeping those guys from working. Throwing a football around and stuff like that." —Timothy Doheny

---

What we call the "Trailer" is an office trailer placed directly across from the Car Garages. It was moved there for the gardeners to have an on-site office to access their emails as well as a location for them to take breaks during the day. The entrance to the Trailer must be Americans with Disabilities Act compliant, so steps and a long metal ramp for a wheelchair were constructed for the entrance.

"WIND"

This was my first interview with Andrea Flores. It took place on April 3, 2018. By now, you've read many of her stories in this book. As you know, she has "the gift." She feels and sees the paranormal with great frequency. At this point, all I knew about Andrea was that she would arrive at night to clean the trailer and the firehouse restrooms. One day I asked her if anything happened to her that she couldn't explain while cleaning at Greystone. This was my introduction to Andrea. Within a few seconds, she's stomping on the floor, recreating something she heard.

ANDREA FLORES
(Janitorial Services)

> Andrea: *I was cleaning the restroom that is inside the trailer. Suddenly I heard, five times, someone stomping on the trailer ramp* [she stomps]. *I thought that one of the guys was playing a joke on me because I told them I was going to go alone. I thought maybe Mario, my supervisor, was here. So I go outside and look around everywhere. There's no one here. I go back into the restroom and keep cleaning and then I hear, three times, on the ramp* [she stomps three times]. *I run out and there's nothing here. But when I run out this time, I felt energy. This "wind" came over me and got me in the face and I thought, "Something happened here." But before, when I looked outside, I didn't feel anything. But now, when I felt the wind, I did get scared, and I don't get scared that easy. It wasn't windy. Nothing at all like that. That's what scared me. We've been here when it's really windy and it's totally different. You feel different. So I kept working. And it wasn't as if I*

was so scared I was going to run away, but suddenly I knew that it wasn't the guys playing a joke on me. I could feel it. And it wasn't normal. I know what I heard. I know that it was someone walking on the ramp.

"ONE STEP"

I've known Karen for over twenty years. We worked closely on the Beverly Hills Art Show and became friends. She is a wonderful person who is very analytical and comes from a science background. With that in mind, she is the last person I know who would believe in the paranormal. When I heard that a series of strange incidents were occurring at her office, which is in the trailer, I was curious what her thoughts would be. And if what was happening might indeed be paranormal, would she be able to come to terms with that conclusion?

KAREN FITCH McLEAN
(Recreation Specialist)

Karen: *This happened not that long after we moved our office into the trailer. It was late afternoon, and you would hear the sound of someone stepping on the ramp that leads to our trailer door. But it would always be just one step. And at first, I was too afraid to check and then after a while I was like, this is ridiculous. I could get to the door right away, within seconds from my desk—we hear it and I look to see if anyone is on the ramp and there's never anyone there. But I can't figure out any explanation. I can't figure out what would be causing that noise except something or someone stepping on it. It makes the same noise we make whenever we step on the ramp. You can't tiptoe on that ramp and not make the noise. For me, it's always been hearing just one step. I think someone else has heard more than one, but for me, and Carolyn, [her co-worker] it's always been the one step, and when it occurs, we both hear it. It's not like I hear it and she doesn't. Or she hears it, but I don't. And I can get out and look immediately, but she's looked too, and there's never anybody there.*

I reminded her that Juan had a theory.

Karen: *So Ranger Juan thought maybe it had something to do with the expansion and contraction of metal late in the day. But whether it's cold weather, or warm weather, I'll still hear it. It's not dependent on heat or cold. He was trying to think of an explanation that would be scientific, but I can't figure out one for this. The only thing I can think of is either it's some sort of science deal I'm not familiar with, or somebody is quickly bouncing on the...* [she starts to laugh] *I don't know, it doesn't make a lot of sense. And why would it only be one step? If it really was somebody on the ramp, why wouldn't it be more steps?*

As a heads-up, there are avocado trees up on a hill about fifty yards away. Wait for it—

Karen: *Every time I check to see if anything fell on the ramp, like maybe some huge avocado* [she laughs again], *but there's nothing, and there's nothing overhead like trees anyway. And even if there were some people around, they're not close to the ramp. You know what I mean? The only time that sound is heard, is when someone is walking on the ramp. I don't hear it in the morning and I don't hear it in the early afternoon. Only later afternoon and evening. It scared me the first time I heard it. It was at night. But it doesn't really scare me now. I guess after a while you kind of get used to it. But I'm curious every time, like, can I find something this time? This is my only experience* [with the paranormal]. *I don't know what it could be because the spirits don't get in touch with me. The ghosts that we've all heard about, generally speaking, you really don't hear about them being down here at the trailer. Who the hell knows who or what this is...*

"Into the Arch"

Feliciano only speaks Spanish, so for this interview, Ernesto Celis-Zarate was there to translate. Feliciano is another worker on the janitorial crew that intermittently works at Greystone. On this night, as Ernesto explained above, he was asked to clean the Trailer. But from the look in Feliciano's eyes, he hopes he never has to clean it again.

FELICIANO RIVERA
(Janitorial Services)

> Feliciano: *The first time I felt so sleepy. I was falling asleep. And then a week later, it was like midnight and I heard and felt five steps. Or like someone was walking outside the trailer on the metal stairs. When I went outside, I heard the steps going down the stairs. Then I saw something going into the arch.*

There's a brick archway that leads back to the horse stables.

> Feliciano: *It looked like a shadow. It was white. I felt afraid. I was scared. I got goose bumps because I was so afraid. I could see through it and I saw it going through the arch and then it just disappeared.*

"Tap"

When I talked to Steve Jaramillo about his experience in October of 2018, his office was in the trailer. So we went into the trailer and recorded the interview in the small room where the incident took place. The room is extremely small, roughly eight feet by ten feet. He had a desk with a computer, a chair, and a small bookcase. When he sat in the chair to show me what happened, it's important to note there was maybe two feet of space, if that, behind him to the bookcase—not a lot of room at all.

STEVEN JARAMILLO
(Park Services)

> *Steven: This was during the day. I was sitting down using the computer in the office and I feel somebody or something tap my shoulder. I was the only one in the building, so it was just kind of odd. I knew nobody was in there with me. All of a sudden, I had a funny feeling about all the stories I've heard, but I knew nobody was there because there's no room behind me. There's the bookshelf right here, so I'd know if somebody is there. So I called my wife to tell her because she has a sense of these things…*

Steve later confided that his wife has "the gift."

> *Steven: …and she said, "Ah, don't worry about it. If they wanted to hurt you, they would have hurt you by now!"* [he laughs]. *So after that, I didn't have any fear. But it felt like someone actually touched me!*

"GHOST RIDER"

I entered the city credit union one afternoon back in 2018. David, who works in a different division, walks in and we started chatting. We've known each other for about fifteen years and enjoy catching up. I told him work was busy, but every chance I get, I'm writing my book. Then it dawned on me that David worked out of the Trailer for about twelve of the past fifteen years. I said, "Hey, wait a minute, I never asked you if you ever had any experiences up at Greystone." When his smile diminished, I knew immediately that something had taken place. He was very reticent to have "that" conversation. "What happened?" I pushed a bit. He slowly shook his head, "I really don't want to talk about it." Now I'm even more intrigued. "David, come on. Five minutes. That's all I need. Do this for me. Five minutes." You could see in his eyes that he wasn't kidding about not wanting to talk. Whatever this incident was, it unnerved him to the

465

point that he didn't even want to discuss it. I tried to convince him one more time, "C'mon, let's go outside to the parking lot. Five minutes. Please." Very reluctantly, David agreed. Well, I lied—five minutes turned into seventeen. His usually calm demeanor became amped up. As we stood in the small parking lot in the mid-September heat, David relived his experience of that night. When he was done, we both had chills and it was apparent why he didn't want to talk about the incident of that night. David took off and I sat in my car for a few minutes just absorbing everything he said. I was completely overwhelmed. As I drove away through the streets of Beverly Hills, I kept thinking, "Could this story be true? Did this really happen?" But the bottom line was clear—walking into that credit union was a fortunate turn of events.

DAVID CARLTON GARRARD
(General Park Maintenance Supervisor)

David: *So it was 2009. The trailer at that time was in the lower area where the new parking lot is located. I came in to work for an event on Rodeo Drive in the middle of the night. I was working all night on an install of holiday flowers until about two-thirty in the morning. We had a break, so I go up to Greystone, to my office, which overlooked the lower parking lot. There were two offices in that trailer and a main lobby area. My office, on the end, was the one that you could look out the window with a view of the parking lot. So I go in there and I sit at my desk and I'm checking emails and I thought to myself, I'm going to take a half-hour snooze because my guys* [co-workers] *are going to come in at 4:30 a.m. So as I'm sitting there, I turn off the computer and put my head back. The door to my office was open, but not the door to enter the trailer* [located in the middle section of the trailer]. *There's nobody there and I'm not asleep. I'm just keeping my eyes closed, just resting for a minute, when all of a sudden, I hear three knocks on the door. Like actual knocks* [he mimics knocking with his hands]. *Now that door has a window, but it's painted black. So you can't see out of it, and no one can see in. Suddenly I hear three more knocks! I look out the window to the parking lot and there is only one light on, a lamp post. There are no cars except for my city truck and I can see when or if people come in the gate. At this time there's no other way to get into Greystone. The Loma Vista gate is locked. And again, there's nobody there, especially at two-thirty in the morning.*

David pauses a long moment to gather his thoughts to move on.

David: *So I hear this knock on the door and it freaked me out. I thought, I'm not going to answer that door at two-thirty in the morning because it's dark and there's nobody up here. But this is the deal, I have seen deer on the property. I have seen deer either walk by the trailer or up on the main lawn. But this was like a knock* [he mimics the sound again]. *I said, "Fuck that. I am not..." It freaked me out. So I close the door to my office and sit there thinking, "Oh my God, what...?" I just froze. I didn't know what to do. But this is what's weird—when I look out the mini blinds, I could see an illumination of something that moves across the back brick wall. I feel and I see this presence of something that is like a ghost. It is like a white illumination of something that went by and I can feel it. I can feel—like the hairs on my arms stand up and I don't know what it is, but what I can see looks like the color of your shirt. Like that white, but sort of purple-ish. Almost translucent. And the blinds are slightly open, but not to where you can see through them. And so whatever that thing is, it went up towards the driveway by the gatehouse above, and out of my sight. And I thought, "I'm not getting the fuck out of this trailer. Victor* [a gardener] *comes in early in the morning, so I'm not leaving here until one of my guys comes in." And I didn't leave. But that's, that's... that's... what I saw.*

Notice how David hasn't told me anything specific as to what he actually saw? He is still reluctant to tell me. And I don't want to push him. I don't want to guess or lead him in any way as to what he witnessed. At this point, I think he may feel that I think he's crazy. Had he been able to read all the paranormal stories in this book, I'm sure it would have alleviated his fears. He gives me a look of "Are you ready for this? Because I'm going to tell you."

David: *I don't know what it was. I sensed it was almost like in New York where they have the horse and buggy that you can rent, where they take you through the park? It was kind of like that. But it was more like a vision of the old Wells Fargo stagecoach from the movie* Tombstone. *And the stagecoach had ornamental motifs at all four corners of the carriage. It almost looked like there was a light shining down from above, which cast shadows on the coach to where it highlighted the wood which appeared to be old barn type wood.*

Holy smokes, the details are flowing now!

David: *There was one horse and it had no real color. In fact, it looked like a ghost. Like in the movie* Ghost Rider. *It was pulling the stagecoach up the driveway. Dude, look!* [he holds out his arm and shows me his goose bumps]. *See!? It gives me the fucking heebie jeebies! But this vision of a horse and stagecoach was like a translucent, bright, purple, like in the movie* Avatar. *That's what it was like. And that was illuminated as it was going up towards the gatehouse, and that's when I lost sight of it. But at the beginning it was in front of my office door, by my window, and it just kind of went by the window and went towards... and I...*

We're in the parking lot and David is reliving the moment—at a complete loss for words, wide-eyed and just stunned.

David: *I... I just freaked out! And I don't get freaked out with stuff like that, but that thing freaked me the fuck out! I mean, it was like an old stagecoach with a horse going up the driveway. But it was a ghost. I don't know. It was real. I mean, this actually happened. I wasn't sleeping and dreaming this. No. It was real and it was weird.*

I asked David if it changed his perception of the location.

David: *Well, yeah. I mean, I choose not to let my mind go there, which is why I've never talked about it with anybody—except to you right now. Because I don't believe in that stuff. But after that night it was hard to say that it didn't happen. Because it did happen. I don't know what the fuck... I don't know what it was. I mean, it was a ghost. And it was... it was weird. And I'd say it was about fifteen feet away from the window on the driveway and I could feel the energy coming off of it. I could feel it and I could see it. There was what looked like a fluorescent, neon light coming from it. It was dark, so if somebody was driving by on Doheny Road or came into the parking lot, how could you not see it? It was that bright.*

So I had to ask him: "So who knocked at your door?"

David: *I don't know. It was three full-on knocks* [he mimics the sound]. *And it happened twice. Solid. If, let's say, a deer, or an animal did that, an animal doesn't knock like a knock. It wasn't footsteps on the ramp. And... it was a knock high up on the door. And that's when I went, "Oh, fuck, I'm not going out there because it's pitch dark, man." And even if you had some crazy bastard out there, and you open up the door, how is anybody going to know if you've been attacked!? But dude, this wasn't a person, this was a horse and buggy, carriage, stagecoach type thing. I didn't see any people. But you could see the reins and how they attached to the horse. You could actually see that! And it went by and it went up the hill and just kind of went to the left and disappeared. So when I finally saw Victor pull in the driveway, maybe forty-five minutes later, to get his coffee, that's when I said, "Okay, I'm going to open up the door to my office." That's how bad it freaked me out. Whatever the hell is going on up there, I don't know. I didn't even want to talk about it. I never did tell Victor what I saw. I've never told anybody. And now, I've told you.*

469

Doheny Greystone Estate

An Estate Built by Edward L. Doheny, Jr.
Designed by Gordon Kaufmann
Landscape by Paul Thiene

HISTORIC LANDMARK NO. 4
Built 1928 Designated 2013

Beverly Hills City Council and
Cultural Heritage Commission
City of Beverly Hills

EPILOGUE

Answered prayers. That's how I view the book you've just read and hopefully embraced. And now that I've come full circle with the process, I realize what a long strange trip it's been (apologies to the Grateful Dead). Initially, I was thinking how labor intensive could it be to research and write a book? I thought I would conduct some interviews, write down some personal stories, hand them over to Chris (my brother and partner in everything creative) and he'd take it from there. Well, I was clueless. Yet here we are—three years later and I'm writing this epilogue. And truth be told, I wouldn't trade the experience for anything. It's been an absolute joy.

As I got into the process of laying out the book, it became quite apparent that it couldn't just be about the paranormal. I wanted you to experience the history of this family's prominence during the growth years of Beverly Hills and surrounding Los Angeles. I also wanted us to envision what it felt like to be a family member or friend and step inside the impressive Grand Entry and gaze at the stunning architecture… what it was like to walk the grounds and see the lush landscapes that once surrounded this celebrated property. The Greystone Historical Report and considerable hours of research contributed tremendously to that effort.

During this journey, I also learned to appreciate the Doheny family—the good times as well as their trials, tribulations, and tragedies. I also wanted you to be as fortunate as I have been to meet some wonderful people from all walks of life that happened to be in the right place at the right time to interact with spirits in a realm we can only imagine.

I realize you may still be questioning whether spirits, ghosts, or entities are real. That's how I felt when I began working at Greystone. Now, nearly one hundred forty stories later, it's hard for me *not* to believe that some of them have merit. But my ongoing mantra through all of this, "Don't believe it until you see it," still rings true with me today. I'm guessing there are those of you who might have felt this way until you experienced your own personal paranormal event. For others, maybe this has opened your mind to the possibility of life on the other side.

What I've also discovered from this deep dive into the *Ghosts of Greystone—Beverly Hills,* and all the scary, funny, horrifying, playful, bizarre, and sad stories that evolved, is that throughout the many years, the spirits here remain ever vigilant to make themselves known to us mere mortals.

It is my hope and desire that you've enjoyed these true stories about the ghosts that haunt this bygone, yet extraordinary estate. But, please note, as the gate closes behind you to end this adventure, *their* journey continues on. Possibly with the hope that we can all visit them again.

EDITOR'S NOTE

It all started three years ago in Peet's Coffee on Beverly Drive in Beverly Hills.

Early every Friday morning, six o'clock early, I'd be trading friendly barbs with "Those Keith Brothers"—Clete and Chris... I love these guys. Writers, filmmakers, theatrical impresarios, and truly the salt of the Earth. We would bullshit about everything and anything. Loud laughter continuously rang forth from our little side table.

One Friday morning, they started telling me about their new book project—a chronicle tracing the haunted history and so-called current ghost reality of Greystone Mansion, the venerable old house that was first built, owned, and occupied by oil magnate, Edward Laurence Doheny, the patriarch of an infamous and royal Los Angeles family... and then later by the American Film Institute. Currently, the mansion with its bucolic surrounding gardens is a city park tucked away in a Beverly Hills neighborhood just north of Sunset Boulevard—a neighborhood populated by the one percent.

What struck me the most when "Those Keith Brothers" told me about their almost-completed book about ghosts roaming the halls of Greystone—terrorizing employees and visitors alike—was how damn serious they were about their research, their on-site recordings, and the umpteen hours of interviews they conducted with a cross-section of eyewitnesses. Once I stopped laughing, out loud, I realized they weren't laughing with me. It was like Ray Liotta's reaction to Joe Pesci in *Goodfellas* when Liotta realizes Pesci is just busting his chops—Liotta: "Get the fuck out of here." Except "Those Keith Brothers" weren't busting my chops. They were dead serious about these ghosts and ghouls and shit that goes bump in the night.

What happened next, over the course of numerous early Friday mornings at Peet's, was an ongoing conversation between me and "Those Keith Brothers" about the *Ghosts of Greystone — Beverly Hills.* As every Friday came and went, I was laughing less and less. And just so you know, I'm a born skeptic—critical of government, religion, corporations, as well as shit that goes bump in the night. But I got the gig editing their book anyway… and after getting to know the interviewees intimately through their words and stories (concluding that these folks were not crazy, just honestly expressing their disturbing experiences)… and then seeing Clete's exhaustive firsthand research and feeling his startling narrative, I found myself open to the possibilities. I'm still a skeptic, but I will tell you this much: something really strange and dark is going on inside this old blood-stained mansion. As famed author Ray Bradbury once offered, *Something Wicked This Way Comes.*

So that new book project "Those Keith Brothers" told me about one Friday morning at Peet's, is the book you now hold in your hands—be it paper or pixels. And I'm telling you straight up about old man Doheny's mansion, I'm not going inside that joint any time soon.

—Stephen Vittoria
Los Angeles, Fall 2020

ACKNOWLEDGEMENTS

To those brave enough to go on record and share their experiences.

Dorothy and Byron
For always stoking the creative fire. Every project has your spirit attached. You are missed.

Chris Keith
Without you there is no book. I create and you bring it to fruition. Your tireless work on every aspect of the publishing process continues to astound me. I ask how something can be accomplished, and you take in on, research it, and it's completed. What a gift you are to me. You are my partner in all things creative. You have always been my best friend. What a journey we've had together. I love you my brother.

Stephen Vittoria
Thank you for joining us and providing your knowledge and guidance. Your insight, editing, and thirst of history was essential for this book.

Christie Mossman
After reading several pages of my first draft, you said you were bored. I came up with every excuse as to why you were wrong. After listening to your reasoning, and starting my next draft, I was fully convinced you were right. What a blessing. Without your thoughts and feelings, this book would be... dare I say... boring! Thank you.

Kacey and Jon Daly
Thank you for your encouragement when we first discussed writing this book. Jon, your enthusiasm helped spark the forward movement of my idea. Kacey, I love you. Thank you for listening to all the stories, and allowing me to hide behind you in the basement!

ACKNOWLEDGEMENTS

Special Thanks

Angie Alaya, Danielle Baccaro, Taylor Bakken, Craig Berenson, Steve Clark, Chip Coffey, Lissa Coffey, Jared Cowan, Claire Danna, Victor DiMichina, Chris Fleming, Clark Fogg, Carrie Gamblin, Hortensia Gomez-Tirella, Kaleo Griffith, Jennifer Grubba, Rob Guillory, Dan Hernandez, Bryan Houser, Sam Houser, Patty Jenkins, Aneta Karapetyan, Raeha Keller, Linda Kyriazi, Steven Lloyd, Martha Mayakis, Karen Fitch McLean, Brad Moylan, Aleksey Murakami, Brooke Putich, Denise Retallack, Ben Reder, Jennifer Riemenschneider, Susan Rosen, Bill Rotella, Linda & Jim Salvati, Erica Santoyo, Ray Scalice, Jasmit Sethi, Sam Sheridan, "The" Ariadna Thau, Ellen Vittoria, and Christopher Worland.

Those Keith Brothers Support

Melodie & Stephanie Baldwin, Shawn Bouyer, Casey, Jamie & Sheila Carter, Denis Cordova, Tammy Crosby, Deb & Rad Daly, Harrison Ellenshaw, John Elsen, Kathy Fitzgerald, Patti & Matt Harrison, Jim Hodson – Advantage Audio, Claire, Emily & Rob Hummel, Nancy Hunt-Coffey, Trisha & George Hunter, Kira Jones, Peggy Kelley, Joe Kite, Mark Laisure, Hal Lewis, Larry Manship, Susan Martin, Diane & Peter McDonald, Mary McDonough, Raymond McIntyre Jr., Roger Michaelson, Gary Migdal, Gomez Mora, Javier Mora, Tyler Mora, Eric Mossman, Debbie Nodella, Diane & Richard Piccuilla, Judie & John Presten, Hope & Tom Quinn, Paul Rahmes, George Rajacich, Barbara Rosenman, Geri & Peter Rotter, Frank Roughan, Brandy Scott, Lynda & Bear Thompson, "Sir Edmund" Thomas Valencia, Steven Villa, John Van Vliet, Karen & Sandy Wood, and Edison "Rock On" Yu.

APPENDIX

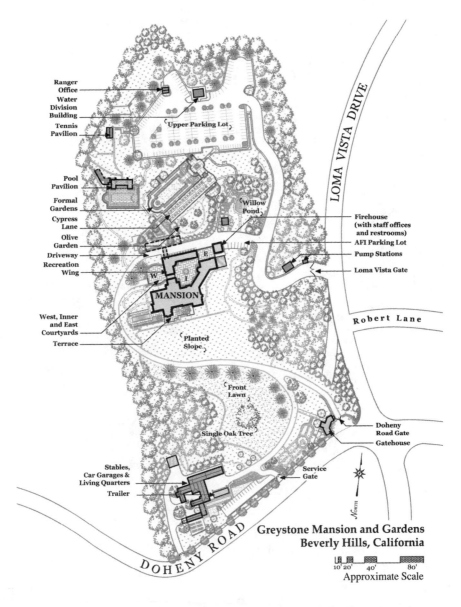

Ranger
Office

Water
Division
Building

Tennis
Pavilion

Upper Parking Lot

Pool
Pavilion

Formal
Gardens

Cypress
Lane

Olive
Garden

Driveway

Recreation
Wing

West, Inner
and East
Courtyards

Terrace

Willow
Pond

E

W I

MANSION

Planted
Slope

Front
Lawn

Single Oak Tree

Stables,
Car Garages &
Living Quarters

Trailer

Service
Gate

LOMA VISTA DRIVE

Firehouse
(with staff offices
and restrooms)

AFI Parking Lot

Pump Stations

Loma Vista Gate

Robert Lane

Doheny
Road Gate

Gatehouse

NORTH

DOHENY ROAD

**Greystone Mansion and Gardens
Beverly Hills, California**

10' 20'   40'   80'

Approximate Scale

© 2020 Karen Fitch McLean

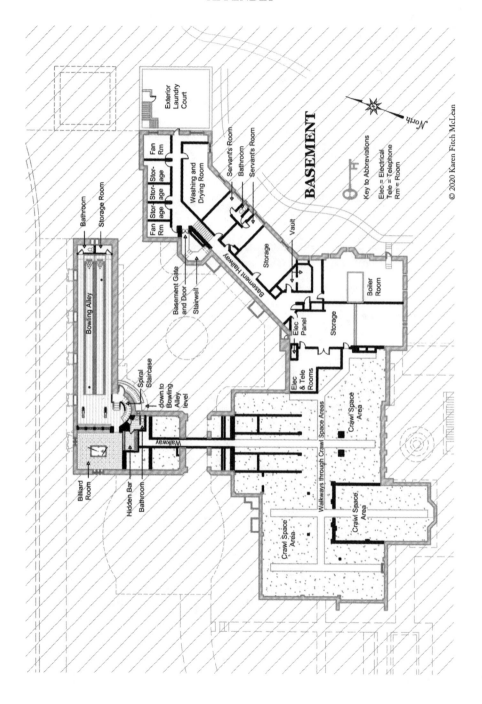

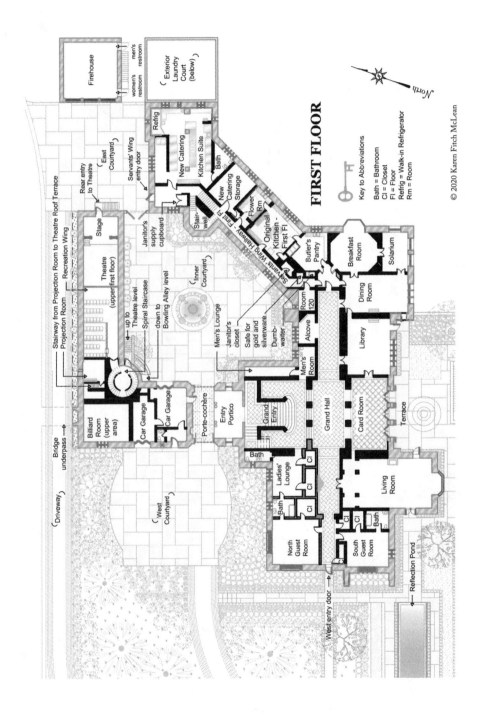

FIRST FLOOR

Key to Abbreviations

Bath = Bathroom
Cl = Closet
Fl = Floor
Refrig = Walk-in Refrigerator
Rm = Room

© 2020 Karen Fitch McLean

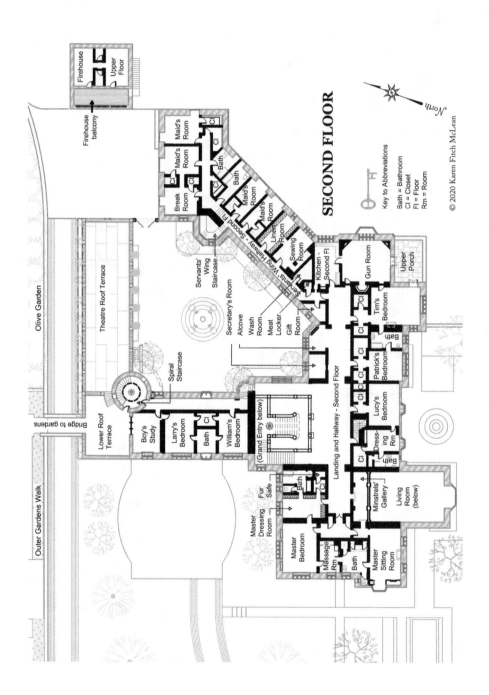

SECOND FLOOR

Key to Abbreviations

Bath = Bathroom
Cl = Closet
Fl = Floor
Rm = Room

© 2020 Karen Fitch McLean

North

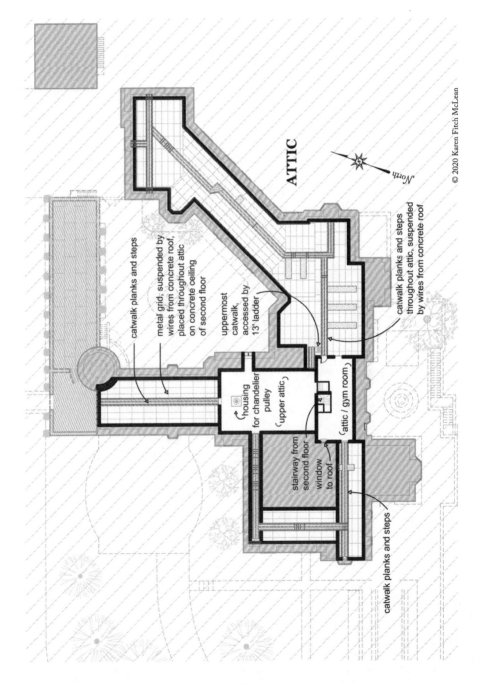

ATTIC

North

© 2020 Karen Fitch McLean

catwalk planks and steps

metal grid, suspended by wires from concrete roof, placed throughout attic on concrete ceiling of second floor

uppermost catwalk, accessed by 13' ladder

catwalk planks and steps throughout attic, suspended by wires from concrete roof

housing for chandelier pulley (upper attic)

stairway from second floor

window to roof

attic / gym room

catwalk planks and steps

INDEX

INDEX

INDEX

During the day, I don't believe in ghosts.
At night, I'm a little more open-minded.

– Unknown